D1474620

Political Theology and Early Modernity

Political Theology and Early Modernity

EDITED BY
GRAHAM HAMMILL AND
JULIA REINHARD LUPTON

WITH A POSTSCRIPT BY
Étienne Balibar

The University of Chicago Press
Chicago and London

Graham Hammill is professor of English at University at Buffalo, SUNY. He is the author of *Sexuality and Form*, also published by the University of Chicago Press.

Julia Reinhard Lupton is professor of English and comparative literature at the University of California, Irvine. She is the author or coauthor of four books on Shakespeare, most recently of *Thinking with Shakespeare: Essays on Politics and Life*, also published by the University of Chicago Press.

The University of Chicago Press, Chicago 60637
The University of Chicago Press, Ltd., London
© 2012 by The University of Chicago
All rights reserved. Published 2012.
Printed in the United States of America

21 20 19 18 17 16 15 14 13 12   1 2 3 4 5

ISBN-13: 978-0-226-31497-6 (cloth)
ISBN-13: 978-0-226-31498-3 (paper)
ISBN-10: 0-226-31497-9 (cloth)
ISBN-10: 0-226-31498-7 (paper)

Portions of Adam Sitze's essay, "The Tragicity of the Political: A Note on Carlo Galli's Reading of Carl Schmitt's *Hamlet or Hecuba*," appeared as "A Farewell to Schmitt: Notes on the Work of Carlo Galli" in *CR: The New Centennial Review* 10, no. 2 (2010), published by Michigan State University Press. Part of Carlo Galli's essay, "*Hamlet*: Representation and the Concrete," first appeared in Italian as the introduction to the Italian translation of Carl Schmitt's *Hamlet or Hecuba, Amleto o Ecuba* (Bologna: Il Mulino, 1983). An earlier version of Étienne Balibar's "Postscript" was published as "Quelle universalité des Lumières?" in *Le Bottin des Lumières*, edited by Nadine Descendre (Paris: ENSBA, 2005), and adapted as "Séjourner dans la contradiction: L'idée de 'nouvelles Lumières' et les contradictions de l'Universalisme," in *Formen des Nicht-wissens der Aufklärung*, edited by Hans Adler-Rainer Gödel (Munich: Wilhelm Fink Verlag).

Library of Congress Cataloging-in-Publication Data

Political theology and early modernity / edited by Graham Hammill and Julia Reinhard Lupton ; with a postscript by Étienne Balibar.
        pages : illustrations ; cm
    Includes index.
    ISBN-13: 978-0-226-31497-6 (cloth : alkaline paper)
    ISBN-10: 0-226-31497-9 (cloth : alkaline paper)
    ISBN-13: 978-0-226-31498-3 (paperback : alkaline paper)
    ISBN-10: 0-226-31498-7 (paperback : alkaline paper)   1. Political theology—
History. 2. Political theology—Historiography.   I. Hammill, Graham L. II. Lupton, Julia Reinhard, 1963– III. Balibar, Étienne, 1942–
    BT83.59.P64 2012
    322'.1094—dc23   2011050365

♾ This paper meets the requirements of ANSI/NISO Z39.48-1992 (Permanence of Paper).

Contents

PART TWO   Scenes of Early Modernity

Illustrations

Acknowledgments

We would like to thank the Humanities Collective at the University of California, Irvine for co-sponsoring the symposium on political theology and early modernity that brought many of the contributors represented in this volume together for a stimulating set of exchanges. UCI's Humanities Collective also provided a generous subvention toward publication costs of this volume. The Baldy Center for Law and Social Policy at the University at Buffalo, SUNY, provided a grant so that the two of us could meet in Buffalo to draft our introduction. Nick Hoffman prepared the initial manuscript for submission, and Richard Allen has provided expert copyediting. C. J. Gordon assisted with the index. Alan Thomas has been an inspiring editor of this and kindred projects at the University of Chicago Press. Finally, we would like to thank our husbands, Richard Ridenour and Ken Reinhard, for their loving support of all that we do.

Graham Hammill and Julia Reinhard Lupton
Buffalo, New York, and Irvine, California

Introduction

GRAHAM HAMMILL

JULIA REINHARD LUPTON

1. The Problem

Let's get this straight. Political theology is not the same as religion. Instead, we take it to name a form of questioning that arises precisely when religion is no longer a dominant explanatory or life mode. Political theology reflects and feeds on a crisis in religion, whether that crisis is understood historically (as Reformation) or existentially (as doubt, skepticism, or boredom). The last two decades have seen excellent work on the centrality of religion in the English Renaissance, from the groundbreaking historical work by Debora Shuger on the Renaissance Bible to the fine collection by Ewan Fernie on *Spiritual Shakespeares*, which explores the varieties of religious experience presented on the English stage.[1] The norms and forms of religious life are, however, not exactly what concerns political theology, which finds its questions rather in the moments where religion is no longer working—but neither are the secular solutions designed to replace it. Such moments include the uncanny transformation of icons into idols under the pressure of reformation, the jarring encounter with strange forms of belief abroad and at home, and the disorienting friction between sacred and secular jurisdictions, calendars, economies, membership protocols, textual operations, and styles of violence.

We take the phrase "political theology" to identify the exchanges, pacts, and contests that obtain between religious and political life, especially the use of sacred narratives, motifs, and liturgical forms to establish, legitimate, and reflect upon the sovereignty of monarchs, corporations, and parliaments.[2] Political theology is less a concept like sovereignty or the state of exception; or a form of government like monarchy, theocracy, or republicanism; or even a moment of historical transition from a worldview that is primarily theological to one that is primarily political. Rather, it is more like a coupling or entanglement of ostensibly discrete domains—the political and the theological—out of which early modern and modern concepts, forms of government, and views of history are born. Although political theology is strongly associated with state formation, its mechanics are also at work in the charters of towns, the operations of guilds and livery companies, the principles of household management and animal husbandry, and even the hieratic clustering of home furnishings.[3] In both Reformation and Counter-Reformation settings, the cumbersome and incomplete transfer of iconographic capital and organizational capacities from the church to a range of civic and civil bodies not only defined and strengthened new centers of authority but also helped transform traditional religious practices and institutions by draining them of a portion of their aura. Bankrupting the Peter of the medieval church in order to pay off the Paul associated with new forms of secular authority also produced subterranean and symptomatic forms of alliance between religion and politics in a modernity founded on their putative division. (On the Peter-Paul alliance, see Julia Lupton's essay on Raphael's cartoons.)

In the study of early modern Europe, political theology is often used to name a gallery of icons, rites, and narratives associated with sacred kingship and the evolving offices of the state, themselves often drawn out of the administrative care of the royal household. In this collection, however, political theology takes on a second, more polemical meaning, in which politics and theology, understood as contest rather than alliance, delineate the schism around which early modernity is constituted. Less an ideology and more of a recursive crisis, political theology unlocks the occasion in which personal sovereignty transforms into its opposites: as citizenship, the *corpus mysticum*, the multitude, or civil society. Political theology is thus bound up in epochal breaks and period definitions: whereas "Renaissance" engages primarily with the challenge of antiquity, "Early Modern" concerns the wars of religion and the attempt to resolve the new heterodoxies and troubling new pluralisms of the Reformation in a secular key.

Political theology, then, is neither a set of themes nor a particular form of government, but rather a scene of recurring conflict—both that which defines the early modern period as the attempt to resolve the challenges of the Reformation and that which continues to unfold today as the impossibility of the state to totalize politics. There are many political theologies, Western as well as non-Western, ancient as well as modern, that could be associated with civil religion—the use of religious belief to ensure obedience to the state or other kinds of political community. In early modern Europe, however, political theology has the status of a founding event—an event that, from the backward glance of the twenty-first century to be sure, makes early modernity *modern*. In post-Reformation Europe, when multiple states and sects individually claimed to embody the one true universal church, a theology that should have led to peace turns into a source of civil war and transnational conflict. Political theology isolates the knot binding religious and secularizing impulses in early modern texts in order to confront the unexpected recurrence of the same conjuncture today. For some writers in this volume, including Victoria Kahn, Étienne Balibar, and Paul Kottman, this means claiming the secular with renewed intellectual vigor and vigilance, while for other writers, including Jennifer Rust and Julia Lupton, this means mining the remainders of theology for conducts of living and styles of comportment that are neither secular nor religious. Whether taken up critically or creatively, political theology confronts its readers as crisis and not content, as recurrent question rather than established doxa.

Although the phrase enjoys a much longer lineage, in contemporary scholarship "political theology" is associated above all with the troubled legacy of the German jurist and sometime Nazi Carl Schmitt, whose short book, *Political Theology: Four Chapters on the Concept of Sovereignty,* declares the homology between religious and political concepts in order to establish the exceptional relationship of the sovereign to a law whose normative legitimacy he is nonetheless dedicated to safeguard.[4] For Schmitt, political theology involves a double movement. Secularized theologies of the state emerge as a solution to the problem of religious division in the writings of Bodin, Hobbes, and the Treaty of Westphalia. But Schmitt also underscores the inadequacy of this resolution, showing how early modern and modern jurisprudence reinforces division and conflict among states, both within Europe, where conflict is provisionally bracketed, and in the New World, which becomes a space of unregulated, wild violence.[5] At first glance, the modern age appears to leave its theological past behind; sacred kingship and its attendant regalia no longer concern the liberal citizen. But upon closer inspection, the modern age redefines and rebinds politics and theology in an attempt to manage its deepest tendencies toward chaos and dissolution. For Schmitt, Hobbes resolves the crisis of political theology by ceding authority to the sovereign who has the capacity to constitute the public as a space free of religious division, while Spinoza founds community on the possibility of heresy and dissensus. Schmitt attempts to foreclose Spinoza's account of political theology by emphasizing Hobbes.[6] Contra Schmitt, the writers in this volume are eager to recapture the democratic promises of Spinoza borne by his iconoclastic re-reading of Scripture. If, as Carlo Galli argues, political theology should be understood as an eruption, or as Jacques Lezra posits, political theology is an always incomplete confrontation between two modes, the political and the theological, then how might this moment be thought in the service of new forms of political community, social life, and artistic invention? A political-theological as well as a biopolitical dimension animates aspects of environmentalism, social media, and DIY labor and community formations, as well as efforts at reading, making, and performance that border on the exegetical in their search for something binding, real, or true.

In literary and cultural criticism, Schmitt's work is often read in tandem—for purposes of decontamination and quarantine as well as comparison—with other figures on the scene of modern German letters, including the German-Jewish lines of thought associated with Ernst Kantorowicz, Walter Benjamin, Leo Strauss, Hannah Arendt, and Sigmund Freud, a list elastic enough to include Benjamin's Italian editor, Giorgio Agamben. In the work of these seminal thinkers, and in the studies pursued by the scholars and critics who have variously taken up their lines of thought, political theology represents not a simple synthesis or transfer, but rather the rendezvous with a constitutive impasse.[7] What is it about politics that finds itself bound up in the archaic charisma of the sovereign? How does politics remain distinct from the content and practices of ethics, economics, and culture while nonetheless bearing on them, and how does politics share this difference with religion, whose irreducibility to culture is exposed precisely in the display, decay, and persistence of political-theological formations? How is "life" in its creaturely and biopolitical dimensions at stake in the differences that obtain between politics, religion, and their others? Finally, what is it about modern and early modern politics that both courts and resists theology, catching civic and religious forms of life in a macabre dance of failed separation and catastrophic rapprochement, skirting the Scylla and Charybdis instanced by the dream of total secularization on the one hand and the nightmare of theocracy and fundamentalism on the other?

Within the lines of inquiry posed by these questions, some scholars focus on political theology as an ideological lure and permanent temptation that requires continued resistance and demystification. (In this volume, see for example the lead essay by Kahn.) For other authors, political theology shelters existential truths about the nature of collective life; if political theology deposits a deep conservatism at the phantasmatic heart of sovereignty, the uneven development of secularization provides openings for the retooling of contemporary existence in response to what Eric Santner has called "the psychotheology of everyday life."[8] (In this volume, see especially the essay by Rust.) Art and literature, moreover, have a role to play in freeing up the hardened nodes of political-theological fantasy so that they can be summoned to perform new cultural and psychic work. We might speak here of a *political theology₁* (inveterate, entrenched, phantasmatic, and reactionary, the stuff of Nazism, racial panic, and the *arcana imperii*), and a *political theology₂* that would rework and refigure those disturbing anchors of psychic life, not only in order to create an easement from their tenacious claim, but also to recover and repurpose whatever it is that makes them so resilient.[9]

Political theology, then, is not itself a politics so much as it is the condition for a range of modern political positions and socio-poetic experiments. Political theology delineates the problem space between dispensations (Old and New Testaments; prophetic and priestly impulses; sacred and profane precincts) where certain kinds of obsessive ratiocination and congregational thinking are allowed to take place and sometimes take flight.[10] What is at stake for political theology is not the truth of religion but the status of theology as operative fiction, whether conceived as an instrument of civil religion, a thesaurus of absolute metaphors, or the part played by myth, fantasy, and affect in the founding and sustaining of collectives. Relevant here is the work of Hans Blumenberg, one of Schmitt's strongest critics, on metaphor and concept formation. (For a discussion of Blumenberg's critique of Schmitt, see Graham Hammill's essay in this volume.) Read from Blumenberg's orientation, the sovereign person of the modern state—whether king, magistrate, or citizen—is not a concept but a metaphor, a fantasmatic crystallization that remains to be thought through, a moment of "imprecision" or a case of "nonconceptuality" that accommodates the real by symbolizing it "without helping us to reach it."[11] In both the literary and the social responses that take shape in this nonconceptual region of disarray, rearrangement, and persistent personation, imagination plays a key role: poets like Shakespeare, Donne, and Milton as well as political theorists such as Spinoza, Hobbes, Bodin, Machiavelli, and Pascal variously reshape the sovereign's capacity to decide, itself linked to the creator's capacity to create, in order to stage new scenes of political making. In some cases, this might mean legitimating imagination on the grounds that it is analogous to sovereignty, as Sidney does in *The Defence of Poesy*, or legitimating literature on the grounds that it is analogous to Scripture, as Dante does in *The Divine Comedy*. Political theology on the scenes of early modernity takes its departure from compromise formations that largely avoid, however, legitimation by analogy, issuing instead in moments in which imagination reclaims the force of making against sovereignties both statist and divine by staging the very effects of sovereign power in and as what literature does.

We began with the proposition that political theology is not religion. Although political theology is sometimes described as a "turn to religion," this is not exactly right: first, because we cannot go back to a religion of the past without devastating consequences, as the brutal delusions of fundamentalism reveal daily; and second, because even if we could time-travel, the religions of the past would fail to meet our expectations of coherence and community. In effect, we have never been religious. The essays in this volume demonstrate that accounting for political theology leads just as readily to a critique of the "religious turn" as it does to its validation. Yet the elusiveness of the religious object also helps us to distinguish political theology from cultural analysis. Cultural studies would take religion to be one element in a series of identifiers, putting religion in its place by turning it into another sign of otherness along-side race, class, and gender. Cultural critique would see religion as a form of mystification either supported or exposed by literary texts. For cultural studies, religion is a positive form of identity; for cultural critique, religion is a negative force of manipulation.[12] Although political theology does not necessarily deny either of those positions, it stakes a third way that conceives of religions as composed of persistent sets of hermeneutic, juridical, and sub-jective processes that jump group lines and are generated from below as well as above. Of course, religions participate in culture, but what distinguishes religions from culture is their survival beyond the local habitations of custom, practice, and power. Political theology takes seriously the recurrence of for-mal patterns, exegetical habits, narrative types, and metaphysical questions (what Hannah Arendt, following Kant, called the "thought-things" of God, freedom, and immortality)[13] that continue to animate forms of thinking, social organization, and everyday life in modernity, and which had peculiar purchase in the Renaissance.

We are not claiming that religion is foreign to culture; rather, we are as-serting that, because of its odd positioning in modernity, religion, like art, requires forms of analysis other than cultural ones if we are to grasp its un-canny ability to retain and transmit its urgencies. Both art and religion can, of course, be explored on purely contextual grounds, by purely contextualizing methods, but do those approaches end up grasping what is distinctive about these forms of human expression? Just as art solicits some kind of formal analysis, religion requires some kind of formal and phenomenological ac-counting in order to apprehend the successive claims for attention, acknowl-edgment, resistance, and reform by means of which religion keeps surviving its various modern overcomings.

In the great poetic projects of Spenser and Milton, the lyric experiments of Donne and Marvell, and the plays of Shakespeare and his contemporaries, we see something called literature emerging against the backdrop of sacred texts. In one account of this transformation, literature founds secular culture. This account offers a narrative in which early modern literature creates a secular public, a narrative in which literature *makes* the break and *is* the break between the secular and the sacred.[14] A counter-narrative would posit that there was no break at all, that each of these great poets was a man of faith, and that the task of the historical critic is to reconstruct the horizon of belief that has become illegible to us today.[15] Political theology remains discontent with both narratives, seeking instead moments of impasse and hence of possibility that elicited imaginative formulations with the power to reveal and consti-tute new norms, communities, and forms of life. Political theology recovers the specificity of literature from the potentially neutralizing force of culture by taking seriously Renaissance literature's definitive disclosure of political making as what is at stake in key moments of revelation and scripture. In this volume, such moments include the signature of circumcision, the violence of sacrifice, the dream of a *corpus mysticum*, the challenge of neighbor love, the unions and disunions of marriage, the dialectic of idolatry and iconoclasm, and the inextricable bond between enlightenment and terror.

2. The Volume

Political Theology and Early Modernity brings together fourteen essays by es-tablished and emerging scholars in early modern studies who share an inter-est in the role that sixteenth- and seventeenth-century literature and thought has played in modern recurrences of political theology. The essays in this volume argue that there is a special relationship between political theology as a critical issue in literature and politics and early modernity as a period and area of study. Political theology is a distinctly modern problem, one that crystallizes in some of the most significant theoretical writings of the twen-tieth and twenty-first centuries, including psychoanalysis, later deconstruc-tion, and Benjamin's Baroque meditations, as well as in a world political stage marked by the resurgence of fundamentalism within a scene scripted by sec-ularity. But political theology also has its origins in medieval iconographies of sacred kingship as distributed and displayed in the political, dramatic, and artistic forms of European civilization, along with the critique of traditional sovereignty mounted by Grotius, Hobbes, Spinoza, Locke, and others in the seventeenth century. *Political Theology and Early Modernity* makes the case not only for the relevance of political theology as a critical discourse in the humanities today but also for the essential role that Renaissance and Baroque literature and thought have played and have yet to play in its contemporary articulations.

Essays in this volume address texts or moments from the early modern period—including works by Shakespeare, Machiavelli, Raphael, Milton,

Donne, Hobbes, Pascal, and Spinoza—that have served as points of departure for later developments of politics and theology in modernity by thinkers
and writers such as Schmitt, Strauss, Kantorowicz, Freud, Lacan, Blumenberg, Auerbach, de Lubac, and Arendt. Our aim in publishing these essays is
to raise two questions at the same time. How does Renaissance and Baroque
literature help to explain the character and persistence of political theology
in modernity and postmodernity? And how does the reemergence of political
theology as an intellectual and political problem in the twentieth and twenty-
first centuries renew and reorient our understanding of the early modern as
a period and an archive? In his essay in this volume, Jacques Lezra writes that
political theology "is not a concept alone but the record of an encounter."
That is, its effects are both imaginary and real, manifest in works of art and
reasons of state; engaging with those effects requires acts of critical imagination that move with precision and grace between past and present, remapping
their relationship in the process.

   As a term, political theology originates in ancient Rome. Marcus Teren-
tius Varro opposes the term *theologia politike* against *theologia mythike* and
theologia kosmike to explain the division of civil religion from mythical and
natural religions.[16] For Varro, political theology is the same thing as civil
religion. As an early modern formulation, political theology gets its fullest and
most explicit articulation in Spinoza's *Theologico-Political Treatise*, published
anonymously in 1670. There, Spinoza defines political theology in terms of
a central contradiction. In one of the *Treatise*'s opening scenes, Spinoza associates political theology with a Tacitean *arcana imperii* or mystery of state.
"The supreme mystery of despotism [*arcanum monarchii*], its prop and stay,
is to keep men in a state of deception, and with the specious title of religion
to cloak the fear by which they must be held in check, so that they will fight
for their servitude as if for salvation, and count it no shame, but the highest
honor, to spend their blood and their lives for the glorification of one man."[17]
In this account, theology is subordinated to the political through the instru-
mentalization of monotheism. If this were all that Spinoza argues, political
theology would be the same as Varro's civil religion. But as the *Theologico-
Political Treatise* continues, Spinoza supplements this scene with a second
one in which monotheism is bound to the state through the social contract.
Taking Hebrew Scripture as his proof-text, Spinoza argues that the Israelites
made a contract with God *before* they made a contract with Moses. Here, all
citizens were "completely equal" and "had an equal right to consult God, to
receive and interpret his laws." In short, Spinoza continues, "they all shared
equally in the government of the state."[18] In this second scene, Spinoza links

religious imagination to democracy, suggesting that the modern state in ineluctably bound to the creative project of rescripting Hebrew narrative. Unlike civil religion, political theology in this sense prompts the reimagination of the political, social, and cultural life. Although Spinoza uses philology to dissolve the authority of Scripture as state-sanctioned revelation, he embraces the generative aspect of what Kahn calls "the cultural artifact we know as the Bible."

Until very recently, political theology has not been a central question in early modern literary studies, especially in Anglo-American circles. Even though Ernst Kantorowicz's study on medieval political theology *The King's Two Bodies* was a central text for much early modern new historicist work, his argument about political theology and the *corpus mysticum* tended to be subordinated to a Foucauldian interest in power and the body.[19] Moreover, work explicitly focused on politics and the state by historians such as Quentin Skinner and literary critics like Annabel Patterson has been decidedly secular. What changed this situation was the end of the Cold War, which brought with it the potential for reimagining Europe and international geopolitics along with a resurgence of religious fundamentalism, sectarian violence, and a war on terror justified and fought as a holy cause. As the promise of a new future began to look like the uncanny repetition of the religious wars of the sixteenth and seventeenth centuries, a number of European intellectuals began to probe with increasing vigor the religious and theological underpinnings of the modern state. It was in this context that a number of contemporary scholars across the humanities began to read Schmitt with renewed critical attention.[20] Based on his readings of Bodin and Hobbes, Schmitt proposes that just as theology assumes a God who can suspend natural law through the creative force of miracles, so too does the modern state assume a juridical sovereign who can suspend positive law and decide exceptions.[21] The implication of Schmitt's argument is that the early modern and modern sense of public space is always and already overdetermined by theological concepts and ways of thinking. To find a way out of religious conflict, early liberal writers like Hobbes and Locke subordinate theological concerns to the secular state, creating a civic space that purports to be free from doctrinal and confessional concerns. But, as Schmitt's critique of liberalism insists, this vision of politics reiterates theological concepts in a different key.

The essays in our volume explore other encounters with early modern texts in order to arrive at new readings of political theology. Do not, however, expect consensus in the arguments and analyses that lie ahead. Our purpose in assembling the essays in this volume is not to develop a single line of argumentation that would answer Schmitt's challenge, but to think through the problems and promises associated with political theology as they appear on the scenes of early modernity, modernity, and postmodernity as well.

3. Essay Descriptions

Rather than reinstating a simple divide between political theology and secular liberalism, the essays in our first section, "Modern Destinations," move from Schmitt's political writings to his literary criticism, and from Schmitt to Strauss, Blumenberg, Kantorowicz, de Lubac, Benjamin, Arendt, and Auerbach, exploring the knotted sites of conflict and concurrence between politics and theology. These essays—by Victoria Kahn, Adam Sitze, Carlo Galli, Graham Hammill, Jennifer Rust, Kathleen Biddick, Paul Kottmann, and Jane O. Newman—share in the effort to shift the locus of political theology from the person of the sovereign to a variety of other nodal points: the *corpus mysticum* of the multitude, rhetoric and metaphor, modes of theological and secular reasoning, and forms of cultural and political making. In the process, these essays reimagine political theology and open new sets of terms for its critique. We continue with a second section, "Scenes of Early Modernity." Traveling back and forth from enlightened despotism to the Reformation and beyond, essays in this section take the literary, figurative, and aesthetic dimensions of political theology as their points of departure. Rather than starting with political thought, these essays—by Jacques Lezra, Julia Reinhard Lupton, Drew Daniel, Gregory Kneidel, and Jonathan Goldberg—begin at the various conjunctions of the secular, the sacred, and the textual, developing in diverse ways the expected forms of community that emerge from a heterogeneous sense of political theology, and exploring the various forms and fantasies of violence by which political theology persists in the secular world. Finally, we are happy to conclude with a postscript by Étienne Balibar that returns us to the problems with which we began, namely the shared ancestry of monotheism and the Enlightenment that turns critiques of political theology into acknowledgments of its longevity.

In the inaugural essay of our first section, "Political Theology and Liberal Culture: Strauss, Schmitt, Spinoza, and Arendt," Victoria Kahn develops a critical account of political theology through her reading of Strauss and Spinoza. The value of Strauss as opposed to Schmitt, Kahn argues, is that he thought about political theology in terms of philosophy. Can there be a version of political philosophy that is based on reason and not revelation? To address this question, Strauss developed a critique of liberal culture, most trenchantly in his work on Spinoza. For Strauss, proto-liberal philosophers like Hobbes and Spinoza attempt to domesticate the problem of religious difference by turning religion into culture. But the cost of this domestication is that proto-liberal theories of culture simply repress the central role of revelation. For this reason, Strauss argues, revelation in politics and religion is an ongoing problem over which liberalism cannot help but stumble. Kahn then shows how Spinoza resists Strauss's reading. For Spinoza, she argues, culture is not a byproduct of religion. Rather, religion, philosophy, and politics are all created by culture. In Kahn's account, culture's central term is imagination. That is, culture assumes a version of imagination that is constitutive and productive, not illusory and false, so that cultural imagination becomes the means by which religion, politics, and reason are differently cultivated. Spinoza's *Theological Political-Treatise* may in fact stage a central conflict between theocracy and culture, but since both are produced by a more fundamental notion of imagination as constitutive, Kahn argues, culture becomes the vehicle for a critique of political theology. But, Kahn suggests, this insight means that contemporary intellectuals need to rethink their understanding of secular culture not just as the site of hegemony but also as the place of invention.

The Italian jurist and Schmitt scholar Carlo Galli develops his account of Schmitt through an innovative interpretation of Schmitt's *Hamlet or Hecuba*, which appeared in German in 1956 and was recently published in a complete and authorized English translation in 2009. In 1983, Galli worked with Simona Forti to bring out an Italian edition of *Hamlet oder Hekuba*; we are very pleased to be able to include Galli's introduction to that edition in this collection, along with a commentary on Galli and Schmitt by Adam Sitze, who co-translated Galli's piece with Amanda Minervini. Sitze's commentary is meant to introduce an English-speaking audience to Galli's groundbreaking work on Schmitt and political theology. In "*Hamlet*: Representation and the Concrete," Galli links Schmitt's *Hamlet* essay to *Nomos of the Earth*, which Schmitt published in 1950 and which he considered to be his most important work. In *Nomos*, Schmitt argues that the long political settlement organized by the Catholic Church was dissolved and replaced in the early modern period by the *jus publicum europaeum*, a form of limited hostility that allowed the European nation-states to control war amongst themselves on the lines of a self-contained game or *Spiel*, but that radically deregulated the state of war in relation to the seas and to nations outside Europe, leading to the genocidal biopolitics of colonialism. *Hamlet*, with its echoes of religious schism, its maritime setting, and its haunting by crises besetting the person of the monarch, unfolds in the space of an early modernity still in transition between forms of geopolitical order. *Hamlet* discloses the protean and unstable other side of the *jus publicum europaeum*, a "barbaric" play of indecision, violence, and catastrophe that is in the mid-twentieth century the European state's undoing. For Galli, *Hamlet or Hecuba* is not an incidental piece of amateur literary criticism, but rather the text in which Schmitt most openly confronted the tragic structure of his own thought.

Graham Hammill keeps his eye on Schmitt but shifts the problem of political theology onto the terrain of rhetoric. In "Blumenberg and Schmitt on the Rhetoric of Political Theology," Hammill shows how Blumenberg develops an understanding of political theology based on metaphor and imagination. Initially Blumenberg used rhetoric as a term of abuse to dismiss Schmitt's account of the theologico-political sovereign, but as the debate continued, he shifted tactics, redefining some of Schmitt's key concepts through a rhetorical understanding of politics in order to underscore the role that invention plays in early modern and modern versions of political theology. As Hammill shows, for both Schmitt and Blumenberg, the key figure is Hobbes. For Schmitt, Hobbes transposes theological concepts into a modern theory of the state, whereas for Blumenberg, Hobbes initiates a linguistic turn in modern political thought that endows the political subject with theological metaphors that can be manipulated and potentially left behind. In Hammill's reading, Blumenberg's account of political theology and rhetoric anticipates and, in many ways, goes beyond Agamben's recent work on economic theology. Aiming to initiate a conversation between political theology and Foucauldian models of biopower, Agamben shows how theologies of the Trinity from the early Church Fathers through the seventeenth century stage various forms of governmentality. Hammill argues that Blumenberg's understanding of political theology and rhetoric offers a more affirmative model of biopower, one that emphasizes the power of metaphor to place the subject within theologico-political models of governance while also underscoring rhetoric as a fundamentally creative form of life.

In "Political Theologies of the *Corpus Mysticum*," Jennifer Rust anatomizes the concept of the mystical body in the writings of Schmitt, Kantorowicz, and the modern Jesuit theologian Henri de Lubac. Rust demonstrates that Kantorowicz uses the lateral sociological imagery of the *corpus mysticum*, the Pauline figure for the body of the faithful united in the institutions of the church, to counter the more personalist and decidedly vertical models of Catholic order put forward by Schmitt in *Roman Catholicism and Political Form* in 1923. Kantorowicz's main ammunition here is de Lubac's *Corpus Mysticum: The Eucharist and the Church in the Middle Ages*, written during World War II and published in 1944. In an argument that would ultimately influence Vatican II, de Lubac argues that the *corpus mysticum* originally referred to both the sacrificial body of Christ in the Eucharist and the social body of the church instituted in communion. Kantorowicz used the institutional dimensions of de Lubac's *corpus mysticum* to argue for a more horizontal, communal, and durable conception of both the Catholic Church and the forms of secular sovereignty produced out of its tropology than that put forward in Schmitt's writings. Yet Rust goes on to show that Kantorowicz also fundamentally flattens the dynamism of de Lubac's account; Kantorowicz substitutes abstraction, fictionality, and legalism for de Lubac's performative and sacramental account of communion and community. As such, Kantorowicz's secular body is the flip side of Schmitt's authoritarianism. Rust proceeds by reading Kantorowicz against Schmitt (for lateral versus horizontal forms of sovereignty) and then reading de Lubac against Kantorowicz (for sacramental, dynamic, and performative versions of the *corpus mysticum* against abstract, juridical, and bureaucratic ones), opening the door to postsecular readings of Catholic political theology conducted in a progressive social key.

In "Dead Neighbor Archives: Jews, Muslims, and the Enemy's Two Bodies," Kathleen Biddick explores recent work by Agamben and Santner, key figures in the translation of Schmitt's ideas into more left-leaning articulations of political theology. Following the writings of early twentieth-century Jewish philosophers and critical thinkers such as Benjamin, Franz Rosenzweig, and Jacob Taubes, Agamben and Santner turn political theology against itself in order to open a new vision of the political. Focusing specifically on their recuperation of messianic time, Biddick shows how contemporary radical politics remains unwittingly caught in the medieval world of Christian typology. An originary moment for her is Peter the Venerable's campaign against Muslims and Jews in the twelfth century, among other things a hermeneutic battle in which both groups were excluded from the miracle of Christian meaning-making. This exclusion surreptitiously continues in the work of Rosenzweig, Benjamin, and Taubes, all of whom stumble over the figure of the undead Muslim, an untimely irritant whose presence keeps the typological machine grinding. Rather than repeatedly deciding on typology and its covert structures of enmity and exclusion, Biddick argues that typology's untimely remainders foster visions of community in the medieval, early modern, and postmodern worlds.

In "Novus Ordo Saeclorum: Hannah Arendt on Revolutionary Spirit," Paul Kottman reconstructs Arendt's attempts to describe the purely human foundations of political authority in secular modernity. Like Kahn, Kottman is concerned with Enlightenment revisitations of the Renaissance, elaborating in Arendt a new vision of the secular that moves beyond the opposition between liberalism and a Schmittian understanding of political theology. Unlike Kahn, Kottman locates secular creation in politics and not in culture. Machiavelli is Arendt's early modern point of departure; in the *Discorsi*, Machiavelli depicts the founding of both Rome and Venice as moments of human constitution that broke from the tyranny of kinship without referring themselves to divine foundations except through the self-conscious poeisis of civic myth. Arendt insists on the necessary relationship between freedom, founding, and politics: politics is acting freely, and action is new beginning, the founding of possibilities for future action. Whereas such a formulation can lead to an aporia—freedom disappears as soon as the foundation it gives birth to congeals into an order—Kottman demonstrates that the "revolutionary spirit" is a form of active recollection—of recollection *through action*—by means of which new generations remain faithful to the promise of freedom made by previous generations through their deeds in the present. Yet modernity for Arendt is ultimately *not* continuous with the Renaissance. In the wake of the revolutions of the nineteenth and twentieth centuries, Arendt tries to rethink the proper role of the revolutionary spirit as the recollection, indeed the mourning, for the complementary failures of the French and the American Revolutions. Whereas the American Revolution, in devoting itself to the pursuit of happiness, failed to account for mass poverty and thus remained a movement of landholders, becoming the nursery of liberal capitalism rather than the seat of a genuine civic republicanism, the French Revolution, by staking its claims in the liberation of the poor from the necessity of hunger, roped the revolutionary spirit to a certain biopolitical program that would constrain politics to the management of life.

Finally, in "Force and Justice: Auerbach's Pascal," Jane O. Newman shows how scholarly work on political theology in post–World War I Germany enacted and enabled resistance to the Nazi state. Newman focuses her analysis on Auerbach's shifting engagement with Pascal, beginning with his 1933 monograph, *The French Audience in Seventeenth-Century France*, and continuing up through his 1941 essay, "The Triumph of Evil," which was revised and reprinted several times over the course of Auerbach's life and was included as a chapter in his posthumously published *Scenes from the Drama of European Literature* (1959). Initially, Newman argues, Auerbach saw Pascal as part of a defanged intelligentsia produced by what he calls de-Christianization, the separation of the City of God from the City of Man that leaves humans in a world of force with no recourse to justice. But as he was rendered an increasingly passive political actor by the Nazi regime, Auerbach came to see Pascal making an argument for the necessary, if also unpredictable, intrusion of the City of God into the world of human force through the figure of the just individual who resists temporal injustice. Moreover, as Newman shows through careful analysis of Auerbach's footnotes, his critical engagements, and reviews of his own work, at issue for Auerbach was the *Kulturkampf*—the attempt before World War I to create a politically unified Germany through German Lutheranism—and its afterlife in Nazi Germany. The very opposite of a Schmittian version of political theology in which theological concepts are embodied in the person of the sovereign, for Auerbach political theology served as a means by which he could give account of himself and of intellectual activity in mid twentieth-century Europe.

The second section of our collection opens with Jacques Lezra's essay, "The Instance of the Sovereign in the Unconscious: The Primal Scenes of Political Theology." Here, Lezra stages a revelatory encounter between psychoanalysis and the story of Don Carlos, the tragedy of a promising young prince sacrificed to the despotic powers of throne and altar. In Schiller's play *Don Carlos* and in Verdi's opera on the same theme, the story came to emblematize for the rest of Europe Spain's turn away from modernity and enlightenment. Schiller's play celebrates secularization by activating the *akedah*, the almost-sacrifice of Isaac by Abraham, a primal scene for the three monotheisms and the forms of sacrifice and anti-sacrifice, of archaism and reform, around which they organize their scriptures, practices, and self-narrations. For Schiller, the despotic monarch's murder of his enlightened son brands as distinctively "Spanish" the intellectual bankruptcy of inquisition and absolutism. And yet this political-theological legacy returns, in the form of the Spanish Catholicism of Donoso and his German Catholic champion Schmitt, indicating the imperfect character of the secularization displaced from Spain onto other parts of Europe. Like Kahn, Lezra is interested in the Enlightenment as the clearing house of certain Renaissance themes and problems; the Enlightenment in effect tries to finish the secularizing projects that the Renaissance initiates, yet its own efforts remain troubled by the phantasmatic energy of the tropes it attempts to lay to rest. Lezra's essay is significant on many counts, not the least of which is his definitive articulation of the symptomatic role of Spain in the broader European imaginary, and the part played by translation (linguistic and mediatic) in hitching the Spanish problem to a series of apparently unrelated projects, including psychoanalysis and liberalism.

Critics as diverse as Leo Strauss and Samuel Weber have criticized Schmitt for ignoring the role that mediation plays in the installation of the theologico-political sovereign. Schmitt's version of political representation tends to cast the sovereign as a distinctly unmediated form of personhood. In her essay "Staging the Sovereign Softscape," Julia Reinhard Lupton approaches political theology from a diametrically opposed point of view: the mediating work of tapestry in producing the fragile, highly mobile, and sublime aura of the theologico-political court. Focusing on a set of tapestries illustrating the lives of Sts. Peter and Paul, initially designed by Raphael for Pope Leo X, acquired by Henry VIII, and sold off by Oliver Cromwell, Lupton considers the various ways in which the Pauline Renaissance takes shape through the rich and textured scenography of design. As objects that can be bought and sold, Lupton argues, Raphael's tapestries map the pathway from the church to the confessional state. As an instance of iconography joining the life of Paul to that of Peter, the arrases disclose the particular in the universal, the Jewish in the Catholic, and the Catholic in the Protestant. As a form of mediation, tapestry helped to create a public life that was at once theological, theatrical, and designed. Like *The Winter's Tale*, which Lupton also considers, Raphael's tapestries in the Tudor and Stuart courts knit together a hybrid space in which Catholic, Protestant, and profane iconographies join together in and as a form of entertainment. And finally, as softscape, tapestry is emblematic of the various threads and connective tissues both real and symbolic that make up the billowing surfaces and temporary architecture of theologico-political spaces. Instead of condensing political theology into the person of the sovereign, Lupton argues for a more expansive and multidimensional approach that allows us to reencounter the layered, infolded, and continually productive character of the Pauline Renaissance as it unfurls on the scenes of early modernity and in contemporary politics.

In "Striking the French Match: Jean Bodin, Queen Elizabeth, and the Occultation of Sovereign Marriage," Drew Daniel offers marriage as a key figure of political theology, one that links sexuality and erotic life to the life of the body politic. Daniel focuses on Elizabeth's possible marriage to the Duke of Alençon and the role that Bodin played in negotiating that marriage in order to ask whether there might be irreconcilable differences between a political theology that takes marriage as its point of departure and one that starts with sovereignty. Recasting a political theology of the absolute and single sovereign through the dynamic sense of coupling that is at the heart of marriage, Daniel rethinks Schmitt's understanding of the agency and temporality of decision-making. In Daniel's account, Elizabeth becomes Schmitt's unlikely partner, as her opacity in relation to her possible marriage to Alençon—her various and contradictory statements, actions, and communications—offers an eccentric perspective on the purity and clarity of Schmitt's solitary, deciding sovereign. In part, Elizabeth's responses to her possible marriage offer historical nuance and texture to Schmitt's account of political theology. And in part, her literary reflections on the marriage disclose strategies of deferral at the heart of political decision-making. Proceeding through a series of couplings—Elizabeth and Alençon, Bodin and Schmitt, Saint Paul and John Stubbs, Elizabeth and Alain Badiou—Daniel's argument orchestrates a ménage à trois among literature, history, and theory in which each plays helpmeet to the other.

Gregory Kneidel focuses on the limits of typological operations. In "Giving Up the Ghost: The Death of Christ in and as Secular Law," Kneidel poses the apparently simple question of why and how the two halves of the Christian Bible came to be called "testaments." The proof text is Hebrews 9:15–19, which moves from testament as covenant or *berit* (the word used for the covenant at Sinai as well as the covenant of circumcision and the covenant with Noah) to testament as last will, coming from Roman testate law. Reading Renaissance biblical commentaries as well as legal treatises, Kneidel teases out a number of possible narratives and scenarios implied in this almost imperceptible yet dramatic slippage between kinds of testament. Typologically, Roman law displaces Hebrew law, and Christ is cast not only as the new Moses but as the new Justinian. But, for Kneidel, typology does not give us the whole story. In probate law, when two wills survive the testator, one testament must be preferred to the other, based on the "spirit" or meaning of the will, to be determined equitably by the probate judge on the presumption of parental "love." Probate reasoning leads to the same conclusion as typology (the New Testament trumps the Old Testament because it is more "loving"), yet it does so via principles of equity and discretion. Kneidel goes on to link these various debates and tensions to the plurality of jurisdictions in early modern England and the drive to both homogenize and secularize them, a debate in which he locates the poetry of John Donne.

Jonathan Goldberg approaches political theology through a reading of Milton's *Samson Agonistes*. A long tradition of Milton criticism sees Samson's decision to massacre the Philistines as the poem's central problem. Is Samson divinely inspired and, therefore, is Milton legitimating religious violence? Or is Samson a rogue actor, misguided in his inspiration, in which case Milton would be distancing himself from religious violence? However, as Goldberg's essay "Samson Uncircumcised" reminds us, the decision—including the decision between these two readings of Milton's drama—is predicated upon a difference whose undecidability exceeds any attempt to resolve it. In Goldberg's account, this undecidability is figured as circumcision. Less a Jewish ritual to be superseded via Christian typology, for Milton circumcision is a mark of difference within the typological imaginary that simultaneously binds, interrupts, and disturbs hermeneutic, political, religious, and sexual oppositions—between literal and figurative, friend and enemy, Christian and Jew, man and woman, homosexual and heterosexual—around which *Samson Agonistes* is organized. *Samson* is Milton's attempt to account for this mark of difference that, Goldberg argues, motivated his revolutionary politics. At the same time, like Daniel, Goldberg draws our attention to the specifically sexual aspects of political theology. As Goldberg argues, the cut of circumcision also prompts a mass of erotic fantasies in *Samson* around phallic potency and castration. One implication of this argument is that the modern state cannot secure the difference between political and religious violence because the state is in fact founded on a secret complicity shared by the two. A second implication is that religio-political violence needs to be understood in its erotic dimensions as well, since this violence draws its resources from erotic fantasies held in reserve by revolutionary politics.

We conclude this volume with a postscript by Étienne Balibar entitled "The Idea of 'New Enlightenment' [*Nouvelles Lumières*] and the Contradictions of Universalism." Recognizing the Enlightenment as a historical moment with its roots in the early modernity of Spinoza, Balibar argues that enlightenment is also an ongoing possibility for thought, political reform, and social organization, a project that finds itself repeated in multiple places and times in history and across the globe. Balibar probes the dialectic between the Enlightenment as a distinctively Western project whose terms European civilization seems doomed to repeat, and enlightenment as a process of thought and emancipation internal to all cultures and systems of belief. For Balibar, universalism—the legacy of the Enlightenment, but also of monotheism—remains a vexed but urgent mandate for global thought today. Universalism, he argues, repeatedly falls short of its own goals, yet cannot simply be inverted or negated by its opposite (particularism, culture, anthropological difference). Instead, our task according to Balibar is to "tarry" within the contradictions of universalism in order to find ways to displace or disarm them, with the hope of achieving genuine moments of community in contemporary politics, thought, and life.

Notes

1. Debora Kuller Shuger, *Sacred Rhetoric: The Christian Grand Style in the English Renaissance* (Princeton: Princeton University Press, 1998); Ewan Fernie, ed., *Spiritual Shakespeares* (Abingdon: Routledge, 2005). For other innovative approaches to religion in the English Renaissance, see Hannibal Hamlin, *Psalm Culture and Early Modern English Literature* (Cambridge: Cambridge University Press, 2004); Phebe Jensen, *Religion and Revelry in Shakespeare's Festive World* (New York: Cambridge University Press, 2008); James Kearney, *The Incarnate Text: Imagining the Book in Reformation England* (Philadelphia: University of Pennsylvania Press, 2009); Peter Lake and Michael C. Questier, *The Anti-Christ's Lewd Hat: Protestants, Papists and Players in Post-Reformation England* (New Haven: Yale University Press, 2002); and

Susannah Monta, *Martyrdom and Literature in Early Modern England* (New York: Cambridge University Press, 2005).

2. Recent contributions to political theology in early modern studies include Paul Cefalu, *English Renaissance Literature and Contemporary Theory: The Sublime Objects of Theology* (New York: Palgrave Macmillan, 2007); Graham Hammill, *The Mosaic Constitution: Political Theology and Imagination from Machiavelli to Milton*, forthcoming from the University of Chicago Press; Richard Halpern, "The King's Two Buckets: Kantorowicz, *Richard II*, and Fiscal *Trauerspiel*," *Representations* 106 (Spring 2009): 67–76; Gregory Kneidel, *Rethinking the Turn to Religion in Early Modern English Literature* (New York: Palgrave Macmillan, 2008); Anselm Haverkamp, "*Richard II*, Bracton, and the End of Political Theology," *Law and Literature* 16.3 (2005): 313–26; Jacques Lezra, *Wild Materialism: The Ethic of Terror and the Modern Republic* (New York: Fordham University Press, 2010); Julia Reinhard Lupton, *Citizen-Saints: Shakespeare and Political Theology* (Chicago: University of Chicago Press, 2005); and Jennifer Rust, "Political Theology and Shakespeare Studies," *Literature Compass* 6.1 (November 2008): 175–90. In German, see Thomas Frank, Albrecht Kokshorke, Susanne Liebermann, and Ethel de Mazza, *Des Kaisers neue Kleider: Über das Imaginäre politischer Herrschaft* (Frankfurt: Fischer, 2002); Albrecht Kokshorke et al., *Der fiktive Staat: Konstruktionen des politischen Körpers in der Geschichte Europas* (Frankfurt: Fischer, 2007); and Björn Quiring, *Shakespeares Fluch* (Munich: Wilhelm Fink, 2009).

3. For some of these latter extensions, see Julia Reinhard Lupton, *Thinking with Shakespeare: Essays on Politics and Life* (Chicago: University of Chicago Press, 2011).

4. Carl Schmitt, *Political Theology: Four Chapters on the Concept of Sovereignty*, trans. Tracy Strong (Chicago: University of Chicago Press, 2006).

5. Carl Schmitt, *Nomos of the Earth*, trans. G. L. Ulmen (New York: Telos Press, 2003).

6. Carl Schmitt, *The Leviathan in the State Theory of Thomas Hobbes: Meaning and Failure of a Political Symbol*, introduced by George Schwab, trans. George Schwab and Erna Hilfstein (Westport, Conn.: Greenwood Press, 1996).

7. There is a growing bibliography of work on political theology that takes up the two terms as the sign of an impasse, not a synthesis (which means leaving aside works of positive theology). Key texts include Eric Santner, *The Royal Remains: The People's Two Bodies and the Endgames of Sovereignty* (Chicago: University of Chicago Press, 2011); Hent de Vries and Lawrence E. Sullivan, eds., *Political Theologies: Public Religions in a Post-Secular World* (New York: Fordham University Press, 2006); Hent de Vries and Samuel Weber, eds., *Religion and Media* (Stanford: Stanford University Press, 2001); Miguel Vatter, ed., *Crediting God: Sovereignty and Religion in the Age of Global Capitalism* (New York: Fordham University Press, 2011); Vincent P. Pecora, *Secularization and Cultural Criticism: Religion, Nation, and Modernity* (Chicago: University of Chicago Press, 2006); and Slavoj Žižek, Eric Santner, and Kenneth Reinhard, *The Neighbor: Three Inquiries in Political Theology* (Chicago: University of Chicago Press, 2005).

8. Eric Santner, *On the Psychotheology of Everyday Life: Reflections on Freud and Rosenzweig* (Chicago: University of Chicago Press, 2001). See also Bonnie Honig, *Emergency Politics: Paradox, Law, Democracy* (Princeton: Princeton University Press, 2009), for inventive readings of Rosenzweig, democracy, and emergency contra Schmitt.

9. Graham Hammill develops this distinction in *The Mosaic Constitution: Political Theology and Imagination from Machiavelli to Milton.*

10. Drew Daniel cites Daniel Dennett on problem spaces in AI research: "An impasse creates a new problem space (a sort of topical workspace) in which the problem to be solved is precisely the impasse. This may generate yet another, meta-meta traffic problem space, and so on." *The*

Melancholy Assemblage, Fordham University Press, forthcoming.

11. Hans Blumenberg, "Prospect for a Theory of Nonconceptuality," in *Shipwreck with Spectator: Paradigm for a Metaphor of Existence,* trans. Steven Rendall (Cambridge, Mass.: MIT Press, 1997), 81, 98. See also Hans Blumenberg, *Paradigms for a Metaphorology,* trans. Robert Savage (Ithaca: Cornell University Press, 2010).

12. See our introduction to *Sovereigns, Citizens, and Saints: Political Theology and Renaissance Literature,* ed. Julia Reinhard Lupton and Graham Hammill, special issue, *Religion and Literature* 38 (Autumn 2006): 1–6.

13. Hannah Arendt, *The Life of the Mind* (San Diego: Harcourt Brace, 1971), 86.

14. For a powerful and highly influential version of this argument, see Richard Helgerson's groundbreaking *Forms of Nationhood: The Elizabethan Writing of England* (Chicago: University of Chicago Press, 1992).

15. For innovative variations of this argument, see for example Maurice Hunt, *Shakespeare's Religious Allusiveness: Its Play and Tolerance* (Aldershot: Ashgate, 2004) and John Cox, *Seeming Knowledge: Shakespeare and Sceptical Faith* (Waco, Texas: Baylor University Press, 2007).

16. Hent de Vries, "Introduction," in *Political Theologies,* 25.

17. *Spinoza: Complete Works,* trans. Samuel Shirley, ed. and introduced by Michael L. Morgan (Indianapolis and Cambridge: Hackett Publishing, 2002), 389–90.

18. Ibid., 540.

19. For an account of the shift from the Kantorowicz of the New Historicism to the Kantorowicz of political theology, see Victoria Kahn, "Political Theology and Fiction in *The King's Two Bodies,*" *Representations* 106 (Spring 2009): 77–78.

20. Perhaps most significant among these intellectuals for the overall project of this volume is Agamben, whose work on sovereignty and law traces the labyrinthine pathways of political theology from the contemporary moment backwards to interwar Germany, early modern Europe, the foundations of the Catholic Church, and the administration of Roman law. These various moments dramatize the persistence of political theology through problems of inclusion and exclusion, sovereignty, and violence as well as dreams of redemption, disturbances in time-keeping, and the return of forgotten possibilities. See Giorgio Agamben, *Homo Sacer: Sovereign Power and Bare Life,* trans. Daniel Heller-Roazen (Stanford: Stanford University Press, 1998).

21. The American reception of Schmitt has tended to focus on *Political Theology* and *The Concept of the Political,* both written during the Weimar period and both locating the problem of political theology in the personal authority of the sovereign, although new work on Schmitt is beginning to focus on his constitutional writings and his theories of representation. This new work is represented, for example, in a special issue of *Telos* (Winter 2010) on Schmitt and Shakespeare, edited by David T. Pan and Julia Reinhard Lupton.

PART ONE

Modern Destinations

1

Political Theology and Liberal Culture:
Strauss, Schmitt, Spinoza, and Arendt

VICTORIA KAHN

Indeed, I barely comprehend how one can be a poet without admiring Spinoza, loving
him, and becoming entirely his.

FRIEDRICH SCHLEGEL

Words are a part of the imagination.

SPINOZA, *The Emendation of the Intellect*

In recent years there has been considerable interest in the problem of political theology, understood as the theological legitimation or religious dimension of political authority. Political events and social movements, from the
Iranian revolution, to 9/11, to the resurgence of the Taliban, to born-again
Christianity in the United States, have prompted Western scholars to revisit
the relationship between religion and the state, in the process frequently
castigating liberalism for cordoning off religion within the sphere of private
experience. And increasingly, modern scholars are returning to one of the
formative moments in the discourse of political theology—that of Weimar
Germany—to conceptualize the problems posed by political theology or to
rethink the relationship between divine law and positive law. It is this turn
that explains the current widespread interest in the work of Carl Schmitt, Leo
Strauss, Ernst Kantorowicz, and other theorists of political theology.

In this essay, I want to complicate the current discussion of political theology by turning to one of the neglected terms of this earlier discussion, that
of culture. In particular, I want to understand what the term meant and why
it was anathema to both defenders (e.g., Schmitt) and critics (e.g., Strauss)
of political theology in early twentieth-century Germany. What work was the
idea of culture doing in the early twentieth-century debate about political
theology? I will suggest that culture for these writers was conceived of as a
product of early modern hermeneutics and the Enlightenment critique of religion. I'll argue that, while its critics saw culture as a symptom of historicism
and relativism, its defenders made culture a bulwark against political theology. Against the political decisionism of conservative figures such as Carl

Schmitt or the religious decisionism of radical Protestant theologians such as
Karl Barth, defenders of culture advanced what we might call a literary decision, a decision in favor of literature, that is modeled neither on law nor on
the idea of the exception. This decision, I'll suggest, is worth recovering as we
think about the work of the humanities today.

This essay is in four parts. In the first, I briefly discuss the stakes of the
idea of culture (*Bildung* or *Kultur*) in early twentieth-century debates about
history and political theology. In the second section, I offer an account of
the early work of Carl Schmitt and Leo Strauss on political theology and its
relation to modern culture (the focus here is Strauss's work on Spinoza).
In the third section, I read Spinoza as elaborating a defense of culture in
response to Strauss. And, in the fourth and final section, I look briefly at a
modern defense of the idea of culture (that of Hannah Arendt) and a modern
defense of the relevance of Spinoza for thinking about literature (Althusser
and Macherey), both of which help us to understand what it might mean to
think of literary culture as a bulwark against political theology and a model
of political judgment.

1. Culture and Historicism

Let me begin by situating the turn to political theology on the part of thinkers
such as Schmitt and the early Strauss as a response to the early twentieth-
century "crisis of historicism." Historicism (German *Historismus*) was a
loose intellectual movement, and sometimes a method of interpretation, that
argued that meaning was immanent in history and that historical events and
texts needed to be interpreted in light of their immediate historical context.
In the late eighteenth and nineteenth centuries, historicist thinking emerged
as a reaction against Enlightenment ideas of universal norms of rationality.[1]
In his pamphlet "Yet Another Philosophy of History for the Cultivation of
Mankind" (*Auch eine Philosophie der Geschichte zur Bildung der Menschheit*)
of 1774, Johann Gottfried Herder criticized the idea of universal principles of
rationality and the view that history manifested itself in the gradual cultivation (*Bildung*) of humanity. Instead, Herder asserted the diversity of cultures
of different historical epochs. Friedrich Schleiermacher advanced a similar
argument in his essays "On Religion" (*Über die Religion: Reden an die Gebil-
deten unter ihren Verächtern*). Schleiermacher's target was those Enlightenment thinkers who equated enlightenment with the overcoming of religious
superstition. Against these "cultured despisers" of religion, Schleiermacher
defended what Jeffrey Andrew Barash has called "the principle of the histo-

ricity of truth as a plea for comprehension of historical divergence of religious beliefs" (5–6). Schleiermacher also advanced the hermeneutical principle that it was the goal of the interpreter to understand texts of an earlier period better than the author understood them himself.[2] (Strauss will later repeatedly attack this claim.) In the late nineteenth century Wilhelm Dilthey elevated this principle of "historicity"—"the historical constitution" of culture and its truths—into a method of historical analysis.[3]

Already in the first decades of the twentieth century there was a reaction against historicism and cultural analysis as forms of relativism. Oswald Spengler's *Decline of the West* in particular was seen as an attack on "the prewar liberal confidence in German and Western culture" and as bringing "into sharp question the forms of liberal historical scholarship through which cultural development" had been interpreted. In 1919, the Protestant theologian Friedrich Gogarten wrote a manifesto entitled *Zwischen den Zeiten* (Between the Times), in which he declared, "We are jubilant over the Spengler book. It proves, whether one agrees with its details or not, that the hour has struck when this fine, clever culture [*Kultur*] discovers, out of its own cleverness, the worm that is eating it; when trust in the development of culture receives the deathblow. And the Spengler book is not the only sign."[4] Gogarten had in his sights liberal theologians such as Ernst Troeltsch and Adoph von Harnack who had studied religion as a historical and cultural phenomenon, as an instance of cultural "values," rather than as an experience of "radical otherness." Gogarten was not alone is seeing relativism as "the inevitable outcome" of the historicist methods of "liberal theology."[5] The German theologian Rudolph Bultmann, Martin Heidegger, and the Swiss Protestant Karl Barth were also struggling to recover a more authentic and personal approach to religious experience. Like Gogarten, Bultmann criticized the cultural approach to religion, emphasizing instead the need for a decision (*Entscheidung*) in favor of faith. This language of "decision" was also used by Heidegger in his lectures on the phenomenology of religion in 1920–21. For Gogarten, Bultmann, and Heidegger, "'decision' involved a return to the individual self, which chose its existence in resolute opposition to the inhibiting factors of the natural or historical objectivity surrounding it."[6] Karl Barth's 1919 commentary on Paul's Epistle to the Romans also stressed the need for a decision in favor of faith and against existing historical conditions. He did so in part as a reaction against "the nationalism of the German theologians, who did not hesitate to see a Divine purpose behind German involvement" in World War I. In charged language that anticipates the later complicity of theologians with the Nazi cause, Barth wrote:

Can religion be of such absorbing interest that it may be welcomed as an enrichment of life, a valuable addition to civilization, or even as a substitute for it? When men are already sufficiently burdened by the inner uncertainty which attaches both to civilization and to barbarism, is it credible that religion should be brought triumphantly into connection with science, art, ethics, socialism, the State, Youth Movements and Race, as though we had not had abundant experience of the waste land of 'Religion and . . . '? . . . The watchman at the gate of humanity has only to take care lest, at the eleventh hour, he too may be compelled to conclude a short armistice with the adversary of whom he is so terrified. Religion, though it come disguised as the most intimate friend of men, be they Greeks or barbarians, is nevertheless the adversary. Religion is the KRISIS of culture and barbarism.[7]

Against the political theology of German nationalists as well as the cultural relativism of liberal theology, Barth asserted the radical otherness of God, his "utter transcendence vis-à-vis the things of this world."[8] This is the intellectual and political context in which both Schmitt and Strauss took up the question of political theology. Both saw historicism as synonymous with cultural relativism, and both were trying to rethink the relationship between politics and religion, positive law and divine law, in ways that responded to political crisis of World War I and the intellectual failures of historicism.

2. Strauss and Schmitt

I think it's fair to say that the most important text in recent discussions of political theology (at least those that try to provide a genealogy of the term) is Carl Schmitt's treatise by that title of 1922. Schmitt used the term political theology historically to refer to the secularization or appropriation of theological concepts for political purposes. More important, he used the term structurally to describe the homology between the theological or metaphysical assumptions of a given age and its dominant political form. And, most important of all, he used the term existentially: a political theologian is one who understands the theological or ultimate stakes of politics. The current widespread interest in Schmitt can be attributed not only to his stringent critique of liberalism but also to his insistence on the theological dimension of political conflict (though what this means is, of course, the subject of considerable debate among readers of Schmitt).

In this section I want to suggest that the work of Leo Strauss—Schmitt's younger contemporary—is equally important for understanding the early twentieth-century debate about political theology, though for complex reasons it has been marginalized within the American academy. Specifically, I propose to use Strauss in order to complicate recent discussions of political theology. By the term political theology Strauss meant a political regime founded on revelation; but by the problem of political theology, Strauss meant the question of the relationship between political theology and political philosophy, or between revelation and reason. For Strauss, this was a "permanent problem" for Western political thought, deriving from its twin heritage of Greek philosophy and the Bible, Athens and Jerusalem. The great political philosophers of the seventeenth century—Hobbes, Spinoza, and Locke—had tried to "solve" the problem of political theology by subordinating religion to the state or by arguing, in proto-liberal fashion, for the separation of state and church, public and private, politics and culture. But, in Strauss's view, they had not so much solved the problem of political theology as repressed it. This does not mean, however, that Strauss was a defender of political theology.[9] Rather, it means he was a critic of liberalism.

In his early work on Hobbes and Spinoza, whom he saw as proto-liberal thinkers, Strauss registered his dissatisfaction with liberal political theory but had not yet found an alternative. In his later work, he became a defender of what he considered the classical notion of philosophy. Thus, while Strauss declared that his whole career had been motivated by a concern with the "theological-political problem," he had a very different understanding of this problem than did Schmitt—and not only because Strauss was Jewish and Schmitt Catholic. Although Strauss entertained the idea of religious orthodoxy as a young man, the mature Strauss was a rationalist who wanted to defend the claims of reason against political theology and the tyranny of revelation, on the one hand, and against liberalism on the other.

In this section, I trace Strauss's critique of political theology, a critique that went hand in hand with an attack on a liberal or Enlightenment idea of culture, which Strauss associated with Spinoza. In the next section, I turn to Spinoza to see what a critique of political theology looks like that defends a liberal idea of culture as a sphere of human activity that makes room for religion while also disabling its claims to theocracy. This comparison of Strauss and Spinoza is designed to bring culture and the imagination to the fore as neglected terms in modern discussions of political theology—not only as sources of *the power* of political theology but also as vehicles of its critique.

Let me begin my account of Strauss's shifting views of the problem of political theology by turning to the autobiographical preface to his first book, *Spinoza's Critique of Religion.* (The book was published in 1930, the preface in 1962.) In the preface, Strauss describes himself at the time of its writing as "a young Jew born and raised in Germany who found himself in the grip of the theologico-political predicament" (1). Here the theological-political problem refers to the problem of the relationship between religion and politics, and specifically to the Jewish question, which is the form this problem takes in nineteenth- and early twentieth-century Europe. Strauss equates the theological-political predicament with the failure of liberalism to solve the Jewish question in Weimar Germany. Liberalism had claimed to solve the Jewish question by making religion a personal matter and treating Jews as equals under the law. But such formal equality, Strauss argued, could not address the ongoing problem of discrimination in the private sphere. Political Zionism was a response to this failure of liberalism to deal with anti-Semitism, but political Zionism was in turn vulnerable to criticism by cultural Zionists for evacuating Judaism of its cultural heritage. Yet even cultural Zionism, Strauss argued, was a diluted form of Judaism, a religion which claims, after all, to be founded on divine revelation. Jewish faith "must regard as blasphemous the notion of a human solution to the Jewish problem" (6), Strauss wrote. And he continued, "One could not have taken this step [of cultural Zionism] unless one had previously interpreted the Jewish heritage itself as a culture, i.e. as a product of the national mind, of the national genius. Yet the foundation, the authoritative layer, of the Jewish heritage presents itself, not as a product of the human mind, but as a divine gift, a divine revelation. Did not one completely distort the meaning of the heritage to which one claimed to be loyal by interpreting it as a culture like any other high culture," he asked.[10] In this analysis, Strauss does not object to liberalism simply because the public/private distinction cannot guarantee freedom from anti-Semitism. Rather, his objection to liberalism is even more fundamental: in his view, Judaism is a political theology and is thus incompatible with the liberal, Enlightenment idea of culture, that is, with a celebration of "product[s] of the human mind" or a belief in "human solutions" to human problems.

Such an objection might suggest that Strauss was sympathetic to modern critics of Enlightenment reason and culture, such as Heidegger. And, in fact, we know that Strauss was deeply impressed by Heidegger's lectures at Freiburg and that he thought of Heidegger as the most important philosopher of the twentieth century.[11] In this light, it's striking that Strauss was critical of Heidgegger in the preface to *Spinoza's Critique of Religion*, and that he used the term "political theology" to refer pejoratively to the secularization of Christian concepts in the work of Heidegger and Franz Rosenzweig.[12] Heidegger and Rosenzweig had rejected Greek philosophy's criterion of reason in favor of an existential experience of a divine call or "being-towards-death." But according to Strauss, this merely amounted to "a secularized version of the Biblical faith as interpreted by Christian theology" (12). Heidegger wanted to "expel from philosophy the last relics of Christian theology like the notions of 'eternal truths' and 'the idealized absolute subject,'" but he ended up rein-terpreting human existence in terms of concepts derived from Christianity, such as "anguish," "conscience," and "guilt" (12).[13] Although Strauss doesn't mention Schmitt in the preface to *Spinoza's Critique of Religion*, Schmitt too might be said to belong in this existentialist camp. For Strauss, all such existentialist "new thinking" was in fact simply old relativism dressed up in new clothes.

Strauss goes on in the preface to imagine the consequences of this intel-lectual desert for the modern Jew. Confronted with the failure of both liberal-ism and modern thinking, the modern Jew (aka Strauss) questions whether a return to orthodoxy might be the best course. In attempting this return, however, he discovers that the way is blocked by Spinoza. That is, any Jew who wants to return to orthodoxy needs to confront Spinoza's critique of orthodoxy in his *Theological-Political Treatise* of 1670 (henceforth *TTP*). This was the task that Strauss set himself in his 1930 book on Spinoza. Spinoza had argued that the Bible provides no evidence for the belief in miracles or, indeed, for a transcendent deity. Instead, the Bible presents moral truths in the form of stories that will inculcate obedience among the uneducated. Spi-noza's stated goal was to show that philosophy posed no threat to religious belief—or vice versa—because philosophy and theology occupied entirely separate spheres. But Spinoza's unstated goal, according to Strauss, was to undermine the authority of Scripture altogether by showing that the Bible was a merely human book, with a complicated textual history involving com-pilation and corruption. According to Strauss, in criticizing political theol-ogy and reducing God to nature, Spinoza founded a new church "not based on any positive revelation" (17), "a Church whose rulers were not priests or pastors but philosophers and artists . . . whose flock were [people of] culture and property. . . . The new Church would transform Jews and Christians into human beings . . . of a certain kind: cultured human beings, . . . who because they possessed Science and Art did not need religion in addition" (17).

According to Strauss, Spinoza's effort to refute belief and found a new "church" of culture failed. This is because belief by definition cannot be refuted by reason. Strauss writes in the preface to *Spinoza's Critique of Religion*:

> If orthodoxy claims to *know* that the Bible is divinely revealed, that every word of the Bible is divinely inspired, that Moses was the writer of the Pen-tateuch, that the miracles recorded in the Bible have happened . . . , Spinoza has refuted orthodoxy. But the case is entirely different if orthodoxy limits itself to asserting that it [merely] *believes* the aforementioned things, i.e. that

they [that is, miracles and other supernatural events] cannot claim to possess the binding power peculiar to the known. For all assertions of orthodoxy rest on the irrefutable premise that the omnipotent God whose will is unfathomable . . . may exist. (28; my emphasis)

But philosophy by this argument is *also* based on belief, specifically the belief in reason: Strauss writes, "philosophy, the quest for evident and necessary knowledge, rests itself on an unevident decision, on an act of will, just as faith does" (29). This means that Spinoza's critique has the same cognitive status as belief. It also means that modern atheism is what Strauss calls an "atheism out of intellectual probity." Such atheism would then be the moral descendant of biblical morality and a modern version of the "will to power" (30). In other words, the rational assertion of the impossibility of a transcendent, inscrutable God is as much a matter of belief as the most devout profession of faith.

Two years later, in 1932, when Strauss wrote a commentary on Schmitt's *Concept of the Political*, he had already moved beyond the critique of reason he articulated in his Spinoza book.[14] We might even say that his commentary amounts to an auto-critique in the guise of a critique of Schmitt's existentialism and subjectivism. *The Concept of the Political* pursued the argument adumbrated in *Political Theology* that liberalism goes hand in hand with a new idea of culture.[15] First and most simply, the liberal idea of human nature dialectically produces an idea of culture. That is, the liberal assumption that human beings first exist in a prepolitical, amoral state of nature gives rise to the idea that humans can be educated to become cultured or civilized. The assumption here is that individuals fashion themselves just as they artificially form the state. This view was anathema to Schmitt, who held that human beings were dangerous or evil by nature, that this evil provided the moral basis of absolute rule, and that politics was not a matter of self-fashioning but of intense existential conflict between friend and enemy, understood as communities rather than individuals. But equally distasteful to Schmitt was the fact that the whole goal of liberalism was to mitigate the existential or religious intensity of politics by turning politics into one activity among others that an individual might engage in—along with law, economics, art, and entertainment. According to Schmitt, culture is another name for this fragmentation of spheres of activity, a fragmentation that obscures the primacy of the political (*Concept of the Political*, 53, 72). Instead of a "politically united people," liberalism breaks down this political unity into "a culturally interested public" on the one hand, and a mass of workers and consumers on the other hand (72).

Strauss agreed with this association of liberalism with a certain Enlightenment idea of culture. In his *Notes* on Schmitt's *Concept of the Political* he seconded Schmitt's insight that "the understanding of the political implies a fundamental critique of at least the prevailing concept of culture," with its differentiation of human activities into spheres of autonomy, including "the autonomy of the aesthetic, of morality, of science, of the economy" and so on (86). And he went on to argue, "If it is true that the final self-awareness of liberalism is the philosophy of culture, we may say . . . that liberalism, sheltered by and engrossed in a world of culture, forgets the foundation of culture, [which is] the state of nature, that is, human nature in its dangerousness and endangeredness" (92). But, Strauss argues, in *The Concept of the Political* Schmitt is still working within the liberal idea of culture, and this vitiates his own analysis of the political. Although Schmitt declares that all genuine concepts of the political assume that man is evil, his own understanding of evil is ambiguous. He sometimes equates this with moral evil, at other times with amoral animal power. In his admiration of amoral power, Schmitt has unwittingly endorsed the new proto-liberal political anthropology of Hobbes, Spinoza, and Pufendorf, an anthropology that gives rise to the liberal idea that humans can be fashioned by culture. According to this new anthropology, human beings in the state of nature are governed by passions and interests rather than any consideration of what is right. This amoral view of human nature dialectically generates the liberal idea of culture, that is, the assumption that human beings, barbarous by nature, can be educated or civilized.[16] But, because the liberal idea of culture that Schmitt unwittingly endorses is not based on a notion of natural or fundamental right, it turns all human preoccupations into matters of merely subjective preference.[17] For this reason, Schmitt needs to move beyond the liberal, individualistic conception of morality and find a new basis on which to affirm the political.[18]

Strauss's critique of Schmitt's entanglement in the liberal idea of culture is also a critique of Schmitt's political theology. In fact, Strauss implies that Schmitt's conception of political theology is merely a continuation of the notion of culture Schmitt attacks. Specifically, Strauss criticizes Schmitt for describing "the thesis of [man's] dangerousness as a '*supposition*,' as an 'anthropological confession of *faith*'" (58). This faith cannot be the basis of the political for Strauss. According to Strauss, "If man's dangerousness is *only supposed or believed in, not genuinely known*, the opposite too can be regarded as possible, and the attempt to eliminate man's dangerousness . . . can be put into practice. If man's dangerousness is *only believed in*, it is in principle *threatened*, and therewith the political is threatened also." And this in turn means that, although Schmitt wants to affirm the political, he can offer no argument for doing so.[19] According to Strauss, then, liberal culture and Schmittian political theology are mirror images of each other, because each is vulnerable to the charge of irrationalism. In the case of liberalism, irrationalism takes the form of historicism and relativism; in Schmitt's political theology, irrationalism takes the form of relativism and existentialism. Against the subjectivism of Schmitt's political theology, Strauss insists that reason rather than faith is necessary to ground the political.[20]

Strauss's critique of Schmitt thus looks forward to Strauss's later work, specifically Strauss's recuperation of classical philosophy. In this later work, Strauss rejected his own 1930 analysis of Spinoza because it framed the problem of political theology in terms of the conflict of modern reason and revelation, while neglecting the classical notion of reason. As he remarked in his 1962 preface to *Spinoza's Critique of Religion*, the 1930 book was "based on the premise, sanctioned by powerful prejudice, that a return to pre-modern philosophy is impossible" (31). Strauss's recognition now of the possibility of returning to premodern philosophy already underlies his comments on Schmitt's *Concept of the Political*. But it is fully developed in Strauss's later work.[21]

In this later work, even as Strauss develops his defense of premodern reason, Spinoza remains a symptom of the failure of modern rationality. In *Philosophy and Law* (1935), Strauss contrasted medieval rationalism to "the world created by the Enlightenment and its heirs, the world of 'modern culture'" (31). Alluding to Spinoza, he went on to say that, in its critique of religious orthodoxy, the Enlightenment failed to prove the impossibility of miracles and succeeded only in showing their "unknowability" (32). In a footnote, Strauss added:

> If 'religion' and 'politics' are *the* facts that transcend 'culture,' or, to speak more precisely, the *original* facts, then the radical critique of the concept of 'culture' is possible only in the form of a 'theologico-political treatise,'—which of course, if it is not to lead back again to the foundation of 'culture,' must take exactly the opposite direction from the theologico-political treatises of the seventeenth century, especially those of Hobbes and Spinoza. The first condition for this would be, of course, that these seventeenth-century works no longer be understood, as they almost always have been up to now, within the horizon of the philosophy of culture. (138n2)

That is, Hobbes and Spinoza should not be understood from within the liberal set of presuppositions they worked to establish. Rather, they should be understood in relation to the theological-political predicament that their works aimed to solve, however unsuccessfully. Really to address the problem

POLITICAL THEOLOGY AND LIBERAL CULTURE 33

of political theology, Strauss suggests, one needs to take it seriously, not assume it has disappeared. But, such a theological-political treatise would not be a work in the style of Schmitt. To the contrary, it would look like the later work of Strauss.

In one of those later works, *Persecution and the Art of Writing* (1952), Strauss returns to Spinoza's *TTP*.[22] Now the problem is not that Spinoza has failed to prove the impossibility of miracles or to rationally refute the belief in miracles. The problem is, instead, that Spinoza's historicism has unintentionally infected his own defense of reason. In Strauss's view, the *TTP* is "*the* classic document of the 'rationalist' or 'secularist' attack on the belief in revelation" (142). But the historicist protocols of interpretation that Spinoza elaborates in the *TTP* make him vulnerable to similar protocols of interpretation and thus undermine his claim to philosophical truth (157–58). In particular, Strauss argues that Spinoza's progressive idea of knowledge—the idea that knowledge develops gradually in history—is at odds with his ambition to reveal what Strauss calls the "whole," or the truth. As a result of this focus on progress, Strauss argues, "the history of human thought . . . now takes the place formerly occupied by philosophy or, in other words, philosophy transforms itself into [the] history of human thought. . . . Once this state has been reached, the original meaning of philosophy is accessible only through recollection of what philosophy meant in the past, i.e., for all practical purposes, only through the reading of old books" (157). While Strauss turns to old books to resuscitate an ancient idea of philosophy, he implies that Spinoza has turned the *TTP* into a different kind of "old book," a mere product of its historical moment or specific culture, which we can evaluate but in which we cannot believe. We can evaluate the work, or in Strauss's words (borrowed from Schleiermacher), claim to understand it better than the author understood it himself, because our historical distance gives us a superior perspective on the works of the past; but, by the same token, our historicist vision makes it impossible for us to accept the work as the truth. It is for this reason, according to Strauss, that Spinoza's effort to found a new church of culture must fail. To put this another way, culture is the name of this failure.

3. Spinoza

I now want to turn to Spinoza to see what kind of resistance the *TTP* offers to Strauss's reading. I'll suggest that in Spinoza we find a critique of political theology that also makes room for a liberal, Enlightenment idea of culture. I'm thinking here of the Enlightenment project as the effort to combine a recognition of the historicity of culture with the transcendence of reason.[23]

The task of the Enlightenment is to acknowledge the historical conditions of prejudice while also asking how reason can emancipate itself from the shackles of prejudice and custom. Two common answers have been that reason unfolds itself teleologically through the historical development of culture (a position associated with Hegel) or that culture makes available a space for the cultivation of reason (a position advanced by Habermas). Spinoza, as we'll see, offers a different defense of the liberal state as a space that preserves the tension between reason and culture or the irreducibility of one to the other. The state is neither the representative of culture, in Schmitt's and Strauss's pejorative understanding of culture as space of conflicting interests; nor is the state simply an instrument of reason. Instead, it's the function of the state to protect both the space of culture and the very different activity of philosophy.[24] How does this work?

As I noted at the beginning of this essay, Spinoza's goal in the *TTP* is to defend the freedom to philosophize and to argue that this freedom is best preserved by republics which grant toleration to different faiths. He does so by arguing that religion and philosophy occupy separate spheres, which means that philosophy poses no threat to religion, but also that religion has no purchase on philosophy. Spinoza makes his argument by elaborating a scriptural hermeneutics, which in turn underwrites a critique of theocracy. Read correctly, the Hebrew Bible demonstrates not only that the prophets have no particular claim to divine inspiration but also that miracles are impossible. This means that the essence of religion is simply a set of basic moral doctrines rather than a matter of supernatural revelation. This "elimination of supernatural agency" from Scripture and from the natural world in turn underwrites Spinoza's critique of theocracy.[25] First, he argues, the theocratic Hebrew state is revealed to be the result of the purely human decision to transfer one's rights to a sovereign, just like any other state (19.240). Once the essence of religion is revealed to be a set of basic moral doctrines rather than a matter of supernatural revelation, the power of superstition is undercut; and, along with this, the power of crafty priests to manipulate the superstitious multitude.

Spinoza supports his critique of theocracy by describing the destruction of the Hebrew state from within, owing to the increasing power of the priesthood (17.228–29). He also argues that it is no longer possible to imitate the ancient Hebrew state because covenants with God are no longer made in ink or stone but "written on the heart by the spirit of God" (18.230). As religion is internalized and universalized by this divine writing on the heart (19.241), it becomes possible to distinguish between internal faith and outward observance. The latter becomes the purview of the state, which, in Hobbesian and

Erastian fashion, firmly subordinates all churches to secular control, but also grants toleration to individuals of different faiths as long as they obey the laws of the state.

From the very beginning of the *TTP* it is clear that, in contrast to Strauss, Spinoza does not think that "religion and politics are *the* facts that transcend culture." To the contrary, along with philosophy, religion and politics are the creations of culture. In Spinoza, the critique of political theology—of a politics based on the claim to revelation—thus goes hand in hand with an elaboration of something like a proto-Enlightenment idea of culture as the historically specific set of beliefs, assumptions, and artifacts produced by a given people.[26] Let me give three examples of how Spinoza's critique of political theology also articulates and defends this idea of culture.

First, the *TTP* presents scriptural hermeneutics as a process of reading (immanently) that turns sacred scripture into stories and religion into culture. Against Calvin, Spinoza rejects the view that the interpretation of Scripture requires a supernatural faculty; and against Maimonides, he rejects the view that Scripture must be judged by the criterion of reason. Instead, Spinoza proposes to interpret the Bible according to the Bible itself. Rather than assuming the truth of Scripture at the outset, Spinoza tells us with revolutionary common sense that the truth of Scripture is what needs to be ascertained through reading. This in turn produces a distinction between meaning and truth, and dictates the reader's focus on the explicit meaning of the text rather than its correspondence to some a priori doctrine.[27] Scripture, traditionally construed as divinely authored truth, becomes instead narrative, parable, and other vividly imagined ways of telling the history of the Jews. Prophecy has no particular claim to divine revelation; instead, the prophets are simply men with unusually vivid imaginations (2.27). Thus, in chapter 2 of the *TTP*, Spinoza describes the different imaginations of the prophets: "For Isaiah saw seraphim with seven wings each, while Ezekiel saw beasts with four wings each; Isaiah saw God clothed and seated on a royal throne, while Ezekiel saw him as a fire. Each undoubtedly saw God as he was accustomed to imagine him" (2.32). Unlike Maimonides, who thought that passages in Scripture that conflict with reason needed to be interpreted metaphorically, Spinoza doesn't simply subject the prophet's imaginations to translation by reason. Instead, Spinoza argues, the Bible itself makes clear that prophecy should be accepted as the imaginative rendering of the divine. By accepting these imaginations at face value as imaginative, Spinoza disables their claim to theoretical truth. The implication of this analysis is that religion is not in principle different from any other cultural artifact. What is required to understand Scripture apart from the knowledge of biblical Hebrew is simply an

understanding of the operation of metaphor, narrative, and allegory, as well
as an understanding of the vagaries of textual transmission.

But—and this is my second point about the positive role of culture in the
TTP—while Spinoza describes prophecy as a function of the imagination,
he doesn't simply condemn the imagination as a source of illusion. He also
focuses on the positive or constitutive function of the imagination. (Here
it's important to remember that, by imagination, Spinoza means, first, "all
thought, including sense perception." But he also construes "imagination
in the more limited and usual sense of the mind's propensity to form ideas
of absent objects. Depending on circumstances and the conclusions drawn,
this propensity can be viewed as either a power or a defect of the mind.")[28]
Spinoza argues that precisely because prophecy is a function of the imagination rather than of reason, the prophets' certainty was "not mathemati-
cal certainty but moral certainty" (2.28). But he then claims that this moral
certainty has a *positive* role to play in the development of ethics: "the reason
why [the prophets] are so highly praised and commended was not for the
sublimity and excellence of their intellects but for their piety and constancy"
(3.35). This means, in the gloss of Yirmiyahu Yovel, that Spinoza "does not
envisage a radical, one-time revolution but a gradual growth of rationality
from within the domain of [the imagination]."[29]

Third, Spinoza elaborates a positive role for culture in his analysis of both
divine law and reason as historical and therefore cultural. Spinoza makes this
point in chapter 16 of the *Theological-Political Treatise* when he argues that
individuals in the state of nature are governed not by reason but by "desire
and power" (16.196); and that reason is instead something that needs to be
"cultivated" (16.197: the Latin phrase is "Rationis cultu"). The same is true of
religion and politics. The state of nature, Spinoza tells us, is "prior to religion
both by nature, and in time. No one knows from nature that he is bound by
obedience towards God" (16.105).[30] Rather, in the state of nature men are absolutely free; they are only bound to obey the law—positive or divine—when
they willingly transfer their natural right to all things to the sovereign. In the
Hebrew Bible, this transfer originally took the form of the Hebrew covenant
with God; but such a transfer of right is later the precondition for the rational
establishment of the secular state and for religion having any force in society
at all. In elaborating this point Spinoza first distinguishes between the state
of nature and the laws of nature on the one hand and divine law on the other:
"For if men were bound by nature to the divine law, or if the divine law were
a law of nature, it would be superfluous for God to enter into a covenant with
men and bind them with an oath. We must admit unreservedly that divine
law began from the time when men promised to obey God in all things by

an explicit agreement" (16.205). In chapter 17, Spinoza then illustrates this point by explaining that when the Hebrews departed from Egypt, "they were not bound by compact to anyone; rather they regained the natural right to all they could get." It was in this renewed state of nature that they "resolved to transfer their right" to God alone. In other words, the covenant with God comes into existence at a particular historical moment, just as the secular social contract does. As Spinoza comments, "this undertaking or transfer of right to God was made in the same way that . . . it is made in an ordinary society" (17.213). The implication of this analysis is to call attention to the secular mechanism of all state formation and political legitimacy.[31]

In chapter 19 of the *Treatise*, Spinoza then performs a similar operation on the relationship between divine law and reason. Here we learn that reason itself brings the divine teachings into existence in society through the secular operation of a transfer of right: "if the teachings of true reason, which are the divine teachings themselves (as we showed in ch. 4 on the divine law), are to have the full force of law, it is necessary that each person should give up his own natural right . . . and it was then and only then that we first learned what justice and injustice, equity and inequity [and all the doctrines of true reason] are." In short, human beings in society produce divine law, and the historical development of society and the state are thus the precondition of religion.[32]

In the end, Spinoza's analysis of culture means he is both a critic of political theology and a defender of it. He is a critic of political theology construed as theocracy, as the contemporary claim of the Jews to be the chosen people (*TTP*, chap. 3), or as the priestly manipulation of theology to subvert the state (17.211). He is a defender of political theology understood as the attempt to think the relationship between philosophy and theology and their mutual dependence upon the state.[33] As Nancy Levene has argued, Strauss ought to have appreciated this aspect of Spinoza since Strauss also wanted to think the relationship between philosophy and theology and their relation to the state. But, against Strauss, in the *TTP* this mutual dependence means that Spinoza's account of the eternal truths of philosophy is not opposed to his argument that these truths emerge in history, which is to say, in culture—including the cultural artifact we know as the Bible.[34]

Spinoza can thus be said to have contributed to the Enlightenment idea of culture by constructing—through biblical interpretation—what Jonathan Sheehan has called the Enlightenment's "cultural bible." Sheehan traces Enlightenment arguments according to which religion is first seen as the source of culture, and then increasingly as a cultural product itself. He argues that this view of the Bible as a cultural product in turn generates a view of culture with some of the characteristics formerly attributed to the Bible. According to Herder, for example, culture names the "entire living picture of the ways of life, customs, [and] needs" of a nation. Such an idea of culture is itself initially dependent on religion: "the real living culture of a people" begins, according to Herder, "with the awakening and cultivation of their language—and this depends on religion." "Religion alone," he wrote elsewhere, "introduced the first elements of culture and science to all peoples; more precisely, culture and science were originally nothing more than a kind of religious tradition." Significantly, Herder singled out the Jews as the "primary model for a *Nationalkultur*," because, in Sheehan's words, their "national religion was the self-contained source of [their] cultural development."[35] As the Bible itself was increasingly treated as a cultural object by Herder and his contemporaries, "the concept of culture took over all those aspects of the Enlightenment Bible—its literary quality, its pedagogical virtues, its philological exemplarity, and its historical depth."[36]

Earlier I showed that Strauss criticized Schmitt's notion of political theology as a continuation of culture when viewed from the perspective of Schmitt's political anthropology. Spinoza's biblical hermeneutics helps us see that there is a more productive traffic between political theology and culture than either Strauss or Schmitt imagined. If we think of biblical hermeneutics as the technique that turns Scripture into a cultural artifact, we can say that Spinoza's hermeneutics anticipates the Enlightenment idea of culture as a bulwark against political theology, construed as the irrational reliance on revelation in matters of politics. But if we think of biblical hermeneutics as a method of reading immanently that allows for the mutual coexistence of philosophy and theology, we can say that Spinoza enacts political theology, understood as this mutual coexistence, in his own writing. In particular, Spinoza's *TTP* dramatizes a textual space that is analogous to the cultural and political space of Spinoza's liberal state, a space that allows for the coexistence of the freedom of philosophy and the freedom of theology, now interpreted as part of a historically evolving culture. Political theology in this second case would be very close to the Straussian project of determining, politically, a space for theology that would not interfere with the activity of philosophy. But for the liberal Spinoza, in contrast to Strauss, the space of politics is understood as sheltering, rather than precluding, the space of culture. The question, of course, that all readers of Spinoza must decide is whether this mutual coexistence is something like a double truth or whether (as I currently think) the very idea of coexistence turns Scripture into secular literature or something like modern textuality. A further question, well beyond the scope of this essay, is whether it does the same to Spinoza's idea of philosophy.

4. Arendt and Althusser

At this point we seem to have come full circle. Spinoza's philological critique of Scripture helped to produce Herder's historicist idea of culture, which in turn generated a critique of historicism and of culture on the part of figures such as Strauss. So how can culture or Spinoza be an answer to Strauss? How can culture be a response to political theology when it so often seems instead to be the source of such religious enthusiasm? One answer to this question would be to reframe the idea of culture in terms of principled judgment; the other (as I've already suggested) would be to see Spinoza as an ally of critical reason and the *TTP* as an instantiation of such reason rather than its historicist subverter. Let me explore the first possibility by turning to Hannah Arendt's essay "The Crisis in Culture." I'll then revisit the second possibility by turning to the reading of Spinoza by Louis Althusser and Pierre Macherey.

Arendt, a Jew who escaped from Nazi Germany to France and then the United States, came from an intellectual milieu in some respects similar to that of Strauss. Although Strauss was raised in an orthodox household and Arendt in a secular one, both deeply identified as Jews and both had studied philosophy at Marburg (among other universities). Like Strauss, Arendt was interested in diagnosing the failure of Weimar and the rise of the Nazi state. And like both Schmitt and Strauss, she saw these political developments as symptomatic of what Ernst Vollrath has called the "particular deficits of traditional German culture," especially the traditional perception that culture (Bildung) was by definition apolitical.[37] But rather than simply accepting this traditional understanding of culture and turning her attention elsewhere, Arendt wanted to rescue culture as an important part of the public sphere of deliberation and political action. In "The Crisis in Culture," Arendt elaborated a defense of the Enlightenment idea of culture and argued for its relevance to contemporary politics.[38] In some ways this is surprising, since Arendt shared Strauss's and Schmitt's sense that both the modern idea of society and modern technology had usurped the realm of the genuinely political in the twentieth century. But, against Schmitt and Strauss, Arendt—no political theologian—argued that modern society and technology had also usurped the realm of culture, which she wanted to defend.[39] With the rise of "modern mass society," she wrote, "society began to monopolize 'culture' for its own purposes, such as social position and status" (201, 202); and in a line of argument reminiscent of Schmitt's critique of the language of values, she argued that, with "the first appearance of modern art," "culture . . . had become what only then people began to call 'value,' i.e., a social commodity which could be circulated and cashed in in exchange for other kinds of value, social and individual" (203, 204). In time, mass society, which was concerned with entertainment rather than culture, devoured the artifacts of high culture and spat them out again in degraded form. Against these developments, Arendt counterposed a notion of art as separate from the world of need, exchange, and consumption. In the Kantian idea of aesthetic judgment, Arendt found a model of political judgment that firmly, if indirectly, linked the realm of culture to that of political action. As a subjective judgment that nevertheless claims the agreement of others, aesthetic judgment liberates itself from the merely subjective (220). As Arendt put it, "In aesthetic no less than in political judgments, a decision is made, and although this decision is always determined by a certain subjectivity, . . . it also derives from the fact that the world itself is an objective datum, something common to all its inhabitants" (222). But while Arendt distanced herself from the arbitrariness of pure (aesthetic, and by extension, political) decisionism, she also defined the realm of politics as outside philosophical claims to truth: "Culture and politics, then, belong together because it is not knowledge or truth which is at stake, but rather judgment and decision, the judicious exchange of opinion about the sphere of public life and the common world, and the decision what manner of action is to be taken in it" (223). Arendt's defense of a Kantian idea of culture is thus at the same time a defense of the realm of politics, conceived of not as a pure decision, or as the conflict of friend and enemy, as Schmitt would have it, or as a threat to philosophical truth, à la Strauss, but rather as an activity of judgment which produces consensus and action. In this way, Arendt also redefines culture: it is no longer signals the degraded activity of fabrication (an ancient Greek prejudice she shares with Schmitt and Strauss [223]); instead, it is a precondition of true politics.[40]

Although Arendt was herself critical of Spinoza, her argument has something in common with Spinoza's praise of freedom of judgment in the concluding chapter of the *TTP*.[41] In his defense of the superiority of democracy, Spinoza writes, "No one . . . can surrender their freedom to judge and to think as they wish and everyone, by the supreme right of nature, remains master of their own thoughts" (20.251). This in turn means that "it is not . . . the purpose of the state to turn people from rational beings into beasts or automata, but rather to allow their minds and bodies to develop in their own ways in security and enjoy the free use of reason. . . . Therefore, the true purpose of the state is in fact freedom" (20.252). And, just as Arendt reasoned from culture to politics, Spinoza reasons from politics to culture, adding that "this liberty is absolutely essential to the advancement of the arts and sciences; for they can be cultivated [*coluntur*] with success only by those with a free and unfettered judgment" (20.255).

Let me now turn to those modern admirers of Spinoza who linked the *TTP* to the modern notion of textuality. Though the notion of textuality has an entirely different valence from that of culture (the former linked to materialism and the critique of the subject; the latter still implicated in humanist notions of agency), I think the two converge on the possibility of an immanent critique of ideology, including political theology. In the short posthumous essay on Spinoza that Althusser intended to include in his autobiography, he wrote that "Spinoza . . . managed to disentangle the mind from the illusion of transcendent or transcendental subjectivity as a guarantee or foundation of every meaning or every experience of possible truth." In *Essays on Self-Criticism*, Althusser elaborated on this point when he linked Spinoza to the Marxist tradition of dialectical materialism:

> Spinoza's "theory" rejected every illusion about ideology. And especially about the number one ideology of that time, religion, by identifying it as imaginary. But at the same time it refused to treat ideology as a simple error, or as naked ignorance, because it based the system of this imaginary phenomenon on the relation of men to the world "expressed" by the state of their bodies. This *materialism of the imaginary* opened the way to a surprising conception of the First Level of Knowledge: not at all, in fact as a "piece of knowledge," but as the material world of men *as they live it*, that of their concrete and historical existence.

In *Reading Capital*, Althusser and Balibar then recast this insight in terms of modern ideas of textuality when they described Spinoza as "the first man ever to have posed the problem of *reading* and, in consequence, of *writing*."[42]

Althusser's student Pierre Macherey drew on this reading of Spinoza to develop his theory of literary production. While Macherey acknowledged that Spinoza was "almost silent" on the topic of aesthetic activity, he argued with Althusser that Spinoza's understanding of textuality and reading foreshadowed something like the critique of ideology. Specifically, literary texts act out their own critique of ideology through a process of internal distantiation. This means that reading is not the deciphering of an a priori truth; instead, the contradictions within the text provide the critic with the elements of an immanent critique.[43] As I have been suggesting and as Macherey knew full well, this is precisely the task that Spinoza takes up in his *Theological-Political Treatise*. The protocols of reading which Spinoza laid out in this work are not only at the basis of the modern, Enlightenment idea of culture; they also point us to the inseparability of a certain idea of culture and the critique of ideology, including the ideology of political theology.

What does it mean, then, to substitute the idea of a "literary decision" (or a decision for literature) for Schmitt's theologically charged existentialist rhetoric of "the decision" or Strauss's classical idea of reason? It means first of all that culture is not simply the sinkhole of relativism. If Strauss can counterpose classical reason to relativism, so Arendt can counterpose an Enlightenment conception of judgment to relativism. In locating a principled exercise of judgment in response to works of culture, Arendt turns culture from the merely contingent product of historical conditions to the occasion for the critical analysis of society as well as the precondition of politics. But why a specifically "literary" decision? Here there is both a historical answer and a theoretical one. Historically, scriptural hermeneutics offers the prime example of the use of reason to dismantle the authority of revelation through the critique of the biblical text. In the process of doing so, it turned Scripture into literature, i.e. into a mere text, rather than the inspired word of God. So we could say that this critique produced a decision for literature, if by decision we mean principled, rational judgment, and if by literature we mean a humanly authored text. But we could also argue, with Althusser and Macherey, that the operation Spinoza performed in his immanent critique of Scripture just is what literary texts do, by definition. Here the "internal distantiation" that is constitutive of the literary text would itself provide the model for what Arendt calls judgment and what Althusser calls the critique of ideology. To parody the theologian Karl Barth, whose manifesto I quoted earlier, we could say that this critique is the KRISIS of theology. If we pressed this argument further, we might even say, with Derrida, that logos understood as reason is always already a matter of logos as the "word" or linguistic representation, and that linguistic representation that knows itself as such is literature. This is undoubtedly farther than Spinoza would want to go, since in preserving the distinction between philosophy and culture, Spinoza could also be said to distinguish between philosophy and literature. But it is clear that at least some of Spinoza's admirers took this additional step—among them, Friedrich Schlegel, who wrote that he could "barely comprehend how one can be a poet without admiring Spinoza, loving him, and becoming entirely his."

I said at the outset of this essay that I wanted to use Strauss to complicate recent discussions of political theology. I hope I've done that by arguing that Strauss saw political theology not as politics founded on revelation or on the existential conflict of friend and enemy but as the problem of the relationship between philosophy and theology. But I've also tried to suggest that there are costs to adopting Strauss's secular critique of political theology, with its distaste for liberalism and a modern, Enlightenment idea of culture—a distaste he shared with Schmitt. This means that if we're interested in the critique of political theology and a *defense* of the idea of culture, we need to respond to Strauss, not Schmitt—and we can do so with the help of Spinoza. Whereas the young Strauss, in seeking to return to orthodoxy, found his way blocked by Spinoza, I suggest that Spinoza can provide a map for those of us seeking to elaborate a critique of political theology that also preserves an Enlightenment idea of culture.

Notes

1. This paragraph draws on Jeffrey Andrew Barash, *Heidegger and the Problem of Historical Meaning*, rev. ed. (New York: Fordham University Press, 2003), chap. 1, "The Emergence of the Problem of Historical Meaning," 1–63, here 3–4. I am grateful to Graham Hammill and Julia Lupton for inviting me to present an earlier draft of this essay at the conference "Points of Departure." I am also grateful to Graham Hammill for probing questions about the penultimate draft of this essay.

2. Schleiermacher: "The task [of hermeneutics] is to be formulated as follows: 'To understand the text at first as well and then even better than its author.'" Quoted in Gerald Bruns, *Ancient and Modern Hermeneutics* (New Haven: Yale University Press, 1992), 151; see Schleiermacher, *Hermeneutics: The Handwritten Manuscripts*, trans. James Duke and Jack Forstman (Missoula, Mont.: Scholars Press, 1977), 112; *Hermeutik*, ed. Heinz Kimmerle (Heidelberg: Carl Winter, 1974), 84.

3. Barash, *Heidegger*, 4, quoting Dilthey.

4. Ibid., 114; quoting Gogarten, 115.

5. Ibid., 142, and 136–37.

6. Ibid., 148.

7. Karl Barth, *The Epistle to the Romans*, trans. from the sixth edition by Edwyn C. Hoskyns (London: Oxford University Press, 1933), 267–68.

8. Barash, *Heidegger*, 138.

9. Here I disagree with the otherwise stimulating article by Miguel Vatter, "Taking Exception to Liberalism: Heinrich Meier's *Carl Schmitt and Leo Strauss: The Hidden Dialogue*," *Graduate Faculty Philosophy Journal* 19 (1997): 323–44. Vatter thinks that Strauss was much closer to Schmitt than does Meier, and that he remained throughout his life a political theologian rather than a political philosopher.

10. Leo Strauss, *Spinoza's Critique of Religion*, trans. E. M. Sinclair (Chicago: University of Chicago Press, 1965), 6. See Nancy Levene on Strauss, "Athens and Jerusalem: Myths and Mirrors in Strauss' Vision of the West," *Hebraic Political Studies* 3 (2008): 124.

11. See "An Introduction to Heideggerian Existentialism," in Leo Strauss, *The Rebirth of Classical Political Rationalism*, ed. Thomas Pangle (Chicago: University of Chicago Press, 1989), where Strauss writes "the only great thinker in our time is Heidegger" (29).

12. Strauss refers to their "neues Denken." The term comes from Franz Rosenzweig's essay "Das neue Denken" in *Kleinere Schriften* (Berlin: Schocken Verlag, 1937). On Strauss's view of Heidegger, see among others Horst Mewes, "Leo Strauss and Martin Heidegger: Greek Antiquity and the Meaning of Modernity," in *Hannah Arendt and Leo Strauss*, ed. Peter Graf Kielmansegg, Horst Mewes, and Elizabeth Glaser-Schmidt (Cambridge: Cambridge University Press, 1995), 105–20.

13. Elsewhere Strauss is critical of the secularization thesis for neglecting "the essential nature of modernity—that is, its will to break with the old theological world." In particular, Strauss rejects the traditional view that "the natural law of modern thinkers is a secularized version

of Stoic-Christian natural law." See Daniel Tanguay, *Leo Strauss: An Intellectual Biography* (New Haven: Yale University Press, 2007), 101, 103; see also 109ff.

14. See Carl Schmitt, *The Concept of the Political*, trans. George Schwab, with Leo Strauss's *Notes on Schmitt's Essay*, trans. J. Harvey Lomax (Chicago: University of Chicago Press, 1996). The pagination is continuous from Schmitt's text through Strauss's. I will refer to both as *Concept of the Political.*

15. In *Political Theology*, Schmitt had assimilated Lockean liberalism to a kind of "aesthetic" rationality, which is concerned with the production of artifacts, including the state as an artifact. In this analysis, technological reason and aesthetics are two sides of the same coin. In the conclusion to *Political Theology*, Schmitt was explicit about the connection: "Whereas, on the one hand, the political vanishes into the economic or technical-organizational, on the other hand the political dissolves into the everlasting discussion of cultural and philosophical-historical commonplaces, which, by aesthetic characterization, identify and accept an epoch as classical, romantic, or baroque. The core of the political idea, the exacting moral decision, is evaded in both" (63). In this note and paragraph, I draw on my earlier analysis of Schmitt in "Hamlet or Hecuba: Carl Schmitt's Decision," *Representations* 83 (Summer 2003): 67–96.

16. *Concept of the Political*, 60 (Schmitt); 86 and 92 (Strauss).

17. Miguel Vatter summarizes Strauss's logic as follow: "If evil belongs to the state of nature only in the sense that it can be eliminated by a transition to the state of culture, then the Hobbesian ideal of civilization entails the loss of the absolute opposition between good and evil" ("Strauss and Schmitt as Readers of Hobbes and Spinoza," *New Centennial Review* 5 [2005]: 175).

18. As Heinrich Meier has shown, Schmitt altered later editions of *The Concept of the Political* in response to Strauss's critique, including replacing various references to culture with "the political" or deleting them altogether. See Heinrich Meier, *Carl Schmitt and Leo Strauss: The Hidden Dialogue*, trans. J. Harvey Lomax (Chicago: University of Chicago Press, 1995), 30–32. Meier also points out that Schmitt addresses Strauss's complaint regarding his admiration for amoral animal power by adding a sentence on Hobbes, Spinoza, and Pufendorf and the state of nature as a state of perpetual danger to the 1933 edition of *The Concept of the Political* (Meier, 58 n. 60).

19. Schmitt fails to see, according to Strauss, that the political "owes its legitimation to the seriousness of the question of what is right" (*Concept of the Political*, 103). As Meier points out in *Carl Schmitt and Leo Strauss*, Strauss criticizes Schmitt for describing "the thesis of dangerousness as a '*supposition*,' as an 'anthropological confession of *faith*' (58). 'But if man's dangerousness is *only supposed or believed in, not genuinely known*, the opposite too can be regarded as possible, and the attempt to eliminate man's dangerousness . . . can be put into practice. If man's dangerousness is *only believed in*, it is in principle *threatened*, and therewith the political is threatened also.' . . . Precisely for that reason Strauss opposes knowledge to faith, and for the same reason he categorically emphasized that faith does not suffice" (51; Meier's emphasis).

20. As Heinrich Meier has argued, it is "precisely for [this] reason Strauss opposes knowledge to faith, and for the same reason he categorically emphasized that faith does not suffice" (*Carl Schmitt and Leo Strauss*, 51).

21. Specifically, Strauss develops his idea of premodern rationalism through his encounter with medieval rationalism, in the work of Maimonides, Alfarabi and Averroes, whom Strauss reads as closet Platonists.

22. Leo Strauss, "How to Study Spinoza's *Theologico-Political Treatise*," in *Persecution and the Art of Writing* (Chicago: University of Chicago Press, 1952), 142–201. The essay was originally published as an article in 1948.

23. See Ernst Cassirer, *The Philosophy of the Enlightenment*, trans. Fritz C. A. Koelln and James P. Pettegrove (Boston: Beacon Press, 1955), 183: "Consideration of the eternal and immutable norms of reason must go hand in hand with consideration of the manner in which they unfold historically, in which they have been realized in the course of empirical historical development. Real 'enlightenment' of the mind can only emerge from the reconciliation and opposition of these two modes of contemplation."

24. I am indebted to David Bates for helping me sort through the ideas in this paragraph.

25. See Benedict de Spinoza, *Theological-Political Treatise*, ed. Jonathan Israel, trans. Michael Silverthorne and Jonathan Israel (Cambridge: Cambridge University Press, 2007), xvi. I have also consulted the Latin text of the *TTP* in *Benedicti de Spinoza opera quotquot reperta sunt*, ed. J. Van Vloten and J.P.N. Land, 3d ed., 2 vols. (The Hague: M. Nijhoff, 1914), vol. 2.

26. See *TTP* 17.225: "Nature certainly does not create peoples, individuals do, and individuals are only separated into nations by differences of language, law and morality. It can only be from these latter factors, namely law and morality, that each nation has its unique character, its unique condition, and its unique prejudices."

27. See Israel, "Introduction" to the *TTP*, on the distinction between textual truth and the truth of fact (xi–xii).

28. Henry E. Allison, *Benedict de Spinoza: An Introduction*, rev. ed. (New Haven: Yale University Press, 1987), 108–9.

29. Yovel goes on: "and he thinks it is the philosopher's task to provide tools for dealing with the various forms of this transition—as he himself does in his theory of allegory, metaphor, and nonscientific discourse generally." See Yirmiyahu Yovel, *Spinoza and Other Heretics*, vol. 1: *The Marrano of Reason* (Princeton: Princeton University Press, 1989), 145. See also Antonio Negri, *The Savage Anomaly: The Power of Spinoza's Metaphysics and Politics*, trans. Michael Hardt (Minneapolis: University of Minnesota Press, 1991). In Negri's brilliant account, Spinoza's analysis of prophecy thus takes place on two levels: "the analysis and identification of the imagination as a constitutive function of falsity and illusion; followed by . . . the analysis of the ontological (differentiated, true) basis of the action of the imagination" (92–93); or, in other words, "a first, static level on which the imagination proposes a partial but positive definition of its own contents and a second, dynamic level on which the movement and effects of the imagination are validated as a function of the ethical constitution of the world" (94–95). See Willi Goetschl, *Spinoza's Modernity* (Madison: University of Wisconsin Press, 2004), chap. 3 on the role of the imagination in Spinoza's *Ethics*: "The imagination's role in the theory of affects casts cognition as the interplay of forces that occurs within the affectual economy and has important implications for aesthetics. . . . Spinoza's revalorization of the imagination accords the aesthetic a new ontological significance" (52). See also Jonathan Israel's introduction to the *TTP*: "Although such universals [in Scripture, such as 'there is a God, one and omnipotent, who alone is to be adored'] are historically determined and are therefore poetic concepts, inexact, limited and vague, and while it is totally impossible to infer from the biblical text 'what God is' or how he 'provides for all things,' nevertheless such universals are not just wholly fictitious or arbitrary intended meanings. To [Spinoza's] mind, they are inadequate but still significant perceptions, that is, vague but natural approximations to the 'truth of things'" (xvi).

30. See *TTP* 16.206: "The laws of nature are not accommodated to religion, which is concerned solely with the human good, but to the order of universal nature, that is, to the eternal decree of God, which is unknown to us."

31. See *TTP* 17.212 on the "stratagem" of pretending government has been "instituted by God rather than by the consent and agreement of men."

32. In a sense this is already true in the theocracy established by Moses, which divided the state into priests and civil administrators: "Thus, God's pronouncements in the mouth of the high priest were not decrees but just responses; they gained the force of commands and decrees only when accepted by Joshua and the supreme councils." See also 19.238: "religion has the power of law only by decree of those who exercise the right of government and . . . God has no special kingdom among men except through those who exercise sovereignty."

33. For an argument that Strauss ought to have appreciated this aspect of Spinoza and not just seen Spinoza as a demystifier of religion, see Nancy Levene, "Athens and Jerusalem," 149, 153–54.

34. See Étienne Balibar, *Spinoza and Politics*, trans. Peter Snowdon (London and New York: Verso, 1998), 36-42, on how Spinoza's notion of nature involves a philosophy of history.

35. Herder, *Auch eine Philosophie der Geschichte zur Bildung der Menschheit*, in *Werke in zehn Bänden*, ed. Martin Bollacher (Frankfurt am Main: Deutscher Klassiker Verlag, 1985–2000), 4:33; "Über National-Religionen" in *Adrastea* in *Werke in zehn Bänden*, 10:612; Herder, *Against Pure Reason: Writings on Religion, Language, and History*, trans. Marcia Bunge (Minneapolis: University of Minnesota Press, 1993), 88. These quotations from Herder are taken from Jonathan Sheehan, *The Enlightenment Bible* (Princeton: Princeton University Press, 2005), 219.

36. Sheehan, *The Enlightenment Bible*, 220. Sheehan traces how the Luther Bible became the cultural Bible in the nineteenth century. The Luther "German Bible simultaneously created a German religion, a German culture, and a German nation." The Luther Bible thus became "a Bible relevant and authoritative even separated from its original theological roots" (227). However, Sheehan also goes on to argue that the cultural Bible in Germany paved the way not only for a more spiritual view of culture but also for a "desecularization" or "revival of religion" (228). See also Steven B. Smith, *Spinoza, Liberalism, and the Question of Jewish Identity* (New Haven and London: Yale University Press, 1997), 15 and ff. on "the Enlightenment's project of emancipation through *Bildung*, or self-formation."

37. Ernst Vollrath, "Hannah Arendt: A German-American Jewess Views the United States—and Looks Back to Germany," in *Hannah Arendt and Leo Strauss*, ed. Kielmansegg, Mewes, and Glaser-Schmitt, 58. On this understanding of Bildung, see also 47, 49, and 52.

38. Hannah Arendt, "The Crisis in Culture," in *Between Past and Future: Six Exercises in Political Thought* (Cleveland and New York, 1968), 197–226.

39. For a recent discussion of Arendt's relation to Schmitt and her hostility to political theology, see Samuel Moyn, "Hannah Arendt on the Secular," *New German Critique* 105 (2008): 71–96.

40. Arendt further elaborated on this reading of Kant's *Critique of Judgment* in *Lectures on Kant's Political Philosophy* (Chicago: University of Chicago Press, 1982). Whether Arendt escapes the existential decisionism of Schmitt and, in some readings, Strauss, is the subject of some debate. See Vollrath, "Hannah Arendt," 38, on the problem of a criterion of political judgment in Arendt.

41. Arendt lumps Spinoza with Hobbes, who equated politics with security. See "What Is Freedom?" in *Between Past and Future*, 150.

42. Louis Althusser, "The Only Materialist Tradition, Part 1: Spinoza," in *The New Spinoza*, ed. Warren Montag and Ted Stolze (Minneapolis: University of Minnesota Press, 1997), 5; Louis Althusser, *Essays in Self-Criticism*, trans. Grahame Lock (London: Schocken Books, 1976), 136. Montag quotes *Reading Capital* in the Introduction, xv. On Althusser's indebtedness to Spinoza, see Christopher Norris, *Spinoza and the Origins of Modern Critical Theory* (Oxford and

Cambridge, Mass.: Wiley-Blackwell, 1991). For further discussion of Spinoza, see also Althusser, *The Future Lasts Forever*, trans. Richard Veasey (New York: New Press, 1993), 215–20.

43. In the gloss of Terry Eagleton this means that "Criticism 'makes speak' what the work must at all costs repress simply in order to be itself. Its job [that is, the job of criticism] is not to extract some secret truth from the work, but to demonstrate that its 'truth' lies open to view, in the historically necessary discrepancy between its various components." See Eagleton, Introduction to the English translation of Pierre Macherey, *A Theory of Literary Production*, trans. Geoffrey Wall (1966; London and New York: Routledge, 2006), viii–ix. See also 72–73 on how "Spinoza's notion of liberation involves a new attitude to language."

In his analysis of Levinas's critique of Spinoza, Hent de Vries asks, "Is it not possible that the model of exegesis, hermeneutics, and inspiration that Levinas attributes to the Talmud presupposes the very ontology of 'expression' that, according to Deleuze, organizes (and unsettles) the Spinozistic system?" De Vries goes on to show that Levinas associated Talmudic exegesis with literary interpretation, with "the coming and going from text to work, of all literature, even when it does not pretend to be Holy Scriptures" (Levinas, "Spinoza's Background," quoted in de Vries). See "Levinas, Spinoza, and the Theologico-Political Meaning of Scripture," in *Political Theologies*, ed. Hent de Vries and Lawrence E. Sullivan (New York: Fordham University Press, 2006), 232–48, here 244.

2

The Tragicity of the Political: A Note on Carlo Galli's Reading of Carl Schmitt's *Hamlet or Hecuba*

ADAM SITZE

In 1983, almost a full decade before Carl Schmitt's 1956 book *Hamlet oder Hekuba* would enter into French and Spanish translation, and more than two decades before it would appear in English, the political thinker Simona Forti rendered Schmitt's text into Italian for the Bologna publishing house Il Mulino.[1] Forti's translation was introduced by a historian of political thought named Carlo Galli, who in 1996 would publish a book called *Genealogia della politica: Carl Schmitt e la crisi del pensiero politico moderno* ("The Genealogy of Politics: Carl Schmitt and the Crisis of Modern Political Thought"),[2] which, at 912 pages in length, has with good reason been called "the most complete, comprehensive, and insightful account of Schmitt's thought ever published."[3] The purpose of this short note is to clarify the way in which Galli's more general reading of Schmitt informs his essay on Schmitt's *Hamlet or Hecuba*, and in particular how the Gallian reading of Schmitt might help us sharpen the questions we raise about the subtitle of Schmitt's text, *Der Einbruch der Zeit in das Spiel*, or, in the felicitous rendering of Jennifer Rust and David Pan, "The Intrusion of the Time into the Play."[4]

First, however, a few words about Galli himself are in order. Carlo Galli is currently *professore ordinario* in the Department of Historical Disciplines at the University of Bologna, where his primary pedagogical duty is to teach the history of political doctrines. Galli's approach to the history of political thought is influenced by the "immanent critique" of the Frankfurt School and, to a lesser extent, the *Begriffsgeschichte* of Reinhart Koselleck.[5] In his various readings of modern political philosophers (which range from Niccolò Machiavelli and Thomas Hobbes to Martha Nussbaum, Paul Gilroy, and Jean-Luc Nancy, from Carl Schmitt and Ernst Jünger to Hannah Arendt,

Herbert Marcuse, Theodor Adorno, and Max Horkheimer), Galli seeks to bring to light the contingencies—the impasses and aporias, the confusions and compromises—that are internal to the basic concepts of modern political thought, and to trace the ways those contingencies have actualized themselves in the crises of the institutions, practices, and theoretical systems founded on those concepts.[6] This is, to be sure, a teaching about the incoherence of modern political thought, for in his writings Galli places special emphasis on the ways in which the traditions of modern political thought we inherit are neither necessary nor inevitable, and above all are not up to the tasks of emancipatory politics demanded of us by our present. But Galli's is also, and for this same reason, a teaching about the need today for imagination in the post-Kantian sense of the word—the task of political thought today is to create new schemas or *Gestalts* with reference to which we can orient our thought in response to the crises specific to the global age.[7]

Like Adorno, Horkheimer, and Koselleck, Galli has pursued this scholarly project not only in the form of books of which he is the sole author, but also through a set of intellectual works that are cooperative in character. With Roberto Esposito, for example, Galli is co-editor of the *Enciclopedia del pensiero politico: Autori, concetti, dottrine* ("Encyclopedia of Political Thought: Authors, Concepts, Doctrines"), which was first published in 2000 and was reissued in 2005 (with newly updated entries for biopolitics, conflict, disobedience, fundamentalism, globalization, war, multitude, and terrorism).[8] At 933 pages, the *Enciclopedia* may be described as a more concise but also—because inclusive of entries on authors ranging from Símon Bólivar, Judith Butler, and Frantz Fanon to Martha Nussbaum, Amartya Sen, and François Touissant L'Ouverture—more contemporary and global iteration of the eight-volume 1972–77 tome whose publication Koselleck supervised (*Basic Concepts in History: A Historical Dictionary of Political and Social Language in Germany*). With Esposito and Giuseppe Duso, meanwhile, Galli is also editor of the journal *Filosofia politica*, which is housed at the University of Bologna, and which, since its inception in 1987, has served as an important forum for rethinking the "epochality of the modern" outside of the explanatory paradigms and hermeneutic horizons according to which the modern proposes to evaluate itself.[9] In its pages, Galli et al. have published many of the same political thinkers who contributed articles to Galli and Esposito's *Enciclopedia*, and who today are increasingly beginning to find readerships in the Anglophone academe (such as Simona Forti, Adriana Cavarero, Sandro Chignola, Sandro Mezzadra, Pasquale Pasquino, Filippo del Lucchese, and Laura Bazzicalupo). Last but not least, Galli has also translated into Italian, and written the introductions to, a number of Schmitt's key works, among them *Political Romanticism, Roman Catholicism and Political Form*, and, of course, *Hamlet or Hecuba*.[10]

As Danilo Zolo has observed, Galli's 1996 book on Schmitt is of a piece with his teaching and writing more generally: Galli's *Genealogia* is an epochal analysis of the concepts of modern political thought, with the aim of deciphering in those concepts the genesis and basis of the institutional crises of liberal democracy.[11] The *Genealogia*'s central claim is that Schmitt's main accomplishment was to have opened himself to, in order to radicalize, the crises that together constitute the origin of the modern epoch. Schmitt is therefore, in Galli's account, a specifically genealogical critic: his single-minded focus, according to Galli, was to understand this origin's strangely double-sided energy or intensity—the way in which it destroys the very institutions and practices it simultaneously creates, deforms the same political forms to which it gives rise, disorders the very systems of thought it demands. By fixing his gaze on this origin, Schmitt discovered that modern political thought (and thus too institutions and practices to which it gives rise) is divided against itself in a nondialectical manner: even as it emerges from and even feeds upon a crisis it is incapable of resolving, it accounts for this incapacity by suppressing the signs and symptoms that point to it, compensating for its impotence with ever more moralistic reaffirmations of its unquestionable necessity. The core problematic of Schmittian thought, Galli will consequently argue, cannot then be reduced to any one of the themes of Schmitt's various texts (the distinction between exception and norm, theology and politics, decision and discussion, friend and enemy, constituting power and constituted power, land and sea, limited and unlimited warfare, play and tragedy, and so on). It is Schmitt's discovery that all modern political forms share a common trait, a birthmark that, in turn, attests to their common origin in crisis: despite the many and various differences between modern political thinkers—indeed as the silent but generative core of those differences—the epochal unity of modern political thought derives from its distinctive doubleness, its simultaneous impossibility and necessity, or, in short, its "tragicity."[12]

"Tragicity," in Galli's lexicon, is not a reference to the tragic drama Aristotle analyzes in the *Poetics* or that Hegel discusses in his *Aesthetics*: it is not the name of a genre. Nor is it the name of a historiographical trope ("the first time as tragedy, the second time as comedy"), an attitude of existential dread (on Galli's read, Schmitt is not a thinker of *Kulturpessimismus*),[13] or a justification of suffering (a "theodicy").[14] As Galli uses the term "tragicity" is a way to gloss Schmitt's attention to a certain sort of rupture—the concrete, epochal rupture at the origin of modernity—that, in Schmitt's view, persists like a scar in all of modernity's institutions, theories, and practices. It is above all a name for the impossibility of giving an adequate name to this rupture (and this, indeed, is what it was necessary for Schmittian conceptual production to assume the form of a metonymic series: the Schmittian *oeuvre* itself is nothing more than a prolonged, repeated attempt to name just this "tragicity"). Above all, on Galli's read, it is a name for a silent force that irrupts into the Schmittian *oeuvre* in much the same way that the "real tragicity of history"[15] irrupts into Shakespeare's *Hamlet.*

It is not then historicism, but rather immanent critique, that leads Galli to "contextualize" the origin of Schmitt's own political thought in a moment in European politics in which inside and outside, peace and war, civil and military, enemy and criminal were entering into the grey of a twilight, in which, as a result, a certain warlike conflictuality was becoming the normal mode of being for political institutions and practices that were supposed to function in and through reasonable discussion, transparent representation, and rational mediation.[16] In Galli's view, Schmitt's contribution was to have attempted to interpret this crisis not from modernity's own various privileged points of internal self-understanding (the state, the subject, society, or reason), but instead critically and genealogically, by leaving his thought permanently open to the catastrophic crisis in and through which modernity itself came into being, namely, the dissolution of the specifically Roman Catholic form of representation that governed political order in medieval Europe.[17] To give a name to this lost form of representation—this peculiar and specifically imperial ability to embrace any and all antitheses (life and death, heaven and earth, God and Man, past and future, time and eternity, good and power, beginning and end, reason and nonreason, and so on) in order to absorb them into a single, unified form—Schmitt took a term from the medieval Catholic thinker Nicholas de Cusa: *complexio oppositorum.* According to Galli, Schmitt understood the *complexio* neither as a dialectical synthesis (a simple coincidence of opposites), nor as an eclectic relativism (an ensemble of plural and variegated qualities), but rather as "a form in which life and reason coexist without forcing," a single hierarchy the integrity of which derives, above all, from the "glorious form" of Christ's Person.[18] For Schmitt, Galli argues, the genealogical significance of the *complexio* is not theological but political: Schmitt is interested in it because of the way in which its mode of representation—the extreme publicity and visibility through which all opposites coincided in the immediate mediacy of Christ's Person—in turn called into being a relatively stable and enduring political order.[19] It is on the basis of this capacity for a mode of representation to constitute a political order (or what Galli calls "morphogenetic power") that Schmitt understands the modern. With the events that together opened the modern epoch (such as the Copernican Revolution, the Wars of Reformation, and the conquest of America), the *complexio* and the order of being it sustained could no longer be treated as a self-evident "given" that could be presupposed by political thought. In the absence of a coherent and integrative Idea in which opposites could coincide without conflict—indeed, under the unprecedented conditions of theological civil war in which the Person of Christ was no longer the basis of European peace but was now precisely both a source of and a stake in European conflict—political and juridical Power became disconnected from theological and moral Good, and the question of how to mediate opposing forces and qualities through representation suddenly emerged as an anxious and explicit question for political thought.[20]

According to Galli, Schmitt understands modern mediation to originate as an unwitting, precarious, and partial response both to this question and to the epochal catastrophe that occasions it. Modern mediation marks the attempt, on the part of a European subject who suddenly finds himself alone in the universe, to accomplish a set of tasks bequeathed to him by the *complexio*—such as the creation of order, the reconciliation of opposites, and the accomplishment of peace on earth—but now only through an *ad hoc* use of his own immanent powers.[21] The task of the modern European subject, put differently, is now to create, *ex nihilo*, the political form, peace, and reconciliation it once could presuppose. It pursues these aims through, on the one hand, instrumental reason (the mathematization and technical mastery of nature, up to and including human nature), and, on the other, through a new form of representation, which seeks to mediate contradictions between opposing forces, but which also recognizes, without also fully realizing why, that its attempts at mediation are somehow already destined, in advance, to failure—that, in other words, the reconciliation of opposites the *complexio* achieved felicitously with reference to the Person of Christ is now the work of an unhappy consciousness, a person in the juridical sense who is capable of peace, reconciliation, and order only at the cost of a ceaseless and restless reflection on division and disorder.[22]

In political terms, meanwhile, modern mediation finds itself in a similar predicament. In the place once occupied by the hierarchical *complexio* of the Catholic Church's "glorious form," Hobbesian political philosophy proposes the egalitarian simplicity of a new beginning—a revolutionary *tabula rasa* that articulates the rational necessity of peace and establishes the impersonal laws of the state through a manifestly geometrical deduction.[23] But the impersonal laws of the state can only produce political form and exercise morphogenetic power in an ungrounded manner, by presupposing the complete separation of Power from the Good. Indeed, the strength of impersonal law (its principled insistence on the formal equality of all persons before the law) is predicated on a displacement of the morphogenetic power of the *complexio* (a hierarchy centered upon the Person of Christ). In the absence of a felicitous use of morphogenetic power, the state finds that law alone is insufficient for accomplishing the aims it inherits from the *complexio*, and discovers itself to be in need of supplements to its impersonal law. The state discovers this supplement by placing instrumental reason (which is to say, the neutralization of conflict through *dispositifs* of discipline, governmentality, and security, but also, if necessary, through the use of military and, later, police forces) at the service of repeated sovereign decisions that reproduce a semblance of the unity and integrity of Roman Catholic visibility and publicity. It sets aside the impersonality of law (with its insistence on formal equality) in order to fabricate a public enemy, whose Gestalt can then serve (*via* a detour of *ressentiment* that is all too familiar today) as the point of reference for the formation of the unity and integrity of a newly secular public.[24] In short, the state achieves the aims bequeathed to it by the *complexio* only to the extent that it now includes exclusion.[25]

Both of these techniques, however, repeatedly undermine the end at which they aim. The state's attempt to create political form and maintain order through the use of force results in an "armed peace" that, in the concrete, amounts to a constant preparation for the next war, even as its attempt to produce and maintain public unity and integrity through decisions on a public enemy constantly reintroduces into the internal space of the state a trace of the same unlimited hostility the suppression of which is (as in Hobbes's elimination of the *bellum omnium contra omnes*) the main justification for state's existence in the first place.[26] The means for resolving conflict within Christian Europe turn out to be plagued by a similar infelicity, only now acted out on a global scale: Europe attempts to expunge and expel the trace of unlimited hostility by instituting the *jus publicum europæum*, which creates an order of limited hostility (formalized warfare) within Europe only by justifying and demanding an order of unlimited hostility toward Europe's exterior (in the form of colonial conquest and genocide).

In every case, in other words, modern political order discovers that it must aim at, but cannot attain, a set of goals—peace on earth, mediation and reconciliation between opposites, the production of political form—that have been set for it, and indeed bequeathed to it, by the very form of medieval representation it also aggressively displaces. Modern political mediation therefore finds itself in a position where it can only fully legitimate its existence with reference to a set of inherited concepts to which it is also especially vulnerable. It discovers that it is fated to attempt a task (the *ex nihilio* "creation" of political form, of peace, and reconciliation) that is both necessary (because the *complexio* is gone, because opposing forces remain, and because peace and order are the raison d'être of the modern state) and impossible (because, above all, in the thoroughly secularized modern epoch, there is no equivalent to the theological concept of "creation": there is only making, fabrication, production, and instrumental reason, the work of *homo faber*).[27] To even approximate the realization of its inner aims—which are, to repeat, not its "own" but those it inherits from the *complexio*—modern mediation seeks to forget the medieval origin that is at once indispensable for it and unsettling to it, and to that exact degree leaves itself vulnerable to destabilization by a genealogy written from a Catholic standpoint.

But though Schmittian thought is thus, for Galli, a Catholic genealogy of the modern,[28] Galli also cautions that Schmitt's relation to Catholicism not be misunderstood as one of religious belief or even nostalgia. When Schmitt thinks the emergence of modern mediation with reference to its secularization of the *complexio*, he does not suppose that a return to the *complexio* is either desirable or possible.[29] Nor, on Galli's read, does Schmitt really even mourn the passing of the *complexio*. Schmitt's achievement is rather to have occupied that standpoint from which a thoroughly secularized modern mediation genealogically derives its innermost aims, through which a thoroughly secularized modern mediation refuses to understand itself, and to which all of its institutions and practices are thus especially vulnerable.[30] Schmitt's idiosyncratic reading of the *complexio* is, in other words, a way to think the "origin of politics" outside of the standard points of self-understanding that modernity privileges in its own self-justifying historical narratives of its emergence. It is an attempt to name a crisis in which the old order (the *complexio*) has irreversibly dissolved and in which the new order (the modern state-form) cannot accomplish the goals it inherits from the *complexio* (reconciliation and peace).[31] Schmitt does not then analyze modernity from the standpoint of a fully intact Catholic faith or ideology; nor does he really even presuppose that his account of *complexio* is accurate (which is why empirical or historicist refutations of Schmitt miss the mark). The *complexio* is simply the blindspot of modern mediation, that concept which enables us to grasp in genealogical terms the reconciliation at which modern mediation must aim but cannot achieve. Indeed, the definitive difference between Kierkegaard's *occasio* and Schmitt's is that for Schmitt the crisis that the *occasio* imposes upon the thought and being of the critic is not the plentitude of an infinity. It is the poverty of a Nothing. It is the utter privation of order, an unsayable opacity internal to the critic's knowledge that is not a trauma in the psychoanalytic sense, but simply an absence of form-giving speech, the lack of any language that can resolve or even merely describe the unprecedented crises of the modern, a vacuum that then serves as the inexhaustible resource for the prolixity of the critic's criticism.[32] And although it would be tempting to make sense of this epochal crisis-event by calling it an *interregnum*, Galli does not, to my knowledge, do so in any of his writings, perhaps because this would be to use a juridical concept for, and to give juridical form to, an experience and an event that, to the contrary, mark the failure of all juridical forms, both modern and medieval, and that consequently would be more properly characterized as an epochal anomie or, as Galli would later write, "chaos."[33]

With this, I think, we are in a position to understand how and why Galli's reading of Schmitt might help us understand the subtitle of Schmitt's *Hamlet or Hecuba*. The time that breaks into the play is not the "time" of phenomenology—the "time-consciousness" that, according to Gadamer, grounds "historically constituted" experience and permits "hermeneutic horizons" to fuse. Nor is it, as Schmitt himself says plainly enough, the time of historicism: this time cannot be understood, in other words, solely or even primarily in chronological or empirical terms, with reference to the events, proper names, or circumstances that immediately surround the play (such as the incidents of 1600 to 1603, the biographies of Mary Stuart and James I, the alignments and intrigues of confessional civil war, or even the transformation of England from a land to a sea power). The time that breaks into the play is rather an epochal reality that expresses itself *in* and *through* these elements. Taken on its own terms, of course, this epochal reality "is" nothing at all. It is nothing more than that dynamic which opens up under conditions where the *complexio* is irreversibly dissolved and where the modern mediation that takes its place cannot reconcile opposites in any felicitous or enduring way. The "time" at issue here, in other words, is a limit to modern mediation that becomes intelligible only once we begin to comprehend modern mediation genealogically, from the standpoint of the catastrophe at its origin (the dissolution of the *complexio*). It is this *limit* to modern representation—this tragic inability of modern representation to achieve the reconciliation, peace, and order that is its main inheritance and justification—that intrudes into the play when James I is "there without being there" in the person of Hamlet, or where Mary Stuart is "there without being there" in the place where Gertrude's guilt could have been staged. The "time" that Schmitt finds in James I or Mary Stuart is not then their empirical existence, their immediate political relevance, or their part in the events of 1600 to 1603. It is rather their concrete epochal status, the fact that in the *absent presence* of their persons (where the

concept of the "person" is understood in a strict *genealogical* sense) we experience the convergence and coincidence of a set of contradictions (namely,
the conflicts of confessional civil war) that were unknown to medieval representation (that, indeed, helped dissolve it) and that modern representation
cannot fully mediate or reconcile. The "time" that steals into the play through
Hamlet and Gertrude, then, is more precisely an *epochal* tragedy, the tragedy
of modern political representation, its inability to achieve the very peace,
reconciliation, and order that together constitute both its *archē* and its *telos.*

But what is it, exactly, *about* the play that cannot accommodate the tragic
contradictions or conflicts that converge or coincide in the persons of Mary
Stuart and James I? Galli argues that one of the reasons why Schmitt wanted
to write about *Hamlet* in the first place was because modern representation
in general arrives at its understanding of political action with reference to the
paradigm of drama, theater, and play.[34] The epochal tragedy that, in *Hamlet*, breaks into the play and reveals, through a sort of intaglio, the limits of
modern representation, therefore presents Schmitt with a situation that is,
as Galli observes, perfectly analogous to the way 'the political' undoes, from
within, the institutions of modern politics that are *founded on* modern representation. On Galli's read, the attribute that modern politics shares with the
theater and with play more generally is the form of the *self-enclosed.* The institutions of modern politics are homologous to a theater or a game because the
actors or players within them conduct themselves according to a set of rules,
and with reference to a mode of mediation, that are together so completely
self-referential that they can apprehend their infinite "outside" as nothing
more than the most powerful effect of permutations internal to their finite
"inside."[35] In short, modern politics is structured like a game because its players are able to represent their most serious decisions *only* with reference to
rules that are at once self-enclosed yet arbitrary, totalizing yet lacking any reference to a "transcendental signified." What is unthinkable and unspeakable
in these terms is that the very *keystones* of modern politics—peace on earth,
reconciliation, order—are genealogically derived from a mode of representation (the *complexio*) that, precisely because it *is* grounded in a "transcendental
signified," is fundamentally incommensurable with modern mediation, indeed, is mutually exclusive with it.

As such, Galli counsels, this genealogical insight is exactly what we need
to comprehend if we are to think both the tragic and 'the political' in their
properly Schmittian sense. Schmitt's concept of 'the political' is not, on
Galli's read, a description of an unchanging essence (such as antagonism,
conflict, or the friend–enemy distinction). It is rather a genealogical concept, a name for a mode of conflict that could not have been reconciled by

the emphasis on the person in the *complexio* (because it is indeed born in and through its dissolution)[36] but that cannot be reconciled by the impersonal law of modern mediation either: 'the political,' in Schmitt, is simply that 'free' or 'unbounded' conflictuality that must but cannot be contained by the normal procedures of the state-form.[37] Schmitt's friend-enemy distinction does not then involve an ontological claim. It is simply a criterion, and a specifically modern one at that, to measure a conflictual intensity—or what Galli has called, from his earliest publications on, a "polemicity"[38]—that comes into being with the dissolution of medieval representation, yet remains constitutively unrepresentable, opaque, and troubling for modern mediation. Schmitt's concept of 'the political,' Galli argues, is neither an "essence" nor a "binary opposition." It is a name for, and a way to measure, the persistence within the theories, practices, and institutions of modern politics of this, modernity's volatile origin.[39]

And this, in turn, gives us a new way to understand Schmitt's reading of *Hamlet*. The "time" that irrupts into "the play" is "political" for the same reason that the hallmark of "the political" is its "tragicity." Just as there is no language, in modern representation, that can fully mediate the contradictions that coincide in the persons of Mary Stuart and James I, so too are there no procedures or norms in the self-referential and self-enclosed institutions of modern politics that can fully mediate the conflictual intensity that presents itself in 'the political.' If, as Galli wrote in 1986, "the basic problem of Schmitt's thought is not its ontologism, but its tragicity,"[40] then Schmitt's *Hamlet or Hecuba* will have been more than merely one among many Schmittian texts. It will have been the text in which Schmitt most openly attempted to think through the structure and conditions of his own thought. It will have provided the synecdoche for the mute but active force which spurred the raging metonymy that was Schmittian political thought.

Notes

An earlier version of this essay was presented at "Points of Departure: Political Theology on the Scene of Early Modernity," a conference sponsored by the Department of English, University of California, Irvine, February 20–21, 2009. For their comments on that paper, I thank Julia Reinhard Lupton, Graham Hammill, and the conference participants. Portions of this essay were previously published in Carlo Galli, *Political Spaces and Global War*, trans. Elisabeth Fay, ed. Adam Sitze (Minneapolis: University of Minnesota Press, 2010), xi–lxxxv; and in "A Farewell to Schmitt: Notes on the Work of Carlo Galli," *CR: New Centennial Review* 10, no. 2 (2010): 27–72. The research for this essay was supported, in part, by a grant from the Amherst College Faculty Research Award Program, as funded by the H. Axel Schupf '57 Fund for Intellectual Life. I thank Nicole Starrett for her editorial commentary and Elisabeth Fay for reviewing my translations from the Italian. All errors are mine.

1. Carl Schmitt, *Amleto o Ecuba: L'irrompere del tempo nel gioco del dramma*, trans. Simona Forti (Bologna: Il Mulino, 1983).

2. Carlo Galli, *Genealogia della politica: Carl Schmitt e la crisi del pensiero politico moderno* (Bologna: Il Mulino, 1996). See also Carlo Galli, *Genealogia della politica: Carl Schmitt e la crisi del pensiero politico modern*, 2d ed. (Bologna: Il Mulino, 2010).

3. Thalin Zarmanian, "Carl Schmitt and the Problem of Legal Order: From Domestic to International," *Leiden Journal of International Law* 19 (2006): 41.

4. Carl Schmitt, *Hamlet or Hecuba: The Intrusion of the Time into the Play*, trans. David Pan and Jennifer Rust (New York: Telos Press, 2009).

5. Sandro Chignola, "History of Political Thought and the History of Political Concepts: Koselleck's Proposal and Italian Research," *History of Political Thought* 23.3 (2002): 531–32, 534–46. See also Carlo Galli, "Alcune interpretazioni italiane della Scuola di Francoforte," *Il Mulino* 22 (1973): 648–71.

6. Carlo Galli, *Contingenza e necessità nella ragione political moderna* (Rome-Bari: Laterza and Figli, 2009), v–viii.

7. Carlo Galli, *La guerra globale* (Roma-Bari: Gius, Laterza and Figli, 2002), 97–101; Carlo Galli, "La pensabilità della politica: Vent'anni dopo," *Filosofia politica* 21.1 (2007): 9; Carlo Galli, *L'umanità multiculturale* (Bologna: Il Mulino, 2008), 84–85; Galli, *Contingenza e necessità*, viii.

8. *Enciclopedia del pensiero politico: Autori, concetti, dottrine*, 2d. ed., ed. Carlo Galli and Roberto Esposito (Rome-Bari: Gius, Laterza, and Figli, 2005).

9. Galli, "La pensabilità della politica," 4.

10. See Carlo Galli, "Presentazione," in Carl Schmitt, *Romanticismo politico*, ed. and trans. Carlo Galli (Milan: Giuffrè, 1981), v–xxxi; Carlo Galli, "Presentazione," in Carl Schmitt, *Cattolicesimo romano e forma politica*, ed. and trans. Carlo Galli (Milan: Giuffrè, 1986), 3–27. See also Carl Schmitt, *Scritti su Thomas Hobbes*, ed. Carlo Galli (Milan: Giuffrè, 1986).

11. Danilo Zolo, "Schmitt e la ragione politica moderna," *Iride: filosofia e discussione pubblica* 3 (1997): 577.

12. Galli, *Genealogia*, 10; Carlo Galli, "Contaminazioni: Irruzioni del Nulla," in *Nichilismo e Politica*, ed. Roberto Esposito, Carlo Galli, and Vincenzo Vitiello (Rome-Bari: Laterza, 2000), 156 n. 7; Carlo Galli, *Lo sguardo di Giano: Saggi su Carl Schmitt* (Bologna: Il Mulino, 2008), 9, 11.

13. Carlo Galli, "Carl Schmitt's Antiliberalism: Its Theoretical and Historical Sources and Its Philosophical and Political Meaning," *Cardozo Law Review* 5-6 (2000): 1603.

14. Theodor Adorno, *Lectures on Negative Dialectics*, ed. Rolf Tiedemann, trans. Rodney Livingstone (New York: Polity Press, 2008), 104.

15. Carlo Galli, "Hamlet: Representation and the Concrete," trans. Amanda Minervini and Adam Sitze, in this volume, 71.

16. Carlo Galli, *Spazi Politici: L'età moderna e l'età globale* (Bologna: Il Mulino, 2001), 117; Carlo Galli, "Introduzione," in *Guerra*, ed. Carlo Galli (Rome-Bari: Laterza, 2004), xxv.

17. Galli, *Giano*, 123.

18. Galli, *Genealogia*, 239–40, 245; cf. Galli, "Presentazione," *Romanticismo politico*, 13–14.

19. Galli, *Genealogia*, 242, 245.

20. Ibid., 4–5.

21. Ibid., 11; cf. Carlo Galli, *Modernità: Categorie e profili critici* (Bologna: Il Mulino, 1988), 8.

22. Carlo Galli, "La 'macchina' della modernità: metafisica e contingenza nel moderno pensiero politico," in *Logiche e crisi della modernità*, ed. Carlo Galli (Bologna: Il Mulino, 1991), 113–20.

23. Galli, "Presentazione," *Cattolicesimo romano e forma politica*, 13.

24. Ibid., 24.

25. Galli, *Genealogia*, 254.

26. Galli, "Carl Schmitt's Antiliberalism," 1598, 1608–9, 1611; Carlo Galli, "Carl Schmitt on Sovereignty: Decision, Form, Modernity," in *Penser la Souveraineté à l'époque modern et contempporaine*, ed. G. M. Cazzaniga and Y. C. Zarka (Pisa-Paris, Edizioni Ets–Libraire Philosophoque J. Vrin, 2001), 465.

27. Galli, "Carl Schmitt on Sovereignty," 469, 473.

28. Carlo Galli, "Il cattolicesimo nel pensiero politico di Carl Schmitt," in *Tradizione e Modernità nel pensiero politico di Carl Schmitt*, ed. Roberto Racinaro (Rome–Naples: Edizioni Scientifiche Italiene, 1987), 21–23.

29. Galli, "Carl Schmitt's Antiliberalism," 1599.

30. Ibid., 1604; Galli, "Carl Schmitt on Sovereignty," 463–64.

31. Galli, "Carl Schmitt on Sovereignty," 467, 470.

32. On these terms, there is no longer any contradiction or inconsistency (as Karl Löwith and many after him have argued) between Schmitt's criticism of political romanticism, on the one hand, and his affirmation of the exception, on the other. The speechlessness—the absence of morphogenetic power—that the political romantic disavows with endless chatter is the same "speechlessness" (or, in Kierkegaardian terms, the "inability to explain") that confronts reason each and every time it tries to think the exception. As Galli observes in his 1983 Introduction to the Italian translation of Schmitt's "Hamlet or Hecuba," Schmitt's interest in Prince Hamlet is simply an attempt to inquire into this same speechlessness from the opposite side. In the silence of his indecisionism, Galli argues, Hamlet is "the tragic counterpart to Romantic indecisionism" ("Hamlet: Representation and the Concrete," 78; see also Galli, *Genealogia*, 212, 218).

33. Galli, *Giano*, 7.

34. Galli, "Hamlet: Representation and the Concrete," 74.

35. The dynamic that governs these institutions is thus not unlike the free play that Jacques Derrida characterized in his 1966 Johns Hopkins lecture as "a field of infinite substitutions only because it is finite," a field that is infinite not because it is "too large," but because "there is something missing from it: a center which arrests and grounds the play of substitutions." See Jacques Derrida, "Structure, Sign, and Play in the Discourse of the Human Sciences," in *Writing and Difference*, trans. Alan Bass (Chicago: University of Chicago Press, 1978), 289.

36. Galli, "Carl Schmitt's Antiliberalism," 1611.

37. Galli, *Spazi politici*, 117.

38. Carlo Galli, "Carl Schmitt nella cultura italiana (1924–1978): Storia, bilancio, prospettive di una presenza problematica," *Materiali per una storia della cultura giuridica*, 9.1 (1979): 153; Carlo Galli, "Carl Schmitt," in *Enciclopedia del pensiero politico*, 753.

39. Galli, *Genealogia*, 736–39, 742.

40. Carlo Galli, "La guerra nel pensiero politico di Carl Schmitt," *La Nottola* 1–2 (1986): 146 n. 4.

3

Hamlet: Representation and the Concrete

CARLO GALLI

Translated by Adam Sitze and Amanda Minervini

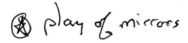

This essay was originally published as the introduction to the Italian edition of Carl Schmitt's *Hamlet or Hecuba: The Irruption of Time into the Play.*[1] On the occasion of its English translation more than twenty-five years later, I find no reason to correct or update it. In fact, while the scholarly literature on Schmitt has since then enormously expanded, not much has been written specifically on *Hamlet or Hecuba.* And even though I have since published two books on Schmitt,[2] each of which goes into more depth on the topics I analyzed in this earlier essay, I nevertheless found that I could, in general, confirm its theses.

At the time that I wrote this essay, I had two goals. The first was to present to readers the postwar portion of Schmitt's thought—deriving from *The Nomos of the Earth,* inside of which *Hamlet or Hecuba* positions itself—which was, at that point, not as well known as it is today. My second objective was to throw into relief the plays of mirrors and references, the allusions and the disputes—between Benjamin and Romanticism, theology and geopolitics, literature and philosophy—that are interwoven into the fabric of Schmittian political science.

Regarding the first goal, I don't have much to add. Through Hamlet, Schmitt speaks about the unsaid of modernity: its obscure origin, its tragic core. He does this starting from a point of view external to the State: the English *Seenahme,* which is to say, England's conversion to modern politics in the maritime, non-terrestrial, mode. For Schmitt, this conversion is a necessary decision if England is to escape the catastrophe of the traditional order, but it is also a decision that did not enter into political consciousness during the epoch of James I. In the character of Hamlet, this catastrophe and incapacity for decision irrupt from the outside, thereby rendering him a living legend.

If, in *Political Theology*, Schmitt captured the unsaid origin of the State in the decision on the state of exception, genealogically apprehending the internal logic of modern statuality, then in *Hamlet or Hecuba*, Schmitt captures the origin of modernity—of the Nomos of the Earth in the modern age—from a 'barbaric' standpoint, which is to say, from a standpoint that precedes and is external to the State. This is, of course, the standpoint of Hamlet's *Spiel*, of a representation that is not yet statual, that is disquieted not by the decision but by its lack. In both instances, it is clear that, according to Schmitt, Order as a Whole implies laceration and decision—of the sovereign on the state of exception in 1922, or of a civilization on the way out of the crisis of the traditional order in 1956. The prince's melancholy and indecision—a mythical theme that is related to the disjointedness of the world axis (as Giorgio De Santillana and Hertha Von Dechend have shown quite well in *Hamlet's Mill*)—make him modern but disoriented, they situate him prior not only to the completely formed and fully disenchanted modernity of the State, but also to England's maritime decision (they would also make him a symbol of Germany, in its excruciating *Sonderweg* between East and West). According to Schmitt, Shakespeare—who the greatest Italian novelist, Alessandro Manzoni, defined in *The Betrothed* as "a barbarian not devoid of genius"[3]—created in his non-statual representation the living myth of a tragic hero. Hamlet reveals—in negative and in a maritime context—the same secret of Hobbes's mortal god, of the Leviathanic representative State: the Origin of politics is a historic-epochal concreteness, an unsaid immediacy that is always operating within modern mediations and representations. It is an Origin that acts as much in the sovereign decision as in the Hamletic indecision, as much in the classic form of the State as in the barbaric form of the *Spiel*.

With regard to the second goal, I should underline that Schmitt's elaboration of the relationship between literature and historical-political reality in *Hamlet or Hecuba* feeds on polemics that were very much alive when the book was written (but not so much today). Against Idealistic Historicism and against the Marxist theory of reflection, against Romantic-bourgeois Aestheticism and against Benjamin's apocalyptic theology, Schmitt elaborates his theory on the relation between concreteness and drama, between the particular event and the universality of the representative *logos*. This is, precisely, the theory of irruption (*Einbruch*)—of that immediacy which renders mediation possible and, at the same time, unhinges it, which renders mediation at once real and impossible ('barbaric' in the case of Shakespeare, 'based on nothing' in the case of the State). Schmitt's peculiar hermeneutics consists in reading the dark clot of the text, penetrating it from the outside and disquieting it. This hermeneutics is the very opposite of Gadamer's, and, indeed, it is not surprising that Gadamer would harshly criticize *Hamlet or Hecuba*. In *Truth and Method*, Gadamer contends that, from the standpoint of the *Spiel*, there is no opposition between *Spiel* and *Zeit*, between play [*dramma*] and concrete historical time. He argues that Schmitt turns *Hamlet* into a roman à clef (*Schlüsselroman*), missing its dramatic and literally concreteness.[4] If anything, according to Gadamer, one can speak of the irruption of play [*dramma*] into time—that is, of the author's assertive intervention into his public and its horizon of expectation—but not, as Schmitt does with his 'bad historicism,' of the irruption of time into play. Evidently, the reasons of hermeneutics and the reasons of genealogy, those of literature and those of politics, of art and of punctual concreteness, are not meant to agree with one another: the relation between what is internal and what is external to the represented form is, for Schmitt and Gadamer, entirely opposite.

One last note. When Schmitt talks about literature (here as elsewhere), he is generally illuminating (his 1919 *Political Romanticism*, for example, would even be praised by the renowned Ernst Robert Curtius).[5] Illuminating—but handle with care. The literary text is always for Schmitt a pretext, an occasion to speak about himself and about his obsession, namely, the ubiquitous and elusive presence of the 'political' in all realms of human activity. The 'political' runs through every human activity, it vivifies and determines it, while at the same time it is disquieted and exposed to an 'immense power of the Negative' that cannot be measured, dialecticized, or exorcised. Works of art interest Schmitt only to the extent that he, with his Janus-like gaze, can see in them the powers that render their measure measureless, that deform their form: the Origin and the End of an epoch.

Bologna
March 15, 2009

✳ ✳ ✳

wow/ "The essay's innermost formal law is heresy," Theodor Adorno once wrote,[6] and in the case of Carl Schmitt's *Hamlet or Hecuba*, this definition is perhaps not out of place. In this essay, Schmitt gives us another example of intellectual vitality, historiographical curiosity, and loyalty to a thought that, always spurred on by new interests and new clarifications, remains determined by the same firm conceptual groundings that the German jurist and politologist established throughout his sixty years of scientific research. Confronting in Hamlet the emblematic personage of indecision in modern man, the theorist of decisionism here performs one of his incursions into territories outside of his professional specialty (his early essay on *Political Romanticism* also comes to mind).[7] Not only does Schmitt's *Hamlet or Hecuba* provide a clever and felicitous solution to a question that is of interest primarily to scholars of English (on this level, however, Schmitt's proposals are not new, as he himself admits: if anything, it is what those proposals imply that's new and stimulating), but he also encounters very broad and engaging problems, which he explicates over the course of a sustained reflection. In this text, Schmitt renews unsleeping polemics whose weight and influence we can perceive with an attentive and meditated reading—a reading which goes well beyond the malicious "understatement," the tone of the "ingenious dilettante," that runs through Schmitt's entire work (with the exception of *Excursus II*, which overtly functions as an orientation to the understanding of the whole book) and that in the "Post Scriptum" melts into a placid and firm (and also, at times, ostentatious) self-justification.

Just as *Political Romanticism* in the end proves itself to be a study on the connection between politics and the intellectual in the realm of a completed secularization, so too in *Hamlet or Hecuba* (precisely because Schmitt's interests exceed the interest of the specialist) Schmitt encounters the problem of the State in the historical moment defined by the dissolution of the medieval symbolic order and by the first affirmation of the new juridical and spatial order of the earth (a concept he renders, synthetically, with the term *nomos*). Schmitt's analysis of the modalities with which this epoch (the beginning of the seventeenth century) understands and represents itself—an analysis he conducts through his interpretation of *Hamlet*—raises a series of broad questions. These revolve around the relationship between representation and reality (such as, for instance, the problematical links between culture and politics, art and history, and between play and seriousness), which Schmitt develops by crossing paths with the critical Marxist Walter Benjamin and by confronting, albeit elliptically, the great German discussion around the essence of the tragic and the function of play. Naturally, this operation also involves questions of method and, in the last analysis, of the philosophy of history.

Although *Hamlet or Hecuba* is ultimately an easy text, it is certainly not without its own restrained and allusive complexity. Neither systematic like Schmitt's *Constitutional Theory* or *The Nomos of the Earth*, nor famous like his *Concept of the Political*,[8] it is affected by that attitude of deliberate simplification (*Vereinfachung*) that marks much of Schmittian thought, and that allows Schmitt to seize the core of complex issues with dazzling lucidity. In *Hamlet or Hecuba*, the topic of the relationship between political reality and forms of representation (which he already sketched in the now classic but, in its time, radically innovative *Political Theology*,[9] and which is really central to Schmittian reflection in general), is reformulated under a different optic.

Hamlet or Hecuba is not, however, a thesis-based book (Schmitt himself rules this out in his "Post Scriptum"). It is rather an instance of Schmittian hermeneutics, in which the object itself (*Hamlet*) is interrogated and left to speak, and where its answer inserts itself into a system of references, a constellation of suggestions, that Schmitt's essay then tries to follow and resolve, although in a purely nonsystematic mode. (And this choice inevitably excludes the possibility that one could enter into the domain of the specialist in English studies to evaluate the philological and documentary consistency of Schmitt's thesis.)

For Schmitt there is no grand entrance, no vestibule, to the temple of knowledge. Rather, the immediacy and uniqueness of historical events, the objectivity of the problems to be analyzed, place before us, from the very beginning, the theme of Shakespeare's work: to unravel an enigma, to account for the causes that not only indeed make *Hamlet* (as many have said before) a drama with the wrong protagonist, but also a drama with an incomplete and incomprehensible plot. By refusing all mediation between text and reader, by putting aside the interpretative and explanatory accretions that, like a gigantic crust, suffocate the Shakespearian masterpiece, Schmitt faces *Hamlet* frontally in order to study its "story"—in order, that is to say, to see where and why it loses its "sure and linear simplicity." This approach only appears to be naïve. In fact, it is a sort of elementary narratology that is designed to eliminate from our interpretation of the drama any aestheticism, any psychologism, and any element of "privatization," and also to go beyond historicist interpretations. It leads Schmitt to the affirmation (which, again, is not altogether new), that, in *Hamlet*, the dramatic word jams up and fails in front of something it cannot speak. The poet faces an ineffable *quid*, covered by taboos; he faces an *excess* that, as compared to the dramatic form, cannot be *told* (and, from this standpoint, *Hamlet* is the opposite of a historical novel, where the narration pretends to exhaust the event). This failure of expression—this *thing* so irremediably distant from *discourse*—is, according to Schmitt, the source of the drama's incomprehensibility. So long as we confine ourselves only to the text of *Hamlet*, we therefore will be unable either to reconstruct a *subtext* (to use Stanislavskij's term), or to explain why *Hamlet* leaves open the question, essential for the development of its "story," of the guilt or innocence of Queen Gertrude, Hamlet's mother. Above all, we will be unable to account for what Schmitt defines as the "Hamletization of the hero," that is to say, of the transformation of the hero of a vengeance drama into a melancholy intellectual who is full of doubts and unable to act, and who, for precisely for this reason, is rendered the drama's protagonist.

By recognizing in the drama of Shakespeare's work a shadow or lacuna that cannot be explained from inside the text, but only by reference to a core of *contemporary historical events* (and we will soon see which ones), Schmitt self-consciously exposes himself to the accusation of effecting a *contaminatio* between art and politics, and thus also of joining with the crassest materialistic determinism. But in this, precisely, consists the originality of the Schmittian position. The fact that Shakespeare could not or did not want to touch the topic of Gertrude's guilt or innocence is something that hides and together reveals, *in negative*, the link between Hamlet's mother and Mary Stuart, who was also at the center of violent discussions about her implication in her husband's death. The fact that Shakespeare could not or did not want to make of Hamlet a typical hero, sure of himself and of his mission of vengeance, hides and reveals—again, in negative—the link between Hamlet and the historical figure of James I, the late defender of the king's divine right, who is condemned to watch the crumbling of his worldview from within ("The time is out of joint. O cursed spite / That ever I was born to set it right!" Hamlet exclaims towards the end of Act I), who sees his own origins and his own royal power transformed into a phantom. This "link" is not meant to be an allegorical superimposition of significations. As Schmitt writes, "the stage character Hamlet is not completely subsumed by the mask. Intentionally or instinctively the conditions and forms of the original context within which the play was written have been brought into the play, and, behind the stage character Hamlet, another figure has remained standing. The spectators of that time also saw this figure when they saw Hamlet."[10] This movement of *hiding* and *revealing*, in sum, does not establish a direct and univocal relationship between structure and superstructure (according to the ideology of someone like Trotsky, who could affirm, "we believe that in the beginning was the deed. The word followed, as its phonetic shadow").[11] Rather, into the autonomy of the drama and its characters, there is an *irruption* (*Einbruch*) of a human and political problematicity that springs from a *contemporary history* that is *transcendental* with respect to the drama itself as well as to its internal logic. This irruption may have effects on the structure of the work, but it does not determine its entire existence as "drama." In other words, the drama does not completely reflect history, and art is not yoked to the cart of the dominant classes. Instead, precisely because it is autonomous, the word cannot express the specific harshness or toughness of the historical reality that faces it ("the rest is silence," concludes the dying Hamlet). External reality is, in sum, autonomous from the text, and *vice versa*. Their only relationship is, on the one hand, *the irruption*, and, on the other, *the scar*, which is to say, the mark of this irruption. The external event is not then sayable from within the text. It is not allegorizable; it does not constitute a pre-text.

The taboo is constituted in this way for two sets of reasons: first of all because of the poet's respect for and fear of (shall we say) certain contingencies, but also, and above all, because of an essential irrepresentability of the external event, which is to say, because of its *tragic* quality (about which we will have more to say later). It is important to note here that Schmitt's emphasis on this taboo in *Hamlet or Hecuba* is not the same as his not infrequent praise of reticence for political reasons (which he used to justify his behavior during the Nazi epoch, as with, for instance, his famous quotation of Macrobius's maxim "non possum scribere in eum qui potest proscribere" ["It is not possible to write against one who has the power to proscribe."]).[12] The concept of irruption, by implying the transcendence of reality from art and the resulting limitation of the inventive freedom of the poet, constitutes an authentic "third way" between the autonomy of the "beautiful appearance" and dialectic materialism[13]—and, methodologically, leads to the dissolution of both subjectivist finalism and historicist teleology (Jakobson's hypothesis of a literature that holds literality as its specific object is, of course, far from Schmitt's thought). In *Hamlet or Hecuba*, in other words, the harsh realism that is characteristic of Schmitt's thought more generally is reconfirmed in the form of a distrust in the ability of the word to seize the thing (and, in this connection, we may also think of Schmitt's *Crisis of Parliamentary Democracy*,[14] his *Political Romanticism* with its critique of the Romantics' "eternal dialogue," and his *Political Theology*, the central concept of which is the exclusion of a relationship of direct and causal continuity—classically 'descendent'—between the juridical universe of reason and the political universe of decision).

In the work of art, there are then neither ideological reflections nor "messages" to be conveyed or pedagogically expressed (the distance between Schmitt and Brecht is, clearly, abysmal). Historical reality does not *found* the drama; rather, it remains an *incognito* within the dramatic dimension of the modern State, becoming transparent only in the political and in public (*Öffentlichkeit*), but only and solely because author and public are together involved in the same historic-epochal event, which imposes itself on both in its incumbent and ineluctable presence.[15] If the Romantic lyric genius can embroider upon his own experience (*Erlebnis*) to the point where it becomes unrecognizable, and if, in so doing, he aims at exhausting the totality of what is expressible, the dramatic genius (Shakespeare, in this case) must be able to distinguish between what is representable and what is not.

But what exactly is the hard core of effectual reality that irrupts into the work of art? Why does the destiny of the Stuarts hold such epochal relevance? What is Schmitt reading in contemporary history that is capable of determining the structure of *Hamlet*? The concept of history in the totality of Schmitt's *oeuvre* is certainly not one of an uncomplicated progression. It is instead, particularly in relation to modern history, that of an *epoch*[16]—*a suspension*— enclosed between two catastrophes that at one and the same time create and dissolve an order (such that the modern order is always "partial" and no longer recognizes the solidarity of the medieval *complexio*).[17] It is worth restating that the novelty of *Hamlet or Hecuba* lies in the fact that, in it, Schmitt interprets the problematic and contradictory formation of the State not in the moment of its baroque and absolutistic construction in political theology (which he examined in *Political Theology* and in his essays on Hobbes),[18] but rather in a Mannerist situation (in a moment, in other words, where an old order goes into pieces, corroded from within by the disquiet of the "melancholy" subject, whose capacity of expressive discourse is hence "beside itself," eccentric, an anomalous elaboration of the elements of the old "style"). However, instead of adopting into his text the historical sequence of Mannerism and Baroque (which has been the object of many discussions, especially in relation to the possibility of applying analogically literary-historical categories to political phenomena),[19] which in any case anticipates as its result a construction of the State that is 'restored' and artificial, Schmitt instead chooses a standpoint that at the same time *precedes* and *is lateral to* the birth of the modern State. Indeed, *Hamlet or Hecuba* cannot be completely explained without reference to the great systematization of the relationship between the earth and the sea that Schmitt gave his research starting in the early 1940s and culminating in *The Nomos of the Earth*.[20] Briefly summarized, Schmitt's works in this period reveal that the European system of the closed continental states (characterized by the temporary suspension and neutralization of the "political," i.e., of the fundamental irrationality of politics that expresses itself in the friend–enemy relation) can no longer be rendered comprehensible solely on the basis of the cessation of religious civil wars and with reference to the implicit contradiction between law and the "political." To this schema, Schmitt argues, one must add the great dichotomy between earth and sea, and also that between European and extra-European lands. Schmitt warns that the birth of European states is determined by a potent element that is neither statual [*statuale*] nor even statualizable [*statualizzabile*], and that consists of the detachment of England from the political forms pertinent to the European state, and of the passage of the island to a form of power that is not statual, but maritime and imperial. It is the English *Seenahme*, Schmitt claims, that permits the *Landnahme* of the European states[21] (or, put differently, it is the English domination of the sea that permits, by balancing it, the European conquest of the lands of the New World), and it is this *Landnahme* that, in turn, permits the formation of "rival" lines of friendship and enmity, under whose protection the continental states are able to proceed with the rationalization of war and the creation of the European and statual *Jus Publicum Europeæum*, only because it is guaranteed by this element that is neither European nor statual. It is this indeed the characteristic of its upheaval, its epochal catastrophe, which is also the germ of its ruin, for Britain's global maritime imperial power will transform the "Law of Nations" into a private international law—a commercial law—and will substitute juridical-statual reasoning, which is essentially founded on the concept of *hostes æqualiter justi*,[22] with a universalistic moralism that is politically dangerous because of its proposal to renew the discriminatory concept of *bellum justum*.

From this standpoint, the great historical event which involves Shakespeare and determines the destiny of the Stuart dynasty is *the formation of the modern nomos of the earth*, which is to say, the birth of the State through wars of religion, the struggle between State and Church, and the opposition of earth and sea—or, in other words, the consciousness of assisting with the end of the medieval *hero*, humanistic *virtú*, and *sacral power* (this sets the stage for the historical and determinant figure of the Stuarts, and of James I in particular). This event—which will leave man alone with his passions, which can no longer be corrected by *natural reason* and thus must be repressed through the artificial *imperium rationis* of the Leviathan, or harmoniously developed as a concurrence of reasonable interests in the liberal State-society[23]—is surely disorienting. In it, Hamlet/James has lost the totality of an order and has not yet understood that, to achieve a new order, there must be a *decision*. And, in fact, the reorientation of England towards a maritime existence will not come from the Stuarts but instead from private entrepreneurs, while the Stuarts will be swept away in the difficult transition towards modernity (which, better to repeat it, is not simply a matter of "the State").[24] We thus find ourselves at the end of the self-understanding of the pre-statual epoch, but not yet at the beginning of self-enclosed political-statual representation. In *Hamlet* there is not yet any political theology.[25]

It is doubtless true that the central interest of Schmittian scientific production consists in his discovery that the absolute sovereign—the master of the exceptional case—properly represents *the Nothing*, which is to say, the necessary *disconnection* between the constitutive elements of the modern State (the public and the private, the juridical and the political, the individual and the State, freedom and authority, lawfulness and legitimacy). Nobody knows better than Schmitt that the "enclosed" self-representation of the State not only cannot satisfy profound demands for collective identification, but also cannot function as anything more than a temporary solution to the problem of the control of the "political" (despite its epochal *efficacy* going from the civilizing process of "good manners" to the psychological construction of the "subject" to the diffusion of "police" control).[26] Even less can the "enclosed" self-representation of the State constitute an answer to the problem of the construction of an order that is capable of going beyond the "political," that positions itself as a new and stable integrality. Thus it is that *Hamlet or Hecuba*, which deals with a "barbaric" level of representation, constitutes not just a variation on the theme of the State, but, by opening up a standpoint that is both anterior and lateral to the State, allows Schmitt to enlarge his field of observation.

The Shakespearean representation is then the metaphor, pre-statual and not yet self-enclosed, of a world that in turn conceives of itself as theater, albeit, as Schmitt affirms, in a still elementary way.[27] In fact, the critical category that interprets England's self-representation during the first years of the seventeenth century is not the baroque but that of the "Elizabethan World Picture,"[28] which is to say, a compromise that tries to integrate the residual elements of a medieval vision of the world with the divine notion of royal power. This is why the theater within the theater in *Hamlet's* Act III (the representation of the so-called "Murder of Gonzago") is the point in *Hamlet* where Shakespeare most holds to life. This meta-theater is not a matter of the sort of game of mirrors and reflections that is typical of the self-representation of absolute power (where the world is represented as if it were seen by the king's eyes).[29] It is instead a matter of a double representation that 'holds up'—that does not collapse into parody—because it is able to receive the tragic seriousness external to the drama,[30] while at the same time retaining its dramatic autonomy. The theatricalization of the world—which Shakespeare emphasizes in the "drama within the drama," and which Schmitt assumes by including in the title of his essay the name "Hecuba" (which refers to the staging of Priam's lament in Act II)—does not then "comprehend" the extradramatic contemporary reality of "Hamlet" (or, rather, the reality in which Hamlet is embedded). This gap between reality and representation is perceptible, much better than in the classic statual tragedy of Corneille and Racine, in a situation that is not yet 'political,' which is to say, in a situation that allows Schmitt to use, referring to the representation, the same word, *Spiel*, to indicate *both* the drama *and* the socio-political context of its staging.[31] *Spiel* here signifies, in a single word, a situation that, in a more advanced epoch,

[handwritten annotations at top: "realty of our present existence" ≠ the "modern state, but rather a la Meier"]

Schmitt would have to designate by referring to representation (*Repräsenta-tion*) (at the properly political level), on the one hand, and tragedy (*Tragödie*) (at the dramatic level), on the other. Thus, the translation had each time to adapt itself to the context, rendering *Spiel* now with "game" [*gioco*], now with "game of the drama" [*gioco del dramma*], now with "drama," and now with "representation."[32] By choosing a historical situation in which representation can be defined as *Spiel*, Schmitt becomes able to demonstrate that, beyond the dimension of the *Spiel*—precisely where it redoubles itself into meta-theater—there is a hard core of irrepresentable reality that, irrupting into the scene from the outside, confirms the distance between artifice and reality, between the secondary system, on the one hand, and the primary elements of politics, on the other. To analyze representation (both dramatic and politi-cal) in a case that is not yet statual nor even yet in the process of becoming statual, is useful after all to create a parallelism, even if only in chronological anticipation, between play and seriousness [*gioco e serietà*], on the one hand, and State and exceptional case, on the other.[33] This parallelism is no coinci-dence; it is instead a more evident and elementary situation, and, in a certain sense, it is also more tangible.

And this is the backbone of Schmitt's argument: "It is inconceivable that Shakespeare intended no more than to make his Hamlet into a Hecuba, that we are meant to weep for Hamlet as the actor wept for the Trojan queen. We would, however, in point of fact weep for Hamlet as for Hecuba if we wished to divorce the reality of our present existence from the play on the stage. Our tears would then become the tears of actors. We would no longer have any purpose or cause and would have sacrificed both to the aesthetic enjoy-ment of the play."[34] In this way, through a sort of reformulation of Diderot's *Paradox of Acting*,[35] Schmitt undoes the thesis of the State as perfect self-representation, absolute and self-sufficient metaphor,[36] which, precisely be-cause it has lost sight of the transcendence of reality from play [*gioco*], will culminate in the theory of the state-spectacle and in the sociology of "simu-lacra" (images of images, which do not represent anything but themselves).[37] This is, in fact, the ultimate outcome of the privatization of the State that was started when the sovereign monarch was substituted by the sovereign citi-zen, who then became a sovereign spectator, capable only of consuming, in aesthetic enjoyment, a representation that made itself, over time, more and more irresponsible and ineffective.

In any case, to return to our point, it is specifically because *Hamlet or Hecuba* moves from a situation that is anterior and lateral to the pure po-litical dimension that it also crosses another series of problems, namely, the relationship between play, the "tragic," and myth. Indeed, it is *Spiel* that is at issue in *Hamlet or Hecuba*—not *Repräsentation*. As such, Schmitt had to grapple with the polysemy of the term 'play' [*gioco*]—that is to say, with the series of meanings that are attributed to it—and, above all, with the problem of play [*gioco*] as a metaphor for the world,[38] and with the theses of those who see, in play, the overcoming of politics and the highest form of freedom.

Schmitt has no doubts, in his realism, about play being a secondary system, to which seriousness of politics is the primary factor. He also has no doubts about the fact that play has its own self-enclosed rules that do not allow for the mediation of any external meaning. And he has no doubts, finally, about the fact that Shakespeare's dramas are "games" [*giochi*] deprived, in other words, of any philosophic intent, of any will to deliver a "message" or to be "engaged." For Schmitt, the encounter between play and seriousness is instead, as we have seen, an *irruption*. The result is not a determinate negation, concept, or *dialectic* between form and content, serenity and engagement, and freedom and necessity.[39] It is rather the potentially nihilistic opening of the word onto the extra-linguistic dimension—over silence (or, we might also say, over the uproar of history at an epochal turning point). For Schmitt, then, the metaphor of *Spiel* is, in and of itself, neither true nor false. It does not "allude" to an Other as True; rather, it involuntarily registers the reality it encounters.[40] This encounter is *tragedy*—modern tragedy—as Schmitt understands it: the barbaric Shakespearian *Spiel*, precisely and only as such, is the only possible representation, during modernity, of the *Tragik*, which is to say, of the real tragicity of history. Classically, the tragic is a serious discourse about the foundations and origins of a political and social system—it is, in other words, the self-certification and self-justification that the link between community and violence had been broken and recreated.[41] The modern destruction of the traditional symbolic order, by contrast, is not fully narratable (it is not "myth," if by it one means *tale*), but can only be present in the negative. Modern tragedy is therefore a tragicity that is without catharsis and without action. It is mute testimony (that is nevertheless recognizable at the public level of the *Öffentlichkeit*) of a catastrophe that has already happened. There is no mediation between *Spiel* and *Tragik*, neither through aesthetics nor through ethics (*Hamlet* is not the tragedy of destiny: it does not involve the sacrifice of the hero, whether that be the unconscious sacrifice of classic tragedy, or the conscious one of which Hölderlin speaks). On Schmitt's reading of modern tragedy, there is only *one source* of the tragic, in one *determinate* moment of history: the catastrophic epochal rupture of the re-orientation of the *Nomos of the Earth*, the birth of the modern State amidst religious civil war. Nailed onto this historical-political fracture between a lost universality and a particularity yet to come, Hamlet/James is the immediate cipher (the living myth) of the impotence of traditional power: the tragic consists in his *inaction*, not in his acts.

Schmitt's insistence on the immediate, non-dialecticizable, relationship between play and seriousness[42]—and ultimately, too, between freedom and necessity—implies a conscious polemic against Schiller, whose discussion of "beautiful appearance" unilaterally developed the concept expressed by Kant in his *Critique of Judgment* of a *Zweckmässigkeit ohne Zweck* ("purposiveness without purpose") and of a *Gesetzmässigkeit ohne Gesetz* ("lawfulness without law"). Schiller's "beautiful appearance," which concluded itself in the project of the aesthetic education of man who in his "aesthetic state" achieves "indifference for reality,"[43] could have had as its emblem the line from the *Prologue* to *Wallenstein*, appropriately quoted by Schmitt: "Ernst ist das Leben, heiter ist die Kunst."[44] But alongside Schmitt's open polemic with Schiller, there is also in *Hamet or Hecuba* a critical allusion to Nietzsche, which is to say, to the last moment of great nineteenth-century German reflection on the tragic. It is certainly not farfetched to argue that, once he had liquidated both the Schillerian and Nietzschean extremes of aesthetic reflection, Schmitt then expressed a negative, if implicit, judgment on what is contained between those two extremes, namely, the notion of the tragic that is proper to German Idealism (in this regard, Schmitt's frequent agreement with Hegelian theses should not cause us to forget that Schmitt is recognizing Hegel's great critical acumen, quite apart from the systematical aspects of Hegel's thought). From Hölderlin to Hegel, German Idealism has turned the possibility of a modern tragedy into the *experimentum crucis* for a freedom that, putting Schiller's concept of the "beautiful soul" through the ordeal of the epoch's infinite laceration (namely, the French Revolution), attempts to affirm itself as *freedom from necessity*. From Hölderlin's sacrifice of subjectivity (in which the subject stays silent because of "fullness," in order to let nature speak, and not, as in Hamlet, out of impotence),[45] to the dialectical solution of the "tragedy of the ethical" provided by Hegel (which, reading *The Phenomenology of Spirit* as a *Bildungsroman* of conscience, still contains the possibility of a 'figural' self-description of the stages of the tragic scission between subject and Absolute),[46] Schmitt implicitly recognizes a path that ends up dissolving its own ethical-political tension into a Nietzschean aesthetic. Nietzsche's thesis on the tragic as conflict between the two "fraternal" concepts of Apollo and Dionysus (appearance and depth), led him, indeed, to a post-tragic perspective, to the vision of "play of the world with itself" [*gioco del mondo con se stesso*], according to which the individual responds with a "yes" to a destiny of play, with a free "superficiality" that is conscious of itself as infinite possibility (Heraclitus's "child at play" [*pais paizôn*]),[47] in a perspective of substantial "innocence of becoming."[48] From the Hegelian "being in difference," we thus arrive at the Nietzschean "playing along" [*stare al gioco*].

Schmitt, of course, inserts himself into this tradition in a reductive modality. For him, the tragic is not the destiny of man in general, such that it could be recognized (as in Hegel) or played (as in Nietzsche). Neither it is a matter of the heroic struggle of "essences," for as much as it is concrete and historically determined in its uniqueness, the tragic has no birth or substance. It is only possible to talk about it as *Ursprung*, which is to say, as the emergence of an epochal rupture. The tragic, for Schmitt, is not then a substantial concept. It is a relational concept—exactly like the political, to which it is indeed, in Schmitt's thought, structurally similar.

Schmitt's debt to Walter Benjamin, besides being declared by Schmitt himself, is especially evident in relation to Schmitt's concept of the tragic. In *The Origin of German Tragic Drama*, indeed, Benjamin distinguishes between the classic *Tragödie*, in which the tragic element was provided by myth, and modern *Trauerspiel* (which is to say, translated literally, a "sad dramatic play" or "mournful representation"), whose tragicity is instead due to history seen in a Christian light, which illuminates it as a panorama of catastrophes and ruins.[49] It is precisely the "glorious" rise of the creature, in baroque drama, that allows for the emergence of a decontextualized creatureliness immersed in its nudity into a history deprived of meaning. In this way, reflective representation opens itself up onto the nothing (and Benjamin is, on this point, explicitly indebted to the analysis of sovereignty Schmitt conducted in *Political Theology*),[50] and modern allegory, which takes the place of symbol, is indeed the dimension where things appear in their own tragic nullity. Yet, Benjamin's intention, in the passage from his dialectical method in *The Origin of German Tragic Drama* to his peculiar materialism in the following years, is to restore to the thing, by working through the catastrophe that emerges in allegory, a new consistency—to illuminate the thing, in other words, not with the human word and its "meanings" but with the innocent and messianic light of the creator's divine word. It is a strange fate that brings Schmitt and Benjamin close.[51] Benjamin's direct citation of *Political Theology*, the 1930 letter in which Benjamin dedicated *The Origin of German Tragic Drama* to Schmitt,[52] and Benjamin's open reference to Schmittian methodology, which he included in a 1928 *Curriculum*—all constitute reasons for reflection. In this last text, indeed, Benjamin mentions Schmitt, together with Riegel, as an example of a method capable of confronting the expressive tendencies of an epoch in a multiform and metadisciplinary mode, under a single religious and political profile. Schmitt's perception of the polysemy at work in the self-representation of a given epoch, as well as Schmitt's will to "integrate phenomena" around a unique center capable of explaining them, was thus what Benjamin saw in Schmitt, with whom he also joined on account of Schmitt's negation of bourgeois and Marxist historicism (through his mythology of the subject-creator) and on account of Schmitt's radical antisubjectivism, which translated itself into a methodology of excess, of the exceptional case (exemplified by Benjamin's claim that "the necessary tendency towards the extreme . . . in philosophical research constitutes the norm in the formation of concepts").[53] This radical antisubjectivism also translated into a vision of catastrophe as the norm of history, and this was marked by an irremediable discontinuity (by the continuous irruption, in the metaphorical universe, of the "political" element). A partial affinity of method and relatively shared thematic horizons (the critique of parliamentarianism, which Benjamin conducts, however, independently from Schmitt,[54] and Benjamin's interest in Romanticism as an aesthetic response to the tragedy of the modern) therefore justify Benjamin's relationship with Schmitt, as a relationship that went well beyond the attitude of those who 'ask their enemy for advice' (*et ab hoste consilium*).

Now, Schmitt's use of Benjaminian categories in *Hamlet and Hecuba* (which includes not only *Trauerspiel* but also Benjamin's notion of *Ursprung*) is, on Schmitt's part, much more than a "flirtation." It is a response that, as with other Schmittian responses,[55] arrives after an incredibly long interval, the space of a generation. It is also, per usual, a partial and tendentious answer, an extremist use of Benjaminian concepts that ends up precisely in a *Gegendeutung* or counter-interpretation. It is, in fact, evident that in *Hamlet and Hecuba* Schmitt uses the concept of *Trauerspiel* to underline and highlight its element of *Spiel*, or play, in order to oppose it to a tragic seriousness that is not, as in Benjamin, a creaturely debris, but is instead a precise epochal turn. It is also evident that, in so doing, Schmitt modifies the *Trauer* component—the mourning—at work in Benjamin's *Trauerspiel*, depriving it of the heuristic and hermeneutic importance it has for Benjamin (Schmitt carefully avoids going deeper into the study of melancholy and into how Benjamin, Panofsky, and Freud used it from the standpoint of a global interpretation of the modern). Thus too, Schmitt barely skims over the topic of allegory, by way of a reference to a footnote of *The Nomos of the Earth* in which Schmitt affirms that the tendency to "personify" the State is a result of medieval subjectivism.[56] Schmitt's distinction between German and English drama[57] is, in the end, an explicit reference to the theory of *nomos*, to a reinterpretation of history that, so concrete and determined, differs from Benjamin's: Schmitt does not want to be part of a metaphysical philosophy of history; he does not, in other words, want to be "used."

The contact between the methods does not rule out that Benjamin and Schmitt follow two very different strategies, ultimately referring to Jewish theology, for the former, and Catholic theology, for the latter: Schmitt is eager to affirm that the modern tragic inheres in history, but that its catastrophic dimension is the result of politically given ruptures, which also require to be controlled politically, with a more integral order than that of the State (an order that "knows better" about the "gravity" of the "political"). Schmitt's distinction between play and seriousness is different from Benjamin's distinction between tragedy and *Trauerspiel*: in Schmitt's version, this distinction is ultimately testimony to Schmitt's effort to take history seriously without also conferring upon it a *telos*—not even one that is messianic and antihistorical.

The nonsensical in *Hamlet's* "story" does not make Shakespeare's drama redeemable on a metahistorical standpoint; it does not make it, as Benjamin affirms, a Christian drama. For Schmitt, the transcendence of history in relation to the play of the drama [*gioco del dramma*] (which is also to say, the transcendence of "the political" from the State), does not refer to another transcendence, or to the creatural redemption that Benjamin sees only just hinted in the presumed Christianity of *Hamlet*.[58] It also makes no reference to the analogy between drama and *Theo*-drama recently introduced by a Catholic theologian, Hans Urs von Balthasar, to explain how the divine Absolute enters history and acts among men.[59] From Balthasar's point of view, *Hamlet* is thus the drama of forgiveness, and the fact that the protagonist spares his mother from his vengeance is the sign that, in the form of drama, modern man looks not for a disguise but for a mirroring as authenticity, and finds that the latter comes from God's action (from the "drama" [*drammatica*]) into the world. From an opposed position, that is, completely finalistic (and the finality is then the overcoming of representation itself while looking for an encounter with the Other, beyond the dimension of "role" and the metaphor of "theater of the world"), Balthasar re-proposes what Schmitt had already excluded apropos of the Lutheran interpretation of Hamlet as an "actor of God," as a sign of the radical senselessness of human action in front of divine will: he re-proposes, that is to say, a religious interpretation of *Hamlet*. Schmitt, on the contrary, only gives an interpretation of *Hamlet through* religion, i.e., through the civil wars of religion that are one of the beginnings of the modern *nomos* of the earth. Schmitt's interpretation of *Hamlet* is, in other words, at root a *political-epochal* interpretation. What interests Schmitt is *Hamlet's* "play" [*gioco*], where play is the metaphor of a culture that is not primary but secondary, a culture that can *make sense* but that, in its meanings, is determined by the external catastrophe (by the end of traditional meanings).

The insistence with which Schmitt elaborates his notion of play [*gioco*] probably has another implicit point of reference. In Schmitt's attribution of primacy to *Ernstfall* ["serious event" or "emergency"] it is impossible not to notice a polemical and direct reference to Johan Huizinga's *Homo Ludens*.[60] In this text, Huizinga argues for the primacy of play by qualifying the ludic space as the convergence of desire for freedom from life, of the agonistic impulse and of the ritual-cultural impulse, in a very ample constellation of meanings, that ends up problematizing the relationship between play and seriousness as such (indeed, for Huizinga, the real contraposition would actually be between play and morality). It is not, of course, by chance that the Dutch historian arrives at this result, not simply on the basis of his Kantism, but more precisely by adopting a polemical stance toward Schmitt, whose concept of the "political" as a friend–enemy relation would remain, after all, inside the rival dimension, but in its primitive, uncivilized form. Schmitt's "struggle for struggle's sake" is, for Huizinga, the real game [*gioco*], while struggle with a finality of objective domination, despite its violation of the "rules of the game," would remain within the realm of the primitive ludic aspiration to "glory." In this way, the *total war* Schmitt theorized in the 1930s—despite its barbarism, which destroys the "game" [*gioco*] of international law—would still result in something ludic, even though primitive, but in any case not serious. Already in 1938 (the same year Huizinga published *Homo Ludens*), Schmitt had indirectly answered Huizinga, restating, under the political stance that interested him at the time, that besides the rival war (in which the enemy is an indispensable "partner," required by the same logic of war), there also exists war as *status*, in which the enemy is presupposed as such.[61] In this type of war, the enemy is existentially and primarily inimical, and the ludic elements of politics—the formalization of war into a "play" that then, in turn, evolves into "fair play" as, for instance, in the humanization and rationalization of war in international law—depend, as secondary, political-statual elements, on the historical happenings of the "political." For his part, of course, Schmitt, excludes the possibility of politics as a "game" completely deprived of conflict.[62]

Even though he is incapable of completely doing without the ludic, Schmitt is therefore, according to Huizinga, a "killjoy." Twenty years later, in his 1957 "Post Scriptum" to *Hamlet or Hecuba*, Schmitt insists on defining himself as such (albeit in the context of his discussion of the method he uses in *Hamlet or Hecuba*), aware of constituting, with his personality and with the scientific content of his thought, a "heretical" element, an element of disturbance, because his introduction of the element of seriousness spoils the serenity of art, the freedom of Spirit, the lightness of play.

The scholar who substituted the notion of *the norm* with that of *the exception* as the core of scientific procedure, who showed how order contains disorder *ab initio*, strongly underlines how that exception and that disorder are the "seriousness," the primary given, the tragic. The time that irrupts into play is the time of *nomos*, precisely because *nomos* itself contains the primal rupture within itself, because the *nomos* is itself upheaval and reorientation that is not temporally and spatially linear (even if it is planned as such), but epochal, and hence tragic in and through its own coming-into-being. Hence, on Schmitt's part, there is no reevaluation of play as re-creation, and there is also considerable distance from some positions on the "carnivalesque," for instance by Rang (who is very close to Benjamin: and in this context, too, one can measure the affinity and distance of their respective positions).[63] It is not "the time of festivity" but the time of the *nomos* that expresses the exception which threatens order. The barbaric in Shakespeare is not then some primitive vitality that is capable of overthrowing the closed and aseptic statual representation. Shakespeare is not, in other words, "irregular."[64] He is the genius who *receives* the sign of the time, and in so doing accepts the negative presence of the tragic event. Only in this way is the Hamletic destruction of subjectivity at once a harbinger and the deep truth of the crisis that relates to full modernity, to its accomplished rationalism. Only in this way is *Hamlet's* tragic not the generic destiny of a clash between the particular and the universal (in Goldmann's and in Hegel's antithetic terms),[65] but the concrete tragic of the lacerating beginning of a new *nomos*, which can be mediated neither ethically nor aesthetically. Only in this way, finally, does it make sense to affirm that, even though Prince Hamlet's tragic quality originates from a precisely historically determined situation, he has become one of the main myths of modernity as such.

Our epoch has, according to Schmitt, a tendency towards the levity of play, towards the Romantic irresponsibility of consumption and enjoyment: the movement of neutralization that characterizes it consists in a continuous migration from one center to the other, in search for ever-expanding neutralizations.[66] In the tendency towards demythicization that is characteristic of our epoch, there is the temptation to read into play the destiny of politics. From Kipling's "Great Game," the fascination with politics as undifferentiated freedom (and not as decision) has gained credibility in our conscience: "Above all I loved the hesitation that precedes the choice, rather than the action that follows. . . . To push the others toward movement, never taking part in it . . . to be afraid of not being able to seize the thousand opportunities of tomorrow any more, these are the rules of an exciting and perverse game."[67] The *whole* modernity cannot be expressed by either Huizinga's cultural play, or by the esthetic and erotic play of Marcuse (who is, on this point, strongly indebted to Schiller).[68] It can be conveyed neither by Nietzsche's joyfully nihilistic play nor by the theological play of Balthasar. Nor, finally, can it be conveyed by the concept of re-creative carnivalesque play. Instead, keen in separating the serious from play, Schmitt goes so far as, not without irony, to foresee the legal definition of play as *spare time*,[69] which is a homage to the ideology of "work while you work, play while you play" [English in the original].[70] But if it is true, as André Malreaux wrote, that "myths do not develop a way in which they determine sentiments, but in a way in which they justify them," this means that the demythicizing process of *Aufklärung* did not happen without leaving remnants, and that the goal of the "mythless man" (*mythenlose Mensch*) was not achieved. The modern metaphor of civilization as play carries with it an unease, which presents itself each time that our culture, by now world-wide, expresses a radical answer on itself. Hamlet, in fact, precisely as modern myth, is not a primal myth, the story around the roots and foundations of a community, but the figure around which—at the level of collective memory—the memory of the painful "schism that has determined the fate of Europe" coagulated.[71] According to Schmitt, given the immediacy of the *Spiel–Tragik* relation, Hamlet is not a myth, in the sense that his figure has been "inflated" with universal and indeterminate meanings. Hamlet is rather a "living" myth, for the catastrophe that started the new *nomos* of the earth, and that Hamlet articulates in negative like a scar, *never finished* (the "political" brackets of the State notwithstanding). It never stopped to be present and operative, hindering any perfect depiction of modernity. In Shakespeare's "imageless imagery" (*unbildlich Bildlichkeit*) there is something premodern that can tell the truth about the modern because the adventure of the Enlightenment (*Aufklärung*) never moved from where it started. "Hamlet," as myth, is not as much the return of the repressed as *the mute testimony of a loss*. It is the tragic counterpart to Romantic indecision: with its irresponsible language, Romanticism strives to express—without being able to—that rupture that Hamlet, with his silence, indicates.

If it is true, as Schmitt often affirms (quoting Virgil's Fourth Ecologue), that "ab integro nascitur ordo,"[72] then *Hamlet or Hecuba* is the analysis not only of the precise moment when traditional integrity is lost, but also of the modalities in which this loss manifests itself (the theory of *nomos* as rupture and catastrophe), and of the effects of "unsayability" that derive from it (the transcendence of the time of *nomos* over the time of *Spiel*). Just as Schmitt's "discovery" of the "political" brought to an end his discourse on power and classic philosophy, so too *Hamlet or Hecuba*—by trials, not systematically—inserts itself into the necessity of Schmitt's thought as the evidence of the gap between reality and representation. It is significant that, although he despises the concept of "engaged" art, Schmitt urges us to participate in *Hamlet*, telling us that it should not be read or enjoyed privately (in other words, one must respect the distance between Hamlet and Hecuba). After all, for Schmitt a privatization of this sort would mean that we would lay claim to the whole *inside* the representation, and hence it would end up in propaganda or *Kitsch* (the outcome of the effort of "authenticity").[73] The integrity from which order is born is *not*, however, to be found inside representation (and what this "place" would be is precisely the problem, well beyond the scope of this essay, of the new, postmodern, *nomos* of the earth). When Schmitt affirms in the "Post Scriptum" to *Hamlet and Hecuba* that his book has no center, he thus perhaps also meant that, above and beyond his own refusal of any systematization, it is ultimately *the eccentricity* of *Hamlet*, and of its protagonist, that express the deep truth and the aporias of the relationship between our civilization and our idea of an order.

Notes

This translation was supported, in part, by a grant from the Amherst College Faculty Research Award Program, as funded by the H. Axel Schupf '57 Fund for Intellectual Life.

1. Carlo Galli, "Presentazione dell'edizione italiana," in Carl Schmitt, *Amleto o Ecuba: L'irrompere del tempo nel gioco del dramma*, trans. Simona Forti (Bologna: Il Mulino, 1983), 7–35.

2. Carlo Galli, *Genealogia della politica: Carl Schmitt e la crisi del pensiero politico moderno*, 2d ed. (Bologna: Il Mulino, 2010); Carlo Galli, *Lo sguardo di Giano: Saggi su Carl Schmitt* (Bologna: Il Mulino, 2008).

3. Alessandro Manzoni, *The Betrothed*, trans. Bruce Penman (New York: Penguin Books, 1984), 141.

4. Hans Georg Gadamer, *Truth and Method*, trans. Joel Weinsheimer and Donald G. Marshall (New York: Continuum Books, 2004), 498–500.

5. "Briefe von Ernst Robert Curtius an Carl Schmitt," in *Archiv für der neueren Sprachen* 218 (1981): 1–16.

6. Theodor Adorno, "The Essay as Form," in *Notes to Literature*, trans. Shierry W. Nicholsen (New York: Columbia University Press, 1993), 1:23.

7. Carl Schmitt, *Political Romanticism*, trans. Guy Oakes (Cambridge, Mass.: MIT Press, 1986).

8. Carl Schmitt, *Constitutional Theory*, trans. Jeffrey Seitzer (Durham: Duke University Press, 2008); Carl Schmitt, *The Nomos of the Earth in the International Law of Jus Publicum Europaeum*, trans. G. L. Ulmen (New York: Telos Press, 2003); Carl Schmitt, *The Concept of the Political*, expanded ed., trans. George Schwab (Chicago: University of Chicago Press, 2007).

9. Carl Schmitt, *Political Theology: Four Chapters on the Concept of Sovereignty*, trans. George Schwab (Chicago: University of Chicago Press, 2006).

10. Carl Schmitt, *Hamlet or Hecuba: The Intrusion of the Time into the Play*, trans. David Pan and Jennifer Rust (New York: Telos Press, 2009), 20–21.

11. Leon Trotsky, *Literature and Revolution*, trans. Rose Strumsky (New York: Russell & Russell, 1957).

12. Carl Schmitt, *Ex captivitate salus: Erfahrungen der Zeit 1945/47* (Köln: Grevern Verlag, 1950), 21. [Schmitt's quotation modifies a passage from Macrobius' *Saturnalia*. When asked to explain his decision not to respond to a satire directed against him by the Emperor Augustus, the poet, orator, and historian Gaius Asinius Pollio responded, "non est enim facile in eum scribere qui potest proscribere" ("It's not easy to write against someone who has the power to 'write you up.'") (2.4.21). Under Roman Law, a *proscriptio* was a "decree of condemnation to death or banishment" (*OED*).—Trans.]

13. Schmitt, "Post Scriptum," *Amleto o Ecuba*, 119. [Schmitt's "Post Scriptum," which is not reproduced in the English translation of *Hamlet or Hecuba*, is a partially revised version of a text Schmitt published in Italian translation under the title "Amleto" in *Il Borghese* 51 (December 19, 1957): 996–97. The German original of Schmitt's essay appeared under the title "Was habe ich getan?" in *Diestland-Europa: Uitgegeven door de Jong-Nederlandse Gemeenschap* 2.1 (1957): 7–9.—Trans.]

14. Carl Schmitt, *Crisis of Parliamentary Democracy*, trans. Ellen Kennedy (Cambridge, Mass.: MIT Press, 1988).

15. Is this not, we might ask, the concept of "horizon of expectation" as it was elaborated by, for instance, Hans Robert Jauss, *Toward an Aesthetic of Reception*, trans. Timothy Bahti (Minneapolis: University of Minnesota Press, 1982)? Not exactly. According to Schmitt, the public's "foreknowledge" is not located on the plane of knowledge of literary sources against which one could then measure the "gap" of the work of art. It must instead, and more immediately, be located in an existential involvement (at least in the case of *Hamlet*). The notion of "horizon of expectation" can, if anything, be applied to the Schmittian concepts of "allusion" and "mirroring," but not to that of "irruption," whose comprehension requires a tragic co-existence (45).

16. Carl Schmitt, "The Age of Neutralizations and Depoliticizations," trans. Matthias Konzen and John P. McCormick, in *The Concept of the Political*, expanded ed., 80–96.

17. The expression "complexio oppositorum," taken from Nicholas of Cusa, is used by Schmitt in *Roman Catholicism and Political Form*, trans. G. L. Ulmen (New York: Greenwood Publishing, 1996).

18. Carl Schmitt, *The Leviathan in the State Theory of Thomas Hobbes: Meaning and Failure of a Political Symbol*, trans. George Schwab and Erna Hilfstein (New York: Greenwood Publishing, 1996); Carl Schmitt, "Die vollendete Reformation," *Der Staat* 4.1 (1965): 51–69.

19. For a political use of these categories, also mediated by Schmitt's disciples such as Schnur and Koselleck, see Emanuele Castrucci, *Ordine convenzionale e pensiero decisionista* (Milan: Giuffré, 1981). On the literary terms of this question, from Curtius to Hauser, from Wölfflin to Hocke, see E. Raimondi's entry on "Manierismo" in *Dizionario critico della letteratura italiana* (Turin: UTET, 1973).

20. Besides the minor essays, partially translated into Italian before the war and not collected in Carl Schmitt, *Scritti politico-giuridici (1933–1942)* (Perugia: Bacco & Arianna, 1983), see, above all, Carl Schmitt, *Land and Sea*, trans. Simona Draghici (New York: Plutarch Press, 1997).

21. [*Seenahme* and *Landnahme* are the names Schmitt gives, in *The Nomos of the Earth*, to the "seizure and appropriation of the Sea" and "the colonization and appropriation of Land." See Schmitt, *The Nomos of the Earth*, 80–83, 172–75.—Trans.]

22. ["Just and equal enemies" or "Enemies who are just and equal." For a discussion of this maxim, see Schmitt, *The Nomos of The Earth*, 124.—Trans.]

23. A. O. Hirschman, *The Passions and the Interests: Political Arguments for Capitalism before its Triumph* (Princeton: Princeton University Press, 1977).

24. Schmitt, *Hamlet or Hecuba*, 63–64.

25. For a different perspective, which tends to read *Hamlet* as a moment of crisis of absolute power, see Franco Moretti, "The Great Eclipse: Tragic Form as the Deconsecration of Sovereignty," in *Sign Taken for Wonders: On the Sociology of Literary Forms*, trans. Susan Fischer, David Forgacs, and David Miller (New York: Verso, 2005), 42–82.

26. Carl Schmitt, "Staat als ein konkreter, an eine geschichtliche Epoche gebundener Begriff," in *Verfassungsrechtliche Aufsätze aus den Jahren 1924–1954; Materilien zu einer Verfassungslehre* (Berlin: Duncker & Humblot, 1958), 375–85. On the notion of manners, it is obvious the reference is to Norbert Elias, *The Civilizing Process: The History of Manners* (New York: Urizen Books, 1936). The bibliography on the individual and the State is vast. On this, see Carlo Galli, "Lo Stato come problema sotrico-politico: Osservazioni su alcuni recenti contributi," *Il Mulino* 32 (1983): 111–31.

27. Schmitt, *Hamlet or Hecuba*, 41.

28. Moretti, "The Great Eclipse," 48.

29. Paola Colaiacomo, "Il teatro del principe," *Calibano* 4 (1979): 53–98. The obvious reference here is to Michel Foucault, *The Order of Things: An Archaeology of the Human Sciences* (New York, Pantheon Books, 1971).

30. Schmitt, *Hamlet or Hecuba*, 45.

31. Ibid., 41.

32. Schmitt himself, in the 1963 Edition of *The Concept of the Political*, affirms that the translation of *Spiel* requires the English term *play* (see, on this point, Heinrich Meier, *Carl Schmitt and Leo Strauss: The Hidden Dialogue*, trans. J. Harvey Lomax [Chicago: University of Chicago Press, 1995], 44 n. 42). [Unlike *Spiel* and *play*, the Italian *gioco* does not preserve the double meaning of "game" and "theatrical play" or "action." In what follows, Galli therefore enters into a detailed discussion of the problems of translating the German and English terms into Italian. This is at the same time a specific issue and general instance where one can observe the various components of the concept of "play" *at play*, taking separate functions according to the word choice. In the course of the present essay, Galli himself usually opts for the term *gioco*, which is equivalent to the English "game." Towards the end, however, Galli will resort to the English words *play* and *game* as the context demands.—Trans.] *Play* preserves a trace of the concept of *agonistic action*. The term *Spiel*, which has also a representative value, could probably be translated fairly by *ludus* and its derivatives, but because, in Italian, the term *gioco* lost any trace of the concept of *azione* (even *represented* action), people used the locution *gioco del dramma* ("game of the drama": *dramma* in fact etymologically contains the "action"). A partial translation into Italian (pages 42–62, 62–67 of the German edition) of *Hamlet or Hecuba*, which appeared in *Calibano* 4 (1979), solves the problem by always translating *Spiel* with *dramma* [although this translation opts for "the irruption of the historical epoch" instead of "of time" for the title—Trans.], while a partial Spanish translation ("Hamlet y Jacobo I de Inglaterra," in *Revista de Estudios politicos* 85 [1956]: 59–91) always renders *Spiel* with *juego*—which, like the Italian *gioco* (which is also used in the quoted occurrence of *The Concept of the Political*), and unlike the English *play*, does not contain the active and representative element of *Spiel*.

33. Schmitt, *Hamlet or Hecuba*, 40.

34. Ibid., 43.

35. On the difference between real tears ("tragic") and staged ones, see Denis Diderot, *The Paradox of Acting*, trans. Walter Herries Pollock (London: Chatto & Windus, and Picadilly, 1883), 16–18.

36. In his *Political Theology II* (Chicago: University of Chicago Press, 2008), Schmitt explicitly contends against Hans Blumenberg's metaphorology (on which, see Hans Blumenberg, *Paradigm zu einer Metaphorologie* [Bonn: H. Bouvier, 1960], as well as Hans Blumenberg, *The Legitimacy of the Modern Age*, trans. Robert Wallace [Cambridge, Mass.: MIT Press, 1983]; and Hans Blumenberg, *Work on Myth*, trans. Robert Wallace [Cambridge, Mass.: MIT Press, 1985]).

37. Mario Perniola, *La società dei simulacri* (Bologna: Cappelli, 1980).

38. William Shakespeare, *As You Like It*, Act II, Scene 7.

39. On the dialectic between engagement and the serenity of art, and on the impossibility of using such categories for the contemporary situation, see Theodor Adorno, "Is Art Lighthearted?" in *Notes to Literature*, trans. Shierry Nicholsen (New York: Columbia University Press, 1992), 2:247–53. On serenity as determined by the attitude of the public, see Harald Weinrich, *Metafora e menzogna* (Bologna: Il Mulino, 1976), 251–67.

40. Schmitt's logic is indeed very far from Adorno, for whom "the anguish of the work created in front of its desperate non-truth" is the allusion, negative-dialectical, to the Truth as Other (Theodor Adorno, *Philosophy of Modern Music* [New York: Seabury Press, 1973]). According to Schmitt, *Spiel* is neither true nor false, and the matter is not its link with Truth, but its connection with the historical-political order.

41. René Girard, *Violence and the Sacred*, trans. Patrick Gregory (Baltimore: Johns Hopkins University Press, 1977).

42. Schmitt, *Hamlet or Hecuba*, 48–49.

43. Friedrich Schiller, *On the Aesthetic Education of Man in a Series of Letters*, trans. Reginald Snell (New Haven: Yale University Press, 1954).

44. ["Life is serious, art is serene."—Trans.]

45. Friedrich Hölderlin, *Sul tragico* (Milan: Feltrinelli, 1980).

46. Peter Szondi, *Theory of Modern Drama*, trans. Paul Fleming (Stanford: Stanford University Press, 2002); G. W. F. Hegel, *Lectures on Fine Art*, trans. T. M. Knox (Oxford: Oxford University Press, 1988), 2:1158 and ff.

47. [Galli is here referring to Heraclitus' Fragment 52. "Lifetime [*aiôn*] is like a child at play, moving pieces in a game. Kingship belongs to the child."—Trans.]

48. Friedrich Nietzsche, *The Birth of Tragedy and Other Writings*, trans. Ronald Speirs (Cambridge: Cambridge University Press, 1999); Roberto Escobar, *Nietzsche e il tragico* (Milan: Il Formichiere, 1980); Morse Peckham, *Oltre la visione tragica* (Milan: Lerici, 1965); Eugene Fink, *Nietzsche's Philosophy*, trans. Goetz Richter (New York: Continuum Press, 2002).

49. Walter Benjamin, *The Origin of German Tragic Drama*, trans. John Osborne (New York: Verso, 1998), 66.

50. Ibid., 105 n. 14.

51. On the irruption, in Benjamin's metaphoric field, of the political horizon qualified by Schmitt on the basis of the friend–enemy relationship, see Michael Rumpf, "Radikale Theologie: Benjamins Beziehung zu Carl Schmitt," in *Walter Benjamin—Zeitegenosse der Moderne* (Kronberg, Scriptor Verlag, 1976), 37–50; Weinrich, *Metafora e menzogna*, 115–32.

52. Letter of December 1930, in Walter Benjamin, *Gesammelte Schriften*, Band I, 3 (Frankfurt

a. M.: Suhrkamp, 1978), 887. In the previous page are the passages of the 1928 *curriculum* dealing with the intellectual relationship between Benjamin and Schmitt.

53. Benjamin, *Origin of German Tragic Drama*, 57.

54. Benjamin's "Critique of Violence" was published in 1921, two years earlier than Schmitt's *Crisis of Parliamentary Democracy.*

55. Schmitt's *Political Theology II* in fact answers to Erik Peterson, *Der Monotheismus als politisches Problem* (Leipzig: Jakob Hegner, 1935).

56. Schmitt, *The Nomos of the Earth*, 144.

57. Schmitt, *Hamlet or Hecuba*, 62.

58. Ibid., 60–62.

59. Hans Urs von Balthasar, *Theo-Drama: Theological Dramatic Theory* (San Francisco: Ignatius Press, 1988), 1:135–257 (on theater as a metaphor for the world) and 465–480 (on Shakespeare's *Hamlet*).

60. Johann Huizinga, *Homo Ludens; A Study of the Play-Element in Culture* (Boston: Beacon Press, 1955), 208–11.

61. Carl Schmitt, "Sulla relazione intercorrente fra i concetti di guerra e di nemico (1938)," in *Le categorie del 'politico': saggi di teoria politica*, ed. Gianfranco Miglio and Pierangelo Schiera (Bologna: Società editrice il Mulino, 1972), 193–203.

62. Schmitt, *Concept of the Political*, 32.

63. Florens Christian Rang, *Psicologia storica del carnival* (Venezia: Arsenale, 1983), with a preface by Massimo Cacciari ("Memoria sul carnevale").

64. [Because the Italian *irregolare*, like the English *irregular,* derives from the Latin *regula,* "rule," it can connote an "exception to the rule." In §46 of *The Critique of the Power of Judgment*, Kant defines genius as "a talent for producing that for which no definite rule can be given."—Trans.]

65. Moretti, "The Great Eclipse," 62.

66. Schmitt, "The Age of Neutralizations and Depoliticizations," 82.

67. Jean-Jacques Langendorf, *Una sfida nel Kurdistan* (Milano: Adelphi, 1969), 15–16, our translation from the Italian.

68. Herbert Marcuse, *Eros and Civilization: A Philosophical Inquiry into Freud* (Boston: Beacon Press, 1974), 172–96 ("The Aesthetic Dimension").

69. Schmitt, *Hamlet or Hecuba*, 40 n. 28.

70. [Theodor Adorno, *Minima Moralia: Reflections from Damaged Life*, trans. E. F. N. Jephcott (New York: Verso Books, 2002), 130.—Trans.]

71. Schmitt, *Hamlet or Hecuba*, 52.

72. ["Order is born out of integrity." As Jan-Werner Müller has observed, this modified quotation from Virgil is a keyword within Schmitt's political thought (*A Dangerous Mind: Carl Schmitt in Post-War European Thought* [New Haven: Yale University Press, 2003], 207). The full quotation (which Hannah Arendt uses as an epigraph for chapter 5 of *On Revolution*) reads, "magnus ab integro saeclorum nascitur ordo," which, as Konzen and McCormick note, is often translated as "a new world order is born" or "a great order of the ages is born anew" (*Concept of the Political*, 96).—Trans.]

73. Schmitt, *Hamlet or Hecuba*, 51.

4

Blumenberg and Schmitt on the Rhetoric of Political Theology

GRAHAM HAMMILL

From the antimodernist writings of Carl Schmitt to the postmodern political theories of Slavoj Žižek, discussions of political theology inevitably center on the person of the sovereign. Despite their differences, these discussions share the assumption that the early modern state emerged as a "quasi-Church" when, to quote Ernst Kantorowicz, "the prince stepped into the pontifical shoes of the Pope and Bishop."[1] The twentieth-century German philosopher Hans Blumenberg takes a different approach. Perhaps best known in Anglo-American circles for his powerful attack on the secularization thesis in *The Legitimacy of the Modern Age*, Blumenberg locates political theology within the domain of rhetoric. Initially, Blumenberg critiques Schmitt for playing rhetorical games, portraying him as an intellectual opportunist who posits an unfounded version of political theology to further his own ends. But as the debate between Blumenberg and Schmitt develops, Blumenberg begins to see that his charge of rhetoric doesn't minimize the force of political theology. It does, however, significantly alter how we might understand that force. The key figure in Blumenberg's shifting position, I shall argue, is Hobbes. Although Hobbes is often read as a particularly prescient theorist of modern sovereignty, in Blumenberg's brief account Hobbes instead theorizes the intersections of rhetoric and modern political power. From that basis, Blumenberg begins to understand political theology as a shaping fiction, one whose strength comes not from a genealogy of the state but instead from the persuasive force of theological metaphors that populate the early modern and modern landscape. Theological metaphors persist in the modern age not because they are structurally necessary, which is Schmitt's argument, but because, like all fictions, theological metaphors serve strategic ends. As fictions, theological metaphors satisfy the need for cogent accounts of the world, and, at the same time, as tactical forms of mediation they shelter against a literal-minded view of politics that, for Blumenberg, polarizes conflict into crisis.

1. Rhetoric at the Scene of the Social Contract

I'll begin by discussing Blumenberg's developing understanding of rhetoric and political theology. Initially, Blumenberg uses rhetoric as a term of abuse   *NB* to dismiss political theology as an intellectual con. In both the 1966 edition of *The Legitimacy of the Modern Age* and the revised 1973 edition, he issues a devastating critique of the secularization thesis and a particularly pointed critique of Schmitt's version of it, the proposition that Schmitt makes in his 1922 monograph *Political Theology* that "all modern concepts of the state are secularized theological concepts."[2] Blumenberg charges that this is actually "metaphorical theology."[3] It would make sense to say that theology is the continuation of politics by different means or to argue that divine authority is metaphorically associated with the person of the sovereign for political ends. Instead, when Schmitt proposes his secularization thesis, he obscures the role of metaphor, arguing that the modern age is a pale imitation of a more authentic theological era. And this, in turn, sets up a loaded critique of democracy. In Blumenberg's analysis, Schmitt justifies political theology rhetorically—that is, cynically and as an act of manipulation—by instrumentalizing religion in the service of absolutist politics while covering up that move with a false sense of history.

Blumenberg's charge provoked Schmitt to revise his earlier arguments in a second monograph, *Political Theology II*, published in German in 1970 and recently translated into English. But Blumenberg issued a more sophisticated, if less obvious, critique a year after Schmitt's monograph was published, in his 1971 essay, "An Anthropological Approach to the Significance of Rhetoric." There, he supplements his early account of Schmitt's rhetorical manipulations with a second, stronger understanding of rhetoric as political practice. Rather than thinking of rhetoric as a term of abuse, Blumenberg makes the case that all modern politics is based in a fundamental way on rhetoric as a metaphorical practice, a mode of understanding circumstances, events, and problems by means of other circumstances, events, and problems that seem to resemble them.[4] This understanding of rhetoric as a metaphorical practice allows Blumenberg to revise key terms from Schmitt's writings—namely, the state of exception and the sovereign decision—in order to argue that rhetoric is a uniquely modern form of political life. Blumenberg's new understanding of rhetoric doesn't lessen his critique of Schmitt, but it does change the emphasis of that critique from the charge of cynicism to the problem of metaphorical mediation. Schmitt can persuasively manipulate theological figures and make them seem to have real effects because of the general role that metaphor plays in the constitution of the modern age. For Blumenberg, Schmitt becomes a symptom of politics as rhetoric, one that underlines and reinforces the persistence of political theology not just as the outcome of a particular ideological position that Schmitt holds but also, historically speaking, as the result of a linguistic turn in political thought that occurs in the seventeenth century with Hobbes in particular and with the constitution of the modern age more generally.

If Blumenberg's critique hasn't received the attention that it deserves, it's due in no small measure to Blumenberg's reluctance to name Schmitt as his primary target. Even though "An Anthropological Approach" takes Schmitt as one its main interlocutors, in that essay Blumenberg never mentions Schmitt by name. And when Blumenberg reworks his critique of Schmitt based on his newer understanding of rhetoric, the term rhetoric fades into the background. In the 1973 edition of *The Legitimacy of the Modern Age*, Blumenberg downplays his understanding of rhetoric as a form of life, even though that understanding is central to his revised critique. Blumenberg's reluctance has to do with more than tact. It indicates his growing awareness that a critique of Schmitt from the point of view of rhetoric doesn't bring an end to political theology so much as it shifts the locus of political theology from the state to the political subject. Whereas Schmitt situates political theology in the formation and collapse of the juridical state as an actor on the international stage, Blumenberg locates the problem of political theology on the more expansive terrain of the political subject as both a historical subject—a subject of the modern age that bears the split between the theological past and the modern present—and a speaking subject—a subject whose political agency crucially involves the capacity and need to represent, manipulate, and shape that split. In Blumenberg's account, the modern age is inscribed through a kind of *translatio imperii* in which the subject's capacity to make history is understood and often denied through the archive of metaphors that the modern age inherits. The emphasis here should go to *imperii* or force as much as it should to *translatio*. The rhetorical subject's capacity to translate herself into a new history is accompanied by the force of theological metaphors that restrain and impel this translation at almost the same time.

The central figure in this debate is Hobbes, whose theory of the social contract combines two scenes through which the state is constituted, each of which has fundamentally different implications for political agency and representation. On the one hand, in *Leviathan* Hobbes argues that the state doesn't exist before there is an artificial person to represent and give unity to the multitude of individuals driven by self-interest who make up the state. This is the scene that he emphasizes and puts forward as the dominant one in his portrayal of the social contract. On the other hand, Hobbes also argues that the state is formed by the consent to be governed, which suggests a sense of unity and agency that precedes the unity brought about by the artificial person of the state. In *De Cive*, Hobbes reluctantly concedes that the act of consent implies democracy as a potential unity, even if the form of government ultimately chosen isn't itself democratic.[5] While Hobbes intends his theory of authorization in *Leviathan* to disable this originary democracy, nevertheless a residue of it remains in his handling of consent. Quentin Skinner suggests that the scene of the social contract as Hobbes depicts it in the English version of *Leviathan* is split in two.[6] Initially, each individual gives up the right of self-governance in the presence of an embodied sovereign who is already there. "*I give up my right of governing myself to this man, or this assembly of men.*"[7] The presence of the sovereign indicates that authority is anthropomorphic and depends on a substance that can't be equated with the act of consent. But as the scene unfolds, Hobbes also intimates that the sovereign is generated by the act of agreement so that the multitude is "united in one person . . . called a COMMONWEALTH" (17.13.114). That is, the agreement of the multitude produces the name "COMMONWEALTH" as a rhetorical effect that confers unity on the multitude before the assumption of a person who will embody it.

Hobbes's version of the social contract implies two distinct readings, one that Hobbes sanctions in which the person of the state confers unity on the multitude, and another that Hobbes attempts to foreclose in which public life is fabricated by the agreement of the multitude. Schmitt develops the first reading, deriving a model of political representation from Hobbes's account of the embodied sovereign and arguing that the sovereign constitutes the people as a unity by bringing into existence the very fact of public life. While certain affinities can emerge through the horizontal identification of individuals, based on "conscious similarities" and other equivalences, nevertheless political unity can only be established vertically, as it were, through the assertion of authority.[8] Responding to Blumenberg's initial charge of rhetoric in the sense of cunning, in *Political Theology II* Schmitt locates the substance of that authority in its relation to the theological utterance. Schmitt cites Erik Peterson's 1925 essay "What is Theology?" where Peterson defines theology as dogma or what Schmitt characterizes as "the continuation of incarnate *logos*."[9] Underscoring the formal aspect of political authority that he developed in *Constitutional Theory* and his earlier *Roman Catholicism and Political Form* (1923), in *Political Theology II* Schmitt takes up and pushes Peterson's thesis in the direction of language as enunciation. Theology, Schmitt writes, is the "performance [*Vollzug*] of the Incarnate Word of God" (PT2 110). More than exegesis, preaching, or prophesy, the theological utterance has an "assertive power" (105) that incarnates authority through the pronouncement of dogma. As a specifically authoritative instance of rhetoric, the theological utterance and its subsequent interpolation into the state establishes the unity of the people through what Schmitt elsewhere calls "the architecture of speech."[10] In the Catholic Church, this authority is embodied in the pope and his delegates, and, in Schmitt's account, Hobbes reasserts the necessity of this kind of authority through the person of the sovereign. As Schmitt puts it toward the end of *Political Theology II*: "Who answers *in concreto* on behalf of the concrete, autonomously acting human being, the question of what is spiritual, what is worldly, and what is the case with the *res mixtae*, which, in the interval between the first and the second arrival of the Lord, constitute, as a matter of fact, the entire early existence of this spiritual-worldly, spiritual-temporal, double-creature called a *human being*? This is the big question posed by Thomas Hobbes, which is as the center of my treatise *Political Theology* from 1922 and which led to a theory of decisionism and of the inner logic of the act" (PT2 115).[11]

In opposition to Schmitt, Blumenberg emphasizes the second half of the scene of the social contract. His aim is to leverage the unity that precedes political representation against any notion of embodied sovereignty. For Blumenberg, Hobbes makes two main moves. First, he assumes a vision of politics as rhetoric that precedes the formation of the state. In Blumenberg's account, the state of nature marks the place of rhetoric as a practice that precedes the state. For the Greeks, Blumenberg writes, rhetoric was located in the polis and was opposed to subjugation by force, which was reserved for barbarians and other noncitizens. By contrast, Hobbes thinks of force as already internal to rhetoric, which encompasses the entire field of conflict and agreement that the state is supposed to regulate. Violence doesn't just emerge when persuasion breaks down. As Hobbes underscores, violence is also an effect of persuasion, polemical speech, and imaginative language. Second, then, Blumenberg uses Hobbes's account of rhetoric to argue that political realism is in fact anti-rhetorical rhetoric. Just as the state attempts to resolve the state of nature, so too does it attempt to contain the field of rhetorical conflict that it assumes. The Hobbesian state disables Hobbes's initial view of rhetorical agency by introducing anti-rhetorical rhetoric "as one of the most important expedients" in the modern age "by means of which to claim the rigor [or harshness, *Härte*] of realism."[12] According to Blumenberg, this anti-rhetorical rhetoric can be discerned in its two most important functions. The first is the literalization of the artificial person of the state, which is first and foremost only ever a metaphorical person. And the second is the reduction of the fictional state of nature to what Blumenberg calls the natural law of "naked self-preservation" (LMA 219). An anti-rhetorical rhetoric that values "res, non verba," things, not words, tends to turn life into a thing that can then be manipulated and controlled by the state (R 454).

Blumenberg is well aware of the paradox of the social contract. The social contract presupposes an agonistic, passion-driven life that it then disciplines in order to allow that life to further its aims. But discipline foments and fosters crisis much more than it resolves it. Life threatens to overstep and rupture the system of discipline, and so, from the perspective of the state, it must be regulated by extralegal and paralegal means—often in the name of defending the social contract that produced this crisis in the first place. By recasting this paradox in terms of an anti-rhetorical rhetoric, Blumenberg aims to uncover a prior understanding of politics as rhetoric at work in Hobbes that might effectively suspend this crisis-driven system.[13] However, Blumenberg's target is Schmitt and not Hobbes. Although he locates his anthropological approach to rhetoric through a reading of Hobbes, he develops that approach through a critique of Schmitt.

Although in "An Anthropological Approach" Blumenberg never mentions Schmitt by name, the essay uses rhetoric to revise key terms from Schmitt's *Political Theology*. Blumenberg's first move is to revise the state of emergency from the perspective of the rhetorical subject. For Schmitt, the state of emergency arises as an exception to the law, as a contingency that can be structurally anticipated by never particularly accounted for before its emergence.[14] In Blumenberg's account, the Schmittian state of exception is a unique instance of a more broadly conceived rhetorical situation, one in which the rhetoric of emergency sets the terms for a plausible but not a necessary course of action.[15] Blumenberg supplements Schmitt's account of the state of emergency by developing two of its central features, what he calls *Evidenzmangel*, or "the lack of norms in a finite situation," and *Handelszwang*, or the "[compulsion] to act" (R 437). For moral philosophy, *Evidenzmangel* or the lack of norms is often a point of critique. Rhetoric lacks the norms that would bind it definitely to the good. But for Blumenberg, this lack of norms is the positive condition for an anti-foundational understanding of rhetorical practice, its enabling feature, in that it allows for the development of new answers where old ones are rejected or found to be lacking. As a "technique of speech," rhetoric is a "special case" within the world of "rule-governed modes of behavior," one that becomes necessary when those modes no longer take hold (431). *Handelszwang*, or the compulsion to act, follows from this lack of norms in the sense of urgency that it produces. Something must be done despite the fact that there are no available norms that would provide a sure course of action, and precisely because there are no available norms, the need for action becomes more urgent.

Blumenberg's second move is to use this account of the rhetorical situation to displace the sovereign decision. For Schmitt, the exception mandates the necessity of the sovereign, but, for Blumenberg, the state of exception points in the more capacious direction of political anthropology. From the point of view of moral philosophy, Blumenberg notes, "Man [is] a rich creature" who possesses truth and only needs rhetoric to give truth ornamentation. But from the point of view of rhetorical practice, "Man [is] a poor creature" who "needs rhetoric as an art of appearance, which helps him to deal with his lack of truth" (430). The compulsion to act emerges from the intersection of temporality with life and its representations, as the deficiency which results from the lack of norms is substantiated in a version of creaturely life exposed to conditions brought about by the lack of endless time. Instead of elevating decision-making to an abstract, semi-transcendental position that rules over the rhetorical situation, Blumenberg proposes that the rhetorical situation is governed by a general "principle of insufficient reason" in which an individual or a group acts to achieve a solution on insufficiently proven grounds (447). Now, this might be a good description of the sovereign, inasmuch as the sovereign decides the state of emergency with insufficient reason. But if this is a good description, it also makes the person of the sovereign nothing other than a metaphor that, as Blumenberg puts it, "expands and occupies" the "empty space" left open by the norms, reasons, or concepts that might otherwise have governed behavior (454). That is, rather than proposing that the sovereign decision is the logical juridical feature of the state of emergency, Blumenberg's revision suggests that the person of the sovereign is only one, particular, metaphorical solution that occupies the place left open by a lack of norms and, as such, is as insufficient as would be any other plausible solution.

2. The Gnostic Crisis

Blumenberg's initial charge of rhetoric is grounded in his general critique of the secularization thesis. Proponents of the secularization thesis such as Schmitt and Karl Löwith argue that the modern age is generated by its Christian past which it systematically denies but which it cannot escape. Like a neurotic individual, the modern age is unwittingly determined by its own repressed past, so the argument goes. It is overdetermined by Christian modes of thought that should have been left behind but in reality are only repeated at higher levels of abstraction. Blumenberg doesn't deny the influence of the past on the present, but he does deny the use of the past to delegitimize the present. In an extraordinarily bold revision of Western intellectual history, Blumenberg replaces secularization with what he calls a reoccupation thesis. The modern age, he argues, should be understood as the intellectual effort to give a second set of answers to questions that Medieval theology tried and failed to answer. As he explains it,

> what mainly occurred in the process that is interpreted as secularization . . . should be described not as *transpositions* of authentically theological contents into secularized alienation from their origin but rather as the *reoccupation* of answer positions that had become vacant and whose corresponding questions could not be eliminated. (LMA 65)

It is important to note that the questions Blumenberg has in mind are not enduring questions for all ages—what is truth? what is justice?—but specific questions that indicate the limits of dominant intellectual paradigms. Instead of seeing the Christian Middle Ages as the origin of the modern age, Blumenberg argues that the modern age is a second—and legitimate—response to the problems first posed by a set of questions that he calls the Gnostic challenge.[16] In his account, Gnosticism posed a fundamental problem for the Church Fathers: how can the omnipotent God who created the world "at the same time make the destruction of this world and the salvation of men from [it] into [his] central activity"? (LMA 129) The question takes shape through a textual problem, the difficulty of synthesizing the Hebrew Scripture's God of creation with the Gospel's God of redemption. But, for Blumenberg, the question's import is largely philosophical. By turning the God of creation into an evil demiurge, Gnosticism puts into crisis both the status of the world and the place of humans within it. With remarkable erudition Blumenberg shows how the Church Fathers and subsequently the Scholastics developed an answer, having to do with doctrine of original sin and the role of the church in caring for the fallen world, that gave legitimacy to the Middle Ages as an epoch discrete from its Classical past. But the Gnostic problem reemerged in late Medieval Nominalism in Ockham's distinction between *potentia absoluta* and *potentia ordinata*, between absolute power and ordered or restricted power, and was given a second—and, for Blumenberg, better— set of answers by early modern philosophers like Bacon and Descartes, who effectively founded the modern age as "an existential program, according to

NB

which man posits his existence in a historical situation and indicates to himself how he is going to deal with the reality surrounding him and what he will make of the possibilities open to him" (138).[17]

As Schmitt sees it, the problem with Blumenberg's argument is that it's based on a concept of politics as reform, which inevitably slides down the slippery slope from reformation to revolution, as demonstrated in the "de-theological continuation" of the Protestant Reformation in the French Revolution and, for Schmitt, its re-theologization in Vatican II and liberation theology (PT2 51). For this reason, he argues, the modern age continually threatens to erupt into the Gnostic crisis that Blumenberg thinks it has resolved. In response to Blumenberg, Schmitt shows how the church failed to contain the Gnostic crisis through the theology of the Trinity. The Trinity transforms the Gnostic conflict between Father and Son into a tenuous peace—a point with which Blumenberg would wholly agree. The difference between the two is that Blumenberg thinks that the modern age has left behind the problem of the Trinity, whereas Schmitt thinks that the Trinity encodes the problem of enmity that no age can leave behind. Schmitt focuses on wordplay within a passage in one of the Church Fathers who is significant in formulating the theology of the Trinity. Gregory of Nazianus aphoristically asserts, *to Hen stasiazon pro heauton.* Pointing out that in Greek the word *stasis* (the root of *stasiazon*) means both tranquility and political unrest, Schmitt notes that the aphorism can mean either, *the One is always at peace with itself,* or *the One is always in an uproar against itself.* "At the heart of the doctrine of the Trinity," he writes, "we encounter a genuine politico-theological *stasiology.* Thus the problem of enmity and of the enemy cannot be ignored" (PT2 123). Moreover, Schmitt goes on to argue, the modern age releases that crisis into political history in the form of revolution. Gnostic dualism, Schmitt writes, "exists inescapably in every world in need of change and renewal" and inevitably intensifies beyond reform into a "hostile struggle" between forces who are enemies "*by definition*" (PT2 125, Schmitt's emphasis).

Like it or not, Schmitt argues, the modern age unwittingly activates the very logic that Blumenberg hopes to avoid. Schmitt concedes Blumenberg's point that the modern age doesn't transpose theological content into an alien form (a major concession that fundamentally admits Blumenberg's critique of *Political Theology*), but he goes on to reassert a version of the secularization thesis as a "structural resemblance between theological and juridical concepts" (PT2 148 n. 2). Simply put, this structural resemblance is necessary because both the church and the state face the problem of the enemy. And, Schmitt claims, Blumenberg can't resolve this problem. In Schmitt's account, the task of resolving this crisis now falls to the state and not the church, but the particular form by which the state handles this crisis comes from the church and its legacy of juridical authority.

Although at first glance it may not be apparent, the stakes of this baroque and abstruse debate could hardly be higher. Once Schmitt interpolates the Gnostic crisis into the Trinity, he also implies that the Son is coerced into the godhead through his suffering and death. This interpolation implies that what substantiates political authority, what allows authority to conjure and shape collective life, is the capacity of the sovereign to inflict pain upon the body of the enemy. If, as Schmitt claims, at the heart of the doctrine of the Trinity we find a politico-theological stasiology, then what supports this claim is the Passion, the switch point by which the conflict between enemies is transformed into an uneasy peace. As Samuel Weber demonstrates, as early as his 1923 monograph *Roman Catholicism and Political Form* Schmitt was fascinated by the promise of political Catholicism insofar as it constituted a public "representable only through its immediate negation, through the depiction of Christ on the cross."[18] Although the Passion is a scene that Schmitt astutely avoids, in *Political Theology II* he hands off the problem of the Passion to Blumenberg, suggesting without directly saying that the reason the modern age cannot bring an end to political theology is that it cannot resolve the biopolitical problem of the enemy.

3. Biopolitics and Confession

Biopolitics is a term that neither Blumenberg nor Schmitt uses, but I want to introduce it anyway because the term suggests what is most important about Blumenberg's focus on an *anthropological* account of rhetoric, an account given from the perspective of the human and of life. In his assessment of rhetoric, I shall argue, Blumenberg offers an affirmative model of biopower. Blumenberg's model responds to Schmitt's account in which the negative is incorporated through its inscription on the body of the enemy. To sharpen the terms of Blumenberg's response and to draw out the implications of that response for an understanding of early modern biopower, I will take a brief detour through some recent scholarship by Giorgio Agamben. In *Homo Sacer*, Agamben revises *Political Theology* through a Foucauldian understanding of biopower, but given the role of the Trinity in the debate between Blumenberg and Schmitt, it would be more fruitful to turn to Agamben's recent work on what he calls economic theology. In *Il Regno e la Gloria*, Agamben shows how important economy, in the Aristotelian term of *oikonomia*, was to the early Church Fathers as they were developing the concept of the Trinity. Agamben's purpose is to develop a genealogy of Foucault's concept of governmentality—the economic model of power that he outlines in *Society Must Be Defended*; *Security, Territory, Population*; and *The Birth of Biopolitics*.[19] By locating governmentality in the theology of the early church, Agamben aims to provoke a more complex conversation between Foucauldian models of modern power and political theology. This conversation is where I would like to place both Blumenberg's account of rhetoric and his reading of Hobbes. In Blumenberg's account, rhetoric becomes a medium of management, governance, and self-governance. Inasmuch as he derives this account from a reading of Book Three of the *Leviathan*, Blumenberg also suggests that Hobbes's writings on religion are a counterplot to the official story of the social contract.

In *Il Regno e la Gloria*, Agamben derives two broad paradigms from the early Church Fathers' writings on the Trinity: political theology, which circulates around "the transcendence of the sovereign" and gives rise to "the modern theory of sovereignty," and economic theology, based on the notion of an immanent domestic order which gives rise to "modern biopolitics up to the present triumph of economy and governance over all aspects of social life."[20] The Church Fathers developed the theology of the Trinity, Agamben argues, in an attempt to solder these two paradigms together.[21] Inasmuch as the Trinity salvages monotheism by making an argument about substance and being, it participates in political theology. And inasmuch as it develops a compromise or uneasy peace between the possibility of two gods, the Trinity also uses the language of housekeeping in such a way that looks forward to the larger problem of governmentality as the management of life. Moreover, Agamben continues, since the Father's management of the Son is at base the management of the crisis of monotheism—the possibility of two equal gods that Schmitt sees implied by the assertion of one single god—economic theology becomes a strategy for managing the exception, disclosing a structural relation between governance and crisis that is analogous to the relation between sovereign and state of exception that he develops in *Homo Sacer*. In *Homo Sacer*, Agamben highlights the exception as a "zone of indistinction" in which life is made vulnerable to sovereign violence, whereas in *Il Regno e la Gloria* he locates the act of governance in a "zone of indistinction between the general and the particular, between calculated and unwilled action."[22] In other words, for Agamben political theology gives structural articulation to the state of emergency, while economic theology preserves the state of emergency in the governance of everyday life.

Agamben argues that in his exchange with Schmitt, Blumenberg wasn't able to see the degree to which "divine *oikonomia*" is at issue in the modern age.[23] But this charge misses the significance of Blumenberg's work on rhetoric. Not only does rhetoric recast and suspend Schmitt's version of political theology. It also anticipates and transforms Agamben's explanation of economic theology. For Blumenberg, rhetoric is a way of testing, shaping, confirming, and reinventing the role or office given to or taken by the speaking subject. Rhetoric is a practice of the self that has the capacity to bend governing forces into something more creative. That is, rhetoric gives form to the subject through efforts to resolve or manage crisis, since in Blumenberg's account, action in the rhetorical situation is predicated on the inevitable contradictions that arise between "role definition" and "role expectation" (R 441). The rhetorical subject inherits roles but never fully inhabits them. Rather, that subject plays at inherited roles and shapes them to a greater or lesser degree, informing both self-understanding and the understanding that others have of oneself. Agamben comes closest to Blumenberg's understanding of rhetoric when he discusses the mode of vicarious government implied by the theology of the Trinity. "Vicariousness implies . . . an ontology," Agamben writes, "or, better, the substitution of classical ontology by an 'economic' paradigm in which no figure of being is, as such, in the position of *arche* but the very trinitarian relation is originary, where each figure *gerit vices*, acts in the place of the other."[24] But rhetoric offers a more affirmative model of biopower than Agamben's dire assessment of life in the state of exception. It doesn't just mediate the exception. It also shapes the exception into a form of life. What's unique about rhetoric is that its relation to reality is "indirect, circumstantial, delayed, selective, and above all 'metaphorical'" (439). Blumenberg puts metaphor in scare quotes to indicate metaphor as the essential component of rhetorical practice, the practice "of comprehending something *by means of* something else." This also applies to the speaking subject. As Blumenberg notes, "the first proposition of an anthropology [of rhetoric] would be, It cannot be taken for granted that man is able to exist" (438). As opposed to anti-rhetorical rhetoric, which conjures life so that it can be managed and governed, for Blumenberg rhetoric becomes a form of life that shapes life through a skeptical and creative approach to the question of human existence.

Blumenberg's anthropological account suggests that rhetoric serves as a third term that takes shape between Schmitt's and Agamben's political and economic theologies. Rhetoric supplements both political theology and economic theologies as a remainder that can't be historicized, naturalized, or finally decided upon as a form of heresy or something altogether less or more substantial. It can, however, be mobilized. Once again, the key figure is Hobbes. Given Schmitt's account of the Gnostic crisis, it's perhaps not surprising that Hobbes developed the social contract alongside an assessment

of the Trinity. Hobbes's central claim is that the three persons of the Trinity
are represented or impersonated in historical time by Moses, who represents
God as a mode of sovereignty; Jesus, who represents God as a mode of obedience; and the apostles, who continue the work of Jesus by teaching that
mode of obedience as a sign of faith. As George Wright has argued, Hobbes
"[conceives] the Economic Trinity in strictly temporal terms, locating the
central events in the Christian narrative in the lives of concrete historical
people."[25] More than just emphasizing the very human means by which divine authority is revealed, Hobbes uses personification to protect the secular order. Hobbes insists on historical impersonation, despite protests from
Bishop Bramhall, because he wants to underscore the contradictions that
result from the use of religion to incorporate the people within the domain
of the state. The problem, as Hobbes understands quite well (and as Schmitt
does, too), is that religion can just as easily turn against the state as support it.
For Hobbes, however, this is a problem of language as much as it's a problem
of monotheism. Moses institutes the literal kingdom of God, "a real, not a
metaphorical kingdom," Hobbes argues, when the Israelites pledge obedience to God through Moses as his proxy (L 35.11.274). The literal here shores
up the distinction between monarch and proxy in an attempt to prevent the
people from turning God against the theocratic state. In Hebrew Scripture
that shoring up fails, however, when the Israelites elect Saul, leaving Mosaic
law as a metaphorical text, or "pretext" as Hobbes calls it, that the prophets
and priests used when convenient to "discharge themselves of obedience"
(40.13.320). The history of ancient Israel discloses a split between the literal
and the metaphorical at the heart of the social contract that maps onto a
whole other series of splits, between monarch and priest, law and custom,
authority and legitimation, the latter always threatening to destabilize and
overthrow the security of the first.

Rather than taking one side or another, Christ triangulates this split, introducing a temporal dimension that interrupts the two poles of crisis and
resolution. As a figure of redemption, Christ promises that the split brought
about with Saul will be repaired at the end of days, when God reestablishes
his literal kingdom on earth. At the same time, as a figure of obedience, Christ
also defers this promise. Christ emphatically *does not* establish a kingdom,
"and thereby [give] a warrant to deny obedience to the magistrates that then
were" (41.4.324). Rather, he personifies God in such a way that secures the
division between religion and state brought about with the election of Saul.
In the process, Christ offers a model of obedience that prepares Christians
for the literal kingdom of God while explicitly *not* claiming that kingdom
here and now. In Hobbes, that is, Christ becomes a paradoxical figure of

the *katechon*, embodying a force to restrain the political realism of the end of days by not giving that force over to the sovereign. Or, to put to point in a different way, Christ offers a model of obedience that protects the secular order by subjecting Christians to the rule of metaphor. Christians may want their state to resemble their church, but this desire needs to be understood first and foremost as a desire for resemblance, a desire that shows political theology to be a metaphor taken literally.

Through the Son, Hobbes develops a mode of obedience that creates space between the fiction of the state and its potential literalization through religion by suspending, without negating, the promise of redemption. And by suspending this promise without negating it, Hobbes is able to open up the more tempered promise of the political. We can see this opening by contrasting Hobbes's depiction of the end of days with his discussion of the obedience that Christian subjects owe to infidel kings. The kingdom of God at the end of days is perhaps the clearest expression of a political realism in which the absolute rule of the sovereign is made manifest in the decision between friend and enemy, the former given eternal life and the latter consigned to not just one death but two, the second being a weirdly interim state of "everlasting death" (38.14.305) in which the enemies of God keep on dying as a sign of God's authority. The model of obedience offered by Christ's example prevents this vision of authority. "What infidel king is so unreasonable," Hobbes asks, "as knowing he has a subject, that waiteth for the second coming of Christ, . . . and in the meantime thinketh himself bound to the laws of that infidel king, (which all Christians are obliged in conscience to do,) to put to death, or to persecute such a subject?" (43.23.401). Through the particular force of obedience inaugurated by Christ, Hobbes proposes, the Christian subject can secure the order of law and displace the more dire forms of the sovereign exception.

Blumenberg explores this mode of obedience in a particularly dense passage on Christian confession in the 1973 edition of *The Legitimacy of the Modern Age*. As he notes, for Hobbes Christianity only requires the confession that "Jesus is the Christ" (L 43.11.394). Hobbes assures his pious readers that this statement may imply a host of theological positions, but he also insists that none of those positions need be articulated or even acknowledged for entry into heaven. Instead of provoking the kind of confessional crisis that, say, Donne agonizes over in *Satire 3*, here confession becomes a rhetorical statement that acknowledges the shaping force of religion but then turns that force against the theocratic state. As Hobbes argues, to say that "Jesus is the Christ" is to say nothing that would preclude obedience to the civil order. For Blumenberg, the double gesture at work in the statement of confession is crucial: on the one hand, the political subject is constituted as a religious subject on the condition that religion is a polite fiction, a representation with no dogmatic substance whatsoever. On the other hand, as a rhetorical gesture confession calls out as fiction any pretense to political theology. "This sort of theology," Blumenberg writes, "corresponds functionally, though not of course in the names and words it employs, to the techniques that Voltaire employed in propagandizing for tolerance with the recommendation that we not take theology in general . . . too seriously, and that we defend God's goodness by no longer asserting His omnipotence" (LMA 95). Hobbes's understanding of confession can certainly turn into a pernicious form of culture, one in which religion becomes an empty form that prompts the moral exclusion of non-Christians and other "uncultured" persons from public life, but because it is a form of rhetoric, Hobbesian confession also sows the seeds of its own destruction, basing belief on empty terms—metaphors wrenched from their dogmatic significance.

Confession goes in the opposite direction of the social contract. Whereas Hobbes's social contract has a literalizing effect that obscures rhetorically produced consensus, Hobbes's version of confession underscores the rhetorical conditions by which sovereignty is manufactured. As I have argued, Blumenberg sees Hobbes consolidating a linguistic turn in the history of political thought. This turn is somewhat paradoxical in that, in the first half of *Leviathan* at least, Hobbes admits rhetoric only to counteract it. He bases his concept of the artificial person of the state on an anti-rhetorical rhetoric that defends against the sense of rhetorical agency and consensus-building implied by submission to the social contract. In order to draw out that sense of agency, in "An Anthropological Approach" Blumenberg reads Hobbes against himself, arguing for a rhetorical understanding of politics that revives and shapes life against its inscription through political realism. Developing this understanding, in the revised edition of *The Legitimacy of the Modern Age* Blumenberg directs our attention to the second half of *Leviathan,* where Hobbes explicitly addresses religion and its relation to the state. In Blumenberg's assessment, the value of Hobbes's understanding of confession is that it chafes against the literalization of the artificial person of the state at the core of Hobbes's anti-rhetorical rhetoric. Hobbesian confession recuperates the force of rhetoric, albeit implicitly, in order to grant rhetorically mediated subjects the capacity to place a limit on the seemingly overawing authority of the "great LEVIATHAN, . . . that *Mortall God,* to which we owe under the *Immortal God,* our peace and defence" (L 17.13.114).

Moreover, confession here also disproves Schmitt's version of the secularization thesis. Professing "Jesus is the Christ" as polite fiction admits the possible synthesis of church and state, but it also reveals that synthesis to be a creative act issued immanently and not a structural necessity required by some secularization process. For Schmitt, Blumenberg cannot account for the persistence of enmity in the modern age. In his assessment of Christian confession, Blumenberg addresses that charge. Instead of supporting a Schmittian version of political theology, Hobbes's emptying out of Christian confession places the political subject at the crossroads between political and economic theologies. That is, for Blumenberg, Christian confession offers a mode of power that displaces the politico-theological sovereign through the self-constitution and self-governance of the rhetorical subject. Furthermore, while this mode of self-governance clearly involves governance, it also cannot be easily conflated with the model of governmentality that Agamben derives from his reading of Schmitt and the Church Fathers. Hobbes's version of Christian confession locates the point at which obedience as self-governance has the capacity to split theology from the state without necessarily doing away with either. This doesn't necessarily mean an end to enmity *tout court*, but it does abate and defer the kind of enmity that Schmitt implies by rearticulating conflict at a higher level, between a political theology based on sovereignty and an economic theology based on management and governance. Economic theology cannot finally break away from political theology, but it can show how political theology amounts to so many metaphors. Once the conflict gets expressed from the perspective of rhetoric, Blumenberg shows how economic theology has already won.

Notes

1. Ernst Kantorowicz, "Mysteries of State: An Absolutist Concept and Its Late Medieval Origins," *Harvard Theological Review* 48 (1955): 66, 67. Also see Kantorowicz, *The King's Two Bodies: A Study in Medieval Political Theology*, intro. by William Chester Jordan (Princeton: Princeton University Press, 1957, rpt. 1997). Kantorowicz's theory of the king's two bodies plays a key role in Slavoj Žižek, *For They Know Not What They Do: Enjoyment as a Political Factor* (London: Verso, 1991), 253–73.

2. Carl Schmitt, *Political Theology: Four Chapters on the Concept of Sovereignty*, trans. George Schwab (Cambridge, Mass.: MIT Press, 1985), 36. Subsequent references cited parenthetically in text as PT.

3. Hans Blumenberg, *Legitimacy of the Modern Age*, trans. Robert M. Wallace (Cambridge, Mass.: MIT Press, 1983), 101. Subsequent references cited parenthetically in text as LMA.

4. For a different account of rhetoric and modern politics, see Ernesto Laclau, "The Politics of Rhetoric," in *Material Events: Paul DeMan and the Afterlife of Theory*, ed. Tom Cohen et al. (Minneapolis: University of Minnesota Press, 2001), 229–53.

5. The intention to found a government, Hobbes writes, "were almost in the very act of meeting a Democraty; for in that they willingly met, they are suppos'd oblig'd to the very observation of what shall be determin'd by the major part." Thomas Hobbes, *De Cive*, ed. Howard Warrender (Oxford: Clarendon Press, 1983), 109.

6. Quentin Skinner, "Hobbes and the Purely Artificial Person of the State," *The Journal of Political Philosophy* 7 (1999): 20. Skinner wants to mend this division by showing how Hobbes imagines the state mediating relations between sovereign and citizens. By contrast, I see a more fundamental schism between these two scenes. For an excellent reading of the paradoxes in Hobbes's theory of the political subject, see Christopher Pye, "The Sovereign, The Theater, and the Kingdome of Darknesse: Hobbes and the Spectacle of Power," *Representations* 8 (1984): 84–106.

7. Thomas Hobbes, *Leviathan*, ed. J. C. A. Gaskin (Oxford: Oxford University Press, 1996), 17.13.114. Subsequent references cited parenthetically in the text as L.

8. Carl Schmitt, *Constitutional Theory*, trans. and ed. Jeffrey Seitzer (Durham: Duke University Press, 2008), 239.

9. Carl Schmitt, *Political Theology II: The Myth of the Closure of Any Political Theology*, trans. and introduced by Michael Hoelzl and Graham Ward (Cambridge: Polity Press, 2008), 41. Subsequent references cited parenthetically in the text as PT2. Schmitt spends the bulk of this short book responding to Peterson and only addresses Blumenberg in a concluding appendix. However, as Anselm Haverkamp notes in his essay on Blumenberg, Schmitt, and *Richard II*, Schmitt "takes Peterson as a pretext and hostage, in order to counter what must have come to him as a shock with Blumenberg's attack" (Anselm Haverkamp, "*Richard II*, Bracton, and the End of Political Theology," *Cardozo Studies in Literature and Law* 16 [2004]: 314).

10. Carl Schmitt, *Roman Catholicism and Political Form*, trans. G. L. Ulman (Westport, Conn.: Greenwood Press, 1996), 24.

11. For further discussion of Schmitt on Hobbes, see Victoria Kahn, "Hamlet or Hecuba: Carl Schmitt's Decision," *Representations* 83 (2003): 67–96; Miguel Vatter, "Strauss and Schmitt as Readers of Hobbes and Spinoza: On the Relation Between Political Theology and Liberalism," *The New Centennial Review* 4 (2004): 161–214; ; and Silke-Maria Weineck, "Invisible Person: Schmitt and the Master Trope of Power," *The Germanic Review* 84 (2009): 199–221.

12. Hans Blumenberg, "An Anthropological Approach to the Contemporary Situation of Rhetoric," in *After Philosophy: End or Transformation*, ed. Kenneth Baynes, James Bohman, and Thomas McCarthy (Cambridge, Mass.: MIT Press, 1987), 454. Subsequent references cited parenthetically in text as R. For a helpful discussion of Blumenberg's argument in this essay, see Jean-Claude Monod's lecture, "A Rhetorical Approach to Politics: Blumenberg's Principle of Insufficient Reason and Its Pascalian Consequences," www.essex.ac.uk/centres/theostud/Blum%20rheto%20chicago.edu (December 8, 2008).

13. Quentin Skinner also emphasizes an anti-rhetorical bias in Hobbes. Skinner maps Hobbes's career through his engagement with, rejection of, and cautious return to a Roman rhetorical tradition associated with civic virtue. Quentin Skinner, *Reason and Rhetoric in the Philosophy of Hobbes* (Cambridge: Cambridge University Press, 1996). Blumenberg would agree that Hobbes represents a watershed moment in the history of rhetoric and politics. However, whereas Skinner focuses on Hobbes's relation to a lost past, Blumenberg argues that Hobbes uses rhetoric to anticipate a new understanding of the human.

14. Schmitt develops his understanding of the state of exception in *Political Theology*, 7–15. Giorgio Agamben substantially expands Schmitt's concept in *Homo Sacer: Sovereign Power and*

Bare Life, trans. Daniel Heller-Roazen (Stanford: Stanford University Press, 1998), 15–48, and *State of Exception*, trans. Kevin Attell (Chicago: University of Chicago Press, 2005).

15. In making this argument, Blumenberg comes close to J. G. A. Pocock's discussion of the state of exception. See Pocock, *The Machiavellian Moment: Florentine Political Thought and the Atlantic Republican Tradition* (Princeton: Princeton University Press, 1975), 25–30. Whereas Pocock draws out the discourses, vocabularies, and models of governance available in early modern Europe for navigating unforeseen contingencies, Blumenberg discusses the implications for political anthropology of an anti-foundational view of the human that strongly links the need to handle unforeseen contingencies with available discursive models for doing so.

16. For a discussion of the role of Gnosticism in twentieth-century German intellectual history, see Benjamin Lazier, *God Interrupted: Heresy and the European Imagination Between the World Wars* (Princeton: Princeton University Press, 2008), 37-48.

17. For a detailed discussion of Blumenberg's argument, see Martin Jay's untitled review essay in *History and Theory* 24 (1985): 183–96.

18. Samuel Weber, *Targets of Opportunity: On the Militarization of Thinking* (New York: Fordham University Press, 2005), 37.

19. Michel Foucault, *Society Must Be Defended: Lectures at the Collège de France, 1975–76*, trans. David Macey (London and New York: Penguin, 2003); *Security, Territory, Population: Lectures at the Collège de France, 1977–78*, trans. Graham Burchell (New York: Palgrave Macmillan, 2007); *The Birth of Biopolitics: Lectures at the Collège de France, 1978–79*, trans. Graham Burchell (New York: Palgrave Macmillan, 2008).

20. Agamben, *Il Regno e la Gloria: Per una genealogia dell'economia e del governo* (Torino: Bollati Boringhieri, 2009), 13. Translations mine.

21. Ibid., 45–46.

22. Agamben, *Homo Sacer*, 19–20; *Il Regno*, 158.

23. Agamben, *Il Regno*, 17.

24. Ibid., 139.

25. George Wright, "Hobbes and the Economic Trinity," *The British Journal for the History of Philosophy* 7.3 (1999): 418. Wright has an excellent discussion of the Hobbes's intervention in the Church Father's attempts to develop a theology of the Trinity. Alexandre Matheron, "Hobbes, la Tinité et les caprices de la représentation," in *Thomas Hobbes: Philosophie premiere, théorie de la science et politique*, ed. Yves Charles Zarka and Jean Bernhardt (Paris: Presses Universitaires de France, 1990), 381–90; Martinich, *The Two Gods of Leviathan: Thomas Hobbes on Religion and Politics* (Cambridge: Cambridge University Press, 1992), 203–8; and Gianni Paganini, "Hobbes, Valla, and the Trinity," *British Journal for the History of Philosophy* 11.2 (2003): 183–218.

5

Political Theologies of the *Corpus Mysticum*: Schmitt, Kantorowicz, and de Lubac

JENNIFER RUST

Fifty years after its publication, Ernst Kantorowicz's *The King's Two Bodies*[1] has generated a flurry of renewed interest. In a recent issue of the journal *Representations*, Kantorowicz's volume garners careful attention from a range of notable early modernists, including Stephen Greenblatt, Victoria Kahn, and Lorna Hutson.[2] Kantorowicz's classic volume holds interest for these critics not so much, as in an earlier generation, as a new historicist work *avant la lettre*, but now rather for the extent to which it responds to, and critiques *sub rosa*, Carl Schmitt's work on political theology, itself recently revived as an object of critical attention by Giorgio Agamben and others.[3] These recent essays decidedly emphasize Kantorowicz's strategy of countering the troubling authoritarian tendencies of Schmitt's thought with an alternative account of premodern political theology, one which stresses the role of fictiveness in transmuting theological concepts into political abstractions.[4] The consensus of the *Representations* writers is that the ultimate value of Kantorowicz's "political theology" lies in its willingness to demonstrate how politics and theology share certain fundamental fictions.

Certainly, Kantorowicz's emphasis on the fictiveness at play in both realms accounts to some extent for the strong appeal of his work in the field of early modern literary studies, where his interpretation of the two bodies doctrine as a structuring principle of Shakespeare's *Richard II* has long had considerable influence. My argument begins in a similar spirit by seeking to reevaluate Kantorowicz's work in light of its potential critical response to Schmitt, but I will pursue this goal through a different trajectory: I show how, via Roman Catholic sources, Kantorowicz develops a concept of the *corpus mysticum* as a mode of communal organization that implicitly counters the authoritarian tendencies of Schmittian decisionism. In turn, this trajectory will suggest a different context for the role of fiction in Kantorowicz's larger claims about premodern developments in political theology.

The year 2007 marked not only the fiftieth anniversary of the publication of Kantorowicz's volume but also the first publication in the United States of the translation of a crucial source for this volume: *Corpus Mysticum: The Eucharist and the Church in the Middle Ages*, by Henri de Lubac S.J., a work of historical theology, first published in 1944, whose effect on modern Catholicism and contemporary theological discourse cannot be overestimated.[5] The influence of this study inside and outside Catholic circles is perhaps comparable to the continuing power of Kantorowicz's monograph within the disciplines of literature and history. Despite great differences in their intellectual commitments, Kantorowicz and de Lubac share some methodological similarities. Both assemble a wide range of primary sources from late antiquity through early modernity in an effort to reveal previously unconsidered dimensions of political or religious tradition. Both excavate the deep history of tradition in order to achieve a new, even radical (in both senses of this term) perspective on familiar institutions, although the primary sphere of their concerns is distinctly different: Western secular political institutions versus Roman Catholic ecclesiastical and Eucharistic theology. Despite these affinities, and despite their enormous impact on in numerous fields of study, the fascinating intersection of these two works has so far been noted only in passing and has yet to be subject to significant critical scrutiny.[6]

The current argument will show how Kantorowicz uses de Lubac's meticulous study of the concept of the *corpus mysticum* in the early church and the Middle Ages to carry out a certain critique of Schmitt's notions of "political theology." This anti-Schmittian agenda is not, however, the only factor that draws Kantorowicz to de Lubac's work. The *corpus mysticum* proves to be a compelling figure for Kantorowicz, one that he weaves throughout the main argument of *The King's Two Bodies*. The key role of this concept is perhaps clearest as Kantorowicz recapitulates the steps of his argument in his concluding paragraph:

> The tenet . . . of the Tudor jurists definitely hangs upon the Pauline language and its later development: the change from the Pauline *corpus Christi* to the mediaeval *corpus ecclesiae mysticum*, thence to the *corpus reipublicae mysticum*, which was equated with the *corpus morale et politicum* of the commonwealth, until finally (though confused by the notion of *Dignitas*) the slogan emerged saying that every abbot was a "mystical body" or a "body politic," and that accordingly the king, too, was, or had, a body politic which "never died."[7]

This statement illustrates the considerable extent to which Kantorowicz's genealogy of the legal doctrine of the ruler's two bodies rests on the discovery of an earlier doctrine of a "mystical body" that designates a corporation bound together by a theologism enabling it, conceptually, to transcend the limits of concrete time and space. In constructing this genealogy of the mystical body, Kantorowicz is deeply indebted to de Lubac's earlier work. To the extent that Kantorowicz constructs a political theological alternative to Schmitt's personalist and decisionist model of sovereignty, he finds in de Lubac an interpretation of Catholic tradition that is not so easily collapsed into authoritarianism. Kantorowicz's adaptation of the corpus mysticum demonstrates that the seemingly disinterested historiography of *The King's Two Bodies* is in fact interwoven with a polemical agenda: to defend the enabling fictions of the liberal constitutional state against the "idols of modern political religions."[8]

However, it is also necessary to question how Kantorowicz himself strategically misapprehends crucial elements of de Lubac's account as he argues that the mystical steadily turns into the fictional in medieval political theology. For de Lubac, as a Jesuit theologian, is emphatically not guided by an impulse to reveal the fictiveness of the *corpus mysticum,* at least in any conventional, secular sense. Indeed, for de Lubac, it is precisely the becoming-fictive of the *corpus mysticum* that represents the signal disaster of collective spiritual life in the Middle Ages. De Lubac seeks to counteract this transformation of the *corpus mysticum* into a political fiction by recovering a more traditional mystical body not so easily translatable into purely fictional or abstract terms. Engaging with a tradition in which "mystical" and "mystery" coalesce as "secret and dynamic" forms of signification,[9] de Lubac discloses dimensions of the *corpus mysticum* that resist sublimation into sheer *corpus politicum.* De Lubac's interpretation of the *corpus mysticum* as a dynamic paradox—simultaneously transcendent and immanent—offers a theological perspective that elucidates the potential inadequacy of both the vertical orientation of Schmitt's account of sovereignty (as personal and transcendent) and Kantorowicz's emphasis on horizontal bureaucracy as a mysticized "body politic."

1. Henri de Lubac and the *Corpus Mysticum*

In this context, it is only possible to indicate briefly the significant impact of de Lubac's work on twentieth century Catholic theology and, indeed, on the very form and liturgy of the Catholic Church itself after Vatican II.[10] De Lubac's early and mid life experience, like that of Kantorowicz and Schmitt, was marked by the wrenching experience of total war and the rise and de-structive fall of fascism in Europe. *Corpus Mysticum* itself was written during the difficult circumstances of wartime France, where Lubac was allied with the Resistance to the Vichy regime in distinct opposition to the "Catholic Rightists ... collaborating with the occupying Germans."[11] Indeed, John Milbank emphasizes that de Lubac's *"political* opponents" were also *"theological* opponents."[12] This personal detail hints at how far the Catholicism manifest in de Lubac's study of the *corpus mysticum* will depart from Schmitt's brand of political Catholicism, which notoriously accommodated itself to the rise of fascism in Germany.

De Lubac's postwar work, most notably the *Surnaturel* of 1946, became controversial, and for a time he was banned from teaching and publishing by the Catholic Church.[13] After some years in the wilderness, he was restored to good standing in the late 1950s and played an influential role in the Vatican II Council in the 1960s. The groundwork for this role, however, was laid by de Lubac's work of the late thirties and forties, most notably in this context, *Corpus Mysticum*. De Lubac's theological influence played a part in enabling a revitalization of the Church by introducing a new way of conceiving of its own tradition that encouraged an effort to overcome the phenomena of an overemphasis on the Real Presence in the Eucharist as a miraculous fact, excessively individualistic piety, and a misunderstanding of church hierarchy as an authoritarian structure. As Hans Boersma argues, de Lubac believed that all of these problems, as well as the earlier political tragedy of a traditional Catholicism that had too readily accommodated itself to fascism in the Second World War, were symptomatic of a general "extrinsicism" which posited "grace as something that came strictly from the outside and had no intrinsic connection with human nature,"[14] and which a Neo-Thomistic separation of natural and supernatural had nurtured. Such a doctrine had eroded an earlier tradition in which the church was conceived as simultaneously sacramental and social; it was this spirit that Vatican II, in its best moments, sought to restore.

De Lubac's work from the thirties and forties, including *Corpus Mysticum*, thus laid out a blueprint for reforming the Catholic Church by returning to its earliest traditions. One of the most influential imperatives that the Vatican II Council derived from de Lubac is succinctly stated in the conclusion to *Corpus Mysticum*, where de Lubac urges a "return to the sacramental origins of the 'mystical body' in order to steep ourselves in it . . . a return to the mystical sources of the Church. The Church and the Eucharist are formed [*se font*] by one another day by day: the idea of the Church and the idea of the Eucharist must promote one another mutually and each be rendered more profound by the other."[15] In this claim, de Lubac urges that both the sacrament and the church be understood in dynamic rather than static terms. This dynamism brings the concept of the "mystical body" into being as the simultaneous mutual relation and interpenetration of the church and the sacrament. In its most originary sense, it contains "an implicit and indirect reference to the action, whatever it is, in which this 'body' is engaged."[16] The Eucharist is thus not an objective Real Presence produced by the intervention of an extrinsic miracle, nor is the church simply a hierarchy channeling this intervention. If we apply the terminology of speech-act theory, we could say that de Lubac is arguing for a *performative* rather than constative understanding of "mystical." In this performative sense, then, "mystical" refers not simply to one entity over against another (church vs. sacrament), but rather evokes a state of affairs in which the relation between these two figures is ceaselessly dynamic—they make each other in an ongoing process. This dynamism is underscored at the beginning of *Corpus Mysticum* as de Lubac emphasizes the derivation of "mystical" from "mystery": "A mystery, in the old sense of the word, is more of an action than a thing."[17]

This dynamic sense of "mystical" also includes a social or communal dimension insofar as the church is encompassed within the sacramental action. De Lubac stresses that, as a term associated with the community of the church, "mystical" stems from the earliest Christian texts. It is evident in St. Paul's First Letter to the Corinthians (1 Cor. 10:17–18), a passage which de Lubac glosses: "The 'communion of the body of Christ' of which St. Paul spoke to the faithful of Corinth was their mysterious union with the community, by virtue of the sacrament: it was the mystery of one body formed by all those who shared in the 'one Bread.' "[18] De Lubac finds his thesis about the intrinsic link between the Eucharist and the church confirmed not only in the Pauline text but also in the writings of the earliest church fathers, especially Augustine. For de Lubac, this performative sacramental and social sense of "mystical" is far removed from the more modern notion of the term "as a watering down of 'real' or of 'true,' "[19] as a synonym, that is, for something immaterial or even imaginary.

The long story of the "degeneration of the *mystical body*"[20] is a major concern of de Lubac's volume, however, and, as we will see, it is the part of this work that most interests Kantorowicz. According to de Lubac, the dynamic, social, and also deeply symbolic traditional logic behind the original sense of the *corpus mysticum* was gradually effaced by a growing rationalism and politicization of the church in the late Middle Ages. For de Lubac, it is actually the political metaphor that comes to inhabit the theological concept, rather than the other way around. Ironically, this shift ultimately "dissolve[s] the social edifice of Christendom" and culminates in the disaster of the Reformation in the sixteenth century, contributing to the "breaking up of the Church itself."[21] The degenerative process that Lubac describes is complex: thus, at the early stage of this process, in the ninth century,

> *mystical body* is in some sense a technical expression that serves, inadequately at times, to distinguish the Eucharist from the "body born of the Virgin," or from the body of the Church, *while at the same time placing it in relation with both one and the other.* By what curious cross-country route (*curieux chassé-croisé*) the "body of the Church" came in its turn, *and precisely in opposition to* the Eucharistic body, to take the name *of mystical body,* is what we will see. . . . [22]

The "curious cross-country route" at issue here is the emergence of a substantial new opposition, between two terms (Eucharist, church) that *mysticum* had effectively linked, even in their distinctness. To make distinctions is not the same thing as to oppose, however, particularly in the paradoxical logic that de Lubac pursues in his argument. In fact, the reason why the transference could take place at all was because of the earlier nuanced relation between the two terms. Indeed it is this traditional relation that enables the work of tracing the "mystical body" back to its Eucharistic roots.

De Lubac's account of this inversion of the "mystical body," particularly the divorce of "mystical" from its sacramental roots, has resonated beyond Catholic circles, and this dispersal is due in part to the influential interpretation of fellow Jesuit, psychoanalytic theorist Michel de Certeau. Certeau's interpretation recasts the main import of de Lubac's *Corpus Mysticum* in post-structuralist terms in his own study of mysticism in the sixteenth and seventeenth centuries, *The Mystic Fable.* Certeau reads de Lubac's book as a narrative of how the "caesura" structuring the "threefold" body of Christ (historical, sacramental, and scriptural), as conceived in the early church, shifted in the twelfth century.[23] After the shift that de Lubac documents, according to Certeau, the mystical loses its "mediating" force, as sacramental and historical bodies are "split off from the Church."[24] This split is the condition of possibility for the Reformation: Reformers privilege the "scriptural" body as the proper "historical" body, while Counter-Reformation Catholics stress the "sacramental" body "recast in the philosophical formality of the sign."[25] Meanwhile, the "mystical body," stripped of its communal mediatory capacity, becomes "other in relation to visible realities," inspiring the growth of early modern "mysticism."[26]

Certeau's synthesis of de Lubac's work is very lucid, but it may be accused of imposing a schematic structure on *Corpus Mysticum* that limits the actual complexity of the work.[27] Nonetheless, Certeau's interpretation of de Lubac, and, more generally a certain reading of de Lubac's entire life's work, has proven very influential in recent theological discourses.[28] Despite de Lubac's prominence in these circles, however, Kantorowicz's early engagement with his work still remains to be fully scrutinized. Before turning directly to Kantorowicz's appropriation of de Lubac in *The King's Two Bodies*, however, it is necessary to explore Schmitt's own approximations of a *corpus mysticum*, as articulated in his early efforts to define Catholicism as "political form," efforts intimately intertwined with his elaboration of a theory of "political theology" in the early 1920s. This exposition will clarify how sharply Kantorowicz diverges from Schmitt in placing the figure of the *corpus mysticum* at the heart of his own account of "mediaeval political theology."

2. Schmitt: *Corpus Mysticum* as the Negation of the "Visible Church"

Carl Schmitt's brief, dismissive reference to the concept of the *corpus mysticum* occurs in an early tract, "The Visibility of the Church" (1917), which is included as appendix to the English translation of *Roman Catholicism and Political Form* (1923), the companion piece to the more celebrated *Political Theology*.[29] A brief sketch of Schmitt's overarching argument in *Roman Catholicism* will reveal the significance of this reference. In this essay, Schmitt seeks to posit the Catholic Church as a public, visible institution that may counteract the dominance of a sphere of modern economic rationalism that Schmitt associates with Protestant private, interiorized religiosity. Schmitt's project is thus in dialogue with Max Weber's *Protestant Work Ethic and the Spirit of Capitalism* throughout.[30] Schmitt agrees with Weber that the Protestant "inner-worldly" ethic in principle opens the way for the reign of economic rationalism, but he seeks to oppose the hegemony of this sphere in modernity by developing the "political" potential of the Catholic Church as a counterweight. Schmitt begins by seeking to understand Catholicism initially through the converse phenomenon of anti-Catholicism: "There is an anti-Roman temper that has nourished the struggle against popery, Jesuitism and clericalism with a host of religious and political forces, that has impelled European history for centuries."[31] He casts this "anti-Roman temper" as a reaction to a "political idea" of the Catholic Church that lies beyond the simple historical fact that the Roman Church is frequently understood as a continuation of the "universalism" of the Roman Empire.[32] Instead, for Schmitt, the "political idea" that provokes such sustained hostility is rooted in two essential characteristics: the Catholic Church as *complexio oppositorum*[33] and its form of "representation" as the realization of divine authority in the "concrete" person (the pope being the most obvious embodiment—in this, Schmitt follows de Maistre).[34] In developing these characteristics of the church, a tension arises in Schmitt's argument. On one hand, he makes statements that imply that he assumes a further underlying opposition between the pure materialism of the "economic" and the inherent need for a transcendent "idea" in the "political." The complex character of "representation" in the church results in its status, in Schmitt's view, as the bastion of the "political" in a thoroughly economic world: "the Church requires a political form."[35] On the other hand, Schmitt's development of the *complexio oppositorum* as an inherent characteristic suggests a potentially less oppositional and also less hierarchically authoritative vision of the church: "There appears to be no antithesis it does not embrace," whether in terms of its governmental structure, its political alliances, or its theology—"this *complexio oppositorum* also holds sway over everything theological: the Old and New Testament alike are scriptural canon, the Marcionitic either-or is answered with an as-well-as."[36] In the *complexio oppositorum*, we could see a concept akin to the paradoxical, dynamic character of de Lubac's *corpus mysticum*. Schmitt, however, tends to short-circuit the potential of the *complexio* in favor of reinforcing a vision of the church that emphasizes the singularity of hierarchical authority.

Schmitt's arguments for the simultaneously personal and political character of Roman Catholic representative authority are motivated, in part, as a polemical response to the Lutheran legal and theological historian Rudolph Sohm, who also deeply influenced Weber's theories of charismatic authority.[37] Sohm posited that the early church, and indeed, all true Christianity, was deeply and exclusively "personalisitic." Sohm cast the ideal Christian community as a "pneumatocracy" and, in classic Protestant fashion, he saw the Catholic Church as a deep corruption of this original reign of the charismatic persona: "The leadership of the Eccelsia comes from *above*, through the medium of the *individual* who is personally endowed by God. The government of Christendom is from first to last authoritative, *monarchical.*"[38] The similarity of Sohm's claim here to many of Schmitt's formulations in *Roman Catholicism* is striking, and indeed, it is no accident that Schmitt directly refers to Sohm at several points in his argument. Schmitt argues against Sohm's dualistic view that the true church of Christ is purely invisible and spiritual in contrast to any worldly order of institutions and laws: "The great betrayal laid to the Catholic Church is that it . . . does not conceive Christianity as a private matter, something wholly and inwardly spiritual, but rather has given it form as a visible institution. Sohm believed the fall from grace could be perceived in the juridical sphere; others saw in it a more grandiose and profound way as the will to world power."[39] *Contra* Sohm, Schmitt embraces the essence of the church as "juridical form,"[40] acknowledging that it does embody the contradiction of the *complexio* in its capacity for representation, but that it has a legitimate claim to connection with the person of Christ animating its authority.

Although "a high-minded Protestant like Rudolf Sohm could define the Catholic Church as something essentially juridical, while regarding Christian religiosity as essentially non-juridical,"[41] this view does not adequately consider the true public nature of the authority of the church, which Schmitt validates by its deep association with "not only the idea of justice but also the person of Christ."[42] In its embodiment of an "idea" the juridical church is like "secular jurisprudence," but in the additional personalistic dimension bequeathed by its linkage to Christ, the church can claim an authority beyond the secular: "It can deliberate as an equal partner with the state, and thereby create new law, whereas jurisprudence is only a mediator of established law."[43] In this claim, we find Schmitt's eagerness to transfer a mode of personal authority, which is proper to the church, directly to the realm of political power. And although Schmitt adjusts the thrust of Sohm's argument in crucial ways, he essentially accepts Sohm's valuation of "personal" charisma. Schmitt insists on personalizing the representative "offices" of the church in order to counter Sohm's claim that the Catholic Church counterfeits the authority of Christ in its establishment of divine offices. This move is also likely intended to rebut Weber's version of Sohm's claim, which emphasizes a depersonalized "office charisma" in the church.[44] Thus, Schmitt defends the notion of the visible church and also positions this church as a reservoir of political power in the modern world.

This personalizing of "offices" may be an effective way to counter Sohm and Weber, but it leads Schmitt to neglect the "mystical body" as a figure for the social and sacramental organization of the church.[45] In 1917, Schmitt anticipates the arguments of the 1923 work insofar as he develops a critique of the overly spiritualized Protestantism that ultimately produces the modern economic state. Schmitt's dismissal of the "*corpus mysticum*" occurs in a passage that insists on the vitality of the visible institution of the church as essential to any properly Christian system of belief:

> One cannot believe God became man without believing there will also be a visible Church as long as the world exists. Every religious sect which has transposed the concept of the Church from the visible community of believing Christians into a *corpus mere mysticum* basically has doubts about the humanity of the Son of God. It has falsified the historical reality of the incarnation of Christ into a mystical and imaginary process.[46]

Schmitt's explicit reference is to a *"corpus mere mysticum"*—"mere," in the Latin phrase, is a variant of "merus" (undiluted, unmixed, pure)—a purely mystical body. In qualifying the idea of the *corpus mysticum* in this way, he associates it with the denial of the visible church, and thus with Sohm's arguments, which, for Schmitt, actually culminate in a denial of any valid political authority. This understanding of the *corpus mysticum* as a spiritualized, seemingly Protestant concept is symptomatic of Schmitt's larger insistence on conceptualizing "authority," whether religious or political, in sheerly vertical terms. A few lines before this passage, Schmitt asserts: "An arrangement making the invisible visible must be rooted in the invisible and appear in the visible. The mediator descends because the mediation can only proceed from above, not from below."[47] The 1917 essay makes it clear that Schmitt develops his claims for the authority of the church from a notion of the "essence" of the church as "mediation,"[48] which is conceived in a particularly hierarchical way. This is consistent with Schmitt's arguments in the later essay on Roman Catholicism, where it is asserted that the church "has 'no representative institutions'" in the modern parliamentary sense because it does not derive its authority from the people, but rather "'from above.'"[49] For Schmitt, it is this vertical, "transcendent" dimension—necessarily personified in the representative authority—that guarantees authentic political force.[50] Modern parliamentary institutions, from this perspective, become depoliticized entities when they are understood in purely horizontal terms; their norms simply replicate the lower bonds of the economic sphere, since they are posited on an absolute separation between visible and invisible realms originally inspired by Protestant doctrine. This insistence on a vertical, transcendent authority is later reiterated in Schmitt's account of decisionist sovereignty in *Political Theology*, where it occurs at the expense of more lateral forms of organization, including those potentially implied by the *complexio oppositorum*.

Schmitt's characterization of the *corpus mysticum* as a concept at odds with any "incarnational" notion of Christianity—as something purely "invisible" and "imaginary"—is a profound misapprehension of this figure within the history of the church, as Kantorowicz and de Lubac demonstrate. The point of de Lubac's study, as we have seen, is to recover an earlier sense of "mystical" rooted precisely in the most vivid incarnational ritual in traditional Christianity, the celebration of the Eucharist. The sense in which Schmitt uses the term, as synonymous with "imaginary" and invisible, is, from this perspective, a later "degeneration"[51] in usage that stems from the transference of the phrase from the sacramental to the institutional realm.

3. Kantorowicz: The *Corpus Mysticum* in *The King's Two Bodies*

Kantorowicz's appropriation of de Lubac's *corpus mysticum* in *The King's Two Bodies* is motivated as a riposte to Schmitt on several different levels. For Schmitt, the quintessence of political theology resides in the instant or *punctum* of the decision: the exception that transcends the norm but also constitutes it. In *Political Theology*, Schmitt famously illustrates his claim that "all significant concepts of the modern theory of the state are secularized theological concepts" with the examples of the "omnipotent God" who becomes the "omnipotent lawgiver" and a further structural correspondence: "The exception in jurisprudence is analogous to the miracle in theology."[52] The corollary to this claim in Schmitt's companion essay on Roman Catholicism is the definition of the political as inherently involved with an idea "from above" that transcends the hegemony of pure economic rationalism. The person of the sovereign with the power to decide the miraculous exception is clearly akin to the Roman Catholic representative who, as mediator, wields transcendent authority. In both cases, authority is concentrated in a singular person and is imagined as an intervention that descends from a metaphysical dimension higher than any normative economy.

In *The King's Two Bodies*, Kantorowicz will go to great lengths to reconstruct a political theology that contradicts Schmitt in crucial ways. Kantorowicz will be keen to show that the theological aspect of the political should actually be understood to reside in the perpetuity, the *longue durée*, of the institution rather than the miraculous instant of the decision. In other words, theology will turn out to belong to the sphere of the norm rather than the exception. In a recent essay, Richard Halpern has shown how Kantorowicz's discussion of the origins of taxation in the "singular emergency"[53] of the *casus necessitatis* works as an "anti-Schmittian parable" that emphasizes "bureaucratic regularity and continuity" over the urgency of the exceptional decision:

> Here the narrative of *The King's Two Bodies* seems implicitly to invert Schmitt's vector of influence running from the theological to the political, since the increasing bureaucratization of both church and state in the Middle Ages demands a God who does not intervene via miracle but rather governs in more predictable fashion: a "chairman God" who acts only in consultation with his corporate board.[54]

Halpern's characterization of Kantorowicz's critique of Schmitt at such moments in *The King's Two Bodies* is apt, as is his contrast between the "theologies" invoked by each theorist. To extend this conceit further, Kantorowicz seems to find a theological figure for God's "corporate board" in the history of the *corpus mysticum* that he has derived from de Lubac's study. *Corpus Mysticum*, adapted to the coordinates of a markedly anti-Schmittian historiography, will also allow Kantorowicz to highlight how, as they become assimilated to the lateral, relatively static institutional bodies, theological tropes become increasingly attenuated into abstract fictions. Kantorowicz uses the narrative of the decline of the sacramental dimension of the *corpus mysticum* to produce an immanent, rather than extrinsicist, political theology.

The *corpus mysticum* is crucial to Kantorowicz's effort to redefine "political theology" in normative bureaucratic terms. As we have seen in the previous section, Schmitt himself appears to have an underdeveloped sense of this concept, providing a void that Kantorowicz's magisterially researched volume seeks to fill. Kantorowicz is particularly concerned with tracing how the *corpus mysticum* as a figure for the institutional body of the church was transferred conceptually to figure the institutional body of the state. To this end, Lubac's 1949 edition of *Corpus Mysticum* is provided with footnotes that are particularly concentrated in the first section of chapter 5 (*"Corpus Ecclesiae mysticum"*), which develops a genealogy of "Polity-Centered Kingship."[55] In a footnote at the beginning of this section, Kantorowicz acknowledges his debt to de Lubac's "excellent evaluation" of the history of the concept: "in the following pages, I have merely ransacked the wealth of [de Lubac's] material (much of which was inaccessible to me) and his ideas."[56] At the same moment that Kantorowicz signals the importance of de Lubac's prior work for his own study, he also implies that his own argument will trespass on or violate in some way ("ransack") the earlier "history of ideas." Kantorowicz works perpetually with and against the tenor of de Lubac's argument throughout this section of the book. While, as we have seen, *"corpus mysticum"* for Schmitt represents a notion that belongs more to the realm of "inner-worldly" Protestantism, Kantorowicz adapts the term from de Lubac's study and restores "mystical" to the context of twelfth-century ecclesiastical and political debate. It now comes to mean something like "fictional, ideal, abstract," particularly insofar as it qualifies the original model for corporate, collective associations that forms a transitional conceptual framework for the modern secular state.

It is important to stress the point that "mystical," the very term that Kantorowicz most avidly "ransack[s]" from de Lubac's work, originates in the ritual practice of Eucharistic celebration. At the end of a summary of de Lubac's account of a ninth-century Carolingian Eucharistic controversy, Kantorowicz highlights the importance of what otherwise might seem an obscure debate. Because the terminology and conceptual framing that Kantorowicz deploys in this passage are crucial for the subsequent argument, I quote at length:

> Here then, in the realm of dogma and liturgy, there originated that notion whose universal bearings and final effects cannot easily be overrated. *Corpus mysticum*, in the language of the Carolingian theologians, referred not at all to the body of the Church nor to the oneness and unity of Christian society, but to the consecrated host. This, with few exceptions, remained, for many centuries, the official meaning of the "mystical body," whereas the Church or Christian society continued to be known as the *corpus Christi* in agreement with the terminology of St. Paul. It was only in the course of a strange and perplexing development—*un curieux chassé-croisé*—that finally, around the middle of the twelfth century, those designations changed their meaning. . . . That is to say, the Pauline term originally designating the Christian Church now began to designate the consecrated host; contrariwise, the notion of the *corpus mysticum*, hitherto used to describe the host, was gradually transferred—after 1150—to the Church as the organized body of Christian society united in the Sacrament of the Altar. In short, the expression "mystical body," which originally had a liturgical or sacramental meaning, took on a connotation of sociological content.[57]

On one level, Kantorowicz is faithful to the outline of de Lubac's claims about the significant change in the idea of the "mystical body" that occurred around the twelfth century—the *curieux chassé-croisé* that transferred "mystical" from a sacramental to a primarily ecclesiastical sense. However, if we recall de Lubac's original text, it is also clear that Kantorowicz flattens out what de Lubac presents as an originally dynamic situation which involves a fluid relation between *ecclesia* and *Eucharist*, to further his own idea of a genealogy of secular polity, one in which theological structures are progressively taken over by political secular forces as metaphors or fictions. For de Lubac, it is simply not the case that in the early Middle Ages *corpus mysticum* "referred *not at all* to the body of the Church *nor* to the oneness and unity of human society" as Kantorowicz insists. Instead, it would be more accurate to say that *Corpus Mysticum* seeks to demonstrate that the "liturgical or sacramental" was always already "sociological" in the milieu of the early church. Kantorowicz seeks to play down the claim about the earlier "sociological" aspect of the "sacramental" because it could interfere with the progressively immanentizing thrust of his larger argument. As theological tropes become sociological in *The King's Two Bodies*, they tend also to be tamed into pliable fictional material for representing specific political, very human, interests, evacuated of all but the barest hint of transcendent content.

Indeed, Kantorowicz directly associates the emergence of the "mystical" designation with the "so-called secularization of the mediaeval Church."[58] This move is most evident in Kantorowicz's analysis of Aquinas as the switching point for the definitive "'seculariz[ing]' [of] the notion of 'mystical body.'"[59] Kantorowicz again turns to de Lubac for the documentary material to substantiate this claim. He cites a passage footnoted in *Corpus Mysticum*: "That last link to the sphere of the altar . . . was severed when Aquinas wrote: 'It may be said that head and limbs together are as though one mystical person.'"[60] Kantorowicz finds here a crucial turning point:

> Nothing could be more striking than this *bona fide* replacement of *corpus mysticum* by *persona mystica*. Here the mysterious materiality which the term *corpus mysticum*—whatever its connotations may have been—still harbored has been abandoned: "The *corpus Christi* has been changed into a corporation of Christ." It has been exchanged for a juristic abstraction, the "mystical *person*," a notion reminiscent of, indeed synonymous with, the "fictitious person," the *persona repraesentata* or *ficta*, which the jurists had introduced into legal thought and which will be found at the bottom of so much of the political theorizing during the later Middle Ages.[61]

In Kantorowicz's footnote 24, de Lubac is cited as the reference for the Aquinas quotation. However, the source of the interpretation of the significance of this moment in Aquinas is not de Lubac at all. In de Lubac's account, while Aquinas may at times appear more modern insofar as he uses "mystical body" in a simple analogical sense "in contrast to '*natural body*,'" the theologian also emphasizes that Aquinas generally tends to stay consistent with the older tradition that identifies sacramental and ecclesiastical bodies.[62] Indeed, Aquinas ultimately illustrates for de Lubac how slowly the tradition actually changed. In order to substantiate the claim that at this moment Aquinas radically changes the character and interpretation of the *corpus mysticum*, Kantorowicz must turn away from de Lubac's text. Interestingly, the source of the sentence, "'[t]he *corpus Christi* has been changed into a corporation of Christ,'" is Rudolph Sohm—Schmitt's Lutheran nemesis in *Roman Catholicism*.[63] Although Kantorowicz inserts this direct quotation of Sohm as if it is a gloss on Aquinas's "mystical person," Sohm does not directly address Aquinas at this point in his text, nor does he explicitly refer to the concept of the *corpus mysticum*. Instead, he is summarizing the passing away of an original "sacramental" and "mysterious" (*geheimnisvolles*) Christian Church at the end of the twelfth century in favor of a church structured like any other earthly community.[64] Superficially, this language appears to have an affinity with de Lubac's project of recovering an earlier "sacramental" sense of *corpus mysticum*; like de Lubac, Sohm finds a crucial turning point in the twelfth century when a newer juridical, dialectical, rationalism effaces an older sacramental tradition.[65] Nonetheless, Sohm's overtly anti-Catholic Lutheran "pneumatology" is not ultimately congenial with de Lubac's effort to reassess the tradition of the early church from within an incarnational Catholic tradition that understands sacramental mystery as equally visible and spiritual, human and divine. Like Schmitt, de Lubac would feel compelled to defend the spiritual integrity of the visible church.[66]

Practically speaking, Kantorowicz cites Sohm in order to make Aquinas into the key element in the transformation of the *corpus mysticum* into the "juristic abstraction" of the "mystical person," a purely legal and ultimately "fictitious" entity. This swerve away from the letter and spirit of de Lubac's account occurs here for at least three interrelated strategic reasons. First of all, giving Aquinas a momentous role in the transformation of the *corpus mysticum* may simply stem from Kantorowicz's desire to make the shift that he is describing seem even more dramatic and authoritative, insofar as it derives from a virtual fiat of the "*Doctor angelicus*,"[67] the "doctor" who, of course, was also distantly related to the subject of Kantorowicz's famous early biography, Friedrich II.[68] Furthermore, Kantorowicz's citation of Sohm, a controversial figure whom Schmitt sharply critiques at length in several important works in the 1920s, strongly reinforces the notion that in this section of *The King's Two Bodies*, as in other places, Kantorowicz is engaged in a subterranean riposte to Schmitt's account of political theology. While Kantorowicz relies more heavily on a newer, Catholic source unknown to the Schmitt of the twenties to develop his own account of "mediaeval political theology," the reference to Sohm, a figure vehemently opposed in several ways to Schmitt, reminds us that Schmitt is a long-term target of this account. Kantorowicz is not simply presenting a disinterested history in invoking the name of Sohm, for Sohm enables Kantorowicz to further dissolve Schmitt's claims for the personalistic authority of the church into matter of mere fictions.

Finally, Sohm may also subtly function as a way for Kantorowicz to ignore de Lubac's more nuanced formulations about Aquinas, a move symptomatic of his resistance to the larger implications of de Lubac's full argument about the original sense of the *corpus mysticum* in the early church. For Sohm, whatever his superficial affinities with de Lubac's claims about the shifting of the ecclesial and legal worlds of the high Middle Ages, ultimately assumes a dualism between spirit and flesh that is antithetical to de Lubac's project of recovering the mysterious unity between them. It may be easier for Kantorowicz to make the *mysticum* into "fictitious" matter if a certain disenchanting juridical interpretation is heightened, beyond the perspective allowed or available in de Lubac's work. Indeed, in the passage above, Kantorowicz strongly emphasizes the increasing abstractness of "mysticum" in the hands of Aquinas. "Mysticum" becomes a curious conceptual matter, the primordial stuff ("mysterious materiality") of secularism, malleable for new ideological purposes once the church has unleashed it from the liturgical sphere. Seemingly amorphous, but also residually charged with ritual religious associations, the *corpus mysticum* will prove the ideal medium for subliming transcendent theology into a substance to be manipulated by immanent politics.

Kantorowicz's claims for the ideological efficacy of the *mysticum* extend beyond the immediate section engaged with de Lubac's work. In the next section of this chapter, "*Corpus Republicae mysticum,*" we find the mirror image of the church's aspiration to the status of a "political and legal organism"[69] in developments on the secular political side of the equation. "The world of thought of statesmen, jurists, and scholars" more easily appropriated the idea of the *corpus mysticum* to the emergent nation-state because it was already "politicized and . . . secularized by the Church itself."[70] The burgeoning nation-state sought to sanctify itself in appropriating such "mystical" terms, but in the process, the "mystical" itself became more than ever a fictional property, a counter to be attached to the abstractions formulated in legal arguments:

> The jurists, thereby, arrived, like the theologians, at a distinction between *corpus verum*—the tangible body of an individual person—and *corpus fictum*, the corporate collective which was intangible and existed only as a fiction of jurisprudence. Hence, by analogy with theological usage as well as in contrast with natural persons, the jurists defined their fictional persons not seldom as "mystical bodies."[71]

Kantorowicz again replicates the structure of de Lubac's argument here in his discussion of secular legalisms. The analogy that he invokes also bears comparison to Schmitt's analogy between the sovereign and God in *Political Theology*; Kantorowicz's analogy is between collective bodies, not single sovereign deciders. Beyond this, Kantorowicz's analogy emphasizes how authentic theological value is depleted, demoted to the realm of the fictional or figural, when it is transferred to the political. Nevertheless, he also implies that something of a sacramental residue yet adheres to the *corpus mysticum*, enhancing its appeal to secular jurists. *Mystical* imports into the commonwealth "some of the super-natural and transcendental values normally owned by the Church."[72] While this "super-natural" aspect would seem severely attenuated in the legal-political developments that Kantorowicz meticulously describes, he still insists that "the designation *corpus mysticum* brought to the secular polity, as it were, a whiff of incense from another world."[73] It is thus not simply its conceptual malleability, its imaginative resources or abstract-ability that accounts for the continued appeal of thinking of political or legal associations as "mystical bodies." Kantorowicz appears to try to have it both ways as he intimates that final total secularization never fully or completely arrives. Even in the desiccated abstractions of the legal realm, the sense of "mystical" retains a trace of the "mysterious materiality" of the sacrament. Curiously, it is only when he turns to the ostensibly "secular" legal realm that Kantorowicz dimly echoes de Lubac's contention that despite the misap-prehension of "mystical" in the late medieval and post-Tridentine Church, it was never completely evacuated of its traditional sense and efficacy, which remain latent, to be recovered on an ongoing basis in modernity. Nonethe-less, such suggestions remain only marginal for Kantorowicz; his emphasis falls on the various ways that the immanent secular sphere overwhelms the theological or "mystical" figures that it takes over from the church.

If Schmitt's "from above" ecclesial authority fatally short-circuits the paradoxical interplay of spiritual and human realms, Kantorowicz's flatten-ing out of the *corpus mysticum* into mere metaphorical material to provide an underlying structure for the secular polity is, in its overemphasis on im-manence, merely the flip side of Schmitt's authoritarianism. While Kantoro-wicz's emphasis on the "mystical body" as a horizontally organized collec-tive body is a necessary corrective to Schmitt, Kantorowicz misses de Lubac's effort to go back behind the modern dualism of nature and spirit, fiction and reality, produced by the dialectics that became dominant in the twelfth and thirteenth centuries. Although Kantorowicz admits to some lingering ambiguities, his dominant understanding of mystical as fictional perpetuates a modern dualism and narrative of progress that de Lubac seeks to put into question. In his appropriation of de Lubac, Kantorowicz ironically rational-izes and substantializes the very tradition that de Lubac is striving to render more fluid and dynamic.

In a later reprise of the arguments of *Corpus Mysticum,* de Lubac provides a striking formula that gives access to his thinking about the relationship be-tween "mystery" and "symbolism": de Lubac claims that the first theologians who had referred to the Church as a *corpus mysticum* had meant "the *corpus in mysterio,* the body mystically signified and realized by the Eucharist—in other words, the unity of the Christian community that is made real by the 'holy mysteries' in an effective symbol (in the strict sense of the word 'effective').'[74] In de Lubac's terms, the "symbolic" or figural need not signal an evacuation of spiritual value or efficacy. If it is understood in a fully dynamic, "effective" (we might prefer "performative") sense, it becomes a paradoxical union of transcendence and immanence. It is only from a static, secular position that figuration or symbolism necessarily takes on the meaning of abstract or empty fiction.

Notes

1. Ernst Kantorowicz, *The King's Two Bodies: A Study in Mediaeval Political Theology* (Princeton: Princeton University Press, 1957).

2. *Representations* 106 (Spring 2009). The articles concerned with Kantorowicz's legacy include: Stephen Greenblatt, "Introduction: Fifty Years of *The King's Two Bodies*," 63–66; Richard Halpern, "The King's Two Buckets: Kantorowicz, *Richard II*, and Fiscal *Trauerspiel*," 67–76; Victoria Kahn, "Political Theology and Fiction in *The King's Two Bodies*," 77–101; and Lorna Hutson, "Imagining Justice: Kantorowicz and Shakespeare," 118–42.

3. See Agamben's comments on Schmitt and Kantorowicz in *Homo Sacer: Sovereign Power and Bare Life*, trans. Daniel Heller-Roazen (Stanford: Stanford University Press, 1998), 91–94.

4. For example, Kahn contrasts Kantorowicz's project with Schmitt's by way of the role of fictionalizing activity in their accounts of political theology: "Unlike Schmitt's 'Catholic political form,' however, Kantorowicz's political form requires a self-conscious act of mythmaking, invoking the deliberate appropriation and manipulation of signs and symbols" (88). Hutson makes a similar point: "Renaissance literary critics focusing on Kantorowicz's use of the word 'mystical' seem not to have noticed how nearly synonymous it is with 'fictional' in the centuries-long intellectual developments that Kantorowicz traces: Aquinas's '*corpus mysticum*' or '*persona mystica*' hardly differed, wrote Kantorowicz, from the *persona ficta* of the jurists. Kantorowicz argues that designations of sacredness are markers of fictiousness and abstraction" (124–25). Kahn and Hutson are largely accurate in their portrayal of the thrust of Kantorowicz's argument; in this context, however, I want to emphasize that in transmuting theology into fiction, Kantorowicz is also partially misrepresenting sources that offer a different theological path toward both critiquing Schmitt and conceptualizing the "mystical." The Aquinas example, in particular, is one to which I will turn in greater detail later in the argument.

5. Henri Cardinal de Lubac S.J., *Corpus Mysticum: The Eucharist and the Church in the Middle Ages*, trans. Gemma Simmonds C.J., with Richard Price and Christopher Stephens, ed. Laurence Paul Hemming and Susan Frank Parsons (Notre Dame, Ind.: University of Notre Dame Press, 2007). In *The King's Two Bodies*, Kantorowicz consistently cites the second French edition of this work: *Corpus Mysticum: L'Eucharistie et l'Église au Moyen Age* (Paris: Aubier, 1949). I will provide page citations for both French and English editions throughout this article.

6. Both M. B. Pranger, "Politics and Finitude: The Temporal Status of Augustine's *Civitas Permixta*," in *Political Theologies: Public Fictions in a Post-Secular World*, ed. Hent de Vries and Lawrence Sullivan (New York: Fordham University Press, 2006), and Regina Schwartz, *Sacramental Poetics: At the Dawn of Secularism* (Stanford: Stanford University Press, 2008), replicate Kantorowicz's use of de Lubac in their own arguments, without assessing the extent to which Kantorowicz is actually accurately representing de Lubac's claims.

7. Kantorowicz, *King's Two Bodies*, 506.

8. Ibid., xviii. This passage of the Preface has been read as a veiled reference to Schmitt by Kahn, "Political Theology and Fiction," 79–80, Halpern, "King's Two Buckets," 67–68, and Agamben, *Homo Sacer*, 91–92.

9. De Lubac, *Corpus Mysticum*, 63; trans., 52.

10. In this section, I draw upon the following accounts for background on de Lubac's life, career, and theology: Hans Urs von Balthasar, *The Theology of Henri de Lubac: An Overview*, trans. Joseph Fessio S.J. and Michael Waldstien (San Francisco: Ignatius Press, 1991); John Milbank, *The Suspended Middle: Henri de Lubac and the Debate Concerning the Supernatural* (Grand Rapids, Mich.: Eerdmans, 2005); Michel de Certeau, *The Mystic Fable*, vol. 1: *The Sixteenth and Seventeenth Centuries*, trans. Michael B. Smith (Chicago: University of Chicago Press, 1992); Lawrence Paul Hemming, "Henri de Lubac: Reading *Corpus Mysticum*," *New Blackfriars* 90.1029 (2009): 519–34.

11. Milbank, *Suspended Middle*, 3.

12. Ibid.

13. Milbank, *Suspended Middle*, 6–14, 33–47, and von Balthasar, *Theology of Henri de Lubac*, 12–19, 63–73, address this controversy and its resolution in greater detail.

14. Hans Boersma, "Sacramental Ontology: Nature and the Supernatural in the Ecclesiology of Henri de Lubac," *New Blackfriars* 88.1015 (2007): 249. See also Boersma's book, *Nouvelle Théologie and Sacramental Ontology: A Return to Mystery* (Oxford: Oxford University Press, 2009).

15. De Lubac, *Corpus Mysticum*, 292–93; trans., 260.

16. Ibid., 62; trans., 51.

17. Ibid., 60; trans., 49.

18. Ibid., 279; trans., 248.

19. Ibid., 280; trans., 249.

20. Ibid., 130; trans., 115.

21. Ibid., 131–32; trans., 116.

22. Ibid., 88; trans., 73–74, my emphasis.

23. Certeau, *Mystic Fable*, 82–85. For the "caesura," see de Lubac, *Corpus Mysticum*, 281–82; trans., 250.

24. Certeau, *Mystic Fable*, 82–85.

25. Ibid,. 84.

26. Ibid., 85.

27. See Hemming's critique in "Henri de Lubac," 524–27.

28. De Lubac is a major inspiration for a largely Anglo-Catholic group of scholars who identify under the label "Radical Orthodoxy" and pursue a project of merging postmodern critiques of secular modernity with a reinterpretation of early church traditions. *Corpus Mysticum*, in particular, appears prominently in several works; see John Milbank, *Being Reconciled: Ontology and Pardon* (London: Routledge, 2003), 122–26, as well as *Suspended Middle*, and Catherine Pickstock, *After Writing: On the Liturgical Consummation of Philosophy* (Oxford: Blackwell, 1998), 121–67. Milbank in particular has more recently entered the wider ongoing interdisciplinary discourse of political theology; see especially the edited collection, *Theology and the Political: The New Debate*, ed. Creston Davis, John Milbank, and Slavoj Žižek (Durham: Duke University Press, 2005).

29. Carl Schmitt, *Roman Catholicism and Political Form*, trans. G. L. Ulmen (Westport, Conn.: Greenwood Press, 1996).

30. See the translator's "Introduction" to *Roman Catholicism* for more details on the relationship between Schmitt's tract and Weber's arguments, ix–xxxvi.

31. Schmitt, *Roman Catholicism*, 3.

32. Ibid., 6–7.

33. Ibid., 7.

34. Ibid., 18–19.

35. Ibid., 25.

36. Ibid., 7.

37. For Sohm's influence on Weber's concept of "charismatic authority," see David Norman Smith, "Faith, Reason, and Charisma: Rudolf Sohm, Max Weber and the Theology of Grace," *Sociological Inquiry* 68.1 (1998): 32–60. Smith argues that Weber actually radically transforms the notion of charisma that he derives from Sohm, ending up with propositions that deeply contradict Sohm's own formulations. However, Wolfgang Fietkau suggests that in Schmitt's view, Weber had indeed replicated some of Sohm's claims about charisma and spiritual authority too closely. See Fietkau's sketch of Schmitt's response to Sohm and Weber in "Loss of Experience and Experience of Loss: Remarks on the Problem of the Lost Revolution in the Work of Benjamin and His Fellow Combatants," *New German Critique* 39 (1986): 169–78.

38. Quoted in Smith, "Faith, Reason, and Charisma," 44. Smith cites a 1904 English translation of vol. 1 of Sohm's *Kirchenrecht*, first published in German in 1892.

39. Schmitt, *Roman Catholicism*, 31–32.

40. Ibid., 18.

41. Ibid., 29.

42. Ibid., 30.

43. Ibid.

44. See Smith's distinction between Weber and Sohm on the issue of "office charisma," "Faith, Reason, and Charisma," 48–51.

45. This point should throw into question the notion that Schmitt presents an authentically "Catholic" vision of representation and authority. Victoria Kahn cites Schmitt's claim that the Catholic Church "represents Christ himself, in person" as symptomatic of a political-theological tendency that will eventually lead Schmitt to embrace Nazi ideology: "Here we see that political theology doesn't simply name the process of secularization for Schmitt; it also refers to a specifically Catholic paradigm, which Schmitt proposes as the solution to the modern political crisis of liberal states. It seems likely that it was precisely this at once 'personalist' and 'institutionalist' notion of sovereignty that inclined Schmitt to support Hitler and the Nazi party in the 1930s, after the failure of the Weimar state" ("Political Theology and Fiction," 83). Kahn moves somewhat too quickly to imply that Schmitt represents the slippery slope that leads from Catholicism to Nazism. It is important to recognize that Schmitt's "personalist" interpretation of the "institution" of Catholicism is inspired, at least in part, by a critical response to the Protestants Sohm and Weber, and that, in making these arguments, Schmitt is effacing other possible interpretations of Catholic tradition.

46. Schmitt, "Visibility of the Church," in *Roman Catholicism*, 52.

47. Ibid.

48. Ibid., 53.

49. *Roman Catholicism*, 26.

50. Ibid., 27.

51. de Lubac, *Corpus Mysticum*, 130; trans. 115.

52. Schmitt, *Political Theology: Four Chapters on the Concept of Sovereignty*, trans. George Schwab (Chicago: University of Chicago Press, 2005), 36.

53. Kantorowicz, *King's Two Bodies*, 285.

54. Halpern, "The King's Two Buckets," 71.

55. Both Kantorowicz and de Lubac acknowledge the influence of a modern revival of the idea of the *corpus mysticum* in the papal encyclical of 1943, *Mystici Corporis*, which affirms the validity of the phrase for describing the communal life of the modern Catholic Church. See Kantorowicz, *King's Two Bodies*, 194 n. 4, and *Corpus Mysticum*, 133; trans., 117. For the text of this encyclical, see http://www.papalencyclicals.net/Pius12/P12MYSTI.HTM. De Lubac discusses the relationship between his account of the *corpus mysticum* and *Mystici Corporis* at greater length in a later work, *The Splendor of the Church*, trans. Michael Mason (San Francisco: Ignatius Press, 1999), esp. chapter 3, 84–125.

56. Kantorowicz, *King's Two Bodies*, 194 n. 4.

57. Ibid., 195–96.

58. Ibid., 197.

59. Ibid., 201.

60. Ibid., 201–2. The sentence cited here is *Summa theologica* III.q.48, a.2, also cited by de Lubac, *Corpus Mysticum* 127 n. 60; trans., 112 n. 60.

61. Ibid., 202.

62. de Lubac, *Corpus Mysticum*, 128; trans., 113: "Nevertheless, we also find [in the Third Part of the *Summa*]: '*the true body of Christ represents the mystical body*,' which takes us back to the origins of the phrase as it is used by Master Simon and the *Treatise of Madrid*."

63. Kantorowicz, *King's Two Bodies*, 202 n. 25, gives Sohm's German: "Aus dem Körper Christi hat sich die Kirche in eine Körperschaft Christi verwandelt," *Das altkatholische Kirchenrecht und das Dekret Gratians* (München; Leipzig: Duncker & Humblot, 1918), 582.

64. Sohm, *Das altkatholische Kirchenrecht*, 582.

65. For a useful précis of Sohm's project in *Das altkatholische Kirchenrecht* and the controversy surrounding it among twentieth-century scholars of canon law, see Bruce Brasington, "Avoiding the 'Tyranny of a Construct': Structural Considerations Concerning Twelfth Century Canon Law," in *Das Eigene und das Ganze: Zum individuellen im mittelalterlichen Religiosentum*, ed. G. Melville and M. Schürer, *Vita Regularis* 16 (Münster, Hamburg, London: LIT Verlag, 2002), 419–38.

66. For de Lubac's defense of the visibility of the church, see *Splendor*, 88. For Sohm's possible influence on the view of the eleventh and twelfth centuries in the work of Yves Congar, a close affiliate of de Lubac's, see Boersma, *Nouvelle Théologie*, 231 n. 225. See also Congar's own essay, "R. Sohm nous interroge encore," *Revue des Sciences philosophiques et théologiques* 57 (1973): 263–94, particularly Congar's critique of Sohm's rejection of the visible church, 280. It is unlikely, however, that de Lubac himself was familiar with Sohm's work at the time of writing *Corpus Mysticum*, as he had insufficient German language ability (*Corpus Mysticum*, "Editor's Preface," x).

67. Kantorowicz, *King's Two Bodies*, 201.

68. Kantorowicz, *Kaiser Friedrich der Zweite* (Berlin, 1927).

69. Ibid., 197.

70. Ibid., 207.

71. Ibid., 209. The pertinent footnote refers the reader back to an earlier note 16, which cites de Lubac on the *corpus figuratum* as the equivalent of the *corpus mysticum.*

72. Ibid, 208.

73. Ibid., 210.

74. de Lubac, *Splendor,* 132.

6

Dead Neighbor Archives:
Jews, Muslims, and the Enemy's Two Bodies

KATHLEEN BIDDICK

1. Messianic Pearls

In the wake of World War I, students of European sovereignty began to ask more urgently what new thinking could unbind politics from sovereignty and its annihilating legacy of internment camps and killing fields. How can the power constitutive of sovereignty—to suspend the law to produce the state of emergency and to name the enemy (who is *not* the neighbor?)—be undone epistemologically?[1] An ongoing search for an antidote has turned contemporary theorists to theology and psychoanalysis as resources for a "cure."[2] A recent reading of the Epistle of Paul to the Romans by the noted theorist, Giorgio Agamben, for example, has inspired him to argue for an unsovereign mode of temporality—messianic time—in which sovereign juridical conditions are transformed such that justice performs without the law, yet, paradoxically without abolishing it.[3] He visualizes messianic time as a pearl inside an oyster. Just as the bivalve secretes its nacre around an irritant, so messianic time contracts around *chronos* (empty chronological time) and brings forth *kairos*, messianic time.[4] Agamben's pearl also exemplifies the centrality of figural thinking to his understanding of messianic time. In messianic figuralism, the type (for example, Adam, or an oyster) and its antitype (Messiah, or a pearl) no longer stand in the "biunivocal" figural relation (Agamben's word) as they once did in the figural exegesis of the Middle Ages; instead, according to him, "the messianic is not one of two terms in the typological relations, it is the relation itself" *and* it is decisive.[5] Students of Carl Schmitt (1888–1985), the brilliant and troubling theorist of sovereignty, will hear in Agamben's rhetorical decisiveness echoes of Schmitt, who famously stated that the sovereign is the one who "decides" on the suspension of the law and the naming of the enemy.[6] Even as Agamben hopes to undo modern sovereignty, formally he participates in what I call typological decision, an act which embodies a historically Christian view of sovereign authority.

Schmitt also claimed that the sovereign exception in jurisprudence is analogous to the miracle in theology.[7] Schmitt was not the first to grasp this political-theological toggle between exception and miracle. Thomas Hobbes, whom Schmitt read closely, astutely observed in his *Leviathan* that one man's miracle is another man's plague, in other words, the toggle can be deadly.[8] It is in this gap between the exception and the miracle that Eric Santner has proposed neighbor-love as an antidote to the sovereign naming of the enemy. In his words, neighbor-love is the "'miraculous' opening of a social link based on the creaturely deposits left by the [sovereign] state of exception that, as Freud indicates, *structurally haunts* the subject in and through the formation of the superego."[9] Santner contends that the past at issue in contemporary theories of messianic time and the miraculous is a traumatic past: "the element of the past that is at issue has the structural status of *trauma*, a past that in some sense never fully took place and so continues to insist in the present precisely as drive destiny, the symptomal torsion of one's being in the world, one's relation to a capacity to use the object-world."[10]

In this essay I want to address something that, from my perspective as a trained medievalist, troubles me in these accounts of messianic and miraculous antidotes to sovereignty. In Agamben's conceptualization, medieval figural thinking is something to be overcome in the messianic; for Santner, who thinks temporality through trauma (sovereignty, he reminds us, is itself a mode of temporality),[11] it could be that the medieval has not yet arrived, and that it always already arrived in the death drive (those implacable forms of repetition compulsion). I am interested in how the messianic and miraculous as conceived by Agamben and Santner seem to contract around each other.[12] What happens, this essay asks, if the messianic and the miraculous are thought in parallax (looking at the same object from two separate vantage points)—does a medieval enemy lodge in the blind-spot of Agamben's messianic; does the despot (the excess of the sovereign) haunt Santner's miracle-making?[13] I answer these questions in the affirmative, showing how the figure of the undead Muslim recurs in the various philosophers and theologians whose arguments support Agamben's and Santner's claims. The undead Muslim as the irritant around which the pearls of messianic time slowly accrete is thus the subject of my study. In what follows, I examine how contemporary messianic thinkers have unconsciously laminated as "dead neighbors" the traumatic irritants productive of the messianic pearl. In order for a messianic pearl to glow miraculously (as Agamben and Santner would wish it to), the new thinking of today needs to engage, I argue, in an act of neighbor-love, whereby it embraces the untimely, undead excarnations of a history of typological damage.[14] Otherwise, I caution, these traumatic dead neighbors remain undead and driven in the drive of critical theories of sovereignty.

2. The Undead Turk

Let me open my archive of indigestible remainders with a brief investigation of what is arguably the most famous modern thesis of messianic time, that is, Walter Benjamin's first thesis in *On the Philosophy of History*, completed in Paris in the winter of 1940 just as the Wehrmacht was breaking through the last line of French defenses. This renowned text reads as follows:

> The story is told of an automaton constructed in such a way that it could play a winning game of chess, answering each move of an opponent with a counter-move. A puppet in Turkish attire and with a hookah in its mouth sat before a chessboard placed on a large table. A system of mirrors created the illusion that this table was transparent from all sides. Actually, a little hunchback who was an expert chess player sat inside and guided the puppet's hand by means of strings. One can imagine a philosophical counterpart to this device. The puppet called "historical materialism" is to win all the time. It can easily be a match for anyone if it enlists the services of theology, which today, as we know, is wizened and has to keep out of sight.[15]

Benjamin's striking image draws upon a famous automaton fabricated in the late eighteenth century.[16] This chess-playing machine, dubbed "the Turk," wended its sensational way through the salons of Vienna, Paris, London, and on to New York. The Turk inspired Benjamin's dialectical image of the relations between historical materialism—philosophy in the guise of a Turkish puppet—and theology—the hunchbacked dwarf hidden in the machine. In a fine illustration (fig. 6.1) of just one of the many efforts made during the eighteenth century to crack the illusionist gimmick of the Turk, the artist, you will observe, exposes the mechanical gears of this automaton as well as the hiding space where, it was speculated, the human agent (imagined by Benjamin as a "buckliger Zwerg," a hunchbacked dwarf) sat and pulled the strings of the puppet, whose gloved hand moved across the chessboard as it played with a contender from the audience.

Benjamin had become acquainted with the Turk through a brilliant essay by Edgar Allen Poe (via its translation by Baudelaire). In 1836 Poe had attended a few performances of the chess-playing machine in Richmond, Virginia. Like many before him, Poe tried to figure out its secret workings. In his

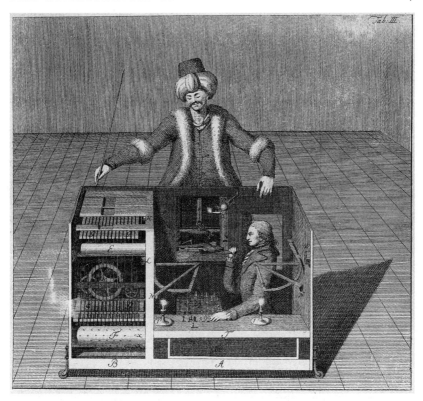

FIGURE 6.1. Joseph Freiherr zu Racknitz, *Über den Schachspieler des Herrn von Kempelen und dessen Nachbildung*, plate 3, *The Turk—small man acting as director of the Turk* (Leipzig und Dresden, 1789). Photograph: The Library Company of Philadelphia.

subsequent publication on the phenomenon, Poe meticulously observed the Turkish puppet, also known popularly as the "oriental sorcerer." Here is an excerpt from his eyewitness description:

> The external appearance and, especially, the deportment of the Turk, are when we consider them as imitations of life, but very indifferent imitations. The countenance evinces no ingenuity, and is surpassed, in its resemblance to the human face, by the very commonest of wax-works. The eyes roll unnaturally in the head, without any corresponding motions of the lids or brows. The arm, particularly, performs its operations in an exceedingly stiff, awkward, jerking, and rectangular manner.

Poe's concise sketch captured what contemporary theorists would term the *undeadness* of the Turkish puppet. Eric Santner, in his two recent studies *On the Psychotheology of Everyday Life* (2001) and *On Creaturely Life* (2006), defines undeadness as follows: "an internal alienness that has a peculiar sort of vitality and yet belongs to no form of life."[17] The undeadness of the chess-playing automaton with its undecidability between what Poe called the "oriental human" and "pure machine" also fascinated Benjamin. He used this undecidability to imagine a transformative temporality, which he called a *Jetzt-Zeit*, a messianic time, in which the undead Turk would be animated and the hunch of the dwarf would be straightened.[18] Historical materialism, Benjamin believed, had the capacity to read a "unique experience with the past" as it flashed in the present.

Benjamin based his concept of the miraculous and messianic *Jetzt-Zeit* on a structure of sign and fulfillment. He hoped that his new philosophy of historical materialism would reconstitute this semiotic structure of the theological miracle. By imagining the dwarf who pulls the Turk's strings specifically as a "hunchbacked dwarf," he further intensified the theological overtones of his dialectical image. Those readers of Benjamin familiar with the Book of Leviticus (21:20), would know that among the list of those blemished chosen people forbidden to make bread offerings to God were included the "crookbacked or dwarf" (according to the King James Bible); the "bucklig oder verkümmert" (according to Martin Luther); and most significantly "ein Buckliger oder ein Zwerg," according to the German translation of the Hebrew text of Leviticus undertaken in the mid-1920s by Martin Buber and Franz Rosenzweig, renowned German-Jewish interlocutors of Benjamin.[19] Students of Leviticus also know that in close proximity to chapter 21 is to be found the famous proof-text of neighbor-love. In Leviticus 19:18–34, God enjoins his chosen people to love their neighbor as themselves. Benjamin's dialectical image of the new thinking of messianic time thus juxtaposes the ghostly visual and acoustical effects of an undead Muslim and the scriptural echoes of a blemished Jew banned by God from ritual acts of sacrifice—but enjoined, nonetheless, to practice neighbor-love.

3. Machines within Machines

For medieval scholars, Benjamin's Turk does not look much different from Christian figural machines eschewed, as we have already seen, by Agamben. In his depiction and discussion of the typological wheel of fortune, Jeffrey Librett has noted that each rotation of the typological gears—from literal, then to figural, and around again to truth—is always reversible and doubled.[20] As the typological wheel turns, the *figura*, the Christian, is always at excarnating risk of becoming Jewish (again), becoming the *littera*, the Jew: "the literal can always come to seem the mere figure of what figures it, which is henceforth rendered literal (or in any case, . . . it can always come to seem the

figure of something else, one knows not what)."[21] What this Christian reading machine radically forecloses is becoming Muslim; such an incarnational
possibility is not even entertained. In order to stop the typological spin that
could render the becoming-Jewish of the Christian, or (even more fearful)
the becoming-Muslim of either Christian or Jew, the Christian typologist has
to decide.

It is just such a typological decision, I argue, that joins medieval typology to the form of sovereignty analyzed by Schmitt. He who decides typology, then, is just like the sovereign, thus typology and sovereignty are
closely bound. With Schmitt's political theology in mind (and Benjamin
knew Schmitt's work), let us take another look at Benjamin's Turk. In his
first thesis, you will recall, Benjamin described how the automaton produced
its illusions through a "system of mirrors" (*ein System von Spiegeln*). Recent
theoretical discussions of Benjamin's notion of *Jetzt-Zeit*, messianic time, especially by Agamben, function, I think, illusionistically, just like the system
of mirrors that had rendered the chess-playing automaton believable to its
viewing public. In their play of illusionary reflections these contemporary
theoretical texts almost manage to vanish the medieval gears of the typological reading machine that are peeking out from Benjamin's image. The
typological relation, as we have seen, is key to Agamben's argument about
messianic time as a cure for sovereignty; he claims, as you will recall, that it
is the typological relation (the relation of *littera* and *figura*) that *suspends* the
sovereign's decision and offers a release, or perhaps an unplugging, from its
undead existence. Agamben further asserts that it is the very typological *relation* itself that transforms temporality from *chronos* (the empty, mechanical
time of typological decision) to *kairos*, messianic time.[22] For Agamben there
can be no reversibility of the *littera* and *figura*; like a sovereign Agamben thus
determines the figurality of messianic time.

4. Mystic Grindings

Agamben is not alone in his figural decisionism, and I want to offer two more
examples of such decisionism drawn from contemporary commentary on
messianic time and miracles. In my first example, a stony piece of medieval
sculpture crops up as an indigestible remainder of messianic thinking. Like
pebbles in a shoe, this carving irritates Jacob Taubes's study, *The Political
Theology of Paul*. Taubes, a professor of Jewish Studies and Hermeneutics
at the Free University of Berlin and an interlocutor of Carl Schmitt, gave
the lectures upon which this book is based in 1987 at Heidelberg, just a few
days before his death from cancer. The frontispiece to the English translation

FIGURE 6.2. Capital: The Mystic Mill (twelfth century). Vézelay Basilica, France. Photograph: Sacred Destinations Images.

features a photograph of one of the famous nave capitals of the Romanesque church at Vézelay, Burgundy (fig. 6.2). The iconography of the carving renders the typological theme of the Mystic Mill. Moses (the *littera*, or type, of Paul) pours grain into the chute of a mill. As its gears grind, Paul, apostle and *figura*, stooped in the corner of the capital, catches the refined flour in a sack. The sculpture, which dates to the third decade of the twelfth century, was carved at a time when Vézelay was a contested node in the monastic network of the abbey of Cluny, arguably the greatest abbey of Western Christendom. Cluny and the popes who reigned over Christendom in the late eleventh and twelfth centuries were closely bound. Less than a generation before the

Vézelay carving, the Cluniac Pope, Urban II, had traveled to Burgundy to call the First Christian Crusade, in 1095. In 1144, Bernard of Clairveaux stood on the church steps at Vézelay to preach the Second Christian Crusade against Muslims.[23]

Why is this particular photograph of a medieval sculpture from the church at Vézelay set as the frontispiece to Taubes's amazing midrashic reading of Paul and of the political theology of Carl Schmitt, with whom Taubes actually met in 1978 to discuss Paul? It should be noted that the same picture of this Vézelay capital had also appeared on the 1969 cover of an influential study of Paul the Apostle by the Gunther Bornkamm, the Heidelberg New Testament scholar. At the moment in his lecture in which Taubes reflected chapter 9, verse 13, of Paul's Epistle to the Romans ("As it was written, Jacob have I loved but not Esau"), he produced the photograph of the Vézelay sculpture for his audience and informed them that he received this copy of the "marvelous picture" from his friend, Jan Assmann (Egyptologist extraordinaire and scholar of religious studies). Taubes went on to say that he treasured the picture and carried it around in his bag, because "with the naïveté of the medieval stonemason, it says everything for those who know how to read."[24] Digressing, Taubes then linked the sculpture at Vézelay with a famous contemporaneous commentary by Suger, abbot (1122–51) of Saint-Denis, Paris. To expound on the grand architectural refurbishments of his abbey, Suger wrote an account with the rather bureaucratic title, "What Was Done Under His Administration" (*de rebus in administratione sua gestis*), the purpose of which was to itemize the considerable costs incurred by the building program. Folded into Suger's laundry list of expenditures can be found a theological gloss to the typological themes represented in a complex sequence of stained-glass roundels designed for the ambulatory of St.-Denis. Here is the text that Taubes extracted from Suger's typological commentary on the Mystic Mill and recited at his seminar:

> One of these [roundels], urging us onward from the material to the immaterial, represents the Apostle Paul turning a mill, and the Prophets carrying sacks to the mill. The verses of this subject are these:
>
> > By working the mill, thou, Paul, takest the flour out of the bran.
> > Thou makest known the inmost meaning of the Law of Moses.
> > From so many grains is made the true bread without bran,
> > Our and angels' perpetual food.[25]

This short poem epitomizes the medieval Christian typological relation. Paul fulfills Moses, and the grain that will baked into the sacred wafer of the Eucharist fulfills the Mosaic Law (from command to comestible).[26] After attentively describing the sculpture of the Mystic Mill and its typological relations, Taubes decisively concluded his ruminations with a vehement disavowal of medieval typology: "Of course, this is not *my* Paul [original emphasis]. . . What I have to say about Moses and Paul is naturally something else."[27] With this emphatic assertion, I argue, Taubes decides on typological decisionism. He seems to be saying, "I know that this medieval Christian typology of Paul is a stony, indigestible exegetical fragment (an always doubled and reversible relation), but I, Jacob Taubes, decide on the meaning of Paul." Put another way, Taubes offers his reader an example of the indigestible remainder of medieval Christian typology. Taubes encounters this indigestible remainder in the form of a chunk of sculpted stone and then decides it away, thus repeating by foreclosure, as I shall unfold for you shortly, the excarnating Christian battle over the semiotics of miracle-making inscribed in the Vézelay capital.

Before turning to an analysis of the medieval crusade about meaning-making, especially meaning-making and miracles, I want to offer the promised second example of typological decisionism at work in the contemporary understanding of political theology. This example moves us from a medieval stone to the accusation of "getting medieval" through magic that surfaced in the treatise, *The Star of Redemption* (1920), by the German-Jewish philosopher, Franz Rosenzweig.[28] In the *Star*, Rosenzweig, like his interlocutor Benjamin, also explicated his vision of a new philosophy capable of reconstituting the miracle in modernity. He argued that the semiotic structure of prefiguration and fulfillment was necessary for miracle-making and further asserted that, because the Quran lacked such a semiotic structure, Islam was incapable of miracle-making. His appraisal of Islam, not atypical of scholarship in the 1920s, has, nevertheless, broad implications.[29] Medievalists will recognize that Rosenzweig repeats almost verbatim the terms of the twelfth century Christian polemic against Islam. That polemic, which justified the declaration of Muslims as the enemy (*hostes*) of Christendom, excluded Islam from the semiotics of miracle-making. Put another way, this polemic foreclosed Muslims from the symbolic order. Muslim bodies thus became the site where incarnation could not occur and thus became the site of excarnation.[30] Moreover, to designate Muslim magic and sorcery, Cluniac monks used the word *mechanicum*.[31]

These examples drawn from Taubes and Rosenzweig persuade me that the undeadness of Christian typological decisionism has insinuated itself into the heart of contemporary political theology and its theories of the philosophical and psychoanalytic miracles—the purported "cure" of messianic time. Taubes and Rosenzweig repeat a traumatic medieval battle over semiotics in which an imperializing Christendom excarnated Jews and Muslims as neighbors and declared them political enemies (*hostes*). If an aim of contemporary theory is to release the undeadness of sovereignty, then it is necessary, I argue, to lay bare the gears that drive its traumatic, theoretical core.

5. Christian Miracles and the Mechanics of Foreclosure

Let me recap briefly the kind of excarnational fantasies impelling medieval polemics at Cluny—the same kinds of fantasies that have crept unconsciously into contemporary theories of messianic time.[32] Such polemics are well known to medieval scholars, so I shall only offer a brief sketch here. Peter the Venerable, abbot of Cluny (1122–60), launched the semiotic crusade against Jews and Muslims in two treatises written in the 1140s: "Against the Jews and their inveterate obdurancy" and "Against the Saracens [Islam] as a sect and heresy."[33] A noteworthy aspect of these polemics was his pioneering use of translated excerpts from the Talmud to argue against Jews and his citations from his commissioned Latin translation of the Quran to attack Muslims (known as Saracens according to popular twelfth-century Christian nomenclature). He intertwined these polemics with Cluniac theories of the Eucharist as the "always and ever" incarnating miracle and also as an "always and ever" incarnating institution.[34] The Eucharistic miracle, as Peter the Venerable theorized, provided the philosophical grounds for foreclosing Jews and Muslims from semiosis and rendering them excarnated bodies.

This is how Peter's argument about semiosis works. He argued that it was only through "signs" (*signa*) that Christianity converted the world, and the world for Peter meant the *nomos* of the earth, *oceans included*.[35] Peter launched his attack from what he called a "congruent place" where his church (Cluny) and the church as a whole (*corpus verum*) conjoined or hinged at the altar of sacrifice, where the monk-priests of Cluny consecrated the bread and wine of the Eucharist. The altars of Cluny served as a sacrificial machine for Christendom (for example, when a professed Cluniac monk died, the monastery would commemorate him with the consecration of thirty hosts per day for a one-month period, which amounted to nine hundred Masses).[36] Peter understood the Eucharist semiotically. He conceived of the Eucharist as an exclusive sign (*signum incommunicatum*) and a perpetual miracle (*miracula*) once and always (*semel et semper*), as he designated the temporality of the miracle in Latin.[37] As the sign of typological truth, the Eucharist once and always fulfilled the Hebrew Scriptures. By implication the perpetual miracle of the Eucharist, as conceived by Peter, foreclosed the typological relation between Jews and Christians by deciding it once and always, since the sacrifice never ceased. Typology thus becomes a perpetual form of Christian sovereignty. By virtue of their power over signs (the Eucharist being the exclusive sign), Christians ruled the world: "because the Christian of the world is not converted to Christ without boundless signs." (*quod Christianus orbis absque signis immensis ad Christum conversus non est*).[38]

Peter acknowledged that there had been miracles in the Hebrew dispensation—those performed by Moses in front of Pharaoh being examples—but these miracles were weak and superseded by the miraculous *signa* of Christ and the ongoing miracle-workings of his apostles and his Christian disciples through time, even down to the monk-priests of Cluny. As for Islam, Peter vociferously denied its access to miracles. According to Peter's concept of miraculous semiosis, Mohammed could be neither a miracle-worker nor a prophet. Peter drew a sharp distinction between Muslim fabulation and *mechanicum* (the arts of sorcery and magic) and the true miracle modeled on the transformation of substance in the Eucharist.[39] Islam, in Peter's eyes. could only triumph by virtue of armed force and seduction.

Peter the Venerable's targeting of Jews and Muslims as enemies of medieval Christendom in his two polemics was nothing less than a semiological declaration of war. The Eucharist was the perfected, perpetual sign through which Christendom ruled land and sea. With the Eucharist, typological relations between the Hebrew Scriptures and the Christian New Testament were miraculously fulfilled once and always, foreclosing any possibility of an ongoing Jewish semiosis, or miracle-making. Islam was utterly bereft of semiotic capacity—its Quran, according to Peter, being only the confabulation of the Talmud and early heretical Christian writings. The Cluniacs, or *Ecclesia Cluniacensis*, under the leadership of Peter the Venerable, fabricated the institutional materiality of the Eucharist in their great Romanesque building programs (the church at Vézelay being an example). They sought to globalize the sign of "the republic of the Christian Church" and conflated the stone of the church altar, the *fabrica* of the Eucharist, with the church as a corporate institution, thus materializing sacred space as a new category. Peter worked to expel Islam from the semiotic *and* geographical space he fabricated and he effectively disincarnated Muslims as dead neighbors, the indigestible remainder of his political theology.

For Peter the Venerable, the perpetual miracle of Eucharistic decision and the monstrosity of undeadness (Islam) are conjoined. We can detect this joining at work in a famous Cluniac sculptural artifact, the main portal to the church of St. Lazare in Autun (fig. 6.3). The tympanum featured a novel example of Christ throned in majesty. The following sovereign inscription

FIGURE 6.3. Tympanum: Punishments of the Damned (twelfth century). Autun Cathedral, France. Photograph: Sacred Destinations Images.

is chiseled on the border of the mandorla: "I alone dispose of all things and crown the just, those who follow crime I judge and punish."[40] In the right-hand corner of the central register of the tympanum, the leviathan rears up from the portals of hell. The sovereign miracle and the pestilential and monstrous are thus closely bound on the tympanum at Autun.

I want to jump from this medieval leviathan to its early-modern neighbor, the Leviathan depicted by Thomas Hobbes in the famous engraved frontispiece (fig. 6.4) of *Leviathan* (1660), which can be productively read as a version of a Romanesque portal or threshold to his treatise. We know that Hobbes based his startling depiction of a composite, artificial, sovereign body, the Leviathan, on an optical device he most likely viewed during his stay in Paris in the late 1640s. The Franciscan polymath, François Niceron, had perfected an anamorphic optical device at that time. To entertain and instruct his audiences, Niceron used fifteen images of Ottoman sultans as the segments of representation that he resolved into the face of Louis XIII (fig. 6.5). Niceron manipulated the heads of the sultans anamorphically to resolve into the singular portrait of Louis XIII.[41] Inscribed then in Hobbes's frontispiece is a paradoxical miracle that produces the Western sovereign through the mechanically manipulated images of Muslim "despots"—the despot being a Western fantasy of an excarnated Muslim sovereign.[42]

FIGURE 6.4. Title page from Thomas Hobbes's *Leviathan, or the Matter, Forme & Power of a Common-wealth, eccesiasticall and civill* (1651). The British Library, London. Photograph: HIP / Art Resource, New York.

FIGURE 6.5. Anamorphic figure of Ottoman sultans coalescing into bust of Louis XIII. From Jean-François Niceron's *La Perspective curieuse*, plate 69 (1638). Photograph: Bibliothèque nationale de France.

6. In the Time That Remains

Just as Jacob Taubes produced the traumatic kernel of messianic time in the form of the Romanesque capital from Vézelay, his lectures gathered in *The Political Theology of Paul* also, paradoxically, provide an opening onto ways of disassociating from this typological undeadness. In his introductory remarks made at Heidelberg, Taubes mentioned his teacher, Gershom Scholem, and Scholem's famous study of Sabbatai Sevi (1626–76), the self-proclaimed

Jewish Messiah who converted to Islam and ended up residing at the Sultan's court in Constantinople. Taubes dramatically asks his audience, "Are we obliged to descend with him [Sabbatai Sevi] into this world of the abyss, Islam?"[43]

Let us pause at this question. In his recent and provocative study entitled *The Jew, The Arab: A History of the Enemy*, Gil Anidjar tries to answer Taubes's query. Anidjar urges scholars to think how the "consistent evacuation of the significance of the theological ('a force without significance' in Scholem's own phrase) repeats the evacuation of the Muslim from the Jews in the double figure of the Messiah—the Messiah and the Muslims, the Messiah and the Musselman—and that it remains, indeed, in force."[44] According to Anidjar's critique, theories of messianic time, as currently understood and argued, especially by Giorgio Agamben, universalize the indigestible remainder of Christian typology as the dead Muslim neighbor, as the Mussulmen of the Nazi camps which Agamben sees as the sovereign's final decision.

I promised at the opening of this essay that I would try to conjure a threshold in the contemporary theory of political theology through which the untimely and undead could pass. I have been arguing that in order for there to be a relation between philosophy and theology that is not a murderous typological one, we need to traverse the symbolic process whereby Christian typology excarnated both Jews and Muslims. The monastic fantasy of the signifier that seized Peter the Venerable, which foreclosed semiosis to Islam, assigning it to a mechanical world of gears, and superseded semiosis for Jews, remains in force, I claim, in Benjamin's first thesis on the concept of history. Indeed, I further contend that it is the Christian fantasy of the force and seduction of Islam and the supersession of Judaism that gives political theology today its incarnational consistency. Is it time for contemporary political theology to descend into its own abyss haunted by the dead neighbors that its typological machine has ground out? By rendering this machine inoperative, we can begin to ask what the untimely of typological time might look like.

Notes

1. The prominent German legal scholar of sovereignty, Carl Schmitt, famously argued for these two criteria of the sovereign in his diptych of works: *Political Theology: Four Chapters on the Concept of Sovereignty*, trans. of *Politisches Theologie* (1922) by George Schwab (Chicago: University of Chicago Press, 1985), and *The Concept of the Political*, trans. of *Der Begriff des Politischen* by George Schwab (Chicago: University of Chicago Press, 1996). For discussion of the murderous effects of sovereignty, see Giorgio Agamben, *Remnants of Auschwitz: The Witness and the Archive*, trans. Daniel Heller-Roazen (New York: Zone Books, 1999) and his *State of Exception*, trans. Kevin Attell (Chicago: University of Chicago Press, 2005). For the epistemological

stakes in separating out European sovereignty from slavery, see Kathleen Davis, *Periodization and Sovereignty: How Ideas of Feudalism and Secularization Govern the Politics of Time* (Philadelphia: University of Pennsylvania Press, 2008). For thoughts on this important work see my review, http://hdl.handle.net/2027/spo.baj9928.0904/006/ (accessed 08/15/2009).

My thanks to Jonathan Gil Harris and Julia Reinhard Lupton for our tender and lively exchange over early versions of this paper at our MLA session (December 2009, San Francisco). The engagement of my fellow colleagues at the Leslie White Humanities Institute (Spring 2009) on *States of Exception* was invaluable to me in further formulating my argument—special thanks to Eric Santner, Don Pease, Klaus Mladek, and George Edmondson. And to other generous interlocutors: Graham Hammill and Nichole Miller.

2. Recent discussions of sovereignty and messianic time include Alain Badiou, *Saint Paul: The Foundation of Universalism*, trans. Ray Brassier (Stanford: Stanford University Press, 2003); Jacob Taubes, *The Political Theology of Paul*, trans. Dana Hollander (Stanford: Stanford University Press, 2004); Giorgio Agamben, *The Time that Remains: A Commentary on the Letter to the Romans*, trans. Patricia Dailey (Stanford: Stanford University Press, 2005); Kenneth Reinhard, Eric L. Santner, and Slavoj Žižek, *The Neighbor: Three Inquiries in Political Theology* (Chicago: University of Chicago Press, 2005); Eleanor Kaufman, "The Saturday of Messianic Time (Agamben and Badiou on the Apostle Paul)," *South Atlantic Quarterly* 107 (2008): 37–54. For the traumatic temporality of sovereignty, see Davis, *Periodization and Sovereignty*. The potential of neighbor love as a way of undeadening sovereignty is explored in *The Neighbor* and in Eric L. Santner, *On the Psychotheology of Everyday Life: Reflections on Freud and Rosenzweig* (Chicago: University of Chicago Press, 2001), and his *On Creaturely Life: Rilke, Benjamin, Sebald* (Chicago: University of Chicago Press, 2006), hereafter *On Creaturely Life*.

3. Agamben, *Time that Remains*, passim, especially, 98, 107.

4. Ibid., 68–69.

5. Ibid., 69, 74. For the temporal implications of medieval typological figuralism, see my study, *The Typological Imaginary: Circumcision, Technology, History* (Philadelphia: University of Pennsylvania Press, 2003).

6. Schmitt, *Political Theology*, 1; *Concept of the Political*, 26. Please note that in this essay I do not intend to deal with Schmitt's typology of the enemy in his *Theorie des Partisanen* (Berlin: Dunckat and Humblot, 1963), translated by G. L. Ulmen, *Theory of the Partisan* (New York: Telos Press, 2007).

7. Schmitt, *Political Theology*, 36.

8. On Thomas Hobbes's seeing that one man's miracle is another man's plague, see his *Leviathan*, ed. G. A. J. Rogers and Karl Schuhmann (Bristol, England: Thoemmes Continuum, 2003), 344–51; for instance, regarding Moses and Pharaoh, Hobbes writes: "And when he [Pharaoh] let them goe at last, not the Miracles persuaded him, but the plagues forced him to do it" (347). Hobbes discusses the sovereign "decision" of the miracle on 350–51.

9. Santner, *On Creaturely Life*, 75.

10. Santner, *The Neighbor*, 126.

11. Santner insightfully observes that sovereignty is a mode of temporalization, but somehow, I think, he fails to work through the implications: Santer, *Psychotheology*, 60–61; Santner, *On Creaturely Life*, 66–67.

12. In so doing it joins with the project of Davis, *Periodization and Sovereignty*.

13. For the fantastical over-proximity of notions of the despot and the sovereign forged in the Enlightenment, see Alain Grosrichard, *The Sultan's Court: European Fantasies of the East*, trans. Liz Heron (New York: Verso, 1998). The psychoanalytic discourse of neighbor-love,

routed through the concept of the Thing ("excessive presence and radical absence") echoes the discourse of the despot in uncanny ways (see note 2 for references).

14. I take this notion of the indigestible remainder from Santner, *Psychotheology*, 29. He discusses the indigestible remainder as a hard kernel that can be "neither naturalized nor historicized."

15. Walter Benjamin, "Theses on the Philosophy of History," in *Illuminations*, ed. Hannah Arendt (New York: Schocken, 1968), 253–64, at 253.

16. For Benjamin's links to the essay by Edgar Allen Poe, see Joshua Robert Gold, "The Dwarf in the Machine: A Theological Figure and its Sources," *MLN* 121 (2006): 1220–36. The essay by Edgar Allen Poe, "Maelzel's Chess Player," *Saturday Literary Messenger*, April 1836, 318–26, is available at http://www.eapoe.org/works/ESSAYS/MAELZEL.HTM (accessed April 27, 2009). For general information about this eighteenth-century automaton, see Tom Standage, *The Turk: The Life and Times of the Famous Eighteenth Century Chess-Playing Machine* (New York: Walker and Company, 2002).

17. Santner, *Psychotheology*, 36.

18. For an interesting exploration of Benjamin's *Jetzt-Zeit*, see Cesare Casarino, "Time Matters: Marx, Negri, Agamben, and the Corporeal," *Strategies* 16 (2003): 185–206.

19. Martin Buber and Franz Rosenzweig, *Die Schrift* (Berlin: Verlag Lambert Schneider, 1934), 3:91.

20. Jeffrey S. Librett, *The Rhetoric of Cultural Dialogue: Jews and Germans from Moses Mendelssohn to Richard Wagner and Beyond* (Stanford: Stanford University Press, 2000); his typological wheel of fortune depicted in fig. 3 is found on 21.

21. Librett, *Rhetoric*, 13.

22. Agamben, *Time that Remains*, 74.

23. The typological rhetoric of such sculptural programs has been elucidated by Rachel Dressler in her study of the West Façade of Chartres Cathedral, a sculptural ensemble contemporaneous with Vézelay. See Rachel Dressler "*Deus Hoc Vult*: Ideology, Identity, and Sculptural Rhetoric at the Time of the Crusades," *Medieval Encounters* 1 (1995): 188–218. Dressler observes and annotates how "typological thinking was deeply ingrained in medieval Christianity and led to the use of an Old Testament paradigm as part of recruiting and victory rhetoric during the First Crusade" (195).

24. Taubes, *Political Theology*, 38–39.

25. Taubes is citing from the translation by Erwin Panofsky, *Abbot Suger on the Abbey Church of St.-Denis and its Art Treasures* (Princeton: Princeton University Press, 1946), 74–75. The original text in Latin reads: "Tollis agendo molam de furfure, Paule, farinam. Mosaicae legis intima nota facis. Fit de tot granis verus sine furfure panis, Perpetuusque cibus noster et angelicus." For background on Vézelay, see Kirk Ambrose, *The Nave Sculpture of Vézelay: The Art of Monastic Viewing* (Toronto: Pontifical Institute for Medieval Studies, 2006) and Kevin D. Murphy, *Memory and Modernity: Viollet-le-Duc at Vézelay* (University Park: Pennsylvania State University Press, 2000).

26. The "truth" of such fulfillment exploded on the sculpted tympanum of the main entry to the church at Vézelay, which grandiosely depicted the theme of Christ commissioning the Apostles to world mission. On the lintel of this tympanum all the Pliny-like monsters, those one-eyed, elephant-eared creatures inhabiting the edge of the world, march inexorably toward Christian conversion. The literature on this innovative portal is voluminous; it is best to start with the critical commentary by Dominique Iogna-Prat, *Order and Exclusion: Cluny and Chris-*

tendom Face Heresy, Judaism, and Islam (1000–1150), trans. Graham Robert Edwards (Ithaca: Cornell University Press, 2002), 267–74.

27. Taubes, *Political Theology of Paul*, 39.

28. Franz Rosenzweig, *The Star of Redemption*, trans. Barbara E. Galli (Madison: University of Wisconsin Press, 2005), 127–29. For the question of Islam in Rosenzweig, see Gesine Palmer, ed., '*Innerlich bleibt die Welt eine': Ausgewählte Texte von Franz Rosenzweig über den Islam* (Bodenheim: Philo Verlag, 2002) and, more broadly, the brilliant essay by Suzanne Marchand, "Nazism, 'Orientalism,' and Humanism," in *Nazi Germany and the Humanities*, ed. Wolfgang Bialas and Anson Rabinbach (Oxford: Oneworld Publications, 2007), 267–305. In his essay, "Miracles Happen: Benjamin, Rosenzweig, Freud, and the Matter of the Neighbor," in *The Neighbor*, 83 n. 12, Eric Santner notes that Rosenzweig excluded Islam from the semiotic structure of the miracle based on prefiguration and fulfillment (the typological relation).

29. Gil Anidjar offers a different reading of Franz Rosenzweig in his *The Jew, The Arab: A History of the Enemy* (Stanford: Stanford University Press, 2003), 87–98. For an important meditation relevant to this argument, see the recent essay by Anne Norton, "Call me Ishmael," in *Derrida and the Time of the Political*, ed. Pheng Cheah and Suzanne Guerlac (Raleigh: Duke University Press, 2009), 158–76.

30. Walter Benjamin, a reader of Rosenzweig, echoes him in thesis sixteen of *On the Philosophy of History*. There Benjamin separated a redemptive philosophy (historical materialism) from the undeadness of the mechanical world (semiosis from mechanics): "This historical materialist leaves it to others to be drained by the whore called 'Once upon a time' in historicism's bordello. He remains in control of his powers, man enough to blast open the continuum of history" (Benjamin, "Theses," 262).

31. See Iogna-Prat, *Order and Exclusion* (107–8), for a compelling discussion of the use of the Latin word *mechanicum* to designate a sorcerer and the scribal slippage that at times rendered this word as "manicheum" (after the heresy); also Ellie Truitt, "Trei poete, sages dotors, qui mout sorent di nigromance: Knowledge and Automata in twelfth-century French literature," *Configurations* 12 (2004): 167–93.

32. Around the time of the Second Crusade (1144), Peter the Venerable took up "the sword of the divine word" (in a kind of semiological Star Wars) to slay the enemies of Christendom, Jews and Muslims. As his secretary famously put it in a letter to Peter: "You are the only one of our generation, who, with the sword of Divine words, slaughtered the three greatest enemies of holy Christianity, the Jews, the Heretics, and the Saracens, in order to humble the satanic pride and arrogance which rise up against the greatness of God Peter of Poitiers" (*Epistola*, ed. Reinhold Glei, in *Petrus Venerabilis Schriften zum Islam*, Corpus Islamico-Christianum, series Latina [Altenberg, 1985], 1:228): The original Latin reads: "Solus enim vos estis nostris temporibus, qui tres maximos sanctae Christianitas hostes, Iudaeos dico et haereticos ac Saracenos, divini verbi gladio trucidastis et humiliare omnem arrogantiam et superbiamdiaboli extollentem se adversus altitudem dei." Other treatises by Peter the Venerable cited in this essay include *Adversus Iudeorum inveteratam duritiem*, ed. Yvonne Friedmann, Corpus Christianorum, Continuatio Medievalis 58 (Brepols, 1985), hereafter cited as *AJ*; Peter the Venerable, *Contra sectam Sarracenorum*, ed. Reinhold Kritzeck, and *Peter the Venerable and Islam* (Princeton: Princeton University Press, 1964). For helpful background on Peter the Venerable and Islam see John V. Tolan, *Saracens: Islam in the Medieval European Imagination* (New York: Columbia University Press, 2002), and Kenneth M. Setton, "Western Hostility to Islam and Prophecies of Turkish Doom," *Memoirs of the American Philosophical Society* 201 (Philadelphia: American Philosophical Society, 1992).

33. R. I. Moore briefly reflects on some of the problems of analyzing the pincer-like movement of Christendom's naming the enemy's two bodies (Jews in Europe and Islam in the West) in the second edition of his famous study, *The Formation of a Persecuting Society: Power and Deviance in Western Europe, 950–1250* (New York: Blackwell, 1987; 2d ed., 2007). The first edition, which appeared in 1987, did not mention Muslims as the targets of a persecuting imaginary and the reflections in the 2007 edition do not really grapple with the stakes of omission.

34. David Bates, "Political Theology and the Nazi State: Carl Schmitt's Concept of the Institution," *Modern Intellectual History* 3 (2006): 415–22.

35. Cited in Iogna-Prat, *Order and Exclusion*, 299. Also, Carl Schmitt, *The Nomos of the Earth in the International Law of the Jus Publicum Europaeum*, trans. G. L. Ulmen (New York: Telos Press, 2003). I am arguing against Schmitt's ahistorical thesis of the ocean as the "free space," free of Christendom; see his chapter 1, "The First Global Lines," 86–100. The citation is from *AJ*, lines 1466–73: "Totum vero orbem dixi, quia licet gentiles vel Sarraceni super aliquas eius partes dominatum exerceant, licet Iudei inter Christianos et ethnicos lateant, non est tamen aliqua vel modica pars terrae, non Tyrreni maris nec ipsius oceani remotissime insulae, quae vel domininantibus vel subiectis Christianis non incolantur, ut verum esse appareat quod scriptura de Christo ait: Dominiabitur a mari usque ad mare et flumine usque ad terminus orbis terrae."

36. Iogna-Prat, *Order and Exclusion*, 236.

37. This discussion is inspired by *Order and Exclusion*, 182–218. Iogna Prat observes that Peter the Venerable's "sociology of Christendom was in the first instance a semiology" (257).

38. *AJ*, 4, 1541ff.

39. *AJ*, 4, 1360–1954.

40. The Latin text of the inscription reads: "Omnia dispono solus meritos corono quos scelus exercet me judice poena coercet." For detailed photographs and mapping of the sculptural program of the tympanum, see Denis Grivot and George Zarnecki, *Giselbertus Sculptor of Autun* (New York: Orion Press, 1961). For basic bibliography and debates over interpretation, see Linda Seidel, *Legends in Limestone: Lazarus, Gislebertus and the Cathedral at Autun* (Chicago: University of Chicago Press, 1999).

41. For a detailed study of optical devices known by Hobbes and their influence on the design of his frontispiece, see the following review essay: "The Title Page of *Leviathan*, seen in Curious Perspective," in Noel Malcolm, *Aspects of Hobbes* (Oxford: Clarendon Press, 2002), 200–33. The engraving of the "Ottoman sultans" can be found on table 49 of J.-F. Niceron's *La Perspective curieuse* (1638) and is illustrated in Malcolm, fig. 4.

42. For the disincarnating Western discourse of the despot, see Grosrichard, *The Sultan's Court*; Guy Le Thiec, "L'Empire ottoman, modèle de monarchie seigneuriale dans l'œuvre de Jean Bodin," in *L'Oeuvre de Jean Bodin: Actes du colloque tenu à Lyon à l'occasion du quatrième centenaire de sa mort*, ed. Gabriel-André Pérouse, Nicole Dockés-Lallement, and Jean-Michel Servet (Paris: Honoré Champion Éditeur, 2004), 55–76; Lucette Valensi, *The Birth of the Despot: Venice and the Sublime Port*, trans. Arthur Denner (Ithaca: Cornell University Press, 1993); Barbara Fuchs, *Mimesis and Empire: The New World, Islam, and European Identities* (Cambridge: Cambridge University Press, 2001).

43. Taubes, *Political Theology*, 9.

44. Anidjar, *The Jew, the Arab*, 161.

7

Novus Ordo Saeclorum:
Hannah Arendt on Revolutionary Spirit

PAUL A. KOTTMAN

It may ultimately turn out that what we call revolution is precisely that transitory phase
which brings about the birth of a new, secular realm.

HANNAH ARENDT, *On Revolution*

Towards the end of his life, Thomas Jefferson began to discuss with John
Adams the possibility of an afterlife. Their exchange turned not on the unan-
swerable question of whether there really is a next world, but more fancifully
on the most appropriate image for an ideal hereafter.

"Obviously, such images . . . if we strip them of their religious connotation," comments Hannah Arendt, "present nothing more nor less than various ideals of human happiness."[1] So, what was, for Jefferson, the ideal form
of human happiness? Was it "the lap and love of . . . family"? Or, "the society
of . . . neighbors and . . . books"? Or, "the wholesome occupation of [one's]
farms . . . and affairs"?[2] These private pursuits of happiness undoubtedly hold
their appeal for Jefferson; nevertheless, his "true notion of happiness comes
out very clearly" when he concludes his letter to Adams with the words:

> May we meet there again, in Congress, with our ancient Colleagues, and
> receive with them the seal of approbation 'Well done, good and faithful
> servants.'[3]

Academics nowadays might find the vision of bureaucratic meetings and debates in the hereafter less than heavenly; but Arendt has no doubts. "Here,"
she writes, "we have the candid admission that life in Congress, the joys of
discourse, of legislation, of transacting business, of persuading and being persuaded, were to Jefferson no less conclusively a foretaste of eternal bliss to come
than the delights of contemplation had been for medieval piety" (*OR* 131).[4]

In at least two respects, Jefferson's letter to Adams provides an appropriate opening for what I have to say in the following pages. First, his remarks
contain an implicit reconciliation of the act of political founding or constitution, on the one hand, and the experience of freedom as "happiness" on

the other. His words describe the happiness of public freedom not only as something that politics makes possible by instituting or expanding civil liberties but as an experience intrinsic to the political activity of founding and re-founding.[5]

Second, Jefferson's description of the happiness of politics as a kind of heaven on earth, in which the words and deeds of the living can reverberate those of the "ancients," sheds light on what I take to be Arendt's basic thesis in *On Revolution*. Namely, that politics lies in a generative tension between freedom and founding that is rooted in a *historical experience* of "revolutionary spirit" perhaps capable of authoritatively binding the living and the dead in a fully secular fashion.[6]

Theology's recent return in sociological and political analysis has led some to point to an emergent crisis in secular politics.

In part, at issue is the incompatibility of faith and reason as such—where by 'faith' we mean not cherished pieties (celebrating religious holidays, for example) or harmless beliefs ("Oh, I missed my train! No matter, God will send another along shortly") but rather faith in its demanding austerity ("I will step blindly off the platform onto the tracks; God will provide"). Because austere faith raises the doubt of reason to the highest pitch, it is this faith—this evil demon, this radical doubt—that self-sufficient reason must overcome. The contours of this split and its framing of secular rationality in modernity are well known and widely discussed.

However, theology's recent return in sociological and political analysis has also been interpreted as a faltering of the notion that humanity's progress necessarily leads to an enlightened modernity rooted in the expansion of atheism, humanism, and secular reason. To a large extent, in other words, what is falling into disrepute is this conflation of secularism with a meta-historical progress—something like a 'forward march of secularism,' say, or the notion that secular politics succeeds only where socio-historical developments can be seen as the relentless advancement of that very success.

But because secular politics need not implicate any 'forward historical progress'—and has nothing to do with "being on the right side of history" (as Bill Clinton likes to say)—it is probably a good thing that this conflation of secularism and progress is on the wane. By the same token, in light of a renewed interest in secular responses to theistic or faith-based politics, we would do well to remember how secular politics itself has been understood *not* to be tied to its own forward march but rather to be rooted *in the experience of past failures to found a fully secular polity.*

On this point Hannah Arendt's *On Revolution* furnishes a crucial rejoinder to those who confuse secularism's political fate with the fate of its progressive, forward trajectory in late modernity. Moreover, because Arendt sees modernity and revolutionary-secular politics as coextensive, she invites us to understand the modern age not as a forward-looking march, but as an era whose politics call for deeper retrospection on lived, historical experience. It is in this light, rather than in light of the incompatibility of faith and reason mentioned above, that she sees the modern revolutionary tradition as incompatible with a theistic politics—incompatible, that is, with any transcendent, absolute, or extrapolitical source of political authority outside human history and experience.

As I will argue in this essay, the revolutionary tradition to which Arendt draws attention—and the secular politics it implies and defends—understands political freedom as founded anew only in the *retrospective* light of past, failed revolutions. Her reflections on revolution thus unfold as the hard-won knowledge that a fully secular politics has no other content than the experience of such new beginnings out of our own past miseries, calamities, and failings.

1. Constitutio libertatis

For Arendt, the authentic sense of politics is freedom. Politics and freedom require, explain, and entail one another. Where political activity is undertaken for the sake of something other than freedom (which Arendt distinguishes from "liberation from tyranny" or "freedom from want"), it ceases to be political; and where freedom is understood in nonpolitical terms (such as freedom of the will), it loses its worldly character.[7] Indeed, it could be said that Arendt identifies any separation of freedom from politics—or, any notion of the one as independent of the other—to be a dire threat to both.[8]

In earlier writings like *The Promise of Politics* and *The Human Condition*, Arendt tends to identify both politics and freedom with a general capacity for "new beginnings" that is rooted in the human condition of natality—the fact that we are all "human, in such a way that nobody is ever the same as anyone who ever lived, lives or will live."[9] Although Arendt does speak of a historical-institutional dimension of political life in those texts (for example, in her discussion of lawmaking in the Greek *polis*), these analyses tend to present politics and freedom as corresponding to the human condition of plurality-natality, whose chief characteristic is the ongoing intervention of unprecedented newcomers.[10]

What distinguishes *On Revolution* from these earlier reflections is the fact that in the later text Arendt offers something like a phenomenological retrospective of politics as the foundation of freedom [*constitutio libertatis*]—

calling it "revolutionary spirit," and tracing its appearance from ancient Rome, Machiavelli, and Montesquieu to the revolutions of the modern age. "Crucial . . . to any understanding of revolutions in the modern age," she writes, "is that the idea of freedom and the *experience* of a new beginning should coincide" (*OR* 29, my emphasis).

It is worth underscoring from the start how these three terms—politics, freedom, and founding—inform one another in Arendt's analysis. When for example, in chapter 4 of *On Revolution*, Arendt describes political foundation as *constitutio libertatis*, she does not mean to suggest that the aim of politics is the establishment of a new order of freedom, or of new spheres for individuals' freedom (civil liberties, rights, and so forth), as if the act of founding could be distinguished from the freedom that is founded. Rather, she aims to show how founding and freedom coincide: namely, how founding is the experience of freedom as new beginning, and how such new beginnings invariably entail the breaking open of any prior 'order' or 'sphere.'

Because freedom means "the experience of a new beginning," the foundation of freedom does not imply the establishment of a new order; rather, it is an attempt to make binding and authoritative the lived tensions inherent in the impossibility of reducing politics to the institution of order.

Put like this, the relationship in Arendt's analysis between freedom and foundation appears aporetic. (In *The Life of the Mind*, Arendt herself speaks of the "abyss of freedom and the *novus ordo seclorum.*")[11] As Miguel Vatter states in his discussion of the "aporetic foundation of political freedom": "Political freedom has an antinomical relation to the possibility of its own founding."[12] Vatter's interpretation is entirely apt; still, I wish to use it to draw attention to the larger thrust of Arendt's argument in *On Revolution*—namely, how she tries to show that this *aporia* actually functions successfully, that it is the historical movement of "revolutionary spirit."

Arendt's first step in this regard is not to show that the aporetic relationship between freedom and foundation is in itself politically authoritative or binding; rather, she makes one further turn by rooting the authoritative tension of freedom and foundation in the historical experience of modernity. Indeed, one of the challenges to which 'revolutionary spirit' responds is the task of finding a source of political authority that is not transcendent, absolute, or extrapolitical—which could be, in other words, authoritative irrespective of human history and experience.[13] Instead, the movement of revolutionary spirit sees the experience of politics as self-authorizing inasmuch as it identifies the 'authority' of political foundations in its own history.

It is in this sense anyway that the revolutionary tradition "brings about the birth of a new, secular realm"; it aims to bind human beings satisfactorily to one another by means of historical tradition, without recourse to divine, natural, or rational foundations for these bonds (e.g., 'God's commandment,' 'biological necessity,' 'violence,' or 'truth'). And it is for this reason crucial that Arendt identifies in revolutionary spirit the very spirit of the modern age—as if modernity and revolutionary spirit were coextensive.[14] Her point is to show how historical experience—as the lived experience of new beginnings—can make itself authoritative through bonds of a tradition or religion [re-ligio] that consequently has no need for a transcendent source of authority. The revolutionary tradition appears, so to speak, as a secular religion: a bond between human beings "according to which power resides in the people" (OR 171) rather than in a pact between human beings and a higher authority. This is why the phenomenological form of On Revolution—its movement from Rome to Machiavelli to Montesquieu to the American Revolution—is inseparable from the content of its argument: the historical experience of freedom and founding is the self-authorization of politics, which thrives when it is faithful to its own past experience, a kind of fidelity between the living and the dead.

2. Potestas in populo

In light of this, we might reconsider the apparent paradox according to which, for Arendt, the end of a revolution is the foundation of freedom (constitutio libertatis)—where freedom is established in the durable way that only a constitution can provide. Clearly, by constitutio libertatis Arendt does not mean simply a constitutional government in the sense of a body of laws designed to define that same government's powers. She makes this explicit when she distinguishes the "covenant" or "act of mutual promise" that characterizes the republican constitution of freedom from the "social contract" or "consent" that establishes a government of laws. (For the sake of clarity, it is worth recalling that by understanding in the term "covenant" something akin to the experience of what she calls "mutual promise," Arendt is consciously departing from the biblical connotation of "covenant.")[15] "Consent" is "accomplished by each individual person in his isolation . . . 'only in the Presence of God' "; that is, in the presence of a transcendent power capable of enforcing the pact.[16] To 'consent' is to implicitly locate the authority of political bonds in a relation of nonreciprocity between the consenter and whatever power underwrites the isolated act of consent (God, sovereignty, law, police violence, and so forth).

By contrast, "the mutual contract by which people bind themselves together in order to form a community is based on reciprocity and presupposes equality; its actual content is a promise," she writes. The crucial point here is that promising is politically binding only inasmuch as it entails the historical experience of having been enacted "in the presence of one another"—and is thus "in principle independent of religious sanction" (*OR* 170–71). In covenant-making, political bonds and power are made authoritative through the *experience* of acting in concert.[17] As an example of this Arendt offers the Mayflower Compact, wherein the 'social contract' theory of politics is confounded since the Hobbesian fear of the state of nature was "accompanied by the no less obvious confidence they had in their own power, granted and confirmed by no one and as yet unsupported by any means of violence, to combine themselves into a 'civil Body Politick' . . . held together solely by the strength of mutual promise" (*OR* 167).

By all rights, Arendt notes, one would have expected the English Puritans—in whom the "eagerness for experimentation, and the concomitant conviction of absolute novelty, of a *novus ordo saeclorum*, was conspicuously absent"—to have been the last people to act as revolutionaries; if anything, one would have expected the early modern social-contract theorists [Hobbes, Locke] to look to the experience of the earliest compacts in colonial America for *proof* of their theories. And yet the remarkable thing—as Arendt points out—is that here "it is an event rather than a theory or a tradition" that is decisive: "No theory, theological or political or philosophical, but their own decision to leave the Old World behind and to venture forth into an enterprise of their own led into a sequence of acts and occurrences in which they would have perished, had they not turned their minds to the matter long and intensely enough to discover, almost by inadvertence, the elementary grammar of political action": promising (*OR* 173).

Notice that Arendt does not wrest a secular, revolutionary politics from the Puritans (who, of course, were themselves anything but secular) by means of conceptual or argumentative force, still less through philological fancy footwork. She simply asks us to think about lived human experience (revolutions, losses, traumas) as authoritative—instead of relying upon theories, doctrines, conceptual traditions, and so forth. In other words, everything turns on making the actual experience of human beings politically binding and authoritative, in a spirit of fidelity to the 'political power' and 'freedom' of which we have been, and remain, capable. Arendt's point, which she never tires of repeating in these pages, is that "experience . . . rather than theory or learning" teaches how "power resides in the people." Thus, conversely, where there has been no lived experience of the "elementary grammar of political action," power cannot reside in the people.

But, if only lived experience can teach "the real meaning of the Roman

potestas in populo," then this very experience—if it is to really 'found' anything at all—must also become authoritative for the future. That is, the lived
experience of *potestas in populo* must be more than a fleeting event or performance, an end-unto-itself; it must become a founding principle capable of
casting its authority (and the auspice of happiness's pursuit) into a worldly
future. "Neither compact nor promise upon which compacts rest are suf-
ficient to assure perpetuity, that is, to bestow upon the affairs of men that
measure of stability without which they would be unable to build a world for
their posterity" (*OR* 182).

What this means, to get right to the point, is rather simple: if power resides in the people and arises from their experience of political action, and
if at the same time this power needs to become politically *authoritative* if
it is to be anything more than a passing moment, then somehow people—
human beings—must themselves become or actualize the 'authority' that
they already (potentially) are.

The achievement of such a political humanism, or secular politics, may of
course sound simple enough. And yet it turns out to be the most intractable
difficulty faced by the revolutionary tradition, by the secular ambition of the
modern age.

This challenge surfaces most immediately in the task of laying down laws;
for instance, in writing a constitution that might provide a future for the
'power that resides in the people.' For what temporal authority could sanction
the making of laws that would be "authoritative and valid for all, the majori-
ties and the minorities, the present and future generations"?[18] This need for a
higher authority, capable of providing stability for 'future states,' is what led
the American revolutionaries to appeal to "religious sanction for man-made
laws" (*OR* 190–92).[19] And it is, perhaps more significantly although no less
piously, what led Jefferson to speak of "self-evident" truths as the basis for the
laws of the new body politic:

> "We hold these truths to be self-evident," combines in a historically unique
> manner the basis of agreement between those who have embarked upon revo-
> lution, an agreement necessarily relative because related to those who enter it,
> with an absolute, namely with a truth that needs no agreement since, because
> of its self-evidence, it compels without argumentative demonstration or po-
> litical persuasion. . . . [T]hese truths . . . are in a sense no less compelling than
> 'despotic power' and no less absolute than the revealed truths of religion or
> the axiomatic verities of mathematics. (*OR* 192)

Arendt's way of avoiding this trap, interestingly, is to try to change the
very notion of 'law' to which authority would correspond; and she does this

by referring to two different historical experiences of law, one indebted to Roman jurisprudence and the other "construed in accordance with the voice of God, who tells men: Thou shalt not." In this way, Arendt aims to introduce a notion of law and authority that would not take the form of an imperative or commandment for future generations whose "model," she says, "was Hebrew in origin . . . represented by the divine Commandments of the Decalogue" (*OR* 189). In a sense, the entire thrust of the tradition of revolutionary spirit—which Arendt traces from Rome to Machiavelli and Montesquieu up to the modern age—is precisely to separate law from commandment; namely, to circumvent the worry about an "absolute which would bestow validity upon positive, man-made laws." All of which is to say that one way to eschew 'absolutism' in politics is to avoid identifying law and authority with command and prohibition.

To accomplish this circumvention, Arendt offers an understanding of Roman law—*lex*—as an "intimate connection" or as a relationship "which connects two things or two partners *whom external circumstance have brought together*" (*OR* 187, my emphasis). This last phrase is, I think, the crucial one— because it shows how the bonds of law need not express transcendent conditions for durable social ties (like self-evident truths, the ever-present threat of punishment, or the fear of an avenging God); the bonds of law might also express and correspond to historically contingent conditions that bring people together—such as the indelible experience of finding oneself and one's fellow Puritans on a storm-tossed ship at sea off the coast of Massachusetts. Or, to give another example furnished by none other than Machiavelli, we can think of the founding of Venice—similarly organized by "peoples who had sought refuge in certain islets at the top of the Adriatic Sea": "There, without any particular person or prince to give them a constitution, they began to live as a community under laws which seemed to them appropriate for their maintenance."[20]

According to Arendt, the constitution of a people from this 'Roman' point of view is an ethnic, tribal, or organic unity that is "quite independent of all laws"—*not* because this unity arises from predeterminate natural (blood, kinship) ties but because "a people" are understood to be bound to one another *by historical experience,* by sheer accident or external circumstance.[21] She also invokes, in this regard, Montesquieu's own definition of the law as *rapport,* or "merely what relates two things and therefore is relative by definition" (*OR* 188–89). In this way, her understanding of the legal foundation of Rome—especially, the founding of the *senatus populusque Romanus*—corresponds to Machiavelli's own interpretation of the foundation of Rome in the *Discourses;* inasmuch as Machiavelli, too, insists that the point of locating the mythical foundation of Rome in Romulus' murder of Remus is to show how the city begins by *overcoming* (albeit violently) the strength of blood-ties or tribal bonds.[22]

However, Arendt also offers a significant re-elaboration of Machiavelli's interpretation of Roman republicanism through her own reading of the Roman poet Virgil's epic *Aeneid*, with which she concludes her chapter on the *novus ordo saeclorum*. She begins her reading through a comparison of the "two 'foundation' legends"—that is, the two stories of political liberation and founding—with which the revolutionaries of the eighteenth-century were chiefly familiar: "the biblical story of the exodus of Israeli tribes from Egypt and Virgil's story of the wanderings of Aeneus after he had escaped burning Troy" (*OR* 205). Both stories, says Arendt, offer not only new beginnings and political foundations; they also contain two different ways of approaching the very problem of absolute beginning. In the case of the biblical exodus story, writes Arendt, "the problem of beginning is solved through the introduction of a beginner whose own beginnings are no longer subject to question because he is 'from eternity to eternity'" (*OR* 206). And she identifies this search for the origin and cause of new beginnings with the philosophical preoccupation with first principles, "the age-old thought-customs of Western men, according to which each completely new beginning needs an absolute from which it springs and by which it is 'explained'" (*OR* 206). To use a kind of shorthand, for Arendt the biblical tradition is complicit with western metaphysics in interpreting the (political) problem of beginnings in terms of the establishment of that which was "in the beginning."

Conversely:

> Inherent in the Roman concept of foundation, we find, strangely enough, the notion that not only all decisive political changes in the course of Roman history were reconstitutions, namely, reforms of the old institutions and the retrievance of the original act of foundation, but that even this first act had been already a re-establishment, as it were, a regeneration and restoration. (*OR* 208)

Rome, as Virgil's poetry attests, understood itself not in relation to an absolute principle of origin but rather "as a second Troy."

It is worth stating the fundamental Roman insight plainly and simply: foundations are always re-foundings; constitutions always re-constitutions; new beginnings always a rebirth. The authoritative principle in question, therefore, is not a 'first principle' or 'original cause' but rather the capacity of human beings to understand themselves and their bonds to one another in the *principium* of many, ongoing new beginnings—which is to say, in view of the principle that human beings are themselves new beginners and self-authorizing.

This is the content of revolutionary spirit, the secular truth of its tradition, so to speak: "What saves the act of beginning from its own arbitrariness is that it carries its own principle within itself, or, to be more precise, that beginning and principle, *principium* and principle, are not only related to each other, but are coeval" (*OR* 212).

3. Lost Treasure

But then why, if all this is true, did the modern revolutionaries of the eighteenth, nineteenth, and twentieth centuries not simply cast their enterprise as Machiavelli did when he—"partly because he was Italian and partly because he was close to Roman history"—imagined a refashioning of Roman law and public glory in the Italian city-states? Or, as John Milton did when he still dreamed of founding "Rome anew"? If even Montesquieu was still able to write his *Esprit des Lois* in the spirit of the *societas Romana*, then why were the founding fathers of the American context—who were well aware, if not downright obsessed, with Roman precedent—unable to speak in the same way?

Put bluntly, if Arendt is able to understand the American Revolution, as could the founding fathers themselves, in light of a "revolutionary tradition" that extends back to Rome, then why is the American Revolution itself not primarily graspable as the extension or 're-founding' of that tradition?

Put even more bluntly—and to cut to the chase—why does Arendt see in the *American* Revolution (and not, after all, in Rome or in Machiavelli or in the French Revolutionaries) the crux and burden of the entire tradition of revolutionary spirit, if it is with the American Revolution that we have both the failure of the revolutionaries to grasp their actions as a 're-founding' in relation to a prior tradition, *and* as a break with the Old World generally?

Why should the *novus ordo saeclorum* also presage the loss of revolutionary tradition, the loss of its "treasure"?

"When the Americans decided," writes Arendt, "to vary Virgil's line from *Magnus ab integro saeclorum nascitur ordo* ["the great cycle of periods is born anew"] to *novus ordo saeclorum* they had admitted that it was no longer a matter of founding 'Rome anew' but of founding a 'new Rome'" (*OR* 212). The "inescapable" reason for this, Arendt concludes, lies in the fact that the American experience gave rise not only to a new body politic but to the beginning of a new national history, not solely in the wake of the breakdown of the European colonial system but in the wake of a more radical break with the tradition of the 'old world.'

In order to better understand this rupture, we must see that Arendt does not finally understand the 'absolute novelty' of the American Revolution primarily in relation to the Roman-European tradition that preceded it; rather, she understands this novelty, so to speak, from the perspective of a break *within* the European tradition *since* the French Revolution. What distinguishes the American *novus ordo saeclorum* from the Roman *Magnus ab integro saeclorum nascitur ordo*, in other words, is not a break that is situated between Virgil and 1776; rather, what "shattered the bonds between the New World and the countries of the old Continent . . . *was the French Revolution*" (*OR* 215, my emphasis).

Put another way: the split that constitutes the predicament of modernity is not a rupture between modernity and what came before, but rather a split internal to modernity itself. Thus, the "loss of tradition" to which Arendt repeatedly refers does not merely indicate, as so many of her interpreters suggest, our separation from an irretrievable, ancient tradition for which we can only be nostalgic. Rather, the point is *to recognize 'loss of tradition' as formative for whatever 'tradition' means in modernity.* "*Notre héritage n'est précédé d'aucun testament,*" in the words of René Char, which Arendt loves to cite. This is the haunting thought with which Arendt begins the book's final chapter, whose title is "The Revolutionary Tradition and its Lost Treasure."

So, again, why should it turn out that the revolutionary tradition be best understood in terms of "lost treasure"; that is, in terms of a break within the secular, revolutionary tradition (*novus ordo saeclorum*)—as if revolutionary spirit were to be better grasped in the 'negative' terms of losses and failures than in the 'positive' terms of a successful, enduring heritage?

To repeat, for Arendt the *novus ordo saeclorum*—the inheritance of modernity, the revolutionary spirit of the modern age from Rome to America— is finally to be perceived in light of the gulf between the American and the French Revolutions; which is to say, in light of the failure of the successful American Revolution to become decisive for the political tenor of the past two centuries, and in light of the success of the failed French Revolution to become determinant for subsequent revolutions in Russia, China, Hungary, and so forth.

What this means most immediately, of course, is that what the revolutions of the eighteenth century have bequeathed to us is not "public freedom, public happiness, public spirit" (recall Jefferson's image of heaven on earth) but rather a darker lesson:

> Forever haunted by the . . . spectre of the vast masses of the poor whom every revolution was bound to liberate . . . the revolutionaries of the nineteenth and

twentieth centuries, in sharp contrast to their predecessors in the eighteenth, were desperate men, and the cause of the revolution, therefore, attracted more and more the desperadoes, namely 'an unhappy species of the population. . . . ' (*OR* 221–22)

These are themes that are dear to Arendt, and she expounds upon the decline of political freedom and the corresponding intrusion of biological necessity (the experience of poverty, or the activity of labor) into the public sphere in many of her writings. In this sense, the historical success of the failed French Revolution among modern revolutionaries lies in its understanding of 'freedom' as mere liberation from necessity, its excessive solicitation of *pitié*; and by the same token, the historical failure of the successful American Revolution lay in its inability to constitutionally account for poverty, for desperation—in the very lack of commiseration implicit in its focus on the "pursuit of happiness."[23]

But—as a summation of these themes—perhaps the clearest sign of the rift between past and future is the palpable separation of the experience of revolution from the experience of happiness, as though the latter were no longer intrinsic to the former. If revolutionary spirit has lost its sense of fun, its *jouissance*, its promise of earthly happiness—and, for us, it clearly has—then it remains not only divided from itself but also doomed to failure, "loaded down with misery" (*OR* 222).[24]

Given all this, one might expect Arendt to speak merely of *loss* and not of *treasure* at all. And yet she does not simply speak of the "loss of the revolutionary tradition"; she refers rather to its "lost treasure," as if the loss were not final so long as we can recall the treasure that is gone.[25] If this means that reflection upon the revolutionary tradition takes the form of a work of mourning, then this is probably not far from Arendt's meaning—although she does not put it in precisely such terms.

Perhaps closer to her own way of expressing matters would be to say that if the split between the French Revolution (e.g. liberation from necessity, commiseration) and the American Revolution (e.g. the pitiless pursuit of happiness) is essential to the "lost treasure" of the revolutionary tradition itself—if this division *is* our inheritance of revolutionary spirit ("*notre héritage . . .*")—then revolutionary spirit is not the historical march of some positive content ("freedom," or "happiness") but rather a different "strange and sad story that remains to be told and remembered" (*OR* 255).

We should discern in revolutionary spirit not "the hidden *leitmotif*" or the "locomotive of all history" as Tocqueville or Marx would have us believe, as if "revolution had been the result of an irresistible force rather than the outcome of specific deeds" (*OR* 255). Instead of a positive content or naïve historical progress, we should now detect in revolutionary spirit Hegel's restlessness of the negative; namely, the traces of past *failures* to found freedom, the fallout of our prior failures to make freedom foundational. The perception in these failures and losses of a potentially sharable heritage is, for Arendt, precisely what allows us to experience the promise of revolution today.

To begin again to make freedom foundational in light of past failed revolutions—knowing now that 'freedom' has no other content than the experience of such new beginnings *out of past failures*—is, finally, what it means to acknowledge the secularity of revolutionary spirit.

Which is to say that the earthly happiness intrinsic to freedom is not separable from its renewed worldly pursuit as politics—from the experience and inheritance of crushed dreams, lost hopes, and thwarted chances for a sharable happiness into which newcomers are born.

Notes

1. Hannah Arendt, *On Revolution* (New York: Penguin, 1965), 131. Hereafter, all citations to this work will appear in parentheses in the text as *OR*.

2. "In short, the privacy of a home upon whose life the public has no claim" (*OR* 129). See Thomas Jefferson in a letter to James Madison, 9 June 1793. Cited in *OR* 523.

3. Cited in *OR* 131.

4. Arendt comments further: "In order to understand how truly extraordinary it was, within the context of our tradition, to see in public, political happiness an image of eternal bliss, it may be well to recall that for Thomas Aquinas, for example, the *perfecta beatitudo* consisted entirely in a vision, the vision of God, and that for this vision the presence of no friends was required (*amici non requiruntur ad perfectam beatitudinem*), all of which is, incidentally, still in perfect accord with Platonic notions of the life of an immortal soul" (*OR* 131).

5. The revolutionaries of the eighteenth-century in France and America, writes Arendt, "had made their acquaintance with 'public happiness,' and the impact of this experience had been sufficiently profound for them to prefer . . . public freedom to civil liberties or public happiness to private welfare" (*OR* 134). By the same token, Arendt thinks the paradigmatic ailment of a depoliticized society is not lack of freedom or rights, but loneliness. See *The Human Condition*, 58–59.

6. The aim of revolutions, according to Arendt, is not only to found or build a new political sphere in which freedom "would receive free play for generations to come," but also "to assure the survival of the spirit out of which the act of foundation sprang" (*OR* 126).

7. With regard to the first point, Arendt repeatedly laments the "failure to distinguish between liberation and freedom" (*OR* 142). See also *OR* 29–30, 299 n. 1. With regard to the second, Arendt suggests that 'freedom of the will' or 'inner freedom' "as a place of absolute freedom within one's own self was discovered in late antiquity by those who had no place of their own

in the world and hence lacked a worldly condition which, from early antiquity to almost the middle of the nineteenth century, was unanimously held to be a prerequisite for freedom" (Arendt, "What is Freedom?" in *Between Past and Future* [New York: Penguin, 1968)], 146–47).

8. For example, the confusion of freedom with 'liberation from necessity' signals for Arendt the collapse of politics into what she calls "the social," and a concomitant failure to distinguish the sphere of politics from the domain of biological necessity.

9. Arendt, *The Human Condition* (Chicago: University of Chicago Press, 1958), 9, 8.

10. In *The Human Condition*, for example, the newness of singular actions only comes to light in the context of a web of human relationships that is, by virtue of the unpredictable arrival of newcomers and the departure of those who die, itself always in flux. Along these lines Arendt distinguishes between the beginning of "something" and the beginning of "somebody," grounding the former firmly in the latter. Citing Augustine, she writes "*[Initium] ergo ut esset, creatus est homo, ante quem nullus fuit* ('that there be a beginning, man was created before whom there was nobody'), said Augustine in his political philosophy. The beginning is not the same as the beginning of the world; it is not the beginning of something but of somebody, who is a beginning himself. With the creation of man, the principle of beginning came into the world itself" (177). Although it may seem as though Arendt is here appropriating a theological trope from Augustine for her own secular-political purposes, I read Arendt as assuming that Augustine is in this regard quite secular. Indeed, Arendt suggests that many early Christian writings are already secular in their political implications (see, for instance, her remarks on Jesus and forgiveness in *The Human Condition*, 239). In this regard, she is very close to Ernst Bloch's *Atheism in Christianity* (New York, Verso, 2009); or to Hegel's thesis about Christianity as atheism. For more on "natality" and Arendt, see my *A Politics of the Scene* (Stanford: Stanford University Press, 2008), especially the Introduction and chapter 5.

11. See the section entitled "The Abyss of Freedom and the *novus ordo seclorum*" in Hannah Arendt, *The Life of Mind* (New York: Mariner, 1981), 195. And in *On Revolution*, she also admits that "the perplexity . . . stated in logical terms . . . seemed unsolvable: if foundation was the aim and the end of revolution, then the revolutionary spirit was not merely the spirit of beginning something new but of starting something permanent and enduring; a lasting institution, embodying this spirit and encouraging it to new achievements, would be self-defeating" (*OR* 232).

12. Miguel Vatter, *Between Form and Event: Machiavelli's Theory of Political Freedom* (New York: Springer-Verlag, 2000), 221.

13. In a recent essay on Hannah Arendt and secular politics, Samuel Moyn claims, puzzlingly and I think wrongly, that Arendt's secularism is "the attempt not to escape from the authority and the sanction that 'the absolute' provides to politics but to find nonreligious versions of them." According to Moyn, Arendt insists "that politics must have continuing recourse to an absolute of the kind that metaphysics in the form of religion provided far more plausibly and efficaciously than revolution could easily succeed in doing" (see Samuel Moyn, "Hannah Arendt and the Secular," *New German Critique* 105 [Fall 2008]: 71–96). As I will argue in the following pages, contrary to Moyn's interpretation, Arendt's notions of revolution, founding, freedom, and secularism all imply a politics without transcendent or absolute grounds, whether explicitly religious-theological or not.

14. See *On Revolution*, chapter 1.

15. This can lead to some confusion, given that she refers to the Mayflower Compact as an instance of mutual promising (and not biblical "covenant") and given that the early American Puritans themselves relied "on the Old Testament, and especially on their rediscovery of the

concept of the covenant of Israel." To avoid confusion, therefore, I am using the term "covenant" here as Arendt does; namely, as the secular experience of "mutual promising" in the lived affair of the Mayflower Compact—although she is well aware that the Puritans themselves understood by "covenant" something distinctly theological. (Elsewhere, Arendt seems to imagine a not-fully-theological sense of covenant within the biblical tradition itself; for instance, she refers to Abraham's "covenants" as acts of promising in *The Human Condition*, 244.) In any case, Arendt's point is that this 'theoretical' understanding of the Puritans is belied by their own lived experience. Here is Arendt: "If there was any theoretical influence that contributed to the compacts and agreements in early American history, it was, of course, the Puritan's reliance on the Old Testament, and especially their rediscovery of the concept of the covenant of Israel, which indeed became for them an 'instrument to explain almost every relation of man to man and man to God.' But while it may be true that 'the Puritan theory of the origin of the church in the consent of the believers led directly to the popular theory of the origin of the government in the consent of the governed,' this could not have led to the other much less current theory of the origin of a 'civil body politic' in the mutual promise and binding of its constituents. For the Biblical covenant as the Puritans understood it was a compact between God and Israel by virtue of which God gave the law and Israel consented to keep it, and while this covenant implied government by consent, it implied by no means a political body in which rulers and ruled would be equal, that is, where actually the whole principle of rulership no longer applied. Once we turn from these theories and speculations about influences to the documents themselves and their simple, uncluttered, and often awkward language, we see immediately that it is an event rather than a theory or a tradition we are confronted with, an event of the greatest magnitude and the greatest import for the future, enacted on the spur of time and circumstances" (*OR* 172–73).

16. "In the so-called social contract between a given society and its ruler . . . we deal with a fictitious, aboriginal act on the side of each member, by virtue of which he gives up his isolated strength and power to constitute a government; far from gaining a new power, and possibly more than he had before, he resigns his power such as it is . . . he merely expresses his consent to be ruled by the government, whose power consists of the sum total of forces which all individual persons have channeled into it and which are monopolized by the government . . . those who 'covenant and combine themselves together' lose, by virtue of reciprocation, their isolation, while in the other instance it is precisely their isolation which is safeguarded and protected" (*OR* 170–71).

17. "The grammar of action: that action is the only human faculty that demands a plurality of men; and the syntax of power: that power is the only human attribute which applies solely to the worldly in-between space by which men are mutually related, combine in the act of foundation by virtue of the making and keeping of promises, which, in the realm of politics, may well be the highest human faculty" (*OR* 175).

18. For Jefferson, as for Thomas Paine, notes Arendt, "it was plain 'vanity and presumption [to govern] beyond the grave'; it was, moreover, the 'most ridiculous and insolent of all tyrannies'" (*OR* 233).

19. "In theory as in practice," writes Arendt, "we can hardly avoid the paradoxical fact that it was precisely the revolutions . . . which drove the very 'enlightened' men of the eighteenth century to plead for some religious sanction at the very moment when they were about to emancipate the secular realm . . . and to separate politics from religion once and for all" (*OR* 192).

20. Niccolò Machiavelli, *The Discourses* 1.1, trans. Leslie J. Walker S.J., (New York: Penguin, 1970), 101.

21. As Machiavelli puts it with stark simplicity at the beginning of *The Discourses*, "all cities are built by natives of the place in which they are built, or by people from elsewhere" (ibid., 100).

22. Machiavelli of course defends Romulus' actions as foundational for a republic that managed to decisively break with the "ancient institutions" of kinship affiliation. Machiavelli's 'proof' of his defense of Romulus lies in the fact that Romulus acted not out of "personal ambition" but for the "common good," as evidenced by his immediate establishment of "a senate" (*The Discourses* 1.9, p. 133).

23. See the discussion of the failure of the American Revolution in this regard in *On Revolution*, 66–73.

24. Consider a complaint often leveled against recent protest movements—against *los indignados* in Spain, for example, or against the Occupy Wall Street movement in the United States and other countries: namely, that such movements display frivolity, and that the manifest enjoyment taken by many of the protesters in their own activity undermines its political status—since, according to some, 'politics' must apparently be deadly serious and no fun at all. I would argue, counter to these complains, that the palpable sense of fun that characterizes the public actions of these movements is perhaps the clearest sign of its remembrance of, and part in, a revolutionary tradition. Far from being mere nostalgia or creative impotence, therefore, contemporary invocations of protest movements from the 1960s, for example, might be better understood as self-conscious demonstrations of a new beginning *out of past failures*.

25. "There is nothing that could compensate for this failure [of the spirit of revolution] from becoming final, except memory and recollection" (*OR* 280).

8

Force and Justice: Auerbach's Pascal

JANE O. NEWMAN

1. Survivals

In March 1948, the famous German-Jewish Romanist and comparatist Erich Auerbach (1892–1957) gave a lecture about Dante's *Divine Comedy* on the campus of Penn State University in State College. Dante "survive[s]" into the present, Auerbach explained, by the force of "the radiation of [his] personality and the evocative power of [his] name" (414).[1] In ways that he could not have predicted, the same could also be said of Auerbach. From out of a tape of the lecture made by R. P. Blackmur, Auerbach's voice enters our "souls," just as Dante's words entered his over and over again throughout his professional life. Auerbach speaks toward the end of his talk of the "terrifying vigor" with which the "men and women" of the *Divine Comedy* emerge for the reader, "strikingly real" and "concrete," out of the lines of Dante's "great poem" (423). On the tape, we hear the scraping of chairs and the bells of the Penn State carillon in the background. In the carefully cultivated voice of the recently arrived immigrant, the disembodied words of the man who wrote so compellingly about the realism of the afterlife—where the "souls" of the dead are so taken aback by the fleshy "presence of a living man" among them that they counter-intuitively press forward in their eternal weightlessness to "give him a full [accounting] of themselves" (424)—press forward into our postmodern world with an equally eerie kind of creaturely everydayness.

It was not just the premodern Dante, however, about whom Auerbach wrote over and over again during his several lives in Germany, Turkey, and the United States. He also returned time and again to the early modern French philosopher Blaise Pascal (1623–62). Auerbach's assessment of Pascal's political theology or, more precisely, of the Schmittian, not to say Dantesque, subject of traffic between the worldly, profane realm, on the one hand, and sacred and eternal spaces, times, and regimes, on the other, captures the "evocative power" that the early modern can have for the modern era and for postmodernity too. Auerbach turned throughout his life to Pascal on the topic of relations between the "civitas terrena" and the "civitas Dei." Of specific interest to him was the question of how terrestrial might and divine right, and thus force and justice, related to one another. Auerbach first wrote about these issues in the fateful year of 1933 in his book, *The French Audience of the Seventeenth Century (Das französische Publikum des 17. Jahrhunderts)*, published when he was still a professor in Marburg. Another version of his thoughts appeared in Turkish in the journal *Üniversite Konferanslari* soon after he began his exile in Istanbul in 1936. In 1941, still in Istanbul, he wrote his first essay devoted specifically to might and right in Pascal, this time in German. The piece was published several years later in the Turkish journal *Felsefe Arkivi* under the title "Der Triumph des Bösen" ("The Triumph of Evil"), with accompanying Turkish translation. Auerbach returned to the topic of force and justice in Pascal several times after his emigration to the United States, beginning with his presentation in 1949 at the Princeton Seminars in Literary Criticism (the so-called Gauss Seminars), whereby he hoped to make the leap from State College to the Ivy League.[2] A version of the Princeton lectures was published as "The Triumph of Evil in Pascal" in *The Hudson Review* in 1951 (the year after he had secured a position not at Princeton but rather at Yale) and then a second time in an altered version as "On the Political Theory of Pascal" in the famous little book, *Scenes from the Drama of European Literature*, that appeared in 1959, two years after his death. Another German version of the Pascal essay had appeared in Switzerland by this time. In these serial articulations of his thoughts about the French seventeenth century, Auerbach, like the denizens of the afterlife in their speeches to Dante the pilgrim, was trying desperately to give an "account" of both himself and the place of the intellectual in the early twentieth century, using Pascal as his Archimedean point in the theorization of the relation between the thinking man's temporal-worldly and eternal-spiritual natures, and thus of his ability to act as a free moral agent and reflective human being.[3]

Auerbach's work on Pascal on these issues intersected explicitly with the thoughts of a number of perhaps less well-known interlocutors, whose readings of the seventeenth century likewise functioned as a commentary on early twentieth-century political-theological thinking. The footnotes in several of the works by Auerbach listed above indicate these men's identities. They are, first, the German Protestant philosopher Gerhard Krüger (1902–72), who studied with Nicolai Hartmann and Heidegger and knew Leo Strauss well, and second, the important purveyor of Christian existentialism, the Catholic theologian Romano Guardini (1885–1968), with whom the young Hannah

Arendt took classes in Berlin. Krüger's and Guardini's work—as well as the work of Auerbach's younger colleague and friend, the German Romanist Werner Krauss (1900–76)—played an important role in Auerbach's approach to the question of how the intellectual could live 'justly' in an unjust world dominated by force, a question both he and they posed in their work on the French seventeenth century and Pascal.[4] The generation of literary critics and historians, of philosophers and theologians, to which Auerbach, Guardini, Krauss, and Krüger, as well as Arendt and Strauss, belonged, turned repeatedly during the interwar years to the texts of the past and to questions associated with pre- and early modern Christian theology in particular. They did so *not*, as Hannah Arendt is said to have suggested of her work on St. Augustine, as "stud[ies] in religiosity," but, rather, as a way of "thinking what [they were] doing" in the literally post-modern era, in the aftermath, that is, of the modernity that began with the conflagration of World War I and ended by exiling so many of them from their homes.[5] In an interesting little essay on Aristotle, written in 1922, Heidegger describes the "history of philosophical research" as philosophy's most proper object, but "only when [research into this history] aims to provide not diverse historical curiosities but rather *radically simple monuments* that evoke thinking."[6] Pascal and the seventeenth century evoked thinking about what they were doing for Auerbach and his contemporaries in this way. Considering his and their nearly obsessive concern with Pascal's understanding of the relationship between force in Man's world and justice in God's allows our own postmodern moment to think what *we* are doing when we undertake research into both early modern and modern political-theological thought.[7]

2. The "De-Christianizing" of the French Seventeenth Century: Auerbach, Krüger, and Krauss

The first of the footnotes that indicate Auerbach's intellectual networks and debts may be found in *The French Audience of the Seventeenth Century*. Before turning to the note, it is important to understand the context of this study. By 1933, when the book was published, Auerbach had already been working on the period of French absolutism for some time; his thoughts there were thus not directly associated with the so-called "Machtergreifung," or seizure of power, by the Nazis that year. Already in a letter dating from 1930, for example, Krauss enthusiastically praises Auerbach for his innovative methodology in treating the phenomenon of French Classicism.[8] The *French Audience* book *was* innovative, even revolutionary, in the context of German approaches to the French seventeenth century at the time. Corneille, one of the greatest of the French 'classical' dramatists, had been considered important in Germany during the late nineteenth and early twentieth centuries, for example, only insofar as his texts could be read as high-cultural artifacts, exempla of Crocean aesthetic unity and greatness, or as articulations of an ideology of selfless patriotism on the part of their heroes. Those of his texts that did not measure up to these expectations were discarded by German Romanists as signs of the disintegration of his 'genius.' After 1918, of course, things changed; everything French, and especially the signature epoch of Classicism, was rejected.[9] To write, as Auerbach did, in the years that followed World War I about the culture of the French seventeenth century at all, but especially in terms of its embeddedness in the social, political, and economic conditions of its time, was thus something like methodological (if not bordering also on actual) treason.

In *The French Audience* Auerbach describes Corneille, as well as Molière, Descartes, and Pascal, as members of a "circle of scientifically and mathematically oriented intellectuals" who belonged to the "upper bourgeoisie," the class from which, he explains, "the majority of the leading intellectuals of the century in any case came" (9–10, 35–37). This class never intended to oppose the state that consolidated around Louis XIII and his minister, Richelieu, and then burst into full bloom around Louis XIV. Rather, they—and thus the intelligentsia writ large—belonged to what Auerbach identifies as a "new" "parasitical" (39, 44) constituency that was forming out the remnants of an aristocracy that was gradually becoming powerless, on the one hand, and a bourgeoisie that was in fact rising, but that did not yet have a political function, on the other (29–45). Together, these classes formed what Auerbach calls the new "audience" for culture at both the court and in the city; its purpose consisted solely in performing a homogenizing "bienséance" and "honnêteté," which allowed both its members and the protagonists of the dramas they watched to adopt high moral profiles while in fact occupying harmless and neutral positions vis-à-vis both authority on stage and the real-life king (26–27, 32–34). This audience, Auerbach writes in 1933, was sheerly incapable of any "resistance that could be taken at all seriously" (45), first because such resistance would have jeopardized its members' newfound privileges, but second, and perhaps even more importantly, because of what he calls the "secularization"—the German is "Entchristung," "de-Christianization" (46)—that was occurring at the same time. Auerbach argues that it was as a consequence of "Entchristung" that the seventeenth-century French intelligentsia and the 'classical' theater of which it was both the author and champion had their debilitating failure of political nerve. This de-Christianizing "worlding" ("Verweltlichung") was thus also a "de-worlding" ("Entweltlichung"), he argues, insofar as the principles of honesty, decorum, and virtue by which they allegedly lived were in fact fictions, visible only on a stage purged of "seasons . . . day and night, sun and rain, sleep and sustenance" by the doctrine of the unities, and thus never translated into the reality of "great movements" in the streets (53).

Auerbach dedicates the final eight pages of his 1933 book to the phenomenon of "Entchristung," investigating in depth its influence on the "educated classes" in particular, classes that ironically—and perhaps somewhat counterintuitively—did not withdraw from "Christian belief" (46) as a result. Rather, some turned to and sided with the Jesuits, who, along with their cardinal, endorsed what Auerbach calls a "questionable mode" of Christian "accommodation" ("Anpassung") to existing political realities. "[M]any others"—and here Auerbach is surely referring to the Jansenists, with whom he associates Pascal—endorsed precisely the opposite stance, namely a neo-Augustinian spiritual commitment to "denying the world." In both cases, the result was the growth of the state's secular power as a result of the intelligentsia's new form of alignment with religious stances that were, respectively, complicitous with or disengaged from a consolidating authoritarian state. As a result, the here-and-now of the world deteriorated into a political "everydayness" ("Alltäglichkeit") no longer illuminated or animated ("durchblutet") by any "Christian light" at all (47). For the author of the 1929 *Dante as Poet of the Secular World*, indeed, for the man who would go on to write *Mimesis*, this kind of evacuated, de-Christianized everydayness would have been an unmitigated existential disaster in the early twentieth-century German sense of that term, as when Arendt, for example, described Karl Jaspers' definition of human "Existenz" as a "shared life of human beings inhabiting a given world common to them all," a world in which Man "experiences the limitations that directly determine the conditions of his freedom," yet understands these limitations as the "basis for his actions" in the world.[10] In Auerbach's "de-Christianized" seventeenth century, the self-absorbed Christian intelligentsia had no such actions in mind. Rather, in espousing 'virtue' as "bienséance" and "honnêteté," its members either opted to serve an aggressively hegemonic state directly, or turned their backs on that state to such an extent that those in power could go ahead and do as they pleased.

Auerbach was not the only German intellectual at the time to be disgusted with the prospect of an either complicit or passive intellectual class. Just two years before, in his friend Walter Benjamin's famous essay, "Left-Wing Melancholy" (1931), the intelligentsia is described as finding its "political" function not in "parties" but in "cliques." Its arenas of activity are "distraction" ("Zerstreuung"), "amusement," and "consumption," Benjamin writes, which do not "correspond[to any] political action."[11] For Auerbach, however, it is the religious affiliations of a defanged intelligentsia that are of particular interest. The subterranean critique articulated here is one associated with the beliefs and events of what has come to be known as the late nineteenth and early twentieth century *Kulturkampf,* or "battle for civilization" in Germany, which created a snug relationship between liberal German Protestantism and the newly unified German state beginning after 1871 and persisting up through the declaration of war in 1914.[12] It was out of this same context that the allegedly opposite—and oppositional—phenomenon of dialectical theology also emerged. During the *Kulturkampf,* a state-identified Lutheran church, following its sixteenth-century historical model quite closely, some would say, endorsed the consolidation of a confessionally pure Germany (Catholics were accused of "racial darkness," "Rassendunkel," for example, and shunned) under the banner of a hegemonic religion. Soon after war was declared, what is known as "war theology" ("Kriegstheologie") developed. "War theology" cast the achieving of victory in the conflict as a matter of a Lutheran Germany's divine mission and thus as part of the state's sacred fate. Intellectuals such as Wilhelm Walther bought into this narrative, hastily publishing his *Germany's Sword as Consecrated by Luther* (*Deutschlands Schwert, durch Luther geweiht*) in 1914.[13] Many famous Protestant theologians signed on in support of war theology's agenda. Others, including Karl Barth, resisted this trend, insisting on the absolute separation of the church from the state. His sometime friend and colleague, Friedrich Gogarten, took Barth's "dialectical theology" even further, suggesting that a full rejection of the world, a turning away from any engagement with the secular, was what was needed. Such issues as were associated with war theology, on the one hand, and with an only apparently resistant, because ultimately quietist, dialectical theology, on the other, were still acute in the interwar period, and are the ones that Auerbach was addressing in *The French Audience,* with the Jesuits and the Jansenists standing in for, or, if that is too strong, then at least representing the same kind of standoff between a religious party that endorsed a state-oriented confessional worldliness and its antithesis, a religious position devoted to otherworldly disengagement in matters of "Existenz." Auerbach indicates as much in a footnote at the very beginning of his excursus on "Entchristung," when he refers to the work of Gerhard Krüger.

True to his sociological approach, Auerbach had begun his discussion of de-Christianization in seventeenth-century France by describing it as part and parcel of what he had argued was the "evacuation [*Entleerung*] of the substance of all class-based functions" of the intelligentsia (49). But de-Christianization also had a more abstract, indeed political-theological and philosophical cause. The main theoretical mastermind, Auerbach argues, of the "worlding" ("Verweltlichung") of the intelligentsia at the time was René Descartes, whose fear about the loss of Man's freedom in view of the incomprehensibly greater power of God led Descartes to his famous retreat into interiority, into "self consciousness" ("Selbstbewusstsein," 47). Since God was ineffably in charge, Man had to stand down; he could maintain *some* sovereign power over himself, but only in this private realm. (For Auerbach, Descartes' God mimics the absolute ruler with His almost personalized "omnipotence" ["Allmacht"] and loses none of His sacred power when He intervenes directly in Man's ability to be free in the world. This is Schmittian political theology in reverse, the de-sacralization of divine hierarchy and rule.) It was the Cartesian removal of God into an unimaginably distant and all-powerful realm, with its undertones of dialectical theology's separation of God's and Man's worlds, that caused the de-sacralization of the world, Auerbach writes. The suggestion is, perhaps understandably, somewhat Weberian. Yet, it is the wheels of absolutist power politics rather than commerce that grind away in Auerbach's version of a "disenchanted" seventeenth-century world. The new audience of the court and the city, and the playwrights who wrote to both edify and amuse its members, responded to the disappearance of God by extending claims about an autonomous *cogito* into notions about a powerful and personal internal *moral* realm, he explains. It was the performance of loyalty to this realm that occupied the heroes of both Corneille's and Racine's plays, performed at the pleasure of the absolutist court.[14] Their actions, being entirely interior, of course had no real "relation to concrete life in the world," he notes (53). In the claim that both the protagonists of French classical tragedy and the audience watching them conceived of themselves as "moral persons" only in a world "outside of and beyond the historical and day-to-day" (53), Auerbach underscores the fact that their respective moral compasses were no more than fictions. Yet, as glorious, even "triumphant" (53), as he claims such theatricalized moral rigor was, the men of the seventeenth century were in fact quite comfortable with only performing it both on and off stage—as well as with the new and better social positions in the absolutist state whose minions they could become if they kept their free will to themselves. Unworldliness and worldliness collaborate nicely here.

At the beginning of his discussion of the Cartesian origins of de-Christianization, Auerbach inserts a footnote, number 48: "I am grateful for having had the opportunity to formulate my theses about the issues I discuss above as a result of having been able to read, in manuscript form, an article by Gerhard Krüger, entitled 'The Origin of Philosophical Self Consciousness,' that the author was kind enough to let me read. It will be appearing in the journal, *Logos,* volume 22, number 3" (48). As noted above, Krüger studied under Nicolai Hartmann and Heidegger in Marburg and probably met Auerbach there. He was also a student and close friend of the Protestant theologian Rudolf Bultmann, and thus moved in circles in which issues associated with war theology and its dialectical counterpart were much debated up into the 1930s. Krüger and Auerbach were apparently more than just colleagues. Indeed, in the winter and spring of 1946, for example, Auerbach asks in concerned fashion after Krüger in several letters to Krauss, inquiring whether Krauss knows if Krüger has survived the war. By October of that same year, the two men have made contact, and exchange letters about the possibility of a job in postwar Germany for Auerbach, who was nevertheless already on his way to the United States by this time.[15] A decade or so earlier, other, perhaps just as pressing, although differently existential concerns appear to have been on the table, including those addressed in Krüger's essay, which did indeed appear in the journal *Logos* in 1933.[16]

In this essay, Krüger examines, among other things, the relationship between the "philosophical self" and human "freedom" in the seventeenth century and above all in Descartes. What interests him most is the question of how Man can, as both a "philosophizer" ("Philosophierender") *and* "as an embodied being" that "belongs to the world," function in the world of the "*polis*" (226). Krüger is interested in these issues because they lie at the origin of what he calls the "catastrophe" of "modern self consciousness" (228), a self consciousness that understands itself as absolutely separate from metaphysical "Truth"; able to know only itself fully, it is suspicious of all that constitutes both Truth and the world. As a result, according to Krüger, a general skepticism and sense of the absolute "meaningless of one's own actions" (228) in the world emerged out of the immense solipsistic doubt on the part of thinkers at the time. The link between such thoughts and Auerbach's analysis of the origin of the impossibility of action by the intelligentsia of the seventeenth century is not hard to discern. At stake in Krüger's article is the question: How did this separation of Man from both Truth and the world come about? Just as importantly: How can reflective Man act in the face of such meaninglessness, if, indeed, he can act at all?

Krüger offers the beginning of an answer to these questions by juxtaposing Descartes with Augustine. (Arendt, who was also at Marburg when Krüger was there, had completed her dissertation on Augustine in Heidelberg under Karl Jaspers' direction just a few years earlier. The parallels between her thesis and Krüger's questions about Man's "freedom" to act are worth considering.) Both Descartes and Augustine see "self knowledge of the self" ("Sich wissen des Selbst") as a "coming to oneself before God" ("Zusichkommen vor Gott,"

232). For Augustine, of course, Man receives the measure of both his earthly and his spiritual existence from the divine; God continues to exist in and for him in the world. For Descartes, however, Man is the only measure of himself. His "self consciousness" is his God; his existence becomes entirely "secularized" ("säkularisiert," 232) as a result. And yet, Krüger writes, while this secularization (which Auerbach subsequently calls de-Christianization) may allow Man—in imitation of God (253)—to be free, not just from the God's frightening power, but also, through judgment, from the dangerous prejudices ("Vorurteile") that the passions and the senses, for example, create (241), Man is always looking back over his shoulder at the all-powerful divine model (250) he has left behind, but Whose power he must imitate and thus acknowledge in order for his own freedom to exist. Hanging uneasily as a disembodied *cogito* between the here and the beyond, between this world and the next, Cartesian Man may well "reject[] Christianity" (243), Krüger writes. But he is still utterly dependent on "Christian tradition" (260). Both powerful and powerless, he is in any case obsessed with proving, over and over again, his freedom from the God on whose transcendent absence as the "oppositional position" (261) he ultimately depends. Ironically un-autonomous in the world, 'enlightened Man' is thus fundamentally un-free to act. This is the catastrophe of modernity of which Krüger writes. The lengthy and byzantine article goes on to address definitions of fate and freedom, hope and virtue, and the notion of progress as it is allegedly present in Descartes. Plato, Aquinas, and Rousseau also make an appearance, as do Krüger's important interlocutors, Heidegger, Husserl, and Leo Strauss, who weigh in on the issue at hand. What Auerbach's footnote 48 to this essay helps us hear, then, is the degree to which commentaries like Krüger's on the religious and existential origins of action (or inaction) in the world by men of the mind were important topics in contemporary philosophical and political-theoretical debates. In his reference to Krüger's thesis about Descartes' secularized world as the obverse of a world ruled absolutely by God, we can observe this context and thus the genealogy of Auerbach's and the others' interest in the theo-political issues behind the passivity of the intelligentsia in seventeenth-century France.

Werner Krauss was familiar with Auerbach's work on the seventeenth century, as noted above, and in 1934 wrote one of the only reviews of his Jewish mentor's *Audience* book that was published in Germany when it appeared.[17] In the review, Krauss praises Auerbach's method, and especially his explanation of the de-functionalization of the intellectuals ("geistig Schaffende," 331) as a result of their class; yet, Krauss was more interested than Auerbach in discovering the possibility of a model for a more active "subject of history"

(330). While it would be difficult to prove that it was Krauss's response to
Auerbach's claims about the failures of the intelligentsia of the seventeenth
century that led, eight years later, to Krauss's work with the Red Orchestra Resistance movement in Berlin, for example, the parallels between the activities
that he would rather have seen on the part of the early modern intelligentsia
and his own engagement in the world are clear.[18] In his review of Auerbach's
book, Krauss suggests a set of alternative interpretations of the phenomenon
the senior scholar had explored; he argues, for example, that there was not a
"loss of [political] function" for the French nobility and bourgeoisie in the
seventeenth century but rather a "change in function" (334). The two classes
may well have been folded into one another and emerged as a new social
group. But rather than becoming powerless, they became "comrades in the
battle" against the "institution of kingship" (337). Krauss's Jansenists were
likewise not quietistic; endorsing, rather, a "Christianity made worldly" ("ein
verweltlichtes Christentum," 339), they engaged intensively with thinking
about their secular role. Even Pascal was called to "action" ("Tätigkeit," 342).
Krauss's seventeenth century thus clearly "evokes" a different way of "thinking the present" with the past than Auerbach's at this point.

Given his assessment—and near reversal—of his mentor's ideas about the
seventeenth century in the review, it is no surprise that in Krauss's own book
about these same issues and figures, which appeared two years later under
the title *Corneille as a Political Writer*, he takes as his topic the issue of the
"sovereignty of the people" ("Volkssouveranität," 345) and its success or lack
thereof in the plays of Corneille. Particularly important to Krauss in 1936 are
questions about whether leaders do or do not defend the rights of the people
and, in turn, about the extent to which the people can act with autonomy
against a "despot" (386) who might betray them.[19] In Krauss's seventeenth
century, Man is not made powerless by the prospect of an all-powerful Godlike sovereign, then. Rather, the people may expect and can demand engagement by that sovereign to preserve their rights. And when the sovereign does
not deliver, the people may justifiably rebel. They nevertheless often do so,
in Krauss's reading, precisely under the banner of "Christianity" ("Christ-
lichkeit"), which, for Krauss, then becomes a prime source of oppositional
strength (354). It is astonishing how open Krauss is here, three years after the
Nazis have come to power, about the parallels he would see between his version of early modernity and more recent times. Richelieu is referred to not
merely as the "cardinal" (358), but also as a "dictator" (359) whose political
aim is the erection of a "Führerstaat," a "state led by the *Führer*" (360). The
pathos of Krauss's reading of Corneille's tragedy *Horace*, with his description of the death of Horace's daughter Camilla, as a symbol of "humanity

undone" when she resists and casts herself up against the "state," the cries of her broken body unheard and un-mourned by anyone within (363), likewise recalls any number of contemporary and future acts of resistance, including those undertaken by Krauss and his young comrades several years hence. In a guest lecture at Freiburg some four years later, which, of all people, Heidegger apparently invited him to deliver, Krauss spoke on "The Martyr Tragedy and the End of Christian Literature in France"; a subsection of the talk was apparently entitled "Martyr Dramas as Literature of Resistance in the Age of Absolutism."[20] The parallels Krauss saw between early modern times and his own are not surprising, given his earlier analysis. It is only remarkable to think that he could have still gotten away with articulating them so openly in 1940. Krauss's Corneille book thus corrects, or, perhaps better, adjusts Auerbach's 'Krüger-ian' reading of the passive alienation of a de-Christianized intelligentsia of the seventeenth century in order to underscore the ways that the intelligentsia could and did become empowered to act in the world—if and when they acted as committed believers.

3. Pascal and Christian Resistance: Auerbach, Krauss, and Guardini

Krauss's *Corneille as a Political Writer* appeared in 1936 in Germany. It would be interesting to know if Auerbach took a copy with him to Istanbul, where he took up a position teaching after the Nazis forced him to resign from his university position in Marburg. But even without any documentation that he did, what is clear is that the provocation of Krauss's call to entertain the possibility of action on the part of intellectuals continued to be a matter of concern to the exile, whose Turkish-language essay based on *The French Audience* appeared in a Turkish journal already in 1936–37. The best proof of this is the piece on the French seventeenth century that Auerbach must have written soon thereafter, namely, the 1941 essay devoted specifically to Pascal, entitled "The Triumph of Evil" ("Der Triumph des Bösen"). Pascal, who in the 1933 *French Audience* had appeared on Auerbach's list of learned men who were "of bourgeois origin" and thus explicitly "without function" (36–37), is now the center of an essay devoted entirely to questions of "political theory."[21]

In "The Triumph of Evil," Auerbach offers a way of reading that later becomes his signature method in *Mimesis*, famously also begun in Istanbul. He opens with a small fragment of text, which he then submits to a penetrating analysis. The text is fragment 298 from Pascal's *Pensées* (in Leon Brunschvicg's edition from 1905), in which the issue is the relation between force and justice:

Justice is subject to dispute;

Might is easily recognizable and is not disputed.

So

We cannot give might to justice, because might has challenged justice,

and has said, it is I who am just.

and thus

being unable to make what is just strong,

we have made what is strong just.

La justice est sujette à dispute, la force est très reconnaissable et sans dispute. Ainsi on n'a pu donner la force à la justice, parce que la force a contredit la justice et a dit que c'était elle qui était juste. Et ainsi, ne pouvant faire que ce qui est juste fût fort, on a fait que ce qui est fort fût juste.[22]

In choosing this passage from Pascal to discuss, Auerbach is clearly continuing his reflections on the same seventeenth century about which he—and Krüger and Krauss, for that matter—had written in the 1930s. In that world and in a time of "an almost completely constituted absolutism" (53), his Pascal's argument goes, those in power, the monarch and his minister, define and determine what is "just." Their might *is* in effect *justice*; it *is* the law. As cunningly phrased as it is, Pascal's argument is nevertheless not just "sophistry," Auerbach insists (51). Rather, "bitterly triumphant," he writes (53), Pascal in fact believed that "on this earth might [*Macht*] represents not only actual positive justice, but legitimate justice" as well (52).

The word that Auerbach uses for "justice" in the 1941 German version of these ideas is revealing: "auf Erden [sei] die Macht nicht nur das wirkliche, positive, sondern auch das 'rechtmäßige' Recht" (53), with "Recht" suggesting positive law, the legal system. Worldly "right," "Recht," the law, acquires "legitimate" ("rechtmäßige") might, moreover, even when, indeed, particularly when it is "arbitrary" and "evil" (58). The somewhat shocking *Realpolitik* of this claim notwithstanding, the phrase "on this earth" signals the embeddedness of the argument in the same Augustinian-Lutheran Two Kingdoms theory that had governed the contest between liberal Protestantism and dialectical theology in the 1910s and 1920s.[23] In this corner, the City of Man with its "worldly political and social institutions," such as the law; in the other, its opponent, the City of God, where "divine justice rules" (55). As separate as the two kingdoms and dispensations may have seemed in *The French Audience*, here a more palpable tension between them has emerged. Indeed, what is stake is how much and what kind of "obedience" Man in the world owes to those "temporal powers" ("weltlichen Gewalten," 55), given their essentially arbitrary nature, which, according to Auerbach, it was Pascal's achievement to have pointed out. In his *Trois Discours sur la condition des Grands* (1660), for example, Pascal underscores not just the effective reality but also the capriciousness of power; only external "respect" and "obedience," and no "inner deference" ("Achtung"), are due to the 'great' of this world, since, he notes, their power is only temporary. A mere turn of the wheel of fortune and someone else will be in charge. (Auerbach actually cites Pascal here to the effect that it is merely a question of a "tour d'imagination" and the essential "poverty and powerlessness" of worldly power are unmasked. The role of the imagination and thus of the mind will become important.) Not based on any "natural or authentic law," the rules of the "great" are also absolutely "opposed to [those of] the kingdom of God," Auerbach writes (59), whose power transcends the "foolish and random" institutions that govern the world (60). In an aside that is all the more powerful because of its understated tone, Auerbach concludes that such thoughts were "widely shared" at the time and "would be exceedingly revolutionary if one failed to contextualize them as Augustinian" (60). With a swerve in logic away from the de-Christianized vision of the seventeenth century of 1933, God's world and divine justice thus actually *do* have an important place in Pascal's system as Auerbach presents it in 1941.

In "The Triumph of Evil," Auerbach argues that the question of what motivates the thinking man to live—and act—justly in a material world from which *justice* is evacuated when it becomes *Recht* is in fact what lies at the center of Pascal's thought. At stake is how one can live "justly" in a world that is "fundamentally and necessarily evil" and thus "in diametric opposition to the kingdom of God" (54) given the infinite chasm between the two realms. It was precisely this chasm that some versions of early modern and modern political theology had tried to bridge by stripping divine power of its otherness and relocating it in the world (as in Schmitt's now all-too-familiar description of the way in which "all significant concepts of the modern theory of the state are secularized theological concepts").[24] Yet, for Auerbach at this point, as for Pascal, secularization of this kind was by no means complete, for there was a crucial remainder of no small import left behind, namely, the all-important residuality of a re-sacralized *justice*—the German word Auerbach uses here is "Gerechtigkeit," divine righteousness, to make the distinction clear (67, for example, and passim)—that continues to pulse just beyond the horizon of Man's world even as—and precisely when—its perverse twin, *Recht*, crosses the divide and becomes law. This justice continues to function as a throbbing reminder—and this is a Krügerian remnant—of how it is that one can in fact live with justice in a world justly determined by force.

Moreover, man *can* live justly in an unjust world, Auerbach goes on to have his Pascal claim—and here, it may be Krauss rather than Krüger whom he is channeling—but only when he (or she) acts as an "instrument" ("Werkzeug," 65) of divine "justice." The two kingdoms can be sutured back together by action. And yet, it is not his own *justice* that Man enacts. Rather, he can only act justly when he acts according to God's will. A "Christian" may "fight for justice and truth," indeed, he "must" fight for truth and justice, Auerbach writes, but he may only do so when he is sure that it "is not in his own interest, but rather in God's service" that he fights (65). Continuing his train of thought from 1933, Auerbach explains that such certainty is not and can never be merely a matter of Cartesian "self examination" (66). Rather, it must result from a steadfast commitment to being at peace with entering the "battle" regardless of the cost and regardless who wins. While martyrdom is not alluded to here explicitly, the call to "endure external resistance with patience" (66) as one fights indicates that it is a distinct possibility. Indeed, even though Pascal's political ideas were in principle very close to those of Machiavelli and Hobbes in terms of the "empirical statecraft" of "*raison d'état*" (72), which acknowledges the "necessity and legitimacy of a powerful state" (73) and leaves the question of justice aside, by 1941 Auerbach's Pascal is said to combine them with what Auerbach labels an Augustinianism predicated on a "positive preoccupation with [one]'s immortal soul" (73). Here, Auerbach allows a second time that such thoughts might seem to contain the "germs of revolutionary social criticism" (74) were it not for their Augustinian setting. He then again dismisses them quickly—so quickly, in fact, that our attention is actually drawn all the more to them as suggesting the possibility of a rebellion against the state legitimated by a religious mandate that encourages neither complicity nor passivity but rather the performance of just action in the world.

In the new situation of his enforced 'passivity' in Istanbul, where he was shadowed by Nazi operatives daily, Auerbach thus uses Pascal to tease out a theory of how to determine moral grounds for intellectual engagement in the public sphere. Neither the terms nor the confessional positions aligned with them are new, however, as he brought them with him out of Weimar Germany. Translating Krüger's theo-existential ideas into the new context and perhaps responding in that context to his own—and Krauss's—concerns about the engagement of the intellectual class in general and of the German intellectual class in particular (whose multidisciplinary membership surrounded him in Istanbul), he finds—or makes—a theory of action immanent in Pascal's thought as a way of challenging both himself and his fellows to think not only "what they were doing" there, but also what they had done in the past—and at the same time updates the theo-political and confessional debates inherited from the *Kulturkampf* and World War I in the context of this new war.[25] Two additional moments in the 1941 essay—and a second important footnote—underscore Auerbach's point about action and the intellectual in relation to the earlier debates.

First, as noted above, in "The Triumph of Evil," Auerbach answers the question of how is it possible to fight for justice in a world where there is no political platform on which the intellectual can base acts of resistance with the argument that "a Christian" can fight for justice in Man's world as long as his actions are based on the righteousness found in God's kingdom. In an interesting "excursus" ("Exkurs," 61) exactly in the middle of the essay, he explains he must take a bit of a detour to explain this claim, arguing that it is important to note that there was for Pascal, in addition to the Two Kingdoms of God and his "infinite love," on the one hand, and of Man and the realm "of material force," on the other, also a third kingdom ("Reich"), the kingdom of "human reason" or "thought" ("des menschlichen Gedankens," 61), whose 'laws' permit a "revolution in the name of the spirit" (or "mind," "Geist") (62). Adding this third "kingdom" may appear a bit "Cartesian" ("erscheint ein wenig cartesianisch gefärbt"), Auerbach suggests somewhat apologetically, but it in fact corresponds to Pascal's theory of Man as a "thinking reed" ("roseau pensant," 61). His project here is, I would argue, to pull Krüger's Cartesian mind over to the positive side of the balance sheet, so to speak, by sacralizing it. That is, even though Auerbach hurries to explain that Pascal in fact never mentions this third kingdom in connection with actual politics, Auerbach locates the possibility of Man's autonomy in the world of his "spirit" or "intellect" ("Geist"). Having planted this seed, his claim a few pages later makes even more sense, when, having asked on what basis a Christian can "fight" for a "true" (and thus not arbitrary) law ("Recht"), Auerbach states forthwith, as noted above: It *is* possible for Man to fight, but only when he is sure that it is in the name of God that he fights (66). It is here that he makes the argument about the unreliability of Man's (Cartesian) ability to "self examine" ("Selbstprüfung") as a way of making sure that it is in God's name that he undertakes the battle. Rather, it must be the "spirit" ("Geist") *as repaired by faith* according to which one acts. With this kind of spirit on one's side, Man can and will fight for a true higher justice, even to the extent of knowing that he will never win, and will do so with such force that he will be able to transcend "normal human courage" (68) and achieve "many meaningful victories." Passive and de-Christianized secularism thus yields to a faith-based willingness to fight even unto "self destruction" ("Selbstvernichtung"). While Auerbach does not use that word here, Krauss had in fact done so five years earlier in his Corneille book when he referred to the self-willed martyrdom of the young Polyeucte in Corneille's play of that name (370). In spite of the differing vocabularies, then, both men—Krauss and Auerbach—clearly think that there is something like a realm of extra-institutional spiritual conviction that can both legitimate and lead to action in the name of *justice*. Again, it is not clear whether it might have been Krauss's review of *The French Audience* or, indeed, his study of Corneille "as a political writer," that functioned as a catalyst for Auerbach, for his commitment, that is, to trying to find in Pascal's work a model in the seventeenth century for moral political action by reformulating Krüger's version of Descartes-with-Augustine in such a way as to develop a theory not of passive disinterest but rather of positive action on the believing intellectual's part. Krüger's orientation towards the transcendent remains, in other words, but out of unworldliness emerges the Kraussian possibility of action in the world.

A second possible source (in addition to Krauss) for this reintroduction of the transcendent into the intelligentsia's world becomes visible in the very first footnote in "The Triumph of Evil." It reads: "On the same topic compare Guardini, *Christian Awareness* [*Christliches Bewußtsein*], Leipzig 1935, pp. 139 ff." (51). As in the case with Krauss's book on Corneille, we do not know whether Auerbach took Romano Guardini's *Christian Awareness* with him into exile. It might have been possible for him to have read it in the Biblioteca San Pietro di Galata in Istanbul, where he did most of the research for the "Figura" essay, for example.[26] The Catholic Guardini (1885–1968) had been a professor of the philosophy of religion in Berlin since 1923 and was very well known, or at least well known enough among Catholics that a few of his books might have been available in the Dominican library in Istanbul. *Christian Awareness* had of course already appeared in Germany in 1935, so it is also possible that Auerbach had already purchased or read it before he had to leave. (It was an entirely different story after 1935, and particularly in 1939, when Guardini openly criticized the Nazi interpretations of Christ in his essay "Der Heiland" ["The Redeemer"] and was forced to resign his university position.[27] His books may have become considerably more difficult to find in Germany over the following six years.) The seriousness with which Guardini in his 1935 book on Pascal discusses exactly the same issues that concern Auerbach in his 1941 "Triumph of Evil," and especially the question of "Man's Status in the Real World" (which is the title of Guardini's second chapter), in any case suggests considerable theological and political sympathies between the two men's work.[28]

The relationship between Guardini and Auerbach is important. What was it that not just readings of Pascal but contemporary German-language Catholic theology in general offered to Auerbach in the 1920s, '30s and even

'40s, after, indeed long after, its liberal Protestant counterpart had utterly
failed to guarantee human justice in the world? What was, for that matter,
the relationship of Guardini's Catholic version of political theology to the
Catholic Schmitt's version of the same? In the context of these larger questions, Guardini's thoughts in the 1935 book that Auerbach cites in 1941 are
relevant not only because they concern Pascal, but also because they address
a specific tradition of theology available in Germany that could serve as the
motor behind the possibility for acts of resistance on the part of the intellectual. Already six years before Auerbach, Guardini had in fact addressed
the relationship in Pascal's thought between three "realms of reality," which
he defines as the 'kingdoms' of the "body," the "mind," and "love," (" 'les
corps'—'les esprits'—'la charité,' " 41). Auerbach's version of Pascal's three
kingdoms may well have found its source here. According to Guardini, these
three 'kingdoms'—and thus state power, one's intellectual life, and one's
faith, which he explicitly aligns with them—were infinitely distant from one
another for Pascal. In 1935, Guardini was thus making the argument for a
theo-philosophical system that separated out these 'kingdoms' from one another for a reason, remembering perhaps an essay he had written some ten
years earlier. His "Redeeming the Political" ("Die Rettung des Politischen,"
1925) originally appeared in the journal of the Quickborn Youth Movement,
Die Schildgenossen (loosely translated: "Comrades in Arms"). There, he warns
of states that "time and again try to transform the power and prestige given to
them by God into their own godlike power . . . it is our duty to be vigilant vis-
à-vis such states and ensure that they stay within their [earthly] bounds."[29]
Guardini's awareness of the impact of the *Kulturkampf* mentioned earlier,
which had of course been much more devastating for German Catholics than
for German Protestants, but also of the intrinsic dangers of Schmittian political theology, is audible here as he insists on the immeasurable distance between the worldly and the divine "orders." By 1935, however, Man, as Guardini finds him in Pascal, *can* fight existentially in the space between the two
kingdoms, and can do so precisely in the all-important space of "Geist," "les
esprits," where, as a thinking human being, he struggles to maintain his balance between the "limited-finite and the unlimited-infinite" worlds, in both
of which he lives (73); Guardini calls this realm the realm of Man's "Genie,"
his "genius," his spiritual strength (83). And yet, according to Guardini, Pascal considers this "Genius" to be—like everything else about Man that is not
divine—tainted and contaminated by evil as a result of original sin.[30] Man
may be able to escape "entanglement in this evil," but only in his "relation
with God" (95). Krüger's de-Christianized self-reflection is in any case not an
option here, in other words.

Auerbach's 1941 reading of Pascal follows Guardini's 1935 argument about Pascal's three kingdoms up to this point. They are in fact nearly mirror images of one another, but only until Guardini maintains that thinking Man, with his spirit ("Geist"), cannot ever really function as an oppositional force or counterweight to events in the world because of original sin. At this point in his 1941 essay, Auerbach abruptly stops reproducing Guardini's reading. Or, perhaps better, he absorbs it in order to take it one step further. Whereas for Guardini's Pascal, "Geist" cannot function as a source of active opposition or resistance, because, like all other non-faith-based institutions, such as society and politics, it is the creature of Evil, for Auerbach, Pascal halts—or hesitates—when it comes to such restrictions on the spirit. Rather, Auerbach explains, even though the realm of the spirit lies at something of a distance from worldly concerns for Pascal, and is even sometimes infected by sin (61), it *must* be able to reach into the world—regardless of how counterintuitive such a claim might seem. "There is no clean and absolute break between power [*Macht*] and spirit," Auerbach nearly shouts—and at this point in the 1941 essay, it is really not at all clear whether he is continuing to ventriloquize Pascal or speaking on his own. "Either there is something earthly, namely, the human spirit [*Geist*], that can successfully challenge power, or power can oppress (or suppress) it" (61–62). Later, when he goes on to assert the necessity that Man fight not in his own interest but rather in God's, as described above, it is clearly the first possibility, the notion, that is, of success, victory ("Sieg," 68), in challenging power that he endorses and believes lies within reach. Again, in the German text, it is almost impossible to tell who is speaking at this point, Auerbach or Pascal, as when Auerbach asserts, for example, that it is difficult for anyone who is "internally invincible" (68) to give in or submit entirely to external force. He (or she) will continue to resist, come what may. In this claim of the possibility that the individual "Geist" can entice something of the divine realm back into the concrete-earthly world as a means of furnishing resistance to temporal injustice, Auerbach's Guardinian Pascal would appear to become more Krauss-like for an instant, capable of defending justice on the ground—even if doing so might mean paying the ultimate price.

4. Conclusion

A much more thorough reading of Auerbach's indebtedness to Catholic theology and to Krüger and Guardini on the political theology of Pascal, also in conversation with similar work by Werner Krauss, would allow us to observe how these men were thinking with the early moderns. For them, the history of early modern philosophy "evoke[d] thinking" as they considered how to act in the world. Yet, theirs was not in any way a purely secularized political-theological discourse. Rather, it was the impact of theological politics in the here-and-now and on the ground with which they were concerned. The early modern forced them to look at the place of the believing intellectual in what they clearly desired to be a *post*-modern world. I am by no means waxing nostalgic for a world in which religious conviction motivates political action. Indeed, both Auerbach and Krauss were committed to understanding how class and political interests were of equal influence in this respect. Yet, along-side theories of political action and state formation based on the seculariza-tion of religious categories and terms, there appears to have existed a clear narrative of the importance of sacred logics in empowering Man to act. We would do well to investigate the power of such logics for these early twentieth-century intellectuals as they looked back to the early modern period for mod-els of how force and justice might interact.

Notes

1. I quote Auerbach's lecture here after the transcription by Martin Vialon of a tape of the lecture made the following August (1949). Erich Auerbach, "The Three Traits of Dante's Poetry," in *Erich Auerbach: Geschichte und Aktualität eines europäischen Philologen*, ed. Martin Treml and Karlheinz Barck (Berlin: Kulturverlag Kadmos, 2007), 414–25. Vialon found the tape of the lecture in 1998 in Istanbul among the papers of the German-Jewish Romanist, Traugott Fuchs, a colleague and friend of Auerbach's, who, like him, fled the Nazis and taught at the Bos-phorus University for many years. See Vialon, "Die Stimme Dantes und ihre Resonanz," also in *Erich Auerbach: Geschichte und Aktualität eines europäischen Philologen*, 46–56. The title of the lecture was assigned by Vialon.

2. On the Princeton lectures, see Robert Fitzgerald, "Paradoxes of a Dwindling Faith: Erich Auerbach on Pascal and Baudelaire," in *Enlarging the Change: The Princeton Seminars in Literary Criticism, 1949–1951* (Boston: Northeastern University Press, 1985), 13–31.

3. These versions of Auerbach's works on Pascal and the seventeenth century may be found in: Auerbach, *Das französische Publikum des 17. Jahrhunderts* (München: Max Hueber Verlag, 1933); "On Yedinci Asirda Fransiz Public'i," *Üniversite Konferanslari* 50 (1937): 113–23; "Der Tri-umph des Bösen: Versuch über Pascals Polische [*sic*] Theorie," *Felsefe Arkivi* 1 (1946): 51–75; "The Triumph of Evil in Pascal," *The Hudson Review* 4.1 (1951): 58–79; "On the Political Theory of Pascal," in *Scenes from the Drama of European Literature: Six Essays by Erich Auerbach* (New York: Meridian Books, 1959), 101–29; "Über Pascals politische Theorie," in *Vier Untersuchungen zur Geschichte der französischen Bildung* (Bern: A. Francke AG Verlag, 1951), 51–74. I would not have been able to compare these various editions of Auerbach's essays without the help of Pro-fessor Martin Vialon (Yeditepe University, Istanbul) and Professor Kader Konuk (University of Michigan, Ann Arbor).

4. On Krüger, see, for example, Hans-Georg Gadamer's introductory remarks in the *Fest-schrift* for Krüger's 60th birthday, "Geleitwort," in *Einsichten* (Frankfurt: Vittorio Klostermann, 1962), 7–10. On Guardini, see Joseph F. Schmucker-von Koch, "Romano Guardini: Christlicher

Realismus und menschliche Selbstbestimmung," in *Grundprobleme der großen Philosophen*, ed. Josef Speck (Göttingen: Vandenhoeck und Ruprecht, 1992), 4:191–228. On Krauss, see *Werner Krauss: Literatur, Geschichte, Schreiben*, ed. Hermann Hofer et al. (Tübingen and Basel: Francke, 2003); *Zum deutsch-französischen Verhältnis: Werner Krauss*, ed. Michael Nerlich (= *Lendesmains* 18, 1993); and Darko Suvin, "Auerbach's Assistant," *New Left Review* 15 (2002): 157–64, and below, note 8.

5. See Joanna Vecchiarelli Scott and Judith Chelius Stark, "Rediscovering Hannah Arendt," in Hannah Arendt, *Love and St. Augustine* (1929) (Chicago: University of Chicago Press, 1996), 115–211, at 116.

6. Martin Heidegger, "Phenomenological Interpretations in Connection with Aristotle: An Indication of the Hermeneutical Situation" (1922), in Heidegger, *Supplements: From the Earliest Essays to Being and Time and Beyond*, ed. John van Buren (Albany: State University of New York Press, 2002), 111–45, at 113.

7. For other contexts in which one might read Auerbach's post-1933 work in Istanbul, see, most famously, Edward Said, as discussed in Emily Apter, "Global *Translatio*: The 'Invention' of Comparative Literature, Istanbul, 1933," *Critical Inquiry* 29 (2003): 253–81; David Damrosch, "Auerbach in Exile," *PMLA* 47.2 (1995): 97–117; and Kader Konuk, "Jewish-German Philologists in Turkish Exile: Leo Spitzer and Erich Auerbach," in *Exile and Otherness: New Approaches to the Experience of Nazi Refugees*, ed. Alexander Stephan (Oxford: Peter Lang, 2005), 31–48. For the post-1946 Auerbach in the United States, see Carl Landauer, "Auerbach's Performance and the American Academy, or How New Haven Stole the Idea of *Mimesis*," in *Literary History and the Challenge of Philology: The Legacy of Erich Auerbach*, ed. Seth Lerer (Stanford: Stanford University Press, 1996), 179–94. Less attention has been paid in English-language criticism to the pre-1933 Auerbach; as an exception, see Martin Elsky, "Church History and the Cultural Geography of Erich Auerbach: Europe and its Eastern Other," in *Opening the Borders*, ed. Peter C. Herman (Newark: University of Delaware Press, 1999), 324–49. For German-language treatments of Auerbach in the Weimar period, see the following, all in *Erich Auerbach: Geschichte und Aktualität eines europäischen Philologen*: Matthias Bormuth, "Menschenkunde zwischen Meistern—Erich Auerbach und Karl Löwith im Vergleich," 82–104; Karlheinz Barck, "Erich Auerbach in Berlin: Spurensicherung und ein Porträt," 195–215; and Leopoldo Waizbrot, "Erich Auerbach im Kontext der Historismusdebatte," 281–97.

8. Krauss was a junior colleague of Auerbach's in Romance Languages at Marburg and his last *Assistent* there. Not a Jew, Krauss was asked to take over Auerbach's duties at the university when Auerbach was forced out in 1935 and did so at his mentor's request. He was no National Socialist lackey, however; already considered politically unreliable by the Nazi authorities, who reviewed his case for a position at the University of Rostock the following year, Krauss subsequently became involved in a series of resistance actions in Berlin, for which he and dozens of young accomplices were arrested and condemned to death in 1942. As Krauss listened to his young friends being led off to be executed, he wrote a little book on the Spanish Baroque political theorist Baltasar Gracian as he waited his turn. Krauss himself survived the war by pleading insanity. His interest in the impact of unjust force on himself and his friends was in any case no abstract matter. On Krauss's work with the Resistance, see Karlheinz Barck, "Werner Krauss im Widerstand und vor dem Reichskriegsgericht," in *Zum deutsch-französischen Verhältnis: Werner Krauss*, ed. Michael Nerlich (= *Lendesmains* 18, 1993), 137–50. Krauss's own "Bericht aus der Todeszelle" is also reprinted there on 157–63. Krauss's letter to Auerbach about *The French Audience* is cited in the notes to the reprint of Krauss's review essay, "Über die Träger der klassischen Gesinnung im 17. Jahrhundert," first published in 1934 in a specialist journal, and repro-

duced in Krauss, *Spanische, italienische und französische Literatur im Zeitalter des Absolutismus*, ed. Peter Jehle, with notes by Horst F. Müller (Berlin/New York: de Gruyter, 1997), 330–43, with notes on 611–12.

9. See Peter Jehle, "Zur literaturwissenschaftlichen Corneille-Rezeption im deutschen Faschismus," *Romanistische Zeitschrift für Literaturgeschichte* 18 (1994): 126–47, and Frank-Rutger Hausmann, *"Vom Strudel der Ereignisse verschlungen": Deutsche Romanistik im 'Dritten Reich'* (Frankfurt: Vittorio Klostermann, 2000).

10. Hannah Arendt, "What is Existential Philosophy?" (1948), in Arendt, *Essays in Understanding, 1930–1954* (New York: Harcourt Brace and Company, 1994), 163–87, at 186.

11. Walter Benjamin, "Left-Wing Melancholy," in Benjamin, *Selected Writings*, vol. 2: *1927–1934*, ed. Michael W. Jennings et al. (Cambridge, Mass.: Harvard University Press, 1999), 423–27, at 424–25.

12. On the *Kulturkampf* and its importance for studying the early modern period in the work of Walter Benjamin and Aby Warburg, see my "Enchantment in Times of War: Aby Warburg, Walter Benjamin, and the Secularization Thesis," *Representations* 105 (2009): 133–67. For an excellent overview of the period, see Helmut Walser Smith, *German Nationalism and Religious Conflict: Culture, Ideology, and Politics, 1870–1914* (Princeton: Princeton University Press, 1995).

13. See Wilhelm Walther, *Deutschlands Schwert, durch Luther geweiht* (Leipzig: Dörffling und Franke Verlag, 1914). Walther explains the "divinely legitimated right" the Germans have to fight the war (1) with the claim: "The war is the will of God" (11).

14. Auerbach cites his own earlier essay on "Racine and the Passions" from 1926 in a footnote here (53, note 53), indicating an even earlier date for when he began to formulate these thoughts.

15. See Auerbach's letters to Krauss of 30 January 1946, 13 April 1946, and 27 October 1946, in Karlheinz Barck, ed., "Eine unveröffentlichte Korrespondenz: Erich Auerbach/Werner Krauss," *Beiträge zur Romanischen Philologie* 26.2 (1987): 301–26, at 311, 313, and 319.

16. Gerhard Krüger, "Die Herkunft des philosophischen Selbstbewusstseins," *Logos: Internationale Zeitschrift für Philosophie der Kultur* 22 (1933): 225–72.

17. Krauss, "Über die Träger der klassischen Gesinnung im 17. Jahrhundert," *Zeitschrift für französischen und englischen Unterricht* 33.1 (1934): 27–38, reprinted in Krauss, *Spanische, italienische und französische Literatur im Zeitalter des Absolutismus* (see note 8), 330–43.

18. See note 8 above.

19. Werner Krauss, *Corneille als Politischer Dichter* (Marburg: Adolf Ebel, 1936), reprinted in Krauss, *Spanische, italienische und französische Literatur im Zeitalter des Absolutismus*, 344–95. All citations are included parenthetically in the text.

20. See Krauss, "Das Ende des christlichen Märtyrers in der klassischen Tragödie der Franzosen," reprinted in Krauss, *Spanische, italienische und französische Literatur im Zeitalter des Absolutismus*, 397–409, with notes, 617–42, that contain transcriptions of various manuscripts about the topic that survive in Krauss's papers.

21. The subtitle of the 1941 essay is "Essay on Pascal's Political Theory." See note 3.

22. Auerbach, 1946, 51, quotes only the French. The English translation here follows Auerbach's citation of Pascal in both French and English in Auerbach, 1959, 102. See note 3 for the references. In what follows, the translations from Auerbach's essay, originally in German, are my own.

23. Auerbach in fact claims that Pascal had adopted the "extreme Augustinianism" of the "men of Port Royal" (54). NB: In the original copy of the 1946 *Felsefe Arkivi*, there is a misprint

in the pagination, with 64 for 54. I cite it here and elsewhere with correct pagination supplied (e.g., 54).

24. Carl Schmitt, *Political Theology: Four Chapters on the Concept of Sovereignty*, trans. George Schwab (Cambridge, Mass.: MIT Press, 1985), 36.

25. It actually appears to have been Krauss, who, after the war, when Auerbach was contemplating a second edition of *The French Audience*, suggested that the final eight pages be dropped; he is in any case pleased, in a letter to Auerbach from 1947, to see the new "de-Krügerized" ("entkrügerte") conclusion, as Auerbach appears to have been preparing it for its publication as the shortened essay "La cour et la ville" in 1951. It may be that in 1947 Krauss had not yet been able to read the Pascal essay, with its resuscitation of "Krügerian" ideas in the direction of "Kraussian" action. The letter is quoted in Manfred Naumann, "Auerbach im Fühlen und Denken von Werner Krauss," in *Erich Auerbach: Geschichte und Aktualität eines europäischen Philologen*, 180–92, at 188.

26. On Auerbach's use of the library of San Pietro di Galata, see Earl Jeffrey Richards, "Erich Auerbach's *Mimesis* as a Meditation on the Shoah," *German Politics and Society* 19.2, issue 59 (2001): 62–91, at 66.

27. See Robert A. Krieg, *Catholic Theologians in Nazi Germany* (New York: Continuum, 2004), 107, 109, and 115–19.

28. Romano Guardini, *Christliches Bewußtsein: Versuche über Pascal* (Leipzig: Verlag Jakob Hegner, 1935). Hereafter cited parenthetically in the text in my translations. The sympathies between the two men may have extended also to questions of methodology. Guardini's approach to reading Pascal in *Christian Awareness* is strikingly similar to Auerbach's, for example; indeed, the debt may have gone the other way, particularly since it was Guardini who, already in 1935, had written that, instead of covering the secondary literature on the philosopher, he will "stay very close to his texts" (22). The first chapter could in fact have been a model for *Mimesis*, or, for that matter, for "The Triumph of Evil" essay itself. Guardini takes as his subject a textual fragment from Pascal's oeuvre, the famous "Mémorial," and writes: "We shall begin with the analysis of this little text" (25).

29. Romano Guardini, "Rettung des Politischen," in Guardini, *Wurzeln eines großen Lebenswerks: Aufsätze und kleine Schriften*, ed. Franz Heinrich (Mainz/Paderborn: Matthias Grünewald Verlag, 2001), 2:207–10.

30. Guardini claims that here Pascal is explicitly criticizing Descartes and his theory of self consciousness as a power over self as only so much "arrogance and hubris" (90). Unfortunately he does not cite Krüger at this point in the argument, as he might have, since their thoughts on the matter are so similar. The two men were in fact very close, and it was in conversation with Guardini that Krüger decided to convert to Catholicism after the war.

PART TWO

Scenes of Early Modernity

9

The Instance of the Sovereign in the Unconscious:
The Primal Scenes of Political Theology

JACQUES LEZRA ⟨*NYU*⟩

And earthly power doth then show likest God's
When mercy seasons justice.
Merchant of Venice, 4.1.196–97

This *analogy* is the very site of the theologico-political, the hyphen [*trait d'union*] or translation between the theological and the political; it is also what underwrites political sovereignty, the Christian incarnation of the body of God (or Christ) in the king's body, the king's two bodies.

JACQUES DERRIDA, "What Is a 'Relevant' Translation?"

There is, I take it, a divided question behind the claim that "Political Theology" finds a place, especially a primary or a primal place, on the scenes of early modernity. On one hand, we might be asking this: "In what ways does our understanding of the early modern period condition how we imagine the encounter between politics and theology? What is the agency, the instance, of the 'early modern' in our formulation of the theologico-political?" This way of posing the question leads us to read Löwith or Schmitt through *Hamlet* or *The Merchant of Venice,* for example, or more precisely through a reading of *Hamlet*'s role, or *The Merchant of Venice's* role, in setting the conditions under which we can make statements about "political theology." (*Hamlet or Hecuba,* yes, but on the condition of understanding the work that *Hamlet* does today in popular as well as high culture, inside as well as outside the walls of the university.) The outcome: a satisfactory critical shuttling between historical positions and critical idioms; a "history of the present"; statements (about terms like "politics" or "theology") that attend to the historicity of their own moment and conditions of enunciation. The risks: the bad conscience of endless mediation, and the radically shifted truth-value of the statements "we" can make about object terms. For "early" one should be able to substitute other fatuous chronological markers ("middle," "late"); the community charged with "understanding," "imagining," or "formulating" changes accordingly; what counts as "politics" and "theology" too. The companion acknowledgement that recognizing mediation's bad conscience changes nothing could easily be taken, rather smugly, as the defining characteristic of a particular post-modernity. (This would be an adequate way to understand Baudrillard's work, and a rather weaker, but defensible, way of understanding Stiegler's.) When we ask about the imaginary construction of the historicity of the encounter (between two concepts, "politics" and "theology"), and ask this question in the awareness of its hyper-mediation, and place under the same historicist lens the criteria for determining the truth or falsehood of the answers to this question—then we are being modern, never more so.

On the other hand, when we claim that "political theology" finds a place on the scenes of early modernity, we are to ask ourselves something like this as well: "Can we identify, in works we group chronologically, the shape of the *encounter* between what we now call 'politics' and 'theology'?" We recognize on this side of the question that we are reasoning from effects to causes, borrowing the subject that we seek out (something called "political theology") from a lexicon that it helps set in place and define. "Politics," "theology," and their relation are of course different subjects of inquiry today than they were yesterday, for instance in the early modern period; what we discover today about the "scene" or "scenes" of early modernity serves primarily to confirm the genealogies of our own thought. Asked this way the question becomes, like many archaeological questions, in part an exercise in historical legitimation. A basic, *substantial* continuity (this is Blumenberg's argument) underlies the specious historiographical break between an "early" modernity in which "politics" trailed clouds of still-unforgotten theological glory, and a "modern," secularized modernity: the more the cultural historian marks the difference from the "early" political theology, the more its mantle drifts to his or her shoulders.[1] The polemic now has another edge. "Political theology" is not a concept alone but the record of an encounter (it is not, for instance, *only* a "borderline concept . . . pertaining to the outermost sphere," as Schmitt describes the concept of sovereignty); the continuing importance of secularization (also not a concept alone) is to be explained by its conversion into disciplinary authority—the migration of the techniques of valuation of culture from the domain of economic elites to the domain of intellectual elites.[2] The discipline, or the technique, of cultural criticism is the most "modern" of political theologies.

If we parse as I have just done the claim that "political theology" finds a place, especially a primary or a primal place, on the scenes of early modernity, we enter a circle, the classic figure for mediation. The concept (borderline, weak, bearing the marks of its construction) of "political theology" is to be thought today in light of the culturally prevailing understanding of the "early modern period." And the concept of the "early modern period" (again, a borderline concept, weak, manifestly fashioned rather than given) is to be thought today by means of a culturally prevailing understanding of "political theology." These are necessarily weak assertions. What *is* a "culturally prevailing understanding" of a concept? (It is not much better to say that "early modernity" or "political theology" are to be "thought" in or through "the lexicon associated with" this or that concept, "political theology" or "early modernity.") Is "culture" synonymous here with "discipline"?

In what follows I'll be trying to answer the following question, while staying as thoroughly as I can within the limits of the circle I have just described. The question: Is there indeed a primal encounter between "politics" and "theology," an early modern "hyphen [*trait d'union*] or translation between the theological and the political" (Derrida) from which the modern understanding of cultural mediation flows? I'm going to approach this question in the context of the crisis of classical, indivisible sovereignty that writers on political theology locate in the early modern period. Where theological concepts *were, there* will, *there* should the modern state *be.*

1. Freud's Schiller

Don Carlo *atterrito.* Cielo! La morte! per chi mai?
Rodrigo *ferito mortalmente.* Per me!

> GIUSEPPE VERDI, *Don Carlos*

Revolutions, I believe, are acceptable only when they are over; and therefore they ought to be over very quickly. What the human beast needs above all is restraint. In short, one grows reactionary, just as incidentally did the rebel Schiller in face of the French Revolution.

> SIGMUND FREUD TO LOU-ANDREAS SALOMÉ, 17 February 1918[3]

Let's start over. It is not controversial, I think, to suggest that we owe to Freud, whose famous, moving line *Wo Es war, soll Ich werden* I am mimicking above, the prevailing account of how, and why, modern subjects are not immediately understandable to themselves. (No particular judgment concerning the accuracy or inaccuracy, truth or falsehood, of Freud's accounts is entailed by this suggestion. It signals the cultural importance of a particular lexicon and of a series of more-or-less conventional transformations of that lexicon; it bears on the place that psychoanalytic discourse occupies at the heart of the practices of mediation, and of the languages in which mediation is imagined, in European and Anglo-American popular and academic culture.) That the hand-off from theology to politics—a hand-off that is of course historically uneven, halting, distributed differently in different domains in which sovereignty is exercised and administered—might have for contemporary political philosophy the characteristics of a *primal scene* means that the encounter between the theological and the political (supposing for now that we can speak of these as if each were distinct from the other) has at the same time the status of a retrospective fantasy; of a compensatory formation or a displacement; of a trauma; and of a fact. It also means that the encounter between theology and politics is imagined to entail an immediate contact between two distinct substances, forms, discursive strategies, *and also* that it is imagined as an utterly mediated, utterly historical relation. "Theology" hands off its sovereign form to "politics" hand to hand, body to body, two distinct, substantial bodies notionally becoming one consubstantial one: the king's body. (In Spanish we say: *se relevan,* and a relay race is a *carrera de relevos.*) But "theology" hands off to "politics" a sovereign form built up of uses and mentions, representations now and then of acts that cultures, and cultures' subjects and users, give different weight and sense to, at different moments, to different effect; as they do to this process that Derrida calls the *trait d'union* (*trait* is not just a line like a hyphen, but a substantivized act: a joining, pulling, tracing, blotting-out, canceling, preserving; rather like what Derrida's essay refers to as *une relève* or as the verb *relever,* his translations not only for "translation," but also and much more famously for the Hegelian terms *Aufhebung* and *aufheben*) and which I've been abstractly calling a "handing-off." For the lines of history, of use, sense, and work, are marked upon the hands that hand-off the sovereign form.

The first step involves a baldly positive assertion. *Wo Es war, soll Ich werden,* the defining, mysterious line from Freud that I have been belaboring— written, Lacan assures us, at the "height of [Freud's] thought"—is not only the definition or the description of a new concept or of a new temporal horizon for the psychic apparatus, it is also and primarily a citation from Schiller's play *Don Karlos, Infant von Spanien,* of 1786–87.[4] Sampled from the field of culture, Freud's famous, "moving" line is the very figure of cultural mediation, and it bears marked upon it the *traits* of Schiller's work, until now more or less unremarked. Written toward the end of Freud's career, in 1933–34, in the *Neue Folge der Vorlesungen zur Einführung in die Psychoanalyse,* the sentence crops up at the end of the thirty-first of Freud's lectures, this one devoted to the subject of "Die Zerlegung der psychischen Persönlichkeit" ("The Dissection [or disassembling, or decomposing, or analyzing] of the Psychical Personality")—as ironic a title as Freud had ever provided. Freud has in mind the struggle to reclaim territory for the ego: this, he says, is the task and the aim of psychoanalysis understood as "therapy," and not the "reconciliation" of *Ich* with *Es,* or the production of some sort of peaceful synthesis between the analytically "dissected" parts of the "personality." Bruno Bettelheim remarked on Freud's unexpected use of the term *Kulturarbeit* in this essay to characterize this struggle; Goethe's *Faust* seems to Bettelheim the most likely source.[5] Freud's metaphors, Bettelheim understands, are at the same time military and hydrological. (This is in part what makes the essay's title ironic: there is no easy way to imagine "dissecting" a fluid, a sea for instance: dykes and dams re-channel fluids, but to section off something, to cut it, to dissect it and have it stay dissected—this requires that the substance in hand be a great deal more concrete than the psychic apparatus proves to be.) *Kulturarbeit* is not only, and maybe not be principally, an intellectual project (the writing of a work like *Faust,* the consolidation of the "civilization" of the Renaissance for the use and enjoyment of a modern European elite), but something on the order of the reclamation of land for cultivation, like draining a marsh, or taming a raging sea. The work that psychoanalysis does to permit "I" to encroach upon "Id" is like work a laborer does upon the land—hand-work, tilling, turning over soil, or building levies, dykes, and dams.

This is Freud's paragraph:

> In thinking of this division of the personality into an ego, a super-ego and an id, you will not, of course, have pictured sharp frontiers like the artificial ones drawn in political geography. We cannot do justice to the characteristics of the mind by linear outlines like those in a drawing or in primitive painting, but rather by areas of colour melting into one another as they are presented by modern artists. After making the separation we must allow what we have separated to merge together once more. . . . Particularly in the case of what is phylogenetically the last and most delicate of these divisions—the differentiation between the ego and the super-ego—something of the sort seems to be true. There is no question but that the same thing results from psychical illness. . . . [Psycho-analysis's] intention is, indeed, to strengthen the ego, to make it more independent of the super-ego, to widen its field of perception and enlarge its organization, so that it can appropriate fresh portions of the id. Where id was, there ego shall be. [*Wo Es war, soll Ich werden.*] It is a work of culture—something like the draining of the Zuider Zee. [*Es ist Kulturarbeit, etwa wie Trockenlegung der Zuydersee.*][6]

It is also, however, "something like" the work of cultural appropriation, or the work of cultural mediation. First, here is Schiller's line. The time—circa 1560. The speakers are King Philip II and the Grand Inquisitor:

KING. But [the Marquis of Posa] / Had been beyond my kingdom's boundaries.

GRAND INQUISITOR. Wherever he might be, there I was also. [*Wo Er sein mochte, war Ich auch.*]

KING (*walking impatiently back and forth*). It was known in whose hands I was—Why then was there / Delay in warning me?

Schiller's great play—a signal achievement of *Kulturarbeit*, surely central to the European *universitas litterarum*—sets before its audience the tragic sacrifices that attend the encounter between the political and the theological domains: the sacrifice of a son, a friend, a wife, a mistress, of the sovereign's undivided authority. Schiller bases himself in the well-known story of the death of Philip's son Carlos of Austria, reputed (in Spain) to have gone mad, and to have died in confinement; but bruited (in the European elites' imaginary, intent on linking the decline of Spain's power to the orthodoxy of its religious institutions) to have been assassinated on his father's orders for sedition, heresy, and finally for having set his sights upon his father's new, third wife, Elisabeth de Valois.[7] The exchange that Freud remembers comes after the play's political plot has resolved itself; the theological struggle will be decided in these lines, and the domestic *denouement* follows, in the play's closing scene. King Philip II, Spain's ruler from 1555 to 1598, summons the Inquisitor. They are discussing the assassination of the Marquis de Posa, Prince Carlos's great friend and interlocutor, on the king's orders. Posa is the play's representative of Enlightened rationalism, and he has been working to convince the king's son to join the party of rebellion in the Netherlands, revolt against his father, and install something like an enlightened republic in the Hapsburg empire.[8] Posa has been captured and—after a remarkable exchange with King Philip—done away with on the king's orders. In the play's penultimate scene the blind Inquisitor reveals that the Inquisition had long nurtured a plan to capture and execute Posa "as a terrible example, / And turn high-vaunting reason into shame." The Inquisitor is highly displeased to have been deprived of his victim; Philip, distraught to find that Posa and Carlos were plotting rebellion, the overthrowing of the confessional and inquisitorial Hapsburg monarchy, and the installation of an alternative form of government, concludes the scene placing his "right to judge" in the Inquisitor's hands, and agreeing to hand over Prince Carlos to the Inquisition. The function of *terror* has been reestablished; after the brief opening that Posa's words and deeds provide, rebellion will once again be bound ("Und Schrecken bändigt die Empörung nur. / Erbarmung hieße Wahnsinn," the king has warned Carlos.) More extensively, the scene that Freud is remembering opens like this:

GRAND INQUISITOR. Why did you commit this murder?

KING. Betrayal without parallel——

GRAND INQUISITOR. I know it.

KING. What do you know? Through whom? Since when?

GRAND INQUISITOR. For years, / What *you* have known since sunset.

KING (*surprised*). What? You had / Already known about this man?

GRAND INQUISITOR. His life / Lies opened and concluded in the holy / Record-ledgers of the Santa Casa.

KING. And he walked free?

GRAND INQUISITOR. The cord on which he fluttered / Was long, but still unbreakable.

KING. But he / Had been beyond my kingdom's boundaries.

GRAND INQUISITOR. Wherever he might be, there I was also.

KING (*walking impatiently back and forth*). It was known in whose hands I was—Why then was there / Delay in warning me?

GRAND INQUISITOR. That question I / Turn back upon you—Why did *you* not ask / When you threw yourself into this man's arms?

KÖNIG. Ein Betrug, der ohne Beispiel ist–

GROßINQUISITOR. Ich weiß ihn.

KÖNIG. Was wisset Ihr? Durch wen? Seit wann?

GROßINQUISITOR. Seit Jahren, / Was Sie seit Sonnenuntergang.

KÖNIG *mit Befremdung.* Ihr habt / Von diesem Menschen schon gewußt?

GROßINQUISITOR. Sein Leben / Liegt angefangen und beschlossen in / Der Santa Casa heiligen Registern.

KÖNIG. Und er ging frei herum?

GROßINQUISITOR. Das Seil, an dem / Er flatterte, war lang, doch unzerreißbar.

KÖNIG. Er war schon außer meines Reiches Grenzen.

GROßINQUISITOR. Wo er sein mochte, war ich auch.

KÖNIG *geht unwillig auf und nieder.* / Man wußte, / In wessen Hand ich war—Warum versäumte man, / Mich zu erinnern?

GROßINQUISITOR. Diese Frage geb ich / Zurücke—Warum fragten Sie nicht an, / Da Sie in dieses Menschen Arm sich warfen?[9]

A few words to fill in the outlines of the cultural reservoir that Freud is drawing from, and to establish the plausibility of this source.

That Freud had read Schiller's play attentively cannot be doubted. He cites from it a number of times in his letters—for instance, in an early letter to Eduard Silberstein he remembers the play's first lines, "Die schönen Tage in Aranjuez / Sind nun zu Ende"—and he refers to these lines again in a letter to Ferenczi of October 1912; in a letter to Martha Bernays, he recalls the lines "*In meinem Frankreich* wischt man solche Tränen / Mit Freuden ab . . . [/]

In meinem Frankreich war's noch anders," from *Don Karlos* 1.6, spoken by the queen and misattributed by Freud in his letter to Mary Stuart, another of Schiller's heroines; in a letter to Fliess from 1895, Freud recalls 2.13: "My theories on defense have made an important advance of which I shall give you an account in a brief paper next time. Even the psychological construction behaves as if it would come together, which would give me immense pleasure. Naturally, I cannot yet say for certain. Reporting on it now would be like sending a six-month fetus of a girl to a ball. We shall not suffer from a dearth of topics to talk about. 'Your battles,' it says in *Don Karlos*, 'and your God'" [Schiller: HERZOG: . . . diese Rosen / Und Ihre Schlachten— ALBA: Und dein Gott—so will ich / Den Blitz erwarten, der uns stürzen soll!]; in a letter to Jung from 31 October 1910 Freud alludes to *Don Karlos* 1.9 ("arm in arm with you"); and Freud mentions the play as late as 1934 in a letter to Arnold Zweig.[10] In 1920 we find him adding a footnote to *The Psychopathology of Everyday Life* of 1901, producing as an example of a literary representation of the slip of the tongue "Shakespeare's *Richard II* (Act II, Scene 2), and . . . Schiller's *Don Karlos* (Act II, Scene 8; a slip made by Princess Eboli)."[11] Freud's circle was at least as interested in *Don Karlos* as was Freud himself—perhaps for obvious reasons. Otto Rank's 1912 *Das Inzest-Motiv in Dichtung und Sage* devotes a long chapter to the stepmother theme in the play. (Carlos's love for the queen, who steps into his mother's position, results in a crudely Oedipal and crudely doubled struggle—for the queen, for the Princess of Eboli, both of them objects of the king's attention, and of the prince's—in which the father does away with the son and the son's protector and proxy, Posa—at a cost to himself that Philip only glimpses late in the play.) In 1914–15, Hanns Sachs had published two linked articles in *Imago* (at the time jointly edited by Freud, Sachs, and Rank) on Schiller's unfinished play *Der Geisterseher*, placing it in dialogue explicitly with *Don Karlos*. Sachs's observations concerning the rivalries at the heart of the play's plot are not especially original; on the other hand, his analysis of the "Polizeistoff" in Schiller's plays, of the "geheimnisvollen Organisation des Katholizismus" in *Geisterseher* and in *Don Karlos*, where the figure of the Inquisitor draws his attention, is striking.[12] In 1924 Lou Andreas-Salomé wrote to Anna Freud referring to *Don Karlos*, and in 1925 Theodor Reik cited from *Don Karlos* in his *Geständniszwang und Strafbedürfnis*.[13]

None of this is conclusive, of course. And it may be that the drive to establish with certainty the famous phrase's sources is itself to some extent a distraction. (It would not be wrong to detect here the interference of "fantasy," or of a compensatory displacement, with the desire to produce a literary-historical "fact.") A complementary but different approach, no more manifestly verifiable and much less "factual" than the source-searching, cultural-reservoir-filling tack I have just taken, would be to ask whether the reference, if it is one, to Schiller *makes sense* in the context of the lecture. "Makes sense" here means: is motivated by the context, arises in a determinable relation to the "dissection" of the "psychic personality," plausibly reinforces Freud's claims in the lecture. Here matters are much trickier, as what we take to *be* Freud's claims in the lecture have come down to his readers built upon the signal mystery of the phrase, a mystery that enables us to read it as the most lyrical enunciation of the therapeutic horizon of psychoanalysis, of what Lacan refers to as "reintegration and harmony, I might even say of reconciliation [*Versöhnung*]" ("Instance . . . ," 435). The context that Schiller's play provides dashes this view of Freud's phrase, and of the great arc of his argument (we no longer move from *Zerlegung* to *Versöhnung*, one might say)—so in an important way the informing mediation of Schiller's text cannot be read within the horizon of the "therapeutic" or humanistic construction of "the goal Freud's discovery proposes to man."

Let's allow the hypothesis that Schiller's scene lies behind Freud's phrase to work, for now. What changes about the "dissection" of the "psychical personality" when *Don Karlos*, Schiller's representation of the encounter between politics and theology in one version of the period of early modernity, enters onto the scene? What changes in our understanding of Freud's career, and in the *Neue Folge der Vorlesungen zur Einführung in die Psychoanalyse*? What changes in the history of the psychoanalytic movement after Freud? Finally, what changes in our understanding of the mediating and determining functions of the notion of "early modernity"?

On the most obvious level, remark that a complicated, flickering pattern of identifications and disidentifications takes shape as soon as Schiller's play steps into Freud's essay. We have seen, from Freud's letter to Lou-Andreas Salomé of 17 February 1918, cited above, how Freud appears to identify with Schiller, the one's Russian Revolution echoing the other's French. The temptation to play out Schiller's dramatic scene with other characters—with Freud's characters and concepts—is irresistible, but it immediately makes Freud's screened allusion thoroughly unreadable, and the phrase's value as a description much less certain (or different). Prince Carlos, infantile and impetuous in Schiller's play, might momentarily capture something about the pleasure principle; his affection for his young stepmother (in evidence spectacularly in Verdi's version of the story, of course), his father's censure, the son's duplication in the father's affection (Carlos, Posa)—all these follow flickeringly a well-known Oedipal plot. Consider also, on a different level, the momentary identification the screened reference invites, between the psychoanalyst and Posa, the character who embodies the sort of rationality that might support the project of a critical "dissection" of the "psychic personality." A certain tragic heroism is solicited for the psychoanalyst, on this reading: destined to exile and death, to supervision, disciplining, sacrifice, all for having followed out egalitarian political principles (Posa) or for having proposed a description of human subjectivity that dethrones old psychic masters, and installs the equally leveling sovereignty of the unconscious.

For Schiller, and then mediately, informingly, for Freud, Hapsburg confessionalism, that old and renewed alliance between politics and theology, lines up against the figure of enlightened analysis, the figure of psychoanalysis and the psychoanalyst; the blind Inquisitor and the king stand in against the enlightened Renaissance, against Posa's and Leonardo's and (later) Burckhardt's Renaissance. They are figures of censure, interdiction, orthodoxy, disciplinarity; Spain stands, reactionary, culturally against Italy and politically against the republican Netherlands; an early modernity that guards the *trait d'union* between theology and politics against a non-theological, resolutely modern secularism.

One is used to these symmetries and duplications in Schiller's work. In Freud, however, matters get messy almost immediately. When the principle of enlightened reason travels beyond the confines of the confessional realm, it does so still under surveillance, and it still acts a part set for it by forces willing for it, willing where it wills. *Wo Es war, soll Ich werden,* or, as the Inquisitor has it, *Wo Er sein mochte, war Ich auch.* With Freud's Schiller, we now imagine the Inquisitor, that blind-but-all-seeing mechanism of the "I" that was always-already wherever the drive to escape—Posa in this little allegory— ever wanted to go. The Inquisitor says: "I was there already, wherever you wanted to go, in the place to which you, Posa, wanted to escape, watching and waiting." Or he says: "The 'I' is in fact nothing other than that structure of watching-and-waiting for the arrival of the desire for freedom, as it arrives where it thinks it is free only to find itself captured or expressed, for instance by the work of 'culture,' by the word of Schiller's play." But if this is so then on the *disciplinary* level—and one should remember that Freud's stories, even his case-histories, are most often also disciplinary stories—Posa no longer stands in for psychoanalysis, or not at any rate for all of the functions of psychoanalysis. Instead, it is psychoanalysis itself, recovering ground for the "I" from the swampy seepages or heroic sallies of the "it," that the blind Inquisitor and the king, theology and politics joined together in this imaginary reconstruction of the primal scene where politics and theology meet—it is psychoanalysis itself that the administrative terror of the theologico-political represents; that the terror of the administrative-confessional, early modern,

Spanish Inquisitorial state represents. Gone, on this Inquisitorial description, is the pathos of renunciation and reconciliation that Lacan and others find in *Wo Es war* . . . Culture works here to drain Freud's *Kulturarbeit* of therapeutic sense. Under the pressure of Schiller's informing scene, Freud's phrase reveals instead the intrinsically supervisory, political function that informs the hydrology or the mechanics of the psychic system.

One result in either case, whether we unfold the antithetical identification of psychoanalysis in the direction of Posa (the psychoanalyst as a tragic figure of rational emancipation) or in the direction of the administrative terror of the theologico-political, toward the king and the Inquisitor: the notions of force, violence, and administrative oversight move from being themes or circumstances subject to ontogenetic, "psychoanalytic" investigation, and susceptible of a therapeutic intervention (for instance, by means of techniques that permit the "I" to take over ground from the "it" or the "id"), to being structuring principles of that investigation. (We are never in a position to abandon *Zerlegung*, dissection, segmentation, analysis: deconstruction.)

And yet even this complicated, contradictory, antithetical picture is incomplete, and in one respect it is crucially wrong. In Schiller's play, the struggle between the king and the Inquisitor over the prince's fate is slight—a disagreement amongst the archaic forces that resist modernization and enlightenment rather than a significant contradiction in the conceptualization of sovereignty. Nor is the outcome really in dispute—not least because the scene repeats the earlier encounter between the king and the prince, when the monarch reminds his son that any course but the application of "terror" would be "madness" [*Wahnsinn*]: because the king has ruined the Inquisitor's plan, a substitute must be found. (The weight of the analogy between the two scenes is carried by the king's acknowledgment to the Inquisitor that "Ich bin / In diesen Dingen noch ein Neuling. Habe / Geduld mit mir." [I am in such matters no better than a novice, a beginner. Be patient with me.]) And into this empty spot, the spot of the sacrificial, exemplary victim, the prince will be delivered by his father.

Except of course that Schiller's scene does not depict the successful coordination of the political and the theological-administrative regimes, the triumph of the Inquisitor, the handing-off of the substantial form of sovereignty from theology to politics or politics to theology, and the marking of the translation or *trait d'union* between the two domains. The history of the Inquisition has a name for one such successful hand-off. The Spanish and American Inquisitions, unable legally to carry out executions, turned over condemned prisoners to the crown, which confirmed and carried out the Tribunal's sentences. These prisoners were referred to as *relajados*, those who have been handed over, or loosened, or released, or eased; from the Latin *relaxo, relaxare,* to "lighten, alleviate, mitigate, soften, assuage; to cheer up, enliven, relax" (Lewis & Short). At least here, however, it is the spectacular failure of the Inquisition and the monarchy to operate in consort, to hand off Posa from one domain to another, that we witness. Posa's death, brought about by the political sovereign, was not anticipated, and highly displeases, the theologico-administrative arm of the Inquisition, which had built itself upon making Posa an example, indeed the very type, of its successful surveillance. This failure flows from and makes patent the dis-coordination of throne and altar; it makes clear that in this case at any rate the two act out of phase, in time to different logics, out of step. In Schiller's play, where the king went in executing Posa, the Inquisitor was not waiting; and through the king, Posa has at last traveled where the Inquisitor was not already: he has reached death. That in a sense this is precisely the place to which the Inquisition would have consigned him—that Posa would at the Inquisitor's bidding have been handed over by the Inquisition for execution, *relajado,* to the crown, which would have done with him what the king has already done, though in this case as an example, as the example of the Inquisition's influence over the crown—this minimal difference (of timing, of the exemplary or representational status of the execution) makes every difference to the way political theology comes on stage.

It is into the spot that Posa has vacated that Philip delivers his son, Posa's fraternal double: for Abraham has acted with haste, and slain his son before the angel's hand can arrest him, before the ram can be produced. The nature of the king's sacrifice is now clear: the son, the sovereign's only son, is delivered up for sacrifice so as to cancel out a previous death, in order to render exemplary what was not, to place a representative death, a death representable within the field of cultural work, in place of another that it cannot quite displace, a prior duplicate, an *analogue* (Derrida: "This *analogy* is the very site of the theologico-political, the hyphen [*trait d'union*] or translation between the theological and the political"), like but unlike inasmuch as it is specifically nonrepresentational. The sovereign's son dies by way of compensation, always *post-festum*: because he cannot stand in for Posa's death—because he is, though the marquis's fraternal double, distinct from him precisely in being destined for a *representative* death—Carlos dies not as a way of suturing the political and the theologico-administrative domains, not as their *trait d'union,* or not as these alone, but as the compensatory mark of their division as well. At the spot of Posa's death, where Carlos will come to die in place of the marquis' death, what waits is not "I," or not at any rate an "I" that waits to capture and form, by means of cultural or pedagogical bonds, lessons and examples, the infant's or the "id's" flight toward freedom. For Schiller's Freud, what waits has *anything but* the structure of watching-and-waiting for the arrival of the desire for freedom, as it arrives where it thinks it is free only to find itself captured or expressed, for instance by the work of 'culture,' by the word of Schiller's play.

Before I try to show where Schiller's Freud takes us, let me look in the reservoir of *Kulturarbeit* from which Freud was drawing for a further mediation, for further confirmation of this drama of failed surrogacy, faulty doublings, mistimed representation, and garbled communication. The greatest, as well as the best known, rendering of Schiller's *Don Karlos* is Verdi's opera *Don Carlos,* which like Schiller's play climactically stages the encounter between the realms of politics and of the theologico-administrative. Verdi's plot is a little different from Schiller's, but the opera's play of doubles carefully captures Schiller's symmetries. In Verdi's version, King Philip, like Carlos, is deeply attached to Rodrigo, Marquis of Posa, made a duke by Philip. Posa turns toward himself the evidence of Carlos's political involvement with the rebels in Flanders ("Il fiero agitator delle Fiandre," Posa tells the imprisoned Carlos, "son io!") as a way of saving the condemned prince and ushering in a new age: "Un nuovo secol d'ôr rinascer tu farai; / Regnare tu dovevi ed io morir per te." But the Inquisitor has approached King Philip and demanded that Philip deliver up his friend: "A te chiedo il signor di Posa." This is the way that the Italian librettists of Verdi's *Don Carlos* render the end of the unforgettable encounter between Philip and the Grand Inquisitor, the king's weak acquiescence to the Inquisitor's demand:

> FILIPPO: Mio padre, che tra noi la pace alberghi ancor.
> L'INQUISITORE: La pace?
> FILIPPO: Obliar tu dêi quel ch'è passato.
> L'INQUISITORE: Forse!
> FILIPPO: Dunque il trono piegar dovrà sempre all'altare![14]

> PHILIP: Father, let peace abide between us still.
> INQUISITOR: Peace?
> PHILIP: You should forget what has passed.
> INQUISITOR: Perhaps!
> PHILIP: And so the throne must always give way before the altar!

The Inquisitor departs; Posa visits Carlos in his cell, where the marquis reveals that he has drawn upon himself the evidence and the charge of treason against the prince. Two men, one dressed in the garb of the Inquisition, the other bearing an arquebus, appear. A shot is fired; Carlos, terrified, cries out: "Cielo! La morte! per chi mai?" Rodrigo answers: "Per me!"

I will return to this exceptionally odd exchange between the prince and the marquis. Achille de Lauzières and Angelo Zanardini, *Don Carlos*'s librettists, have been making this argument: threatened by complex pressures (parental devotion, friendship, love) the old peace between the king and the Inquisitor can only be brought back to its proper spot, "residing" or "abiding" ("alber-gàre," an odd word in this context) between the sovereign and the authority of the theological-administrative realm, when the Inquisitor "forgets what has happened."[15] The Inquisitor will not forget, or may not forget—but in any case the decision lies with him, and the king's request cannot rise to the level of a command, the verb "dovere" ("Obliar tu dêi") lodging, resident, like Freud's verb *sollen*, somewhere between the registers of moral obligation (the Inquisitor *should* forget), of the command (the Inquisitor is *ordered* to forget), and of the suggestion, even the plea (the Inquisitor is *requested* to forget, or *implored* to do so). "Forse" is the Inquisitor's tense, difficult answer. What is it an answer to? The king's assertion or plea—"tu dêi," as in "Perhaps it is true that 'I ought' to do what you say, yes, after all, you are the king"? Or perhaps, *forse*, to its content—as in "Perhaps I will forget . . ."? *Forse*: the word harbors and discloses the fundamental asymmetry of the relation between the two characters, and between the two institutions, traditions, and forms of power they represent for Verdi: *trono* and *altare*, politics and theology. *Forse*: the word may even be said to produce this asymmetry, working not only as a hyphen between "politics" and "theology," not as a *trait d'union* alone, but also and simultaneously as a *trait de division*. The Inquisitor's word bends the sovereign's will, not by appealing to a stronger will, or to a more general or more universal law, or to a more proximate relation to instituting or administrative violence, the twin *ultimae rationes regum*. The altar bends the throne before it because the church holds in reserve the decision to remember or to forget, to act or not to act. From the point of view of this reserve, any action that the state, the throne, or the political domain might take finds itself housed in advance in the *altar*: the reserve of the theological domain is itself theologically obscured, it is in the nature of the terror of theology.

In Schiller, and in Verdi, rational enlightenment shapes a genealogy for itself from the field of culture, and then installs that genealogy as the organizing principle of that field. (When I say "in Schiller and in Verdi" I mean that this double process of "shaping" and "installing" happens *in* their works and more broadly *by means of* their works.) In them the drama of secularization and modernization features an archaic plot: a benighted early modernity—confessional, Inquisitorial—where the substance of theological sovereignty is handed off to a political sphere thus shaped to it; facing and opposing it, a larval principle of freedom, resembling that first, benighted early modernity as one brother might resemble another, as Abel for instance might resemble Cain. At stake: land, culture, primogeniture, thought. A sacrifice is required, or two; on each side, doubled figures: the Inquisitor and the king on one side, Carlos and Posa on the other. The genealogy of secular, rational enlightenment takes shape in and from the sacrificial death of its early modern defenders. With Carlos and Posa's deaths, a new age, "un nuovo secol d'ôr," is reborn. "Rinasce" is Posa's word: a second, enlightened Renaissance.

The genealogy of confessional political theology takes shape in the same moment, by the same gesture, joined to or translated into secular, rational enlightenment by a *trait d'union*. The prince's death, or in its place the marquis' death, joins together theology and politics, marks the spot where *trono* yields to *altare* in accepting from the altar the relay, the *relajado,* that it will put to death as an example. And here the attentiveness of Verdi's librettists is remarkable. Where Schiller embeds a *trait de division* into *Don Karlos,* in the shape of the relation of non-substitutability between Carlos and Posa, in the shape of the temporal and representational difference between the two characters' deaths, Verdi's librettists provide the astonishing spectacle of a death announced on stage, and then as it were *fought over* by two twinned characters. For what can it mean that the prince does not know whether he or Posa has been hit? Whether it is his body or his double's body—the body of the man who has stepped into his place, taken his death from him—that has been touched by the bullet? "Per me!" exclaims Posa: "I have seized it, this death is mine, I have made it mine; it was waiting for you; where you were to go it already awaited, but I stepped forth and made it mine!" The story of the emergence of secular, rational enlightenment is the story of a death and a rebirth, of fratricidal conflict, of a sacrifice—in short, its shape, tropes, and materials are those of the theologico-political domain, whose *cultural* substance is turned to other use, seized and appropriated as Posa seizes and appropriates the death intended for Carlos. And on the other hand, however, the story of the persistence of confessional political theology—as told by Donoso and Schmitt, for whom the figures of Abel and Cain are also central—is the story of the failure of a sacrifice, of the unbreachable difference between the death of the sovereign's son and the man he will not be able to represent, of an unhinged and mistimed hand-off or relay, of a mistranslation, of a Reformation. In short, the tropes and cultural materials from which, and in which, the genealogy of confessional political theology takes shape are always and already located where that genealogy is not waiting, where it does not reach.

2. Lacan's Renaissance

We all still show too little respect for Nature which (in the obscure words of Leonardo
which recall Hamlet's lines) "is full of countless causes [*ragioni*] that never enter experience." Every one of us human beings corresponds to one of the countless experiments in
which these "*ragioni*" of nature force their way into experience.

    SIGMUND FREUD, "Leonardo da Vinci and a Memory of his Childhood"[16]

Allow me now to move toward a conclusion on a slightly different level. I have
been worrying questions preliminary to any investigation into how, under
what circumstances, to what purposes, and with what limitations "political
theology" comes onto the scene of "early modernity." I've moved between
Freud and Schiller, and through the determining ways that the Enlightenment and its Freudian recasting and critique sought to shape the Renaissance, so as to suggest that a contradictory, even antithetical construction of
early modernity shapes the cultural materials available to us today for imagining the encounter, or hand-off, or *relève* between politics and theology.
My hypothesis has been that this antithetical construction of early modernity
conforms to two genealogies for modernity that shape, limit, and contradict
each other. I have referred to this series of encounters, contradictions, shap-
ings, and limitations rather generally as if they constitute a group of primal
scenes, the primal scenes of political theology, intending the genitive in its
most extensive senses: to indicate that the concept, if it is one, of political
theology *suffers from* "primal scenes" proper to it (traumatic encounters, fantasies, prohibited scenarios, etc.); and also to indicate that political theology
produces for us traumatic encounters, fantasies, prohibited encounters that
help constitute our psychic and disciplinary identities. Let me close with an
example of the way in which the double fantasy of early modernity's relation
to political theology inflects how we understand cultural mediation more
broadly.

    There is a subclass of writings within the psychoanalytic canon that bear
explicitly on the problem of political theology. Each of us will no doubt be
able to come up with his or her own list of these, ranked differently and
reflecting quite different senses of what a "psychoanalytic canon" might be;
I suspect that *Moses and Monotheism* might make most lists, as would *Anti-
Oedipus* and some of Marcuse's works; less obvious, more interesting, might
be some of Kohut, and not a few of Klein's and Winnicott's works. Lacan's
essay on the "Instance of the Letter in the Unconscious," which has been
keeping us company surreptitiously thus far, belongs to this baggy group—
though much less clamorously than either Freud's or Deleuze and Guattari's

works. "The Instance of the Letter in the Unconscious," first delivered at the Sorbonne's *amphithéâtre* Descartes as a talk to the university's literature students, strives to hinge the languages and disciplines of philosophy, philology, and psychoanalysis to each other within "l'*universitas litterarum de toujours*," "the age-old *universitas litterarum* . . . the ideal place [for the institution of psychoanalysis]," as Lacan has Freud say, evidently also thinking of the location and occasion of his own talk. (The essay was delivered as a lecture on 9 May 1957 to the Groupe de Philosophie of the Fédération des étudiants ès lettres-Sorbonne.) In that sense "The Instance of the Letter in the Unconscious" also forms part of the subclass of writings in the psychoanalytic tradition that treat openly the relation between the concepts of psychoanalysis, its institutional, technical, and therapeutic aspects, and its material and practical conditions—much as the *New Introductory Lectures on Psycho-Analysis* propose to do.

In order to hinge these different disciplines to each other, Lacan's essay imagines a language sufficiently formalized, or a language sufficiently universal, that in and through it the different sorts of claims (to completeness, to truth, coherence, etc.) of different disciplines can be translated into each other, and can come under some sovereign rule (the rule of translation, of relation). The essay performs the mediating and translating function it will ascribe to "reason since Freud" by perching itself, Lacan says, midway between the written and the spoken word; it closes upon an image of similar topological complexity, concluding that "through his discovery Freud brought the border between object and being that seemed to mark the limit of science within its ambit" (Freud par sa découverte a fait rentrer à l'intérieur du cercle de la science cette frontière entre l'objet et l'être qui semblait marquer sa limite). The characteristic turn to topology is attenuated (these are, after all, *étudiants ès lettres*), or rather it is carried out at a different level from the one to which many others of Lacan's works of the period turn: here it is the "borders" of Lacan's writing that are brought within the circle of his essay. This invaginating movement runs rigorously through "The Instance of the Letter in the Unconscious." It is first a formal principle: Lacan's literary examples bring into his work samples from the reservoir of culture, the *universitas litterarum*; these samples work instrumentally, discreetly, and discretely, as a citation from Valéry might do, to illustrate this or that point; but each is a figure for the *universitas litterarum* as well. Or rather: each "sample" stands in for what I've rather inexactly, rather too hydrologically, been calling the reservoir of culture, and stands in *both* as a metaphor, a condensed representation of that *universitas litterarum* of which Lacan's essay, "The Instance of the Letter in the Unconscious," is a part and a product; *and* as a metonym, a contingent substitute expressing the endless *desire* to bring within the circle of the essay that which, being brought within it, brings along more than the essay's "borders" know how to contain.

This complicated principle of *topo*logical and *tropo*logical translation bears an additional weight in the essay, where it enters into rich conversation with an *onto*logical vocabulary that Lacan draws in some measure from his reading and translation of Heidegger's essay on "Logos," just published in *La Psychanalyse.*[17] It's a well-enough known encounter, but it is worth underscoring that when Lacan mentions that "when I speak of Heidegger, or rather when I translate him, I strive to preserve the sovereign signifierness of the speech he proffers" (je m'efforce à laisser à la parole qu'il profère sa signifiante souveraine), he makes himself into a cultural example—a "sample" from the "cultural reservoir" of readers of Freud, and Heidegger, and so on—and brings himself explicitly, and as problematically as in the case of the literary examples I briefly mentioned, within the "ambit" of his essay.[18]

I mentioned that Lacan's essay opens situationally and performatively, commenting on the circumstances of its enunciation, broadly and indexically gesturing to the auditorium, the various disciplines knotted together in the institution, the space, the audience. But this is not quite right, for the published version of "The Instance of the Letter in the Unconscious" has a different border and opens earlier, upon a scene it wishes to bring within its border, a scene both prophetic and historical, both anticipatory and symptomatic. And this description refers openly, indeed spectacularly, *to the Renaissance.* I'm referring to the epigraph to the essay, borrowed by Lacan from Louise Servicen's translation of Leonardo's *codex atlanticus*, which Servicen has taken from the Italian original edited by Jean Paul Richter, but also and primarily from Richter's German translation. Here are the famous lines. They are drawn from the first section of the so-called "Division of the Prophecies" within Leonardo's *codex,* the section "of things relating to animals." They bear on the constitution of the city:

> *Of Children Bound in Bundles.*
> O cities of the Sea! In you I see your citizens—both females and males—tightly bound, arms and legs, with strong withes by folks who will not understand your language. And you will only be able to assuage your sorrows and lost liberty by means of tearful complaints and sighing and lamentation among yourselves; for those who will bind you will not understand you, nor will you understand them.[19]

This is Servicen's translation:

Des enfants au maillot
O cités de la mer, je vois chez vous vos citoyens, hommes et femmes, les bras
et les jambes étroitement ligotés dans de solides liens par des gens qui n'en-
tendront point votre langage, et vous ne pourrez exhaler qu'entre vous, par
des plaintes larmoyantes, des lamentations et des soupirs, vos douleurs et vos
regrets de la liberté perdue. Car ceux-là qui vous ligotent ne comprendront
pas votre langue, non plus que vous ne les comprendrez.[20]

And the Italian:

De fanciulli che stanno legati nelle fasce
O città marine, io veggo in voi i vostri cittadini, così femmine come maschi,
essere istrettamente dei forti legami colle braccia e gambe esser legati da gente
che non intenderanno i vostri linguaggi, e sol vi potrete isfogare li vostri do-
lori e perduta libertà mediante i lagrimosi pianti e li sospiri e lamentazione
infra voi medesimi, chè chi vi lega non v'intenderà, né voi loro intenderete.[21]

Annabel Patterson leaned on this epigraph to mount an attack on Lacan's,
and through him on psychoanalytic criticism's, "elitism," which Patterson
associates with the discipline's resistance to history and politics, and with the
individualism entailed in what Lacan calls "la difficulté de la référence au réel."
"If one places Leonardo's fable," writes Patterson, "not only in his whole collection (which is pervasively interested in the political and social meanings of
liberty) but also in the documentable history of the fable, from antiquity on-
ward, as a strategy for evading censorship, it stands rather in an oblique and
antagonistic relation to Lacan's essay than as its aphoristic essence."[22] What
happens if we read the reference to Leonardo as it were through the fantasy
or fantasies of early modernity—or, more properly, of the Renaissance—that
this "universal genius," already "admired even by his contemporaries as one
of the greatest men of the Italian renaissance," as Freud calls him, brings
within the ambit, the borders, of Lacan's essay?[23] What happens when we
read Lacan's Leonardo through Freud's Schiller (or Schiller's Freud)? What
happens to the "political and social meanings of liberty" that "The Instance
of the Letter in the Unconscious" may disclose?

   The questions are too broad and too consequential to treat briefly. Let
me sketch out some possible approaches. We are not surprised to find that
Freud's 1910 monograph on Leonardo opens citing from Burckhardt: it is
partly Leonardo's place in the "age-old *universitas litterarum*" that is in question in Freud's essay; Freud's diagnosis of Leonardo, flawed and partial as it
may appear, forms part of a number of roughly contemporaneous works that
treat the narcissistic attachment of European culture to fantastical constructions of the *universitas litterarum* of precursor and legitimating "civilizations"

and "cultures," most prominently the cult and culture of the Renaissance.[24] Bear in mind, then, the role that Leonardo has in Freud's thought on the work of culture. For now, let us agree that the lines that Lacan cites from Leonardo's rather mysterious *codex* bear first and most obviously on the notion of *binding*—on its relation to citizenship, to speech, to force, violence, the distinction between the human and the animal, and so on. What Leonardo might mean by "binding," however, is partly eclipsed in the French translation that Lacan cites, which stresses the sense of "maillot" as a swaddling cloth for infants. (Académie Française: "Pièce ou bande de tissu utilisée pour envelopper le corps et les membres d'un nourrisson. Un enfant serré dans un maillot. Un enfant au maillot, un très jeune enfant."[25] The rich connection of *maillot* to *maille,* mesh, is subterranean.) Servicen's stress on the constraint this "maillot" places upon the *infans*—part comfort, part education—chimes nicely with much of the explicit content of Lacan's essay—an ontogenetic movement of psychic maturation, education, and confinement that each child experiences, in hand with the phylogenetic realignment of the relation to being that Heidegger announces and deplores, conceived perhaps in developmental terms, as if each child, and human history as well, underwent something like Enlightenment. Richter's English—"Of Children Bound in Bundles"—restores some of the image's odd violence (a bundle of children, as well as children individually bundled, or children bound and bundled together with other things), and attends more carefully to the placement of the fragment in Leonardo's notebooks (the surrounding prophetic images are all deliberately disjunctive).

But to allow Leonardo's Italian, *De fanciulli che stanno legati nelle fasce,* to seep anachronistically or achronically into Lacan's essay makes matters even more disturbing. (Leonardo's Italian is not immediately present in Lacan's text, any more than Verdi's Italian is in Freud's *Neue Folge der Vorlesungen zur Einführung in die Psychoanalyse.* Has it perhaps been imported, brought within the essay's ambit or borders, according to a metonymous, hydro-logical conception of the field of culture? Of *Kulturarbeit?*)

Remark the quiet link between Leonardo's *dei forti legami . . . legati* and the Italian *legge,* law; recall the lexical and conceptual importance for Lacan of *legein,* binding-together and letting-lie-in-unconcealment, in the Heraclitus fragment that Heidegger treats, and which Lacan translates and mentions in "The Instance of the Letter . . ." Lacan's use of the prophecy of citizens bound by laws (*legge*) into *fasces* willy-nilly brings into the ambit of his essay, brings within its borders, that "réel" that Patterson calls for—though in a less than naked way, the Heideggerian lexicon of *legein* rhyming with Leonardo's figure of discipline and legal binding in a quiet reference to the historical situation from which Europe had just emerged. The "difficult . . . reference to the real" of *fascism* has been with us all along, from the beginning, before indeed we even began to read (*leggere, legein,* and so on).

We do not need to travel quite so far downstream to make the point. Leonardo's cities of the sea are metaphors only—vivid tropes employed perhaps as Patterson says to avoid censure, perhaps for different reasons. The "fable" Lacan finds in Servicen's edition nestles among the surrounding prophecies, which concern anthropomorphized trees, dogs, rats, and so on. Leonardo's citizens are in the first instance nothing but fish, bound in nets, male with female, unable to converse with the humans who have netted them. In order to apply the fable to human society—Florentine republic, the Papal state, the various duchies that Leonardo knew well—we cross species, a routine enough matter in political fables of the time (Machiavelli's little menagerie: foxes, lions, wolves . . .). We read "human" society into and by means of these cities of the sea; the condition of boundness and confinement, the untranslatability of fish-language to the language of humans, these "translate" into descriptions of human circumstance, and serve as *types* of the situation of the human: human cities, human citizens, are figured in these fish schools. A coherent, well-known, Terentian doctrine is enunciated: the human is the universal (*nil a me alienum puto*); it contains multitudes, is the summation of all created beings; every form of life can be translated into the human. The association of the "universal genius" of Leonardo with the universality of what Cassirer famously called the "Renaissance philosophy of man" rests upon, and supports, this metaphoric translation. Burckhardt's Leonardo, as Freud reminds his readers, is precisely this universal figure, and figure of human universalism. And Leonardo's thought-image also and necessarily works in reverse. What we know as human activity, indeed as the foundational human activity, the foundation of political life or of life as biopolitics, is available to us symptomatically *only* or *primarily* in the figure of these cities of the sea. A clutch of double translations, in the form of a circle: from the city of the sea to the human, from the human to the citizens bound in bundles; from human laws (*legge*) to binding ties, and from the ties that bind Leonardo's fish together (*legare*) to the human city's laws; where the animal was, there will the human be—and vice-versa as well.

What does it mean, then, that at the heart of Leonardo's strange and surreal thought-image lies the violent drama of non-translation? That it is non-translation, that is, the refusal of substitution and of representation, the violent rejection of linguistic or cultural similarity and mediation, that "substitutes for" or "translates" or "represents" (none of these words now being correct) the condition of citizenship? A wholly different doctrine concerning early modernity stands forth. (Nicholas Rand might say: is encrypted within the image.)[26] Fishers of men; speakers of Latin to the ignorant and the *infans*; a species apart; cities in the sky. One need not be quite so literalistic. (Leonardo's heterodoxy sometimes comes close to anticlericalism, but he is careful: he translates himself; he censors himself.) For my purposes, Leonardo's image need only yield, in addition to the *trait d'union* or principle of translation between species and humans that we find in the thought-image's many circles, a *trait de division* or instance of radical and violent untranslatability. It will then provide us not only with a Renaissance philosophy of man, a principle for handing the indivisible sovereignty of the theological sphere over to a waiting, consubstantial humanist political sphere, attending where the theological domain will come; *but also* with an early modernity in which citizenship rests upon violence, division, miscommunication or non-communication, coercion. Nothing will mediate between these two figures of thought and of civic identity; they are the same image, the same mark or *trait,* the same word; and they represent an antinomy; they (it) mark the limit of *mediation.* It is the work of culture, or of ideology, to bind them together— no longer in the fatuous ties provided by a sufficiently formalized or formal language, in the imagined and fantastical space of "l'*universitas litterarum* de toujours," much less in the physical space of the *amphithéâtre* Descartes, but in the *maille* or *maillot,* the imprisoning, forming, educating net with which the infant, the *infans* and the citizen, learns to speak his name.

It is this scenario that Lacan seeks to capture, on a different, technical order of argumentation, when he recalls, at the close of "Instance of the Letter," "the goal Freud's discovery proposes to man," "defined at the height of his thought in these moving terms: *Wo Es war, soll Ich werden.* Where it was I must come into being. This goal is one of reintegration and harmony, I might even say of reconciliation."[27] The same steps: if we began in violence and coercion, Lacan's essay *appears* to say, we end on a note of disciplinary and civic reconciliation. No longer do we find ourselves, as at the infancy of Enlightened modernity or "before" Freud, speaking different tongues, the philologians ruled by the philosophers or vice-versa, fish ruled by fishermen, believers by the clergy, citizens by blind or supervisory sovereigns. Rather, the *Kulturarbeit* of civilization (in the verbal sense)—the civilizing effect of the Renaissance and its proxy, Freud's account of "reason," serve to bind the infant, to naturalize the violence of the theologico-political encounter, and to translate that violence into a tongue in which the sovereign's, or the fisherman's, "no" or "yes" saves or condemns, and which all of us understand: a common tongue, commonly understood. (Posa stands in for Carlos,

Carlos for Posa: the two deaths are made the same, or analogous at least; we lose their constitutive difference.)

But this therapeutic and conciliatory reading of Freud's line, Lacan then shows, is topologically and tropologically inaccurate, inasmuch as it ignores the "self's radical ex-centricity to itself." For Lacan, Freud's famous phrase shockingly discloses this very ex-centricity, which it expresses in three internal antinomies: a difference of substance, between *Es* and *Ich;* of mode (*sollen*, the figure of command, but also of supposition, of counterfactuality); and of time (*war* against *werden*, a historical description and a providential or an ethical injunction: "I" must or should come to, arrive at, where "it" was). This ex-centricity of the self with respect to the position it imagines itself to occupy, and with respect to the position it wishes to occupy, or imagines itself at some point to arrive at—these two *topological* and *tropological* non- or mistranslations line up with an *ontological* misprision as well: the self is not what it is (what it thinks it is); I think where I do not think I think, says Lacan, revising Descartes. Revising Descartes, but also echoing the strange way that Leonardo's prophecy of the "Cities of the Sea" builds into itself a fantasy of translation and of non-translation; of consubstantiality (between humans and their animal analogues) and of absolute disanalogy; a *trait d'union* and a *trait de division*. Echoing Leonardo, but also, whether he knows it or not, reading Freud's Schiller's as well, attending to the sovereign signifiedness of Freud's words, which themselves, whether Freud himself remembered it or not, bring Schiller's contradictory fantasies of early modernity "within their ambit."

In 1918, fifteen years before Freud pens the line from *Neue Folge der Vorlesungen zur Einführung in die Psychoanalyse* on which Lacan closes "The Instance of the Letter in the Unconscious," Freud tells Lou-Andreas Salomé that he identifies with the older Schiller, that he wishes the revolution over as soon as possible (so that it will be "acceptable"), and that "what the human beast needs above all is restraint." It is altogether remarkable that at the "height of his thought" and toward the end of his career Freud should have remembered (or allowed within the ambit or borders of his essay on the structure of the psychic apparatus) an earlier Schiller, who in turn was recalling the complex *beginning* of a revolution he considered still unfinished, a new golden age or new Renaissance that turned on the epochal divisions at the heart of secularization and of the hand-off, the *relève*, between politics and theology. We need not imagine a late, pathos-ridden return to the heroic vein: by this time Freud has seen too much to hazard much heroism of that trivial sort. The French and Russian Revolutions may hasten to their *denouement*, to the place where they are attended by their institutionalization or by the terror of the administrative state (in the case of the French Revolution, called properly "the terror"). But Freud has understood—though *Don Karlos* is not directly before him—that Schiller's early play marks out in early modernity, in the fratricidal conflict between the play's two early modernities, a spot where revolutions *perpetually begin,* not where they end. Where Posa differs from Carlos; where one death cannot stand in for another, cannot be grasped in place of another, cannot be its sacrifice or its *analogue*—there, Freud understands, a different, *primal* scene is acted out, and something, call it freedom or citizenship, *begins.*

Notes

The epigraph is taken from Jacques Derrida, "What is a 'Relevant' Translation?" trans. Lawrence Venuti, *Critical Inquiry* 27.2 (2001): 197. In French, Jacques Derrida, "Qu'est-ce qu'une traduction 'relevante'?" in *Jacques Derrida,* ed. M. L. Mallet and Ginette Michaud, Cahier de l'Herne (Paris: L'Herne, 2004), 561–76, at 574. First published in *Quinzième Assises de la Traduction Littéraire* (Arles: Actes Sud, 1999), 21–48.

1. Hans Blumenberg, *The Legitimacy of the Modern Age,* trans. Robert M. Wallace (Cambridge, Mass.: MIT Press, 1985), 94–101.

2. Carl Schmitt, *Political Theology: Four Chapters on the Concept of Sovereignty,* trans. Gorge Schwab (Chicago: University of Chicago Press, 2005), 5. Important discussions of the "concept" of political theology (the quotation marks are intended to indicate that it remains a matter of controversy whether it *is* a concept, and if so of what sort) may be found in Heinrich Meier, *Carl Schmitt and Leo Strauss: The Hidden Dialogue,* trans. J. Harvey Lomax (Chicago: University of Chicago Press, 1995); and Jan Assmann, *Politische Theologie zwischen Ägypten und Israel* (Bonn: VG Bild-Kunst), 1992; and, more recently, in Samuel Weber, "Taking Exception to Decision: Walter Benjamin and Carl Schmitt," *Diacritics* 22.3/4 (Autumn–Winter, 1992): 5–18, esp. 9–10, and Peter Osborne, *The Politics of Time: Modernity and the Avant-Garde* (London and New York: Verso, 1995), 144–59. See also the essays collected in Creston Davis, John Milbank, and Slavoj Žižek, eds. *Theology and the Political: The New Debate* (Durham, N.C.: Duke University Press, 2005), and the excellent introductory essay by Michael Hollerich in *The Blackwell Companion to Political Theology,* ed. Peter Scott and William T. Cavanaugh (London: Wiley-Blackwell, 2004), esp. 110–20.

3. From *Sigmund Freud and Lou-Andreas Salomé: Letters,* ed. Ernst Pfeiffer, trans. William and Elaine Robson-Scott (New York: Harcourt Brace, 1966), 75.

4. "The goal Freud's discovery proposes to man was defined by Freud at the height of his thought in these moving terms: *Wo Es war, soll Ich werden.*" Jacques Lacan, "The Instance of the Letter in the Unconscious or Reason since Freud," in *Écrits: The First Complete Edition in English,* trans. Bruce Fink (New York: W. W. Norton & Co., 2006), 412–41. Fink returns to the word "instance" in place of the polemical "agency" favored by Alan Sheridan in his translation, *Écrits: A Selection* (New York: W. W. Norton & Co., 2002), 138–69. The original is Jacques Lacan, "L'instance de la lettre dans l'inconscient," in *Écrits* (Paris: Seuil, 1966). The essay was first published in *La psychanalyse* 3 (1957): 47–81.

5. Bruno Bettelheim, *Freud and Man's Soul* (New York: Knopf, 1983), 61–64. Bettelheim makes the remark concerning the Zuider Zee in the context of an extended and highly inflammatory critique of Strachey's translations in the *Standard Edition*. See Morris N. Eagle, *Recent Developments in Psychoanalysis: A Critical Evaluation* (New York: McGraw-Hill, 1984) for the consequences of retranslating Strachey's "reclamation work" as "cultural achievement."

6. Sigmund Freud, *New Introductory Lectures on Psycho-Analysis*, in *The Standard Edition of the Complete Psychological Works of Sigmund Freud*, trans. James Strachey, vol. 22 (1932–36): 79–80. I've translated "something like" in place of Strachey's "not unlike" for "etwa wie." The German is from Sigmund Freud, *Gesammelte Werke*, vol. 15, *Neue Folge der Vorlesungen zur Einführung in die Psychoanalyse* (London: Imago/S. Fischer, 1940), 86.

7. The long history of the incident's role in the creation of the so-called "Black Legend" of Spain's benightedness has been the subject of a number of important studies. Especially helpful for an account of its literary and musical treatments is Andrée Mansau's *Saint-Réal et l'humanisme cosmopolite* (Lille–Paris: Université de Lille III, 1976). A more recent account in Jean-Frédéric Schaub, *La France espagnole: Les racines hispaniques de l'absolutisme français* (Paris: Seuil, 2003).

8. Posa is traditionally, and not unreasonably, understood as Schiller's proxy in the play, though with important reservations that flow from the character's portrayal by Schiller himself in his "Letters on *Don Carlos*." Here is how a recent critic has put it: Schiller "[hat] seine literarischen Helden zu Sprachrohren seiner selbst gemacht. In *Don Karlos* ist es Posa, der Schwärmerische Weltbeglücker aus dem Geiste der Aufklärung, der nicht nur scheitert, weil das Jahrhundert (dass 16) für seine Ideen noch nicht reif war, sondern auch, weil er sich in den selbstgesponnen Netzen politischer Taktik verfängt. Sein Versuch, den Freund durch ein Selbstopfer zu retten, mußte dessen Untergang beschleunigen, weil Posa vorbeischaute an der alles beherrschenden Macht der Inquisition, der Freiheitsparolen willkommene Anlässe waren, ihre Macht zu stabilisieren. Am ende des Stücks hat Schiller den Marquis weit von sich abgerückt" (Norbert Oellers, "Schiller, der 'Heros': Mit ergänzenden den Bemerkungen zu einigen seiner Dramen-Helden," in *Schiller: National Poet—Poet of Nations: A Birmingham Symposium*, ed. Nicholas Martin, Amsterdamer Beiträge zur neueren Germanistik 61 [Amsterdam and New York: Rodopi, 2006], 70). A more elaborated discussion, including a review of scholarship on Schiller's Posa since André von Gronicka's influential "Friedrich Schiller's Marquis Posa: A Character Study," *Germanic Review* 26 (1951): 196–214, in Fabian Elias Gebauer, *Zu Friedrich Schillers "Don Karlos": Genese, Funktion und Problematik des Marquis Posa* (Norderstedt: GRIN, 2008). I find particularly useful Maria Carolina Foi's observation, in her "Recht, Macht und Legitimation in Schillers Dramen," that Posa's appeal to the king recaptures in dialogue the process of emergence and formation [*Entstiehungsprozess*] of the modern state. In *Friedrich Schiller und der Weg in die Moderne*, ed. Walter Hinderer, Alexander von Bormann (Würzburg: Königshausen & Neumann, 2006), 227–42, esp. 229. Hans-Jürgen Schings' *Die Brüder des Marquis Posa: Schiller und der Geheimbund der Illuminaten* (Tübingen: Niemeyer, 1996) argues for understanding Posa as an Illuminatus, or a forerunner—and makes the point that Schiller's distance from the character (after the first sketches of the play and its first published versions, the so-called "Thalia-fragments") represents Schiller's fear that the Illuminist, even the Enlightenment, critique of Jesuit obscurantism might nonetheless end up relying upon the Order's methods—as Posa seems to do at the play's end.

9. The English translation is taken from *Friedrich Schiller: 'Don Carlos,'* trans. Robert D. MacDonald (London: Oberon Books, 1995), 222. Translations of the Grand Inquisitor's "Wo

Er war . . ." have varied. Johann Gustav Fischer's translation reads "'Where'er he travel'd I was at his side,'" in *Schiller's Works*, ed. J. G. Fischer (Philadelphia: Barrie, 1883), 90; Charles Passage has "'Wherever he might be, there I was also,'" in *Friedrich von Schiller: 'Don Carlos, Infante of Spain,'* trans. Charles E. Passage (New York: Ungar Publishing, 1959), 208. The German is from *Friedrich Schiller: Don Karlos, Infant von Spanien: Ein dramatisches Gedicht (Letzte Ausgabe 1805)*, ed. Helmut Nobis (Frankfurt a. M.: Suhrkamp, 2007), 224–25 (ll. 5151–65). Nobis notes about these lines: "Mit diesem Äußerungen des Großinquisitors werden die im Drama dargestellten Machtverhältnisse einer neuen Sicht unterworfen und zeitigen Konsequenzen für die Gesamtinterpretation. Die ungeheure Machtfülle der kath. Kirche und ihrer Institutionen schränkt Philips absolutistische Stellung radikal ein, zeigt ihn als Marionette der Inquisition und neutralisiert die von Posa in III:10 entwickelten Ideen und Gedanken über Freiheit und Menschenrechte." Nobis refers his reader here to Niels Werber, "Technologien der Macht," *Jahrbuch der Deutschen Schillergesellschaft* 40 (1996): 210–43. The beginning of the scene is subtly changed from the 1787 version. See Paul Bockmann's edition of the earlier work, *Schillers Don Karlos: Edition der ursprünglichen Fassung und entstehungsgeschichtlicher Kommentar*, ed. Paul Bockmann (Stuttgart: Ernst Klett Verlag, 1974), 329–31 (ll. 6792–6816), as well as his commentary on the sources—in Rousseau and Montesquieu—of Posa's earlier, and contrasting, arguments to Philip II (490–507); and for a *variorum* of the initial editions, see *Friedrich Schiller: Dramen II*, ed. Gerhard Kluge, vol. 3 of *Werke und Briefe* (Frankfurt a. M.: Bibliothek Deutscher Klassiker Verlag, 1989). Kluge observes that "Ein Auftritt des Großinquisitors gehörte offenbar zu den ältesten Plänen Schillers" (1344); points out that the Inquisitor functions as Posa's opposite; and concludes: "Es gibt in Schillers Werk schwerlich eine Szene oder ein Gestalt, in der der Gegensatz zur Freiheit (sei sie politisch, moralisch oder als Naturrecht des Menschen verstanden) und das Böse samt der Mechanik seines Handelns eindringlicher dargestellt sind."

10. The letters are "Letter from Sigmund Freud to Eduard Silberstein, April 23, 1876," in *The Letters of Sigmund Freud to Eduard Silberstein, 1871–1881*, ed. Walter Boehlich (Cambridge, Mass.: Harvard University Press, 1990), 150–56; *The Correspondence of Sigmund Freud and Sándor Ferenczi: 1908–1914*, vol. 1, ed. Eva Brabant, Ernst Falzeder, Patrizia Giamperi-Deutsch; trans. Peter T. Hofferp (Cambridge, Mass.: Harvard University Press, 1993), 408; "Letter from Sigmund Freud to Martha Bernays, March 19, 1886," in *Letters of Sigmund Freud, 1873–1939* (London: The Hogarth Press, 1970), 212–14; "Letter from Freud to Fliess, June 12, 1895," in *The Complete Letters of Sigmund Freud to Wilhelm Fliess, 1887–1904* (Cambridge, Mass.: Belknap Press, 1986), 131–32; "Letter from Sigmund Freud to C. G. Jung, October 31, 1910," in *The Freud-Jung letters: The Correspondence between Sigmund Freud and C. G. Jung* (New York: Taylor and Francis, 1977), 365–69; "Letter from Arnold Zweig to Sigmund Freud, May 12, 1934," *International Psycho-Analytic Library* 84:76–79. On the general topic of Freud's use of Schiller's work, see Lewis W. Brandt, "Freud and Schiller," *Psychoanalytic Review* 46.4 (1959): 97–101.

11. Sigmund Freud, *The Psychopathology of Everyday Life*, trans. Alan Tyson, in *The Standard Edition of the Complete Psychological Works of Sigmund Freud*, vol. 6 (London: The Hogarth Press, 1991), 99. It seems likely that Freud—who has kings, sovereignty, and different sorts of threats to them very much on his mind, as the reference to *Richard II* suggests—is thinking here of the moment at the scene's close when the princess lets slip that the letter she wants back from Don Carlos was sent to her by the king, his father. "O Himmel!," cries the princess: "Wie schrecklich hab' ich mich verstrickt! . . . Was hab' ich Unbesonnene gewagt!"

12. Hanns Sachs, "Schillers Geisterseher," *Imago* 4.2 (1915): 69- 95; and *Imago* 4.3 (1915): 145–79.

13. "—als käm ich heim zu Vater und Schwester": *Lou Andreas-Salomé-Anna Freud: Brief-wechsel 1919–1937*, vol. 1, ed. Inge Weber (Göttingen: Wallstein Verlag, 2001), 357–59; Theodor Reik, *The Compulsion to Confess*, in *The Compulsion to Confess and the Need for Punishment*, ed. J. Farrar (New York: Farrar, Straus, and Cudahy, 1959), 176–356; cf. Reik, *Geständniszwang und Strafbedürfnis: Probleme der Psychoanalyse und der Kriminologie* (Vienna: Internationale Psychoanalytisch Verlag, 1925); 2d ed. in *Psychoanalyse und Justiz*, ed. Alexander Mitscherlich (Frankfurt a. M.: Suhrkamp, 1974), 9–201.

14. Giuseppe Verdi, *Don Carlos: Opera in Four Acts* (New York: Fred Rullman, 1920), 45–50. The translation is mine.

15. The original French of Philip's line, by Joseph Méry and Camille Du Locle, is quite different: "L'orgueil du roi faiblit devant l'orgueil du prêtre." The exceptionally complex textual history of Verdi's opera (the composer produced three versions of different lengths: in French, Italian, and German) is the subject of a number of specialized works, the recent ones heavily indebted to Ursula Günther's "La Genèse de *Don Carlos*, opéra en cinq actes de Giuseppe Verdi, représenté pour la première fois à Paris le 11 Mars 1867," *Revue de musicologie* 58 (1972): 16–64 (part 1), 60 (1974): 87–158 (part 2). Lucio Lugnani's *"Ella giammai m'amò": Invenzione e tradizione di Don Carlos* (Milan: Liguori, 1999) is an intertextual study of Verdi's sources, especially the French libretto for the opera.

Something of a thickener for my own plot: *Don Carlos's* performance history in the years directly before Freud sets about writing the *New Introductory Lectures on Psychoanalysis*. With no fast evidence one way or the other, I imagine Freud aware, at least, of the rumblings that shook the *tout monde* of the Viennese opera establishment, and the musical world about him. In the years from 1926 to 1934 various German and Austrian productions attempted what Grundula Kreuzer has called the "re-Schillerization" of Verdi's opera—various cuts intended to bring the libretto in line with Schiller's original (in her remarkable "Voices from Beyond: Verdi's *Don Carlos* and the Modern Stage," *Cambridge Opera Journal* 18.2 [2006]: 151–179). The most important event in this small, odd history was the Viennese production on 10 May 1932 of *Don Carlos*, in a new adaptation by Franz Werfel. Commissioned by Clemens Kraus for the Vienna Staatsoper, Werfel's adaptation was highly controversial. Kreuzer gives examples of the titles of contemporaneous reviews: "For instances of the debate, see Ernst Decsey, 'Guiseppe [*sic*] Verdi—Franz Werfel—und die Kritik,' *Die Musik* 24/10 (1932), 786–7; Victor Junk, 'Wiener Musik', *Zeitschrift für Musik*, 99 (1932), 600–7; Ferdinand Scherber, 'Franz Werfel als Großinquisitor,' *Signale für die musikalische Welt*, 9 (1932), 526–8; and Franz Werfel, 'Verdis *Don Carlos* und seine Kritiker,' originally *Neues Wiener Journal* (15 May 1932), repr. in idem, *Gesammelte Werke: Zwischen Oben und Unten* (Prosa, Tagebücher, Aphorismen, Literarische Nachträge), ed. Adolf D. Klarmann (Munich, 1975), 351–3" (Kreuzer, "Voices from Beyond," 160 n. 37).

16. Sigmund Freud, "Leonardo da Vinci and a Memory of his Childhood," in *S.E.* 11:137; the German is from *G.W.* 8:210–11.

17. Heidegger's essay first appeared in the *Festschrift für Hans Jantzen*, ed. Kurt Bauch (Berlin: Verlag Gebr. Mann, 1951), 7–18. Lacan's translation, "Logos," appeared in *La psychanalyse* 1 (1956): 59–79.

18. This is how Lacan puts it:

> Que ceci soit le symptôme et le prélude d'une remise en question de la situation de l'homme dans l'étant, telle que l'ont supposée jusqu'à présent tous les postulats de la connaissance, ne vous contentez pas, je vous prie, de cataloguer le fait que je le dise comme un cas d'heideggerianisme,—fût-il préfixé d'un néo, qui n'ajoute rien à ce style

de poubelle par où il est d'usage de se dispenser de toute réflexion en un recours au décrochez-moi-ça de ses épaves mentales.

Quand je parle de Heidegger ou plutôt quand je le traduis, je m'efforce à laisser à la parole qu'il profère sa signifiante souveraine.

This is the symptom of and prelude to a reexamination of man's situation in the midst of beings [*dans l'etant*], as all the postulates of knowledge have heretofore assumed it to be—but please don't be content to classify the fact that I am saying so as a case of Heideggerianism, even prefixed by a "neo-" that adds nothing to the trashy style by which it is common to spare oneself any reflection with the quip, "Separate that out from me from its mental jetsam." When I speak of Heidegger, or rather when I translate him, I strive to preserve the sovereign signifierness of the speech he proffers. (438)

19. *The Notebooks of Leonardo Da Vinci,* vol. 2, compiled and edited from the original manuscripts, trans. Jean Paul Richter (1888; New York: Dover, 1970), 354. Compare MacCurdy's translation: "Of children who are wrapped in swaddling bands. O cities of the sea, I behold in you your citizens, women as well as men, tightly bound with stout bonds around their arms and legs by folk who will have no understanding of our speech [*sic*]; and you will only be able to give vent to your griefs and sense of loss of liberty by making tearful complaints, and sighs, and lamentation one to another; for those who bind you will not have understanding of your speech nor will you understand them" (*The Notebooks of Leonardo da Vinci,* trans. and ed. Edward MacCurdy [New York: Reynal and Hitchcock, 1938], 2:499). MacCurdy's "no understanding of our speech" is provocative, but possibly only a mistake (for "your speech").

20. Leonardo da Vinci, *Carnets,* trans. Louise Servicen (Paris: Gallimard, 1942; 1951), 2:400.

21. Leonardo, *Scritti Scelti di Leonardo da Vinci,* ed. Anna Maria Brizio (Torno: Unione Tipografica-Editrice, 1952; 1966), 333.

22. Annabel Patterson, *Reading Between the Lines* (Madison: University of Wisconsin Press, 1993), 320–21.

23. Freud, "Leonardo . . . ," 63.

24. Freud's essay on Leonardo, he says, does not seek to " 'blacken the radiant and drag the sublime into the dust' " (Freud is quoting Schiller), but the analysis is threefold: Freud seeks to understand Leonardo's "enigma"; he seeks to understand the place that Leonardo holds, in part as a result of that "enigma" at the heart of his works, in the imagination of later societies; and he seeks to locate, through his analysis of Leonardo, a limit or a border for psychoanalysis itself: "We are left, then, with these two characteristics of Leonardo, which are inexplicable by the efforts of psycho-analysis: his quite special tendency towards instinctual repressions [*Triebverdrängungen*], and his extraordinary capacity for sublimating the primitive instincts [*Triebe*]. Instincts and their transformations are at the limit [*sind das letzte*] of what is discernible by psycho-analysis. From that point it gives place to biological research" ("Leonardo . . . ," 136; 209).

25. "Par méton. *Dès le maillot,* dès la plus tendre enfance (on dit plus couramment '*Dès le berceau*'). Bande ou morceau d'étoffe dans lequel on enveloppait les membres et le torse d'un nouveau-né; lange dans lequel sont enveloppés jusqu'aux aisselles les jambes et le torse d'un nouveau-né. Être dans un maillot, être dans la première enfance."

26. Rand adopts language from Abraham and Torok to describe a mechanism of encryption at work in this essay, by means of which one language discloses what another holds within it. In this case, one might say: that humans are anthropomorphic animals, and that the ties that

bind them into citizenship are to be imagined as incommunicable, and violent, to the very extent that they are foundational of the class of "citizens." Nicholas Rand, "The Political Truth of Heidegger's 'Logos': Hiding in Translation," *PMLA* 105.3 (May 1990): 436–47.

27. Lacan, "Instance . . . ," 435 (Fink). Compare Sheridan's translation: "The end that Freud's discovery proposes for man was define by him at the apex of his thought in these moving terms: *Wo es war, soll Ich werden.* I must come to the place where that was" (*Écrits,* 171).

10

Pauline Edifications: Staging the Sovereign Softscape in Renaissance England

JULIA REINHARD LUPTON

Among a suite of hangings purchased by King VIII from one John Baptist Gualterote, merchant of Florence, in 1542, is a tapestry that depicts Paul preaching in Athens, a scene illustrating Acts 17 (see fig. 10.1).[1] Woven in Brussels, the tapestries were based on cartoons by Raphael, who had designed a set of hangings for Pope Leo X to grace the lower walls of the Sistine Chapel. Raphael's radical designs transferred the monumental interests and perspectival space of Italian narrative painting into the flatter, more artisanal, and decidedly Northern planes of tapestry, forever changing the subsequent course of tapestry production. In 1623, Charles I, then Prince of Wales, admired the tapestries enough to buy Raphael's cartoons for use at the Mortlake tapestry works that his father James I had established in 1619.[2] The Rump Parliament sold off the tapestries in 1650, after the execution of the same Charles in 1649. Although the cartoons would remain in England, the tapestries eventually landed in the Kaiser Friedrich Museum in Berlin in 1844, where they were presumably destroyed during Allied air raids on the city in 1945. Before their destruction, however, the tapestries had been photographed on site in Berlin, and the images are now housed at the Getty Research Institute in Los Angeles as part of a massive archive of photos amassed by the American tapestry and furniture historian George Leland Hunter (1867–1927).

Wrapped up in the story of these tapestries is a series of interfolded processes, including the transfer of apostolic imagery from Leo's Rome to Henry's England; the *translatio* of the Italian style from south to north via cartoon, tapestry, and print; the possible uses and meanings of such tapestries in the political theology of the Tudor and Stuart courts; and the link between arrases and theater in both dramatic performances and the spectacular life of the English monarchy. Rereading Paul, whether in the light of his Jewish

FIGURE 10.1. *Paul Preaching at Athens.* Unknown workshop (Brussels?) after a cartoon by Raphael (ca. 1540). Wool, silk, and gilt metallic thread. Presumed destroyed in the Kaiser Friedrich Museum, Berlin, 1945. Photograph: The Getty Research Institute, Los Angeles (97.P.7).

sources, his messianic claims, or his contributions to both philosophy and anti-philosophy, constitutes a major strand of contemporary political theology.[3] This essay supplements my efforts elsewhere to apprehend the meanings of Paul in the English Renaissance, in order to illuminate the stratified, conflicted, and often existential texture of England's peculiar engagement with religious traditions. In this essay, I show how Paul's mixed destinies in the Renaissance extend to the media by which his life and letters were transmitted. Raphael's tapestries invite us to seek out the Apostle not only in explicitly theological print works, where we expect to encounter him, but in forms such as tapestry, architecture, and theater, each bearing its own special forms of publicity (*Öffentlichkeit*) as well as its own conditions of reproduction and distribution. In these other media, the *logos* of the Bible undergoes new lives as well as new deaths, by passing through emerging scenes and regimes of performance and visualization, evincing what Manfred Schneider calls "the medial hybridity of divine communications."[4]

In the theater of Renaissance sovereignty, tapestry played a major role not only in adorning the courts of monarchs such as Henry VIII, Philip II, Francis I, and Charles V, but also in draping the streets for civic entries and lining the tents erected for kingship on the move. Tapestry is a transitional object between the fine and the decorative arts, at once a species of represen- tation and a kind of home furnishing.[5] The flow of fabric among the domestic offices that tended to the person, image, comfort, and environments of the monarch help us capture what I call in this essay *the sovereign softscape*: the real and virtual layers of fabricated significance that helped shape, shelter, and communicate the life of the monarch to himself, his court, and their audiences. Subsisting at the billowing interface between the royal household and the public display of sovereignty, tapestries render visible the tremulous membrane connecting the scripts, furniture, and menus of domestic enter- tainment to the life of the state, an interface that also often concerned the ongoing tension between confessions during the traumatic sea changes of reformation and secularization. Put otherwise, in the banqueting houses of the Renaissance courts, *biopolitics* (commensal entertainment as a form of communicative action) could also be *political theology* (the pressing of re- ligious narratives into the service of secular forms of legitimacy).[6] Raphael's tapestries, designed for a Medici pope and then copied and distributed to the great courts of the Continent and England, display some of the tensions resi- dent in the secularization process, as Renaissance princes adopted religious iconography for their own purposes, in the troubled context of confessional controversy, international war, administrative reorganization, and territorial consolidation.

1. Paul in Rome, 1519

In late 1514 and early 1515, Pope Leo X commissioned Raphael to design a set of tapestries illustrating the lives of Sts. Peter and Paul, to be hung beneath the fresco cycles of the Sistine Chapel, thus joining Raphael's artistry to that of Botticelli, Michelangelo, and Perugino, and allowing the Medici pope to leave his mark on the chapel renovated so magnificently by Pope Sixtus IV. Raphael completed a scheme and first sketches by summer 1515, with finished cartoons—full-sized paintings made with tempera on paper—early in 1516. The tapestries themselves were probably woven in the Brussels workshop of Pieter van Aelst, and the first seven arrived in Rome in 1519, in time to be dis- played on December 26 of that year, as part of Christmas festivities.[7] The suite of ten tapestries, reduced from what was likely an original sixteen tapestries, was designed to hang above *trompe l'œil* frescos of painted tapestry executed under Sixtus.[8] The presence of the frescoed fabric beneath the woven panels reminds us that major tapestries would only have been on view for holidays and festivals. On ordinary days, the painted frescoes would have sufficed; it's possible as well, following the practice in some northern churches, that Raphael's cartoons, clearly painted in order to survive the weaving process, were intended to stand in for the tapestries during the days when the latter rested in storage.

By systematically pairing the lives of Peter and Paul, conceived as the two princes of the early church and the double fonts of papal authority, Leo aimed to celebrate the sovereignty as well as the magnificence of the papal office, and to preach the unity of the Church after the conciliar schisms of the fourteenth and fifteenth centuries. As a "Medici" or Medicine Man, Leo cast himself as the physician for an ailing church, and scenes of miraculous healing from the lives of both Apostles emphasize this role.[9] Leo is depicted just behind the Apostle in *Paul Preaching at Athens*; seated next to him is a portrait of Janus Lascoris, a leading Greek scholar and part of Leo's humanist circle. The presence of Leo and Janus, along with the clusters of Epicureans and Stoics (Acts 17:18) who listen attentively to Paul's speech, construe Rome under Leo as a second Athens in which philosophy and theology will be unified in a new Christian humanism, a synthesis itself brilliantly exemplified in Raphael's art.[10] Closest to us in space is the transfixed figure of Dionysius the Aeropagite, as well as a woman named Demaris, both "recorded in the Bible as believers."[11] The sunken space of the tapestry, dipping below the picture frame, places us in the space of the Aereopagus, as part of Paul's audience.[12]

The scene of Paul at the Aereopagus in Acts 17 is above all a *mise en scène* of the encounter between theology and philosophy. The French phenomenologist Jean-Luc Marion provides a strong modern Catholic reading of this encounter, a reading that also touches on the phenomenology of the image in Paul's letters. Marion writes that "Paul enters into a city (and therefore into a politics) that he (and he alone) sees to be 'devoted to idols' (17:17)." According to Marion, "everything happens as if the philosophers also came under the jurisdiction of idolatry—only having purified it, that is, having conceptualized it" (24). For Marion, the scene in Athens sets *conceptual idolatry* and *visual idolatry* on a continuum; to replace God with a concept (such as reason) is no better than replacing God with a marble statue. For Marion, idolatry is "effaced only before the absence of a concept, an absence that is definitive and that initiates another approach to God as the 'unknown God' (17:24)."[13] Paul is seen to institute here a kind of negative theology, in which the withdrawal of God from all ideation finally yields the face of Christ: "Thus Paul evokes the only imaginable face of the invisible, the risen Christ (17:31–32), 'icon of the invisible God.'"[14] Whereas "idol" for Marion refers to every attempt, even or especially atheist ones, to identify God with a concept, the icon is that which emerges in the space from which God as concept has withdrawn. Marion defends the Catholic icon, conceived here as that which appears in the clearing of concepts, against both Protestant iconoclasm and philosophical atheism. For Marion, Paul, far from belonging to Luther's party *avant la lettre*, is himself a phenomenologist of the icon in its punctual appearance and disappearance through the eyes and ears of faith.

The medieval source for Marion's modern phenomenology of the image is Pseudo-Dionysius, the fifth-century Greek theologian mythically identified with the Dionysius mentioned in Acts, depicted in the left corner of the *Paul in Athens* tapestry.[15] Raphael's design, not unlike Marion's reading of the scene from Acts, is divided between physical and conceptual forms of idolatry. The worship of statues organizes the background, where the figure of Mars stands behind and above the assembled philosophers, overseeing his circular temple, which houses additional sculptures. Yet Paul's primary address is to the Stoics and Epicureans; it is idea, not idol, or rather *conceptual idol* rather than *physical idol*, that could be said to occupy Paul here. Extending upwards to the heavens, Paul's hands try to grasp the unknown god *as unknown*, to index without picturing the majesty of the Lord. The tapestry itself will be an icon and not an idol: not a material substitute for God, fixed in space in order to stabilize time, but an image furled and unfurled in response to the exigencies of the liturgical calendar, repeating in its drape and movement, its disappearance and its disclosure, the temporal phenomenality of the image as such. "Distance," writes Marion, "implies withdrawal as a mode of advent."[16] Just as winged altarpieces afford opening and closing, tapestry affords hanging and unhanging; the periodic removal of tapestry—its "deposition" if you will—is the precondition for its reappearance on feast days, a process that stages religious iconicity as a temporal one, its miraculous *Jetztzeit* requiring repeated, but not relentless, solicitation.[17] Epiphany means manifestation: what is revealed behind the curtain, but also what is revealed by means of the curtain, and even perhaps what appears on its woven surface.

Paul participates here in an act of edification, a building up of the church as a holy community composed of its human members. As John Coolidge argued in *The Pauline Renaissance*, edification is a key term in Paul's letters. From the verb *oikodomeo*, to build a house, edification in the Old Testament indicates the building up of the households of the semi-nomadic patriarchs through reproduction, the physical building of the Temple of Solomon, and the creation of a holy community in exile, understood as a "living building," the household (*oikos*) of God (cf. Eph 2:19–22).[18] *Edification* links *education* to

the construction of an *edifice*: preaching is "edifying" because it is addressed
to distinct communities in order to build them up as the church. Designed
for the Sistine Chapel, the tapestries identify edification with the physical site
of papal majesty. If the tapestries adorn the hardscape of the Sistine Chapel
in order to celebrate its identity with the Temple of Solomon, they are themselves a form of softscape, portable hangings that echo the nomadic structures
of the patriarchs as well as Paul's own vocation as a tentmaker (Acts 18:3).[19]
The epistle itself, Paul's favored form of communication, is aimed at edifying distinct communities from a position defined by distance and mobility;
Randall Martin writes that humanist training in epistolary form encouraged
Renaissance writers to "read Paul's epistles as situationally mobile transac-
tions among writers, scribes, messengers, and listeners/readers."[20]

Signs or conditions of edification, as depicted in the tapestries, include
a rhetorically dynamic speaker engaged in gesture and speech; a responsive
audience; a stage, rostrum, or other platform for speaking; and the presence
of a framing architecture, an edifice or sheltering building enshrined in an
established urban locale. Sharon Fermor notes the distinctive compositional
attributes of the tapestries, which include "an almost exaggerated clarity of
dramatic action" that is "concentrated in the foreground," in a space that is
"limited and well-defined, almost stage-like in nature, concentrated towards
the front of the picture plane."[21] Such features show Raphael adjusting the
requirements of Albertian perspective and *istoria* to the traditionally shallow
space of tapestry, while also playing up the edifying nature of the majority
of episodes depicted in the cycle—their capacity not simply to teach, but to
build communities within specific settings whose affordances (of sheltering,
harboring, displaying, or guarding, for example) are amplified by these rhetorical acts.

Take, for example, the tapestry depicting St. Peter healing the lame man
on the porch of the Temple of Solomon (fig. 10.2.) The act of healing, linked
to Leo's medical ambitions, occurs before an audience of onlookers, who
are edified by the spectacle. The scene takes place on the porch of the Temple (the *porta speciosa*), identified as both a specific edifice and a canonic
scene of edification by the twisted Solomonic columns. Medieval exegetes
cast the Temple porch as a figure of interpretation, its latticed structure both
inviting and delaying the hermeneutic process by managing access to the
Holy of Holies within.[22] The two main columns butt right up against the picture plane, both framing Peter's act of healing and celebrating him as *janitor*
or gate-keeper of the mysteries behind him. The receding lines of columns
give depth to the image, while the massive frontality of the main columns
respect and sustain some of tapestry's native flatness. Finally, the intricately

FIGURE 10.2. *Healing of Lame Beggar at the Beautiful Gate of the Temple of Solomon by Ss. Peter and John*. Unknown workshop (Brussels?) after a cartoon by Raphael (ca. 1540). Wool, silk, and gilt metallic thread. Presumed destroyed in the Kaiser Friedrich Museum, Berlin, 1945. Photograph: The Getty Research Institute, Los Angeles (97.P.7).

depicted swirl of the columns themselves renders them into an image of the affordances of fabric: the tendency of textiles to twist, drape, and sway. If the tapestry is designed to adorn and celebrate a specific edifice—the Sistine Chapel as the new Temple of Solomon—that same tapestry will also refer to its own rhetorical mobility, its capacity to address and dress up multiple historical contexts and speech situations, a mobility figured in part by the openness and visual detachability of the porch as a kind of permanent tent.[23]

We might take *Paul in Athens* and *Peter Healing the Lame Man* as templates for grasping the different orientations of these two founding Apostles in the early church and in its diverse legacies. Peter stands on the porch of the Temple in Jerusalem, directing the mission to the Jews from the administrative center. Keeper of the Keys, Peter is the *janitor* or gatekeeper who oversees a guarded universality, admitting newcomers but only according to traditional membership protocols such as circumcision and dietary laws. For Protestants, Peter would be associated with the Catholic Church, of course, but also with the Jewish strain in Christianity. Paul, addressing the Athenian philosophers from the open platform in front of the classical *stoa*, is the Tentmaker; "all things to all men," his mission to the gentiles erects a more open universality that operates by rendering traditional membership practices *adiaphora*, theologically in-different. Yet despite the efforts on the part of Protestant readers of Paul to divorce him completely from the legacy of the Jews, Paul retains an embodied and embedded relationship to Judaism, manifested for example in his double address to the mixed congregation of Jewish and Gentile Christians in his Epistle to the Romans. The compelling presence of Paul here, on the walls of the Sistine Chapel in Rome, reminds us that Paul remains firmly affiliated with Peter in the institutions of Catholicism, which maps Rome as the new Jerusalem, the administrative center of the temple cult. Moreover, it is Paul more than Peter who knit the Hebrew Bible into the scriptural consciousness and indeed unconscious of the West, transmitting the Jewish bases of a Christianity always ready to foreclose its origins. Whereas Peter and Paul oppose or complement each other in their orientations towards Athens and Jerusalem, a division that would be exacerbated in the struggles of the Reformation, their uneasy compromises also suggest the power of their ongoing affiliation, the existence of a Petrine core at the heart of Paul's universal project. In critical theory, we might point here to Badiou's emphasis on Paul's absolute break with Judaism, the vision of Paul contra Peter dramatized in his play, *Incident at Antioch*, and Agamben's emphasis on the messianic, which is to say Jewish nature, of Paul's project, which he derives in part from a reading of Jacob Taubes.[24]

Although the tapestries made from the cartoons are often referred to as the *Acts of the Apostles*, two scenes from Peter's life are taken from the Gospels, not from Acts. John Shearman, the preeminent historian of the cartoons, argues that the ordering of scenes suggests rather a sermon delivered on the Feast of Sts. Peter and Paul (June 29).[25] The tapestries, in other words, do not illustrate Scripture so much as enhance liturgy. *In situ* in the Sistine Chapel, Raphael's tapestries disperse sound, attention, and interpretation across multiple surfaces according to a festal rhythm of withdrawal and display. As woven objects designed to be taken down and hung up, the tapestries engage the tactile imagination in a space resonant with the measured magnificence of liturgical performance. Walter Ong would say that the tapestries contribute to an "oral-aural" theology of the Word, since their rhythmic appearance and disappearance across the year reflects the celebration of the Word made flesh in sacrament rather than its inscription in a book.[26] Indeed, the tapestries may even help mold the acoustic character of the chapel.[27]

In *Paul Preaching in Athens*, Raphael aimed to incarnate the prototypical: Shearman writes that "his representational task was the ultimate test of his power of imagining the perfect antique style, as Paul's sermon to the Athenians was the ultimate test of *his* rhetoric, scholarship and rightness of cause. The result in each case was a set piece."[28] The many niches, rostra, and stages depicted in the tapestries, which emphasize the edifying conditions and dimensions of these Apostolic *Acta*, are *stages for prototypicality*, elevated platforms that promote and display the exemplary character of Raphael's genius for design. What is *prototypical* (exemplary in its responsiveness to decorum) can also become a *prototype*: suitable for reworking in other media. Aby Warburg wrote of tapestry, "In the history of methods of reproduction and dissemination it figures, in a sense, as an ancestor of printing—the same craft whose cheaper product, wallpaper, has appropriately enough usurped the position of tapestry in the bourgeois home."[29] It is certainly no accident that Raphael's designs, even before the tapestries themselves were complete, would swiftly spread through Europe as engravings and woodcuts, hitching the future of design to the destiny of the book.[30] If the tapestries qua tapestries remained part of Catholicism's cool media remix, the Sistine hangings considered from the standpoint of their designs helped heat up (in McLuhan's sense) the medium of visual art in league with technical innovations in printing and mechanical reproduction. As tapestries designed for a liturgical space-time sensorium, as masterpieces of the High Renaissance, and as a major act of intermedial communication between Italy and the Netherlands and between painting, weaving, and printing, Raphael's cartoons are transitional objects in the history of design.[31] The cartoons are Raphael's letters to northern Europe, acts of missionary edification on behalf of Italian *disgeno*. Both a set of the tapestries and the cartoons themselves would end up in England, whose Protestant reception of Paul exists in some tension with Catholic understandings of the apostle. It is to this story that I will now turn.

2. Paul in Whitehall, 1542–1649

In her Booker Prize-winning novel, *Wolf Hall* (2009), Hilary Mantel recounts the fall of Cardinal Wolsey by describing the packing up of his extraordinary collection of tapestries:

> They take down the tapestries and leave the bare blank walls. They are rolled up, the woolen monarchs, Solomon and Sheba; as they are brought into coiled proximity, their eyes are filled by each other, and their tiny lungs breathe in the fiber of bellies and thighs. Down come the cardinal's hunting scenes, the scenes of secular pleasure: the sportive peasants splashing in ponds, the stags at bay, the hounds in cry, the spaniels held on leashes of silk and the mastiffs with their collars of spikes: the huntsmen with their studded belts and knives, the ladies on horseback with jaunty caps, the rush-fringed pond, the mild sheep at pasture, and the bluish feathered treetops, running away into a long plumed distance, to a scene of chalky bluffs and a white sailing sky.[32]

Wolsey's arrases are images in motion; in the words of Aby Warburg, tapestry "was a mobile support for the image."[33] Sliding off the wall and rolling inward on themselves, there is something cinematic in Mantel's waving of the woven histories, their images suddenly adrift in the folds and drape of their disassembly. Mantel's prose reveals tapestry's participation in four dimensions. As flat images, they inhabit a two-dimensional plane; artisanal arrases have traditionally embraced their flatness through the use of graphic ornamentation and stacked, layered, and frontal pictorial space. Yet as weavings, tapestries tend to warp, sag, drift, or bulge, introducing an element of mutation and distortion that subjects the two-dimensional figure to topological as well as temporal shifting. Tapestries counted as *mobilia, meubles, Möbel*: movable furnishings that, unlike frescos, can be taken down, folded up, and rehung. (Wolsey is reported to have changed his tapestries once a week.)[34]

The dismantling of Wolsey's tapestries not only indexes the cardinal's personal fall but also anticipates Henry's break with the Catholic Church. The rolling up of those tapestries is also the rolling up of an era; when Solomon and Sheba appear again in the novel, York Place has been taken over by Henry as the core of what will become Whitehall. Overseeing the apartments of Ann Boleyn, Solomon and Sheba, images of a universal church, gaze out on a world in the process of being unmade and new-made by the king's divorce and its ramifications in theology, liturgy, and life.[35] (Noting the progress of the tapestry is Mantel's anti-hero, Thomas Cromwell, who will go on to supervise the dissolution of the monasteries.) Yet as every housekeeper and conservator knows, stored rugs, canvases, and linens also harbor the dust of seasons past, clouding the bright air of the now with spectral spores, the motes and molds of prior feasts and fasts. Wolsey's hangings, then, exhibit a *manifold mobility*, encompassing everything from the transport of furnishings in an era when all movables lived up to their name, to the uncanny undulation of images on fabric, to the epochal shifts and residual memories of confessional and political change.

Stored in the King's Wardrobe, rolled up alongside specimens from Wolsey's expropriated collection, lay Henry's set of Raphael tapestries.[36] According to Thomas Campbell, woven images constituted Henry's favored visual tool for political-theological communication; his major sets would have been seen by "the leading members of the three estates," and "they must have contributed to the intellectual climate that created the Reformed Church in England."[37] Henry's acquisition of Raphael's tapestries and cartoons raise interesting questions about the confessional complexities of the English case. Henry consistently professed an affinity with Paul, as John N. King demonstrates in his classic study of Tudor royal iconography. The frontispiece to the Coverdale Bible, designed by Hans Holbein, represents Henry at the bottom center, flanked by David and Paul, his Old Testament and New Testament predecessors. Henry holds the sword and the book, attributes of Paul, identifying him an evangelical king. Meanwhile, in a quadrant at the right towards the top, the multiplication of keys given to the Apostles served to contest papal authority by diluting Peter's claim to be the *janitor* of heaven, participating in the Tudor "displacement of St. Peter as the ultimate source of spiritual authority."[38]

In 1538, Henry bought a nine-piece set illustrating *The Life of St. Paul*, referred to in the Great Wardrobe accounts of 1539 as "xi [*sic*]" pieces of "Arras novum" illustrating the "Actibus Apostolum"; Campbell concludes that these were *not* the ones woven from Raphael's cartoons, but rather depicted scenes from the life of Paul alone, unaccompanied by Peter. The set likely issued from the workshop of Pieter Coecke van Aelst, whose work was already influenced by the designs of Raphael and his students Giulio Romano and Gianfrancesco Penni; thus Raphael's tapestries first entered England not directly, but via their mediated impact on Netherlandish design.[39] For Henry and the English reformers, Paul represented both an alternative to Petrine supremacy and an affirmation of secular authority (Rom 13:1). Even before the Reformation, Paul bore a special relationship to England; he was the patron saint of the Corporation of London, and legend had it that Paul had actually visited England in his missionary travels.[40] (Holinshed refers to the tale, though he passes it over as a "conjecture.")[41]

London itself, of course, was closely identified with one of its most famous buildings and public meeting places as well as its main book market, St. Paul's Cathedral.[42] In the architectural view from England, St. Peter's in Rome stands against St. Paul's in London. The spire and the dome distinguished them architecturally, even when the spire itself became a kind of phantom limb after it burned down in 1561. When Christopher Wren rebuilt St. Paul's in the image of St. Peter's, the interior of the dome sported images of Paul largely without Peter, painted by James Thornhill in a classical style that clearly recalls the cartoons of Raphael.[43] The lining of the London dome with images borrowed from the Sistine Chapel, but laundered through the media regimes of the Reformation, completed not only the Englishing but also the Paulinizing of Raphael's papal designs.

Given England's historic preference for Paul over Peter, it makes sense that Henry's first version of the *Acts of the Apostles* came without Peter in the picture.[44] The Raphael tapestries, procured a few years later, present a somewhat different backdrop for political theology, since here Paul most decidedly comes *with* Peter by his side, as party to a systematic defense of papal supremacy and the unity of the church. Whereas Peter and Paul represent twin pillars of the church in medieval iconography, whether on church facades or on the outer wings of altarpieces, under the pressure of the Reformation, Peter becomes a more ambiguous figure. The incident at Antioch (Gal 2:11–14), when Peter and Paul quarrel over circumcision and table fellowship, was cited by both Luther and Calvin as grounds for rejecting papal authority.[45] The English Catholic poet-martyr Robert Southwell wrote a poetic monologue called "St. Peter's Complaint"; taking up Peter's despair at his denial of Christ, Southwell is surely interested in proferring Peter as a model of spiritual exercise for English Catholics.[46] Dürer's Luther-inspired *Four Apostles* altarpiece famously prefers Paul to Peter, tucking Peter in the left background and giving Paul pride of place, foreground right.[47] El Greco's double portrait of Peter and Paul is one of the most eloquent and compelling Counter-Reformation testaments to the continuing alliance between the two main apostles of the early church; a kind of brutal melancholy charges the relationship between the keeper of the keys and the bearer of the book, their hands both interfolded and kept apart and their gazes pointedly not meeting. Antioch, it seems, is still between them.[48]

What could a suite of tapestries celebrating the double apostleships of Peter and Paul as the fonts of papal authority have meant in the court of Henry VIII after the Act of Supremacy? An observation by George Peacham in 1622 places the tapestries in the Banqueting House at Whitehall, and Thomas Campbell believes that Henry commissioned the set for the renovations of the Banqueting House in the early 1540s, as part of a general Italianate sprucing up of the London palace.[49] Margaret Mitchell muses that "it is difficult to understand the unbroken silence about the presence of the tapestries in England during Henry's reign; it extends even into the visual arts where no trace of their direct influence can be felt."[50] Is it possible that the papal origins and arguments of the tapestries limited their impact in Tudor England, even while their Italian design made them appropriate décor for an ambitious sovereign? Campbell thinks not, arguing that Henry's propagandists had successfully reclaimed Peter for the Protestants. As demonstrated on the Coverdale frontispiece, the Reformers argued that Christ gave the keys of His kingdom to *all* the Apostles, allowing an image like Raphael's *Christ's Charge to Peter* to be understood as the inauguration of a more general apostolic succession. Such a script would place Henry himself, as head of the English Church, in the line of Peter, and not in conflict with him. Campbell concludes, "In effect, Henry had appropriated and transferred the splendor and trappings of apostolic succession from the papal palace in Rome to his own palace at Westminster, the visual focus of the Tudor court in London."[51]

Despite the marked English preference of Paul over Peter, the Tudor monarchs clearly made their peace with the coupling of the two apostles in Raphael's tapestries, since the set adorned Westminster Abbey for the coronation of Elizabeth I.[52] The Stuart court certainly appreciated the full fabric of the tapestries' presentation of Scripture and sovereignty. James, the son of a martyred Catholic queen, was considered more open to Catholic influences than Elizabeth; James's wife Queen Anne converted to Catholicism, and the king preferred Catholic marriages for their offspring in order to further his pacifist policies through ecumenical alliances.[53] (Elizabeth Stuart, however, married a Protestant, Frederick V, Elector Palatine, who became the Winter King of Bohemia in 1619.) After acquiring the cartoons for use at Mortlake, Charles went on to order several weavings from Raphael's designs, using working cartoons made by Francis Cleyn.[54]

We do not have any clear accounts of when and how the Peter and Paul tapestries were displayed, but John Astington has provided a fascinating reconstruction of how another major Henrician cycle, the Abraham tapestries, on view today in the Great Hall of Hampton Court Palace, were ritually displayed during James's reign.[55] In April or May of 1621, an entertainment entitled *The History of Abraham* was staged in the new Banqueting House designed by Inigo Jones, then in its final stages of completion, in honor of the Feast of the Knights of the Garter, held on St. George's Day, April 23.[56] Preparations would have included not only the laborious hanging of the tapestries themselves, but also assembling the temporary architecture that accompanied sovereignty itself: "Whenever the monarch was present the royal state—dais, throne, hangings, and canopy—had to be constructed in advance in any chamber where it was not a usual fixture."[57] The festivities demonstrate the full array of elements that constituted the sovereign softscape: the tapestries themselves, as an iconographic backdrop celebrating the English monarch as the father (Abba and Abraham) of his people; the outlining and sheltering of the person of the monarch in the elaborate canopies and cloths of state; the splendid ritual clothing of the king and the assembled party; and the celebration of the garter as a fashion accessory associated with both military and festival adornment.

Presumably Raphael's tapestries were displayed according to a similar curatorial protocol as the backdrop for major ceremonial events at court, not only for coronations but also annual holiday celebrations. The ceremonial care and political-theological self-consciousness with which the Abraham cycle was treated would surely have been shared with the several equally ambitious and dramatic Paul cycles, all bearing the impress of Raphael's designs, that rested in the care of the Great Wardrobe in the seventeenth century. Astington notes that the new banqueting hall designed by Inigo Jones was built the same year that James started up the Mortlake tapestry works, and under the leadership of the same court personnel, as part of a "'general renewal of the State Apartments at Court.'"[58] The acquisition of the cartoons by Charles effectively organized English royal tapestry production around the designs of Raphael and the twinned images of Peter and Paul displayed in them; by the early eighteenth century, a poet like Anne Finch could write an ecphrastic poem about a tapestry "*made after the Famous Cartons of* Raphael."[59] We even have some indication that Pauline tapestries would have had some play in the broader public imagination in the earlier seventeenth century: in Beaumont's *Knight of the Burning Pestle*, likely first performed at Blackfriars in 1607, the Wife asks the Citizen about the subject matter displayed on a painted arras: "now sweet lambe, what story is that painted upon the cloth? The confutation of Saint *Paul?*"[60] A painted arras depicting the conversion of St. Paul survives in the Hardwick House collection; images of Paul were likely common on the painted arrases that decorated both greater and meaner houses in the period.[61]

It is interesting to consider the extent to which Shakespeare's later dramas, often performed in the Banqueting House at Whitehall, might have shared space if not time with the Peter and Paul tapestries. First performed at the Globe in 1611 and at Blackfriars Playhouse in 1613, *The Winter's Tale* was also performed at Whitehall, most likely at the Banqueting House, as part of the festivities associated with the marriage of Princess Elizabeth to Prince Frederick the Elector Palatine, in winter, 1612–13. At the Banqueting House, it's highly unlikely that Raphael's Peter and Paul tapestries would have been on display during performances of *The Winter's Tale*; minor rather than major arrases would have warmed the walls during theatrical performances.[62] Yet the members of the audience, consisting of the court of James I, would have seen *at alternating times* both Shakespeare's and Raphael's late masterpieces. One must not risk making too much of this. No direct threads knit the tapestries to *The Winter's Tale*, nor do the stories narrated in the two works reflect each other in any direct way. Yet we can say at the very least that Raphael's arrases and Shakespeare's play not only shared a *common space* (the Banqueting House at Whitehall), but they also shared a *common world*, understood both theologically and in terms of media. Theologically, it was a world uneasily occupied by both Peter and Paul, by both Catholic and Protestant theories of sovereignty and the sign, as they intermixed uneasily with each other in the testy atmosphere of James's court. Both works, moreover, participated in the shimmering softscape of Whitehall, itself consisting of modern Italianate acquisitions already stamped by the medium of print and older, more medieval

layers inherited from a less divided England, including the collection appropriated from Cardinal Wolsey.

The Winter's Tale is arguably at once Shakespeare's most explicitly Pauline play *and* his most Catholic one.[63] Featuring a character named Paulina,
who affiliates herself with the working of grace and the redemptive power
of faith, the play also stages markedly Catholic forms of architecture, spiritual discipline, and image-making, including a red thread of Mariology that
weaves a decidedly Catholic figure into the play's *mille fleurs* carpet. Usually
commentators place the Pauline and the Catholic elements in tension with
each other; in the algebra of confessional criticism, to cite Paul is to support a Protestant agenda, while Catholic reminiscences must represent some
remainder of or resistance to the Pauline Renaissance. Exemplary here is
Houston Diehl's fine reading of Paul in *The Winter's Tale*. Far from presenting a purely spiritualized or Marcionite Paul, Diehl addresses the mixed and
bodily character of Paul for Shakespeare. Arguing that Paul's "preaching emphasizes the imperfection of every human being and celebrates the 'grafting'
of the new man onto the old," Diehl aims to "examine the way Shakespeare
draws on Protestant constructions of the historical Paul for his conception
of Paulina."[64] I would insist that those same forms of hybridization extend
to Paul's dual citizenship in Catholic and Protestant regimes of worship and
reading. Paulina, both the clerklike keeper of a sacred chapel that houses the
miraculous image of a saintly mother *and* the canny wielder of a rhetoric of
rebuke and grace, presents a fascinating cipher of the regrafting of Protestant
and Catholic iconographies in the court of James, evident above all in the soft
architecture and moving pictures of the statue scene.

We first learn of the statue in Act Five, Scene Two: "The princess hear-
ing of her mother's statue, which is in the keeping of Paulina—a piece many
years in doing and newly performed by that rare Italian master Giulio Romano" (V.ii.92–95). Although Romano is not Raphael, he *was* one of the most
talented and famous of Raphael's students, *and* he almost certainly assisted
Raphael on the painting of the cartoons.[65] Romano, too, then, is present on
the walls of the Banqueting House. Vasari makes no mention of Romano's
tapestry work, but he does record Romano as a participant in the courtly
softscape of festival: "Giulio devised many superb decorative arches, scenery
for plays, and many other things in which he had no rival for invention; nor
was there ever anyone more fanciful in devising masquerades and design-
ing extravagant costumes for jousts, festivities and tournaments."[66] Perhaps
the link between Romano and court pageantry encouraged Shakespeare to
use the word "perform" in the place of "sculpt" or "make" in his account
of Romano's artistic agency. The name "Romano," moreover, effectively

romanizes Paulina's chapel-gallery, tagging the Roman setting shared by the Sistine tapestries and by Paul's most famous Epistle.[67]

When Paulina bids us to approach the statue in the final scene of the play, a curtain hides the figure of Hermione: "*Paulina draws a curtain, and reveals Hermione standing like a statue.*"[68] At the Globe, the curtain would have hung over the discovery space, with the actor playing Hermione posed within. Bruce Smith compares the use of the curtain here to "the religious custom of shrouding the crucifix during Lent with a curtain . . . and opening it on Easter."[69] At Whitehall, the entire mini-chapel/statuary niche might have been constructed out of fabric, a piece of tentwork like the baldachins or canopies of state that sheltered and back-dropped the king wherever he sat.[70] Throughout the scene, Paulina keeps motioning to close the curtain, instituting the rhythmic motion of closure and disclosure that measured the liturgical display of tapestry in the Catholicism. Richard Wilson describes the curtained space of *The Winter's Tale* as "one of those women's alcoves . . . referred not to the empire of the gaze but to the claustral interiority of a suspect woman, or the sororial enclacve of an enclosed nun."[71] When Hermione steps outside her curtained closet, breaking the illusion that she is a petrified, even Petrine, statue, she does not abandon representation for reality so much as incarnate another form of representation, suspended (but in movement) between idol and icon, or between statue and tapestry, marrying the three dimensions of sculpture to the fourth dimension of arras, which embraces the cinematic drift and drape, the slide and wrinkle, of fabric.

Renaissance tapestry floated and flowered at the intersection of entertainment, sovereignty, and theology. In the Tudor and Stuart courts, the Office of the Great Wardrobe was responsible for the care of tapestry, along with the other major textile holdings of the monarch; the Office of the Tents, periodically expanded into the Office of the Tents and the Revels, administered the display of tapestry for specific occasions.[72] A softscape composed of assorted tapestries, rugs, balduchins, and bedclothes not only dressed the space of Whitehall, but also helped build the moveable scenery of sovereignty as the prince passed from palace to palace, transited through the streets of the city, or held court in offshore locales. The phrase "edify" was sometimes used to denote the erection and outfitting of temporary structures for revels and banquets.[73] A form of attire for walls, tapestry was married to both architecture and festival, and it had a special role to play not only in celebrating sovereignty, but in bodying forth its shifting, billowing character during a period of religious strife and political consolidation. *The Winter's Tale*, along with plays such as *Hamlet, Othello,* and *Cymbeline,* shares materials, both representational and physical, with the sovereign softscape. Both the court and the theater used tapestry not as permanent adornment but as a form of temporary and indeed *temporal* décor. Tapestry was a form of *mobilia,* kept in motion as part of the continual rezoning efforts undertaken both by the court as a scene for the display of sovereignty and by the theater as part of its iconographic arsenal. In both situations, fabric provided not only a flat backdrop for the choreographies of politics and theater alike, but also contributed a key element to the creation of three-dimensional structures for the framing of a political-theological aura as fragile as it was sublime.

Finally, both theater and tapestry drew on a layered history of religious images, repurposed architecture, and representational practices that could be used to announce breaks with previous dispensations, but they did so via media characterized by flow and fold, echo and reverb. If Henry and his heirs desired to use the tapestries to celebrate a firmly Protestant Paul, what comes forward in the history of Raphael's designs is a softer, more layered scape. England, well before the Reformation, showed a marked preference for Paul over Peter. (We might even, in psychoanalytic terms, speak here of an object choice or a *Neurosenwahl,* a primal decision made against a ground not yet mapped by reason.) The Reformation brings that choice into greater clarity, refiguring Paul and Peter's uneasy partnership as an antagonism: Paul against Peter, faith against works, the Book against the Keys, London's spire against Rome's dome. In this scenario, the ancient English affinity for Paul testifies to England's always incipient Protestantism. On the other hand, the Anglican Church's permanent nostalgia for the Roman rites projects an England always falling back into crypto-Catholicism. Henry VIII's own erratic mood swings in matters concerning theology and matrimony alike anticipate the persistence of a Petrine Paul on England's shores. Certainly Henry's ability to retrofit a glorious piece of papal apology to the requirements of his own propaganda machine indicates the elastic meanings of Peter and Paul for the England that Henry helped build. This was a world that accommodated folded layers of iconography in its Great Wardrobes, linen closets, and prop shops. Where we might want to see conflict or contradiction, the audiences of the Tudor and Stuart courts may have simply enjoyed a glorious weave of wool and linen interspersed with threads of gold. "Everything is of use to a housekeeper": this proverb, attributed to the Anglican poet-pastor George Herbert, also characterized the Tudor-Stuart softscape in all of its biopolitical complexity. Like Herbert's housekeeper, the stewards of the Great Wardrobe and the officers of Tents and Revels put up with a great deal of contradiction, without, however, requiring a theory of tolerance to manage the seams. In pursuing their curatorial and sumptuary duties, these stewards nonetheless helped transmit the mixed legacy of Paul's Epistles, including their legacy to liberalism, a process in which Shakespeare, too, participated.[74]

3. Coda: Paul in Los Angeles

The Raphael tapestries would remain in the possession of the monarchy until 1650, when the Rump Parliament began the work of selling off the king's household goods. The sale, writes Jerry Brotton, "represented a conscious act of political iconoclasm as much as a brutal piece of financial asset stripping."[75] The inventory included over sixteen hundred tapestries, most appraised at ridiculously low prices. In the great fire sale of royal goods, devotional panels once belonging to Cardinal Wolsey were valued as low as a pound, perhaps because of their "Popish" subject matter.[76] Since their original execution in 1518, Raphael's cartoons for Leo X had become ambassadors for the Italian style, which, swiftly moving north, infiltrated territories associated not only with print but also with reform, a reform driven, moreover, by a strong reading of Paul, whom Manfred Schneider dubs Luther's favorite "media and semiotic specialist."[77] In these north-south exchanges, Leo's Paul, at once humanist and Catholic, meets Luther's Paul, via Raphael's pact with print culture and the possibilities for design that print promoted. No wonder Cromwell was confused. The Lord Protector did hold onto Henry's Abraham tapestries, which commanded the highest price of the whole collection, and ended up not being sold.[78] It is interesting to imagine that Cromwell might have found the Old Testament themes easier to reconcile with Puritanism than Raphael's paeans to the papacy, though many Old Testament cycles, as well as Henry's first St. Paul set, were de-accessioned in the rush to pay off royal debts.

Destroyed in Berlin during Allied air raids, Henry's tapestries were photographed before the War, and the photos, along with other refugees, ended up in Los Angeles. The photos of Henry's tapestries live in a large green box devoted to several series of tapestries originating in Brussels and depicting the Acts of the Apostles. Most of the photos depict tapestries that still exist somewhere, whether at Hampton Court Palace, or the Palacio Real in Madrid, or the Bijlokemuseum in Ghent. The sepia prints from the Berlin Gemäldegallerie, however, are ghosts without bodies, sodium sulfide shrouds that can never be replaced by fresher, more faithful recordings. At the back of the green box, in a 1620 Apostles series composed from designs by Raphael and Pieter Coecke van Aelst the Younger, I found a subject not depicted in Leo's program. Catalogued as *St. Paul Burns the Books of Gentiles at Ephesus*

FIGURE 10.3. *St. Paul Burns Books of Gentiles at Ephesus*. Tapestry, Flemish (ca. 1620). Designed after Pieter Coecke van Aelst the Younger, in the workshop of Jan Raes I. Tapestry in Palacio Real de Madrid. Photograph: The Getty Research Institute, Los Angeles (97.P.7).

(fig. 10.3), the tapestry depicts a startlingly serene Apostle overseeing a holocaust of classical codices, perhaps associated with sorcery (Acts 19:1–19). Great cushions of smoke and flame spread up and out from the right hand side of the image. It is as if the tapestry itself were on fire, though in the black and white photo, the billows resemble heavenly clouds. In the echo chamber created by that box of photographs, Paul's burnt offering backlights the later fate of Henry's tapestries, and I cannot help asking what Paul has to do with the destiny of Henry's tapestries.[79] Paul himself was no Marcionite. Never ceasing to declare himself a Jew, Paul remained committed to the chosenness of Israel, even as he reengineered prophesy and law in his effort to come to terms with what he judged to be the messianic event. In the Epistles themselves, the dualities that measure the rhythm of Paul's thinking—letter and spirit, works and faith, Jew and Greek—were always kept in motion by the rhetorical exigencies imposed by his mixed and multiple congregations. Yet those same oppositions would harden into the fatal machinery of anti-Judaism and anti-Semitism in the centuries after the messianic moment had closed up, eventually flaring up as holocaust and blitzkrieg, a sequence uncannily materialized, through a kind of spectral analysis, in the proximity of these affiliated photographs in the green box at the Getty. I choose to glean at least a stitch of irony in the fact that Henry's great Abraham tapestries, with their extraordinary representation of the circumcision of Isaac, survived the war, while the weavings of Peter and Paul, architects of Christianity, did not (fig. 10.4).[80]

To what extent, then, do Raphael's tapestries represent a point of departure for political theology? Anselm Haverkamp distinguishes between a "weaker," largely descriptive and sociological approach to political theology, and "stronger" accounts that test the structural translations between theology and politics that concern the media and signifying systems of the state.[81] Raphael's tapestries most certainly participate in political theology in the weaker sense, insofar as they supported the ideological apparatuses of the papacy, the great courts of the continent, and the Tudor and Stuart monarchies as they tried to fashion modern theories of sovereignty out of the narratives of authority and succession embedded in the earliest history of the primitive church. In these pages, however, I have also tried to set a more multidimensional, temporally infolded, scene. Swaying in space, unfurling across time, and repeatedly deposed, rolled up, and hung anew, Raphael's Peter and Paul tapestries bear both contradictions and potentialities in the dynamic topology of their woven surfaces. The reliance of early modern sovereignty on the *mobilia* of arrases points to a certain mobility within sovereignty itself as it struggled to attach itself to single administrative centers and fixed territorial borders. The padding, tenting, and framing of sovereignty by fabric awnings and woven backdrops suggests the precarious quality of the prince's real and symbolic existence, which needed to be decked, sheltered, clothed, and glossed with the pomp and circumstance of statist liturgies. The Great Wardrobe had much to contribute to the "tradition, form, and ceremonious duty" that allowed the king "a little scene, / To monarchize."[82] The sovereign softscape at once shelters and figures forth the even softer scape of the king's mortal body, exposing the biopolitical lining of political theology. Meanwhile, billowing in the background, the strange journey of Henry's Raphael tapestries through reformation, revolution, and blitzkrieg indicates the enigmatic presence of Paul, both fronting off against Peter and continuing to build alliances with him, on the scenes of early modernity.

FIGURE 10.4. *Circumcision of Isaac*. Tapestry, woven in Brussels, workshop of Willem de Kempeneer (1541–43). Likely designed by Pieter Coecke van Aelst the Elder. Hampton Court Palace. Photograph: The Royal Collection © 2012, Her Majesty Queen Elizabeth II.

Notes

A first draft of this essay was composed for the conference "Cultures of Communication, Theologies of Media," organized by Ulrike Strasser and Christopher Wild for the Clark Library, Los Angeles, December 2009; I also had a chance to share it with colleagues at the University of Texas at Austin. My thanks to Jane O. Newman and Jayne Lewis for their generous responses, and to Tracey Schuster at the Getty Research Institute for guidance in using George Leland Hunter's collection of tapestry photos.

1. Although scholars had speculated that the tapestries were a gift from Leo X to Henry before the Act of Supremacy, Thomas Campbell has argued persuasively for the later date and different origin. See "School of Raphael Tapestries in the Collection of Henry VIII," *Burlington Magazine* 138.115 (February 1996): 73. For the papal legend, see Margaret Mitchell, "Works of Art from Rome for Henry VIII: A Study of Anglo-Papal Relations as Reflected in Papal Gifts to the English King," *Journal of the Courtauld and Warburg Institutes* 34 (1971): 178–203.

2. W. G. Thomson, *A History of Tapestry* (1906; rpt. East Ardsley, U.K.: EP Publishing Ltd., 1973), 278–80. See also Linda Peck, *Consuming Splendor: Society and Culture in Seventeenth-Century England* (Cambridge: Cambridge University Press, 2005), 81.

3. For a sampling of the debate, see John D. Caputo and Linda Martin Alcoff, eds., *St. Paul Among the Philosophers* (Bloomington: Indiana University Press, 2009). I summarize some of the recent work in Renaissance studies in "The Pauline Renaissance: A Shakespearean Reassessment," *European Legacy* 15.2 (April 2010): 215–20. Since then, see for example, Jonathan Goldberg, *The Seeds of Things: Theorizing Sexuality and Materiality in Renaissance Representations* (New York: Fordham University Press, 2009), for a powerful reading of Pauline iconography written in response to Badiou and Agamben.

4. Manfred Schneider, "Luther with McLuhan," in *Religion and Media*, ed. Hent de Vries and Samuel Weber (Stanford: Stanford University Press, 2001), 201.

5. On the use of tapestries in outdoor settings, see Adolfo Salvatore Cavallo, *Medieval Tapestries in the Metropolitan Museum of Art* (New York: The Metropolitan Museum and Harry Abrams, Inc., 1993), 29. On the use of the tapestry on the Renaissance stage, see Sarah Ann M. Ill, "Visibility and Resonance: Tapestries on and around the Early Modern Stage" (Master's thesis, Mary Baldwin College, 2007). See also Juliet Fleming's account of the inscribed character of Renaissance space, *Graffiti and the Writing Arts* (Philadelphia: University of Pennsylvania Press, 2001).

6. On the interrelation between biopolitics and political theology, see Eric Santner, *The Royal Remains* (Chicago: The University of Chicago Press, 2011).

7. Thomas Campbell, *Tapestry in the Renaissance: Art and Majesty* (New York: Metropolitan Museum of Art, 2002), 187–97.

8. Ibid., 187.

9. John Shearman, *Raphael's Cartoons in the Collection of Her Majesty the Queen, and the Tapestries for the Sistine Chapel* (London: Phaidon, 1972), 77.

10. Ibid., 73.

11. Sharon Fermor, *The Raphael Cartoons* (London: Victoria and Albert Museum, 1996), 82.

12. Shearman, *Raphael's Cartoons*, 133.

13. Jean-Luc Marion, *The Idol and Distance: Five Studies*, trans. Thomas Carlson (New York: Fordham University Press, 2001), 24.

14. Ibid., 25.

15. On the importance of the Pseudo-Dionysius to medieval image theory, see Georges Didi-Huberman, *Fra Angelico: Dissemblance and Disfiguration*, trans. Janice Todd (Chicago: University of Chicago Press, 1990), 50–55.

16. Marion, *The Idol and Distance*, 23.

17. On the "deposition" of images as part of their religious phenomenology, see Amy Powell, *Perpetual Motifs: Scenes from the Late Medieval Church and the Modern Museum* (Cambridge, Mass.: Zone Books, forthcoming).

18. John S. Coolidge, *The Pauline Renaissance: Puritanism and the Bible* (Oxford: Clarendon Press, 1970), 23–54. For a literary application of Coolidge's account of Pauline edification, see Gregory Kneidel, "Samuel Daniel and Edification," *Studies in English Literature* 24.1 (Winter, 2004): 59–76; reworked in Kneidel's brilliant book on Paul and English Renaissance literature, *Rethinking the Turn to Religion in Early Modern English Literature* (London: Palgrave Macmillan, 2008). Rebeca Helfer explores the link between edifices and edifications in *Spenser's Ruins and the Art of Recollection* (Toronto: University of Toronto Press, forthcoming).

19. Shearman notes that the tapestries are "uniquely architectural," and comments on a series of metaphors and identifications, including the Sistine Chapel as the Temple of Solomon and Christ as Cornerstone of the Church. *Raphael's Cartoons*, 80–84.

20. Randall Martin, "Shakespearian Biography, Biblical Allusion, and Early Modern Practices of Reading Scripture," *Shakespeare Survey* 63 (2010): 212–24. Manfred Schneider also comments on the medial mobility of the epistolary form: "That the canonical texts of the Christian tradition also includes letters can be seen as a sign of the openness and modernity of the early Christian movement." "Luther with McLuhan," 201. Paul writes to the Corinthians, "see that ye may excel to the edifying of the church" (1 Cor 14:12; KJV). Cf. 1 Cor 14:5, "that the church may receive edifying."

21. Sharon Fermor, *The Raphael Tapestry Cartoons* (London: Scala Books and the Victoria and Albert Museum, 1996), 76.

22. Georges Didi-Huberman writes of the *limen templi* that it "hides but also gives access to what we could call the Holy of Holies in the scriptural sense" (*Fra Angelico*, 38).

23. On porches as detachable architecture, see Ellen and Julia Lupton, "Porch Envy," in *Design Your Life: The Pleasures and Perils of Everyday Things* (New York: St. Martin's Press, 2009), 28–33. On the architecture of tents, see Charlie Hailey, *Campsite: Architectures of Duration and Space* (Baton Rouge: Louisiana State University Press, 2008) and *Camps: A Guide to 21st Century Space* (Cambridge, Mass.: MIT Press, 2009).

24. I develop the contrast between Badiou and Agamben and the necessity of both perspectives to a reading of Paul in Shakespeare in *Thinking with Shakespeare* (chapter 6: Paul Shakespeare). The key texts are Alain Badiou, *Saint Paul: The Foundation of Universalism*, trans. Ray Brassier (Stanford: Stanford University Press, 2003) and his unpublished play, *Incident at Antioch*, which dramatizes the conflict between Peter and Paul (translated by Susan Spitzer with an introduction by Kenneth Reinhard for Columbia University Press); Giorgio Agamben, *The Time That Remains: A Commentary on the Letter to the Romans* (Stanford: Stanford University Press, 2005); and Jacob Taubes, *The Political Theology of Paul*, trans. Dana Hollander (Stanford: Stanford University Press, 2004).

25. The Feast commemorates the double martyrdom of Peter and Paul in Rome, a scene not depicted in the tapestry cycle.

26. Walter Ong, *The Presence of the Word: Some Prolegomena for Cultural and Religious History* (New Haven: Yale University Press, 1967).

27. Bruce R. Smith comments on the acoustic properties of tapestry, *The Key of Green* (Chicago: University of Chicago Press, 2009), 212.

28. Shearman, *Raphael's Cartoons*, 125.

29. Aby Warburg, "Peasants at Work in Burgundian Tapestries" (1907), in *The Renewal of Pagan Antiquity*, trans. David Britt (Los Angeles: Getty Center, 1999), 315.

30. On Raphael and print culture, see Lisa Pon, *Raphael, Dürer and Marcantonio Raimondi* (New Haven: Yale University Press, 2004).

31. See Thomas Campbell: "Through the medium of engraved and woven copies, the *Acts* were among the most effective ambassadors of the Italian High Renaissance in northern Europe in the second quarter of the sixteenth century, and through their influence on Netherlandish artists such as Bernaert van Orley and Pieter Coecke van Aelst, they fundamentally altered the subsequent development of Netherlandish tapestry design" (*Tapestry in the Renaissance*, 187).

32. Hilary Mantel, *Wolf Hall* (New York: Henry Holt, 2009), 40.

33. Warburg, "Peasants at Work," 315. I also borrow the phrase "image in motion" from Aby Warburg; the Renaissance softscape, composed of textile *mobilia* subject to drift and flow and suited to spectacle and festival, clearly resonates with Warburg's investigations into an Italian visual culture organized but not fixed by the idea of *disegno*. See Warburg's landmark essay on Botticelli, which emphasizes the painter's depiction of "accessories in motion," including fabrics, in *Renewal of Pagan Antiquity*, 88–156, and commentary by Phillipe-Alain Michaud, *Aby Warburg and the Image in Motion*, trans. Sophie Hawkes (New York: Zone Books, 2004).

34. Thomas P. Campbell cites the Venetian ambassador Sebastian Giustinian, who, visiting in 1519, "reported to the Signory that Wolsey 'had a very fine palace, where one traverses eight rooms before reaching his audience chamber and they are all hung with tapestry, which is changed once a week'" (*Henry VIII and the Art of Majesty: Tapestries at the Tudor Court* [New Haven: Yale University Press, 2007], 140).

35. Mantel, *Wolf Hall*, 164.

36. In an inventory of 1542, the tapestries are called "10 Arras of thistorie of thactes of thapostles." Tom Campbell, "School of Raphael Tapestries in the Collection of Henry VIII," *Burlington Magazine* 138.1115 (February 1996): 73.

37. Campbell, *Henry VIII and the Art of Majesty*, 335.

38. John N. King, *Tudor Royal Iconography: Literature and Art in an Age of Religious Crisis* (Princeton: Princeton University Press, 1989), 54–64.

39. Campbell, *Henry VIII*, 238–39. Campbell argues that the subject of Paul suited Henry's new project of Reformation, and suggests that Ann Boleyn may have introduced a specifically Protestant reading of Paul's letters to the king.

40. Corporation of the City of London, *The Guildhall of London* (London: Court of Common Council, 1899), 134. The association between Paul and London "goes back to earliest times. . . . As the cathedral's patron, Paul was the embodiment of the church—in a memorable phrase, its 'undying landlord.'" Christopher Wren modeled the dome of St. Paul's after St. Peter's, and the English were highly conscious of the comparison. Derek Keene, Arthur Burns, and Andrew Saint, eds., *St. Paul's: The Cathedral Church of London, 604–2004* (New Haven: Yale University Press, 2005): 113, 200, 345.

41. Raphael Holinshed, *First Volume of the Chronicles of England, Scotlande, and Irelande* (1577), 9.

42. On the architectural and social history of St. Paul's, see Keene, Burns, and Saint, eds., *St Paul's: The Cathedral Church of London, 604–2004*.

43. On the history of the commission, see Carol Gibson-Woods, "The Political Background to Thornhill's Paintings in St. Paul's Cathedral," *Journal of the Courtauld and Warburg Institutes* 56 (1993): 229–37.

44. Campbell writes, "The recurrent citation of St. Paul as a role model for Henry in texts and sermons generated by the court during the mid- to late 1530s, provides circumstantial evidence that the purchase of this set was motivated by an intention to celebrate the parallel between Paul, the main propagator of Christ's teachings, and Henry, the latter-day evangelist who was responsible for introducing the Great Bible to every church in the country" (*Henry VIII and the Art of Majesty*, 241).

45. Thus Luther writes unequivocally of Peter, "Peter, the prince of the apostles, lived and taught contrary to the Word of God," and he goes on to cite the incident at Antioch, as recounted in Galatians, as the proof-text for Luther's rejection of papal authority (*Lectures on Galatians* [1535], cited in *The Writings of St. Paul*, ed. Wayne Meeks and John T. Fitzgerald [New York: Norton, 2007], 236n). The same point is made in Article 29 of the Thirty-nine Articles: "As the Church of *Jerusalem, Alexandria,* and *Antioch,* have erred; so also the Church of *Rome* hath erred, not only in their living and manner of Ceremonies, but also in matters of Faith" (*39 Articles of the Church of England* [London: J. G. and F. Rivington, 1834], 47). For a survey of Patristic, Medieval, and Reformation accounts of the incident at Antioch, see John Riches, *Galatians through the Centuries* (Malden, Mass.: Blackwell Publishing, 2008), 108–14. Michael Goulder tracks the conflict between Peter and Paul as formative of the Gospels themselves, with Mark representing a more Pauline position and Matthew a more Petrine one. See *St. Paul Versus St. Peter: A Tale of Two Missions* (Louisville: Westminster/John Knox Press, 1995). On Peter in the New Testament, read from both Catholic and Protestant perspectives, see Raymond Brown, *Peter in the New Testament: A Collaborative Assessment by Protestant and Roman Catholic Scholars* (Minneapolis: Augsburg Publication House, 1973).

46. Robert Southwell, *Saint Peters Complaint* (London: Printed by I[ames] R[oberts] for G[abriel] C[awood], 1595; STC (2d ed.) / 22956). Gary Kuchar emphasizes the Catholic character of Peter as a choice for lyric-dramatic representation: "By recognizing Peter as the first apostolic model of true compunction before Christ, a reader testifies to the authority of the communion of saints—thereby activating the poem's distinctly Catholic features. Read this way, Southwell's Peter becomes more than an individual sinner, he emerges as the first Apostle of the Church and thus a symbol of the Catholic communion as such" (*The Poetry of Religious Sorrow in Early Modern England* [Cambridge: Cambridge University Press, 2008], 36).

47. Albrecht Dürer, *The Four Apostles*, 1526; Alte Pinakothek, Munich. David Hotchkiss Price writes, "Dürer seems to have arranged the biblical writers according to a Protestant hierarchy so as to display, in their foreground placements, the primacy of Paul and John" (*Albrecht Dürer's Renaissance: Humanism, Reformation, and the Art of Faith* [Ann Arbor: University of Michigan Press, 2003], 258). See also King, *Tudor Royal Iconography*, 64–67.

48. For further images of Peter and Paul, and a brief commentary on the El Greco image, see Riches, *Galatians through the Centuries*, 109–11.

49. Campbell, "School of Raphael Tapestries," 78.

50. Margaret Mitchell, "Works of Art from Rome for Henry VIII," 299.

51. Campbell, *Henry VIII*, 275. Campbell suggests that Henry ordered the first set of Paul tapestries for Hampton Court Palace, and acquired the second set, the ones made from Raphael's cartoons, for Whitehall, "to ensure that all the key palaces were equipped with imagery appropriate to Henry's vision of himself as both patriarch of, and apostle to, his people" (*Henry VIII*, 332).

52. The Raphael tapestries were hung in Westminster Abbey, along with scenes from Genesis, likely including the Abraham tapestries. Campbell, *Henry VIII*, 349.

53. Shakespeare, *The Winter's Tale*, ed. Stephen Orgel (Oxford: Oxford University Press, 1996), 47–48. All citations from *The Winter's Tale* are taken from this definitive edition.

54. Campbell, *Renaissance Tapestry*, 202; Shearman, *Raphael's Cartoons*, 144–64.

55. The Abraham tapestries, composed of ten pieces, entered the Great Wardrobe in 1543–44. On the design and iconography of the cycle, see especially Campbell, *Henry VIII*, 283–97. They were likely designed for the Great Hall at Hampton Court Palace, where they hang today, but they were also used at the coronation of James II in Westminster Abbey in 1685, and possibly at Elizabeth's coronation (along with the Raphael set). Astington places them at Whitehall in the 1620s, and also at the important first Christmas celebrations held by James I at Whitehall in 1603–1604, so they seem to have been on the move between palaces.

56. John Astington, "A Jacobean Ghost, and Other Stories," in *Medieval and Renaissance Drama in England*, ed. S. P. Cerasano (Cranbury, N.J.: Associated University Presses, 2005), 40. The original entry appears in the *Dramatic Records in the Declared Accounts of the Treasurer of the Chamber, 1558–1642*, ed. David Cook and F. P. Wilson, Malone Society, Collections VI (Oxford: Oxford University Press, 1961–62), 119.

57. Astington, "A Jacobean Ghost," 38.

58. Ibid., 42.

59. Charles Hinnant, *The Poetry of Anne Finch: An Interpretation* (Cranbury, N.J.: Associated University Presses, 1994), 124. My thanks to Jayne Lewis for this reference.

60. It turns out that what's hanging over the discovery space is a painted cloth depicting the Rape of Lucrece (comically rendered as the "Rafe of Lucrece" in the interchange between the Wife and the Citizen). Francis Beaumont, *The Knight of the Burning Pestle*, ed. Herbert S. Murch (New Haven: Yale Studies in English, 1908), III.i.580–83. See Sara Ann M. Ill, "Visibility and Resonance," 32. My thanks to J. K. Barrett for the initial reference.

61. For a comprehensive reading of the Hardwick House hangings and their reliance on prints, see Anthony Wells-Cole, *Art and Decoration in Elizabethan and Jacobean England: The Influence of Continental Prints, 1558–1625* (New Haven: Yale University Press, 1997), 275–85. The Hardwick House hangings, stunning in their own right, do not show any influence from Raphael's *Acts*.

62. John Astington movingly reconstructs the hanging of the Abraham tapestries for the "the procession and feast of the Knights of the Garter on St. George's Day, 23 April." When the Banqueting House was used for theatrical events, Astington writes, tapestries would have been moved out "to their storeroom, or to the Great Chamber" ("A Jacobean Ghost," 40). On the Great Chamber as another performance space at Whitehall, see James Shapiro: "The great chamber was the most intimate playing space at Whitehall. Sixty feet long by thirty feet wide, with a twenty-foot ceiling, it had a wooden floor, a wooden fire place, and *was decorated with woven tapestries*" (*A Year in the Life of William Shakespeare: 1599* [New York: Harper Perennial, 2005], 29).

63. On Paul and the philosophers in *The Winter's Tale*, see Ken Jackson, "'Grace to Boot': St. Paul, Messianic Time, and Shakespeare's *The Winter's Tale*." Unpublished. Presented at the Shakespeare Association of America conference, 2009. For a brilliant reading of the Catholic elements in the play, see Richard Wilson, *Secret Shakespeare: Studies in Theatre, Religion and Resistance* (Manchester: University of Manchester Press, 2004), 246ff. In *The Idolatrous Eye: Iconoclasm and Theatre in Early-Modern England* (Oxford: Oxford University Press, 2000), Michael O'Connell argues that the statue scene reincarnates Catholic image regimes (141). See also

James R. Siemon, *Shakespearean Iconoclasm* (Berkeley and Los Angeles: University of California Press, 1985), on theological image theory in the play. In *Afterlives of the Saints: Hagiography, Typology, and Renaissance Literature* (Stanford: Stanford University Press, 1996), I argued for the importance of Catholic iconography as well as Protestant iconoclasm to the world of *The Winter's Tale.*

64. Huston Diehl, "'Doth Not the Stone Rebuke Me?': The Pauline Rebuke and Paulina's Lawful Magic in *The Winter's Tale,*" in *Shakespeare and the Cultures of Performance,* ed. Paul Yachnin and Patricia Badir (Aldershot: Ashgate, 2008), 70, 72. Phebe Jensen mounts the same critique: "Since St. Paul was important to Counter-Reformation as well as Reformation devotion and theology, the guidance of a Pauline figure in this scene does not necessarily, as Huston Diehl argues, associate the ritual at the end of *The Winter's Tale* with Protestant theology" (*Religion and Revelry* [Cambridge: Cambridge University Press, 2008], 226–67). On grafting in St. Paul and the Pauline Renaissance, see Lisa Freinkel, *Shakespeare's Will: The Theology of Figure from Augustine to the Sonnets* (New York: Columbia University Press, 2001).

65. Frederick Hartt summarizes the significance of Giulio Romano as "an artistic personality strong enough to have influenced some of the greatest geniuses of the Renaissance and Baroque," a key element in the "crystallization of an anti-classical or proto-Mannerist phase in the Raphael school" ("Raphael and Giulio Romano: With Notes on the Raphael School," *Art Bulletin* 26.2 [June 1944]: 67–68).

66. Giorgio Vasari, *Lives of the Artists,* vol. 2, trans. George Bull (Harmondsworth, U.K.: Penguin Books, 1987), 227.

67. According to Richard Wilson, "Romano's purported workmanship . . . raises this instant of connoisseurship into the heady atmosphere of the Counter-Reformation, and gives this Roman detour its climax" (*Secret Shakespeare,* 264).

68. Stage direction from the Folio, following 5.3.19.

69. Bruce R. Smith, *The Key of Green,* 235.

70. Streitberger notes that the Office of the Tents, which merged with the Office of the Revels, was "an ancient office" in the English monarchy, dating at least from the period of Henry I. Its functions were both military and festive, and suited an "itinerant court" (19). When the court became more settled around the region of Westminster, "there were still wars to be fought, tournaments to be held, receptions to be organized, banqueting facilities to be built, and progresses to be supported, all of which required the services of the Tents" (18–19).

71. Richard Wilson, *Secret Shakespeare,* 249.

72. On the King's Wardrobe, see J. Cornforth, "Repositories of Splendor: Henry VIII's Wardrobes of the Robes and Beds," *Textile History* 29 (1998): 134–56. On the Office of the Tents and Revels, see W. R. Streitberger, *Court Revels, 1485–1559* (Toronto: University of Toronto Press, 1994).

73. Streitberger notes that in 1546, "the officers of the Tents were occupied with setting up and 'new Edifying' a great timber house. . . . It appears that the king's timber tents were set up to form something like a temporary palace." Such palaces were decorated with hangings and usually sported canvas roofs; they formed part of the Renaissance softscape of Tudor sovereignty (*Court Revels,* 179).

74. I address Paul, Shakespeare, and liberalism in *Citizen-Saints: Shakespeare and Political Theology* (Chicago: University of Chicago Press, 2005).

75. Jerry Brotton, *The Sale of the Late King's Goods: Charles I and His Art Collection* (New York: Macmillan, 2006), 217.

76. The inventory conducted by the trustees in charge of the sale listed one set of tapestry as "'rich hanging but Popish" (cited in ibid., 222).

77. Manfred Schneider, "Luther with McLuhan," 206.

78. Campbell, *Henry VIII*, 356. See also Roy Sherwood, *Oliver Cromwell, King in All But Name, 1653–1658* (New York: St. Martin's Press, 1997), who notes that retaining the Abraham tapestries contributed to the "process of investing Cromwell with at least some of the princely splendor to which his predecessors had been accustomed," an investiture that required "a large number of tapestries" (33). See Arthur MacGregor, ed., *The Late King's Goods: Collections, Possessions and Patronage of Charles I in Light of the Commonwealth Sale Inventories* (London: Alistair McAlpine and Oxford University Press, 1989), for a complete account of the inventories. The chapter on "textile holdings" is of special interest. Campbell sketches the political-theological significance of the Abraham tapestries for Henry: "Abraham, founder of the Hebrew nation and first of the great patriarchs, was the Old Testament model most congenial for Henry as he sought to establish a new Church of England centered on the Tudor dynasty" (*Henry VIII*, 289).

79. *St. Paul Burns Books of Gentiles at Ephesus*, based on cartoon by Pieter Coecke van Aelst (the Younger), from the workshop of Jan Raes I (weaver), c. 1620; Madrid, Palacio Real de Madrid; photo at the Getty Center, GCPA 0238474. The Geneva gloss associates the books with "conjuring and sorcerie" (Acts 19:19, note 5; 1603 edition). The unusual subject is also depicted in one of the sectors of the ceiling of St. Paul's Cathedral, painted by James Thornhill in 1715. These undistinguished paintings certainly show the influence of Raphael's cartoons. See Teresa Sladen, "Embellishment and Decoration, 1696–1900," in Keene et al., *St. Paul's: The Cathedral Church of London*, 233–57.

80. I address the political theology of the Abraham tapestries in "Soft *Res Publica*: On the Assembly and Disassembly of Courtly Space," *Republics of Letters* 2.2 (2011); http://rofl.stanford.edu/node/96.

81. Anselm Haverkamp, "*Richard II*, Bracton, and the End of Political Theology," *Law and Literature* 16.3 (2005): 314. Jennifer Rust revisits Haverkamp's distinction in "Political Theology and Shakespeare Studies," *Literature Compass* 6.1 (November 2008): 175–76.

82. *Richard II*, 3.2.164–73, ed. Kenneth Muir (New York: Penguin/Signet, 1963; 1988).

11

Striking the French Match: Jean Bodin, Queen Elizabeth, and the Occultation of Sovereign Marriage

DREW DANIEL

By the time Jean Bodin arrived in England in 1581 as secretary to the Duke of Alençon's mission to finalize the longstanding possibility of marriage with Queen Elizabeth, Bodin's monumental text *Six livres de la République* was already in circulation at the English universities.[1] Cambridge undergraduates would have read in Bodin's text a stirringly direct summary of the nature of sovereignty: since sovereignty consists in "the absolute and perpetual power of a commonwealth," sovereignty fundamentally cannot be shared.[2] The matrimonial cause that provided the occasion for Bodin's visit proved fruitless, but that very impasse might well have looked to contemporary observers like a striking confirmation of the lonely implications of Bodin's definition. After over a decade of intimate letters, ritualized gift-giving, diplomatic shadowplay, ambassadorial feints, and the incremental progress of intimacies both known and unknown between the queen and the man she nicknamed her "frog," the so-called French match collapsed. Which prompts a question: Are there irreconcilable differences between the theory of sovereignty and the practice of marriage?

I take it as axiomatic that marriage is simultaneously included in political and theological discourses. As an institution regulated by the state and subject to legal restrictions and norms, marriage is, then and now, included in politics. As a sacrament that joins subjects to each other and to the church that sanctifies their union, marriage is, then and now, included in theology. Yet this double-citizenship of multiple inclusion seems to functionally exclude the topic of marriage from easy residency within the frame of political theology as an account of historical change. Marriage's recalcitrant simultaneity as political institution and religious sacrament rubs historical narratives of secularization the wrong way, tenaciously lodging a counter-exemplary rock in the progressivist river of secular modernity. Does marriage perform a similar function for theories of political theology that assume the gradual sublation or smuggling of the formerly theological into the presently political? What place, if any, does marriage hold within the historical trajectory of Jean Bodin's theory of sovereignty, and does that place, or placelessness, hold fast within the discourses informed by its descendant, Carl Schmitt's *Political Theology*?

Acting as both narrative glue within drama and a conceptual solvent within jurisprudence, royal marriages are exceptional occasions, loosening the explanatory hold of many of the standard frames through which civilian marriage tended to be understood in the period (banishing, for example, the necessity of the doctrine of the proprietary absorption of the wife into the inventory of the husband's possessions known as "coverture" in favor of laboriously tailored prenuptial couture). But if royal marriages break free of certain constraints, they do so by being subject to *more* statist regulation, intervention, and protocol, rather than less. If Hegel's conception of the trilogy of state, civil society, and family defined three distinct political spheres, royal marriage constitutes a politico-theological quilting point that joins them together. The political/amorous event of a royal marriage marks the creation of a new family which ideologically models the institution itself for the families of the sovereign's royal subjects, ripples across civil society with affective disturbance and excitation in the form of national "moods" of celebration or anxiety, and, at least in the case of the marriage of two sovereigns of different nationalities, royal marriage forces the ligature of their corresponding states into a tentative and temporary alliance whose terminal reversibility trumps idealized metaphorics of "one flesh" in favor of a strategic pact between new kindred who remain potential rivals-to-be.

Granting the possibility of intimate or *sub rosa* spheres of informal marriages for common people, and the ad hoc privacy of clandestine weddings in which courtiers found a last resort in the handfasting regularly practiced by their inferiors and still legally recognized in England after its continental abolition, the necessarily public nature of royal marriages cannot be thought outside of the full dress of the theologico-political matrix. They are displays of sovereign power; the decision to marry would seem to be the sovereign decision par excellence, as it insists upon making a radically constitutive exception out of one particular subject-spouse. Given that, I want to pour out a cascade of possibly unfair questions: What relations might there be between Bodin's theoretical account of sovereignty and Queen Elizabeth's rejection of the French suitor that Bodin accompanied? If the answer "none whatsoever" settles readily within the mind, what might this very non-relation tell us about the constraints imposed by that theory? If the collapse of the French match tell us nothing about sovereignty as Bodin, Schmitt, and Agamben have variously yet cumulatively deployed that term, does the vacant place set for the seemingly anomalous situation of sovereign marriages within recent theories of political theology provide any critical purchase upon those theories? In particular, does Elizabeth's cumulative sequence of mixed messages and her intimate declarations in poems and letters that she denied Alençon against her will place limits on the explanatory utility of theories of politics that insist upon starkly defined absolutes (friend/enemy, norm/exception, absolute power/shared power)? Alternately, does the ultimately negative outcome of these negotiations ratify that theory's decisionism despite this particular sovereign's gainsaying? Or, to finally translate this interpretive problem into the terms of Alain Badiou's formal metaphysics of the subject, should we read the failed courtship as an evental site for a political truth or an amorous truth, and, in either case, can we locate Elizabeth's stance towards the non-Event of this marriage-that-never-was within his subjective figures of production, denial, occultation, or resurrection?

To sketch out some possible scenarios through which to answer these questions, I propose to create in this essay a series of arranged marriages, some joining persons (Queen Elizabeth and the Duke of Alençon, Jean Bodin and Carl Schmitt, Saint Paul and John Stubbs, and finally, Queen Elizabeth and Alain Badiou) and others joining concepts (aporia and consensus, choice and desire, sovereignty and marriage). Like any collection of amorous experiments, some will prove lasting and loving, others fraught and brief.

1. The Marriage of Aporia and Consensus

First, a bluff. The question of the "true" nature of Elizabeth's feelings for the Duke of Alençon cannot be answered. To admit this impasse is, of course, only to transpose that very question to a melancholic, aporetic key. But aporia and consensus have a way of circumventing their chaperones and arranging secret meetings. A journey through the historical and biographical archive of this particular courtship largely repeats the scholarly gestures and attitudes attendant upon all of the other foreign marriage proposals vetted during Elizabeth's reign: counterfactual speculation spiced with xenophobia. Across a range of narrative accounts, it seems very difficult for any writer to entertain the possibility that Elizabeth might have sincerely intended to marry. The biographers clearly relish the opportunity to stud their physical descriptions of Alençon with barbed, crypto-eugenic epithets that limn this "young foreigner" with the "pockmarked face" and "bandy legs" and "mock-heroic" middle name (Hercule) as a priori unsuitable. Housed within the standard fawning admiration of what modern business culture would call Elizabeth's leadership style, Lytton Strachey's glib judgment of the matter is typical: "It needed a lion heart indeed to spend twelve years in convincing the world that she was in love with the Duke of Anjou, and to stint the victuals of the men who defeated the Armada; but in such directions she was in very truth capable of everything."[3] Everything, it seems, but falling in love. If the brazen prosopoeia of *Elizabeth and Essex: A Tragic History* embarrasses us, it must be said that Strachey's estimation of the affair was shared by many early modern observers. One such was King Philip of Spain, whose letter to his ambassador bluntly states: "I have always looked upon the idea of a marriage between the queen and Alençon as a mere invention. I nevertheless believe they will continue to discuss it, and even may become reconciled for the purpose, but I believe that she herself is the person who will refuse."[4] The aporetic irritant (what was she thinking?) at the core of this subject finds a soothing analgesic in the negative outcome, and that negative outcome seems to retroactively define the process itself as a purely political game of chess. The failure to successfully produce marriage is taken to mean that these affairs were never serious in the first place, permitting historians to become brisk: "she had no intention of taking the Duke of Anjou or anyone else as her husband."[5] The end crowns all. Then and now, there is a striking consensus among these primarily male scholars that this courtship, like all the others, was just a charade.

These claims have their basis in evidence, but they seem to stem from a prior decision about personal character that then guides selective quotation from a mass of archival material as it reconfirms its premise. Again, Strachey is usefully blatant: "In reality, she succeeded by virtue of all the qualities which every hero should be without—dissimulation, pliability, indecision, procrastination, parsimony."[6] If one accepts this view of Elizabeth as the Great Procrastinator, one might regard the collapse of the Alençon match as merely "typical" of her evasive managerial style. At a stretch, one could even regard its lightness of touch in shaking off alien attentions as proleptic of the collapse of the Armada to come seven years later: a risky and treacherous foreign entanglement cancelled due to rain. As the privileged candidate for the triumphant political Event of Elizabeth's reign, the withdrawal in defeat of the Spanish Armada, like the withdrawal in defeat of the French suitor, could thus be regarded not as positive occurrences so much as convenient negativities.

How ought we to understand the relationship between knowledge and non-knowledge produced by this reading of the Elizabethan archive? It seems that the things we do not (cannot?) know about this woman generate out of their void the compensatory feeling of an all-too-familiar psychology, the well-nigh Theophrastan "character" of Queen Elizabeth as She-Who-Cannot-Decide. This ready-to-hand picture of a dilatory monarch who drove her exasperated privy council members and courtiers to ever greater rhetorical exertions because she could not, or would not, choose (to execute Mary, to marry, etc.) is familiar from countless historical and biographical expeditions across Tudor documents, but one wonders if ignorance about what underwrote her decisions has not been back-projected into supposed evidence of coquetry. When we consider, for example, the mingled timidity and impatience openly displayed on 6 October 1579, when the council members write "to require hir Majesty, to shew hir own mynd ... that [their own] resolutions might not be to the Contrary," one senses that the biographers and historians simply reduplicate the frustrated gestures of the councillors themselves.[7] Reducing Elizabeth's habitual deferrals from a policy to a personal, static "quirk" relieves some of the pressure generated by this refusal to "shew hir mynd."[8]

A newer generation of scholarship on Elizabeth and marriage has tried to replace these old answers with new questions, with mixed results. Suggesting that "the contradiction between female power and marriage has no practicable resolution" in *Marriage and Violence: The Early Modern Legacy,* critic Frances Dolan poses a useful rhetorical question about whether we place the emphasis upon the rejection of marriage or the embrace of solitude: "Should we define her by the marriage she refused or failed or couldn't manage, or by the alternative state she positively chose?"[9] By contrast, historian Susan Doran questions whether "choice" is even appropriate in the first place. In *Monarchy and Matrimony: The Courtships of Elizabeth I,* Doran argues that we ought to reject the standard narrative's collapse of a highly variegated history into a single display of the Virgin Queen's frigidity or willful self-possession altogether, and with it the related reification of "choice" upon which this narrative rests:

> Elizabeth did not reject marriage from either psychological motives or political reasons associated with her gender. I question whether Elizabeth *chose* at all to remain single. It is clear to me that she did want to marry on two occasions: once on the death of Lord Robert Dudley's wife in September 1560 when most contemporary observers believed that she was seriously contemplating marriage to her favorite, and again in 1579 when she demonstrated a strong desire to wed Francis duke of Anjou.[10]

I am sympathetic to Doran's position, particularly her laudable refusals to indulge in speculative psychobiographical narratives about motivation, or to collapse the multiple courtships into a single narrative pattern as so many writers before her have done. Against the devotees of the "Great Procrastinator" theory, she asserts the optative mode, and suggests that at least twice Queen Elizabeth might well have decided to marry, and nearly did so. But Doran's account of the relationship between "desire" and "choice" seems to me still in need of further theoretical articulation, and this renders her abandonment of psychoanalytic thinking precipitous insofar as it is precisely psychoanalysis that might allow us to think in a way that is orthogonal to agencies of "choice," or at the very least might provide some insight into the pleasurable compensations at work within apparently self-frustrating and self-punishing decisions *not* to choose. If the nonequivalence between "who one loves" and "who one chooses to marry" is at issue because of the political complications inherent in a queen regnant marrying a male subject necessarily at once beneath her by the logic of sovereignty and above her by the logic of marriage, this seems to me to occasion a crisis about the very possibility of decision which is both "psychological" in its mediation and "associated with her gender" in its political reality. And it is here that psychoanalysis can find its own helpmeet, if not "other half," in the political theology of the sovereign decision.

2. The Marriage of Jean Bodin and Carl Schmitt

Though space prevents us from surveying the political reality of sixteenth-century Europe as a site in which the emergent theoretical framework of absolutism entered broad circulation and wrought its own concrete effects *as theory* upon the very world it attempted to describe, some consideration of Jean Bodin as its putative "author" is in order. On the other side of Bodin's appropriation by Carl Schmitt, I shall also consider the theoretical marriage of convenience that Schmitt effected between himself and his predecessor, and their shared custody of "sovereignty." Bodin's definition of sovereignty as "the absolute and perpetual power of the republic" primes and anticipates Carl Schmitt's account of the sovereign decision in *Political Theology* with a bond of early modern filiation that Schmitt both courts and seeks to delimit.[11] Schmitt's lavish praise for Bodin ("he stands at the beginning of the modern theory of the state") rests upon Bodin's capacity to anticipate Schmitt's own thesis of the sovereign exception: "the decisive point about Bodin's concept is that by referring to the emergency, he reduced his analysis of the relationship between prince and estates to a simple either/or."[12] Though Schmitt maintains that this insight is what makes Bodin "modern" and not the more frequently quoted definition of sovereignty itself, it is hard not to see that the simplicity of the "either/or" follows from the very absolutist definition of sovereignty itself that Schmitt sidelines: to the extent that sovereignty for Bodin is precisely what is indivisible and cannot be shared, it is thereby "absolute," and insofar as it is "absolute," it is subject to the decisive cut of the "either/or." Either power is in the hands of the prince absolutely or it is not, and to share any part of it is to lose what makes it sovereign—by definition. The "perpetuity" of Bodin's account of sovereignty drops from view, but the functional importance of sovereignty's absolute indivisibility is crucial, and Schmitt treats this proposition as itself decisive and irreversible: "This is what is truly impressive in his definition of sovereignty: by considering sovereignty to be indivisible, he finally settled the question of power in the state."[13]

In the eighth chapter of Book I of the *Six livres de la République*, Bodin also makes clear what he means by "absolute." It is not that law grants and conditions the extent or nature of sovereign power; rather, sovereignty grounds law:

> . . . a subject who is exempted from the force of laws always remains in sub-
> jection and obedience to those who have the sovereignty. But persons who are
> sovereign must not be subjects in any way to the commands of someone else
> and must be able to give law to subjects, and to repress or repeal disadvanta-
> geous laws and replace them with others—which cannot be done by someone
> who is subject to the laws or to. persons who have power of command over
> him.[14]

Julian Franklin's own definition of the sense of "absolutism" operative in Bodin hinges crucially upon "consent," which we shall see is the very term at the heart of debates about the nature of marriage: "Absolutism in the sense here used is the idea that the ruler, however much he may be responsible to God for observation of the higher law, *does not require the consent of any other human agent* in making public policy."[15]

The consequences of this absolutist vision are many, but here I specifi-cally wish to flag the matrimonial difficulties set in place by the foreclosure of shared power, for they bear upon Elizabeth's predicament in deciding whether or not to run the risk of losing status and sharing her authority through subjection to a husband. Here we stand at a historical divide. From the other side of an ongoing debate about the persistence of the biblical poet-ics of marriage within the present moment of a secular modernity that thinks otherwise, is not a marriage precisely an example of what it would mean to share power, for power to flow between partners, insofar as Edenic married helpmeets must pledge at the moment of their union to fuse into "one flesh"? Bodin's text offers only a relentlessly negative series of answers. Sovereignty ceases at the moment that companionship begins:

> For the prince or the Duke, who has power to give law to all his subjects in general and to each in particular, is not sovereign if he also takes law from a superior or an equal—I include equal because to have a companion is to have a master—and he is even less a sovereign if he has this power only in the capacity of a vicar, lieutenant or regent.[16]

In the original French no less than in the Latin and (later) English translations, Bodin is equally emphatic: "Je di egal, par ce que celui a maistre, qui a compagnon."[17]

Unsurprisingly, Bodin is just as emphatically negative in his accounts of women monarchs. Indeed, his account of the political disasters attendant upon the marriages of female monarchs is so forthright that one wonders why he was chosen to attend Alençon on a matchmaking voyage in the first place. Seeing double, one is tempted to see Bodin as, in this respect, rather like Schmitt after all: someone whose views remain disturbing when considered from a contemporary liberal democratic standpoint (they foreclose the possibility of collaboration, reciprocity, and the sharing of power) and yet which feel insistently, scandalously apt as an analysis of the political logic of the present conditions they describe. For all their utterly conventional patriarchal chauvinism, Bodin's remarks on the problems attendant upon "gynecocracy" eerily anticipate the standard historical analysis of the collapse of the French match, to such an extent that one must remind one's self that they predate that event by seven years:

> But dangerous as elections to the crown are, for the reasons we have already given, should there be a failure of heirs male, this expedient is to be preferred to the succession of women, for that means outright gynecocracy in defiance of natural law. Should the sovereign princess marry, as she must do to secure the succession, she must marry either a subject or a foreigner. If a subject, it is a great abasement for a princess to marry one of her servants, seeing that the greatest sovereign princes in the world have found all sorts of difficulties follow marriage to a subject. There is besides the risk of great and powerful nobles, in the contempt they always feel for men of inferior station, if she insists on marrying the man of her preference. . . . On the other hand no foreign prince who tries to rule over an alien people can be secure of his life unless he lives behind fortifications, and goes about strictly guarded. But if he thus has control of the armed forces he can control the state, and in order then to make himself the more secure, he is tempted to advance his own compatriots. This is a thing which no

nation of the world will endure. . . . If the foreigners are not the stronger party,
they get their throats cut on the slightest provocation by patriots.[18]

Though Bodin goes on to relate stories from thirteenth-century Naples, this
passage seems to be describing all too precisely the fate suffered by Philip II
and his entourage in England during his courtship and eventual marriage to
Mary, which Elizabeth's counselors feared would occur with redoubled force
if she married a Catholic foreigner.[19] The gradual purging of Spanish courtiers from the realm after a series of disastrous brawls and assaults upon the
visiting foreigners provided a vivid and recent illustration of Bodin's principle that the marriage of a female sovereign to a foreign suitor would trigger
a bloody battle for the upper hand between a hostile populace of murderous
patriots and the husband's occupying force. Were the marriage to take place,
it would of necessity compromise the sovereignty of one of its partners, and it
would ripple outwards into conflict for supremacy between the nations each
partner governed.

3. The Marriage of Elizabeth and Paul

If Elizabeth finds herself all too clearly scripted into the subordinate-or-be-
subordinated dilemma posed by Bodin's articulation of sovereignty, does this
carry forward into the analytic framework of Carl Schmitt's *Political Theology*
as it builds upon that legacy? Before answering that question, I want to locate
Elizabeth within the backstory of Schmitt's narrative arc. If we take Schmitt's
sententious opening declaration that "all significant concepts of the modern
theory of the state are secularized theological concepts" to be an essentially
historical argument about the disavowed sources of modernity, then that
would seem to place Elizabeth off limits, out of theoretical orbit.[20] Insofar
as her reign precedes this secular dawn, she can neither provide evidence
for, nor against, a theoretical assertion about a modernity she did not live to
experience.[21] Yet even a cursory perusal of her *Sententiae* reveals Elizabeth's
fluency in the mingled creole of theology and politics, with her initial section
De Regno [On Rule] asserting the presumptive foundational synthesis upon
which Schmitt's own narrative of separation and secularization operates.
Elizabeth's text begins by translating Saint Paul:

> DE REGNO
> *Quae sunt potestates a Deo ordinatae.* Rom. 13
> The powers that be are ordained of God.
> *Quisquis resistet potestati, Dei ordinationi resistit. Ibidem*
> Whoever resists power, resists the ordinance of God.

Qui restiterint sibi ipsis iudicium accipient.
Those who resist will bring judgment upon themselves.
Principes non sunt terrori, bene agentibus sed male.
Rulers are not a terror to those doing good but to those doing evil.
Princeps Dei minister est in bonum et, qui quod bonum est facit.
For the ruler is the minister of God for the good of him who does what is
    good.[22]

These citations of Paul hold out the promise of an encounter across historical distance, with an absolutely synthetic moment of a theological politics
without apology, before the fall, with the commonplace book functioning
as a rope-bridge thrown back from the sixteenth century toward the beginnings of Christian universalism. But thanks to the undecidably decon-
structive iterability of such textual practices, we cannot know if this is a
heartfelt and passionately mutual embrace of theology and politics as immanently coextensive or simply a carefully pious performance, the solitary re-
inscription of the received wisdom that they had once been so regarded. If we
read "sententious passion" as a historical long-distance love affair inflected
by the pressure of a need to rewrite the text of Paul to the letter, can we sense
what might have been on the line in the habitual relay of these phrases, and
to see the analogous resemblance between Elizabeth's historical backwards
glance and Schmitt's own declaration that there was once a moment of fusion? How married to Paul was Elizabeth?[23]

Here we might upend Schmitt's assertion that Bodin, in resembling Schmitt,
was thereby "modern"; rather, in resembling Bodin, it is Schmitt who remains
"early modern." For Schmitt's own argumentative logic in *Political Theology*,
insofar as it hinges upon the poetic assertion of an analogy as an argument
unto itself, feels rather early modern. Schmitt legislatively insists upon an optic
of similitude, an aspectual seeing of one thing under the terms set by another:
"The exception in jurisprudence is *analogous* to the miracle in theology. *Only
by being aware of this analogy* can we appreciate the manner in which the philosophical ideas of the state developed in the last centuries."[24] Sublunary political
matters are made in the image of divinity ('as above, so below'), but only if we
can maintain our focus upon this double vision, suggesting that the critic must
squint slightly to see the family resemblance across the centuries.

Exceptional to this temporal form, marriage is thereby critically transformative in the work it performs upon Schmitt's structure: instead of seeing
one thing as "like" another thing, the simultaneity of marriage's inclusion
in both the sphere of theology and the sphere of politics becomes the origin
point of the theologico-political idea's gradual metamorphosis from coex-
tension to metaphor to simile. All who are called to marry may return to

this origin in the singularity of marriage: in the *Augenblick* of ceremony, the political is no longer "like" the theological as an analogous relationship we must be aware of at the level of judgment. In the sacramental legality and legalized sacredness of its binding moment, marriage permits those granted access to it to experience political theology as a lived state of fusion rather than an analogical vantage point. If Schmitt's formation of political theology defines a work of separation extended across time, marriage performs a work of juncture within time, for all time: the coming into being of a truth.

Then as now, such junctures are contested battlegrounds between marriage as intersubjective fusion and marriage as hierarchy, and both traditions lay claim to the same scriptural origin. Entwining the three paired groupings of husband and wife, Adam and Eve, and Christ and the Church into each other, "The Form of Solemnization of Matrimony" within *The Book of Common Prayer* signals the ideological work of marriage vows as reification of the church's interpellating institutional force, and figures therein the power of the sovereign monarch over the nation to which they too are said to be metaphorically "wedded." But it also suggests the possibility that hierarchy might be surpassed or healed over in a union of mirroring helpmeets. Touching upon all of these meanings, the service begins:

> Dearly beloved friends, we are gathered together here in the sight of God, and in the face of his congregation, to join together this man and this woman in holy matrimony, *which is an honorable estate, instituted of God in paradise in the time of man's innocency, signifying unto us the mystical union, that is betwixt Christ and his Church:* which holy estate Christ adorned and beautified with his presence and first miracle that he wrought in Cana of Galilee, and is commended of Saint Paul to be honorable among all men. . . . [25]

As the vows progress, both parties pledge to honor and love each other; after consideration of the obligations of a husband to his wife, the closing passages of the service turn towards the corresponding obligations of wives to their husbands in terms set by quotations from Ephesians that seem to set in place the inherently and fundamentally hierarchical nature of marriage:

> Now likewise ye wives hear and learn your duty toward your husbands, even as it is plainly set forth in Holy Scripture.
>
> Saint Paul (in the forenamed Epistle to the Ephesians) teacheth you thus, Ye women submit yourselves unto your own husbands as unto the Lord, for the husband is the wife's head even as Christ is the head of the Church. And he is also the savior of the whole body. Therefore as the church or congregation is subject unto Christ, so likewise let the wives also be in subjection unto

their own husbands in all things. And again he saith, Let the wife reverence her husband. And (in his Epistle to the Colossians) Saint Paul giveth you this short lesson, Ye wives submit yourselves unto your own husbands, as it is convenient in the Lord.[26]

What are we to make of the narrow space forged between these distinct quotations from Paul? Does Colossian "convenience" drive a wedge within Ephesian subjection, in the process insisting upon some trace elements of prerogative, choice, and autonomy? In a luminous gloss on this passage driven by her characteristic emphasis upon the radically universal potentiality of the Pauline author against the conservative undertow of his own corpus, Julia Lupton takes pains to maximize the role of consent within this ceremony:

> The bride is *she who consents to submit*, who enters freely and equally into a contract that will henceforth install a law above her. The conditions and limits of that law—the retention of any rights and immunities, the possibility of divorce, and the problem of custody—then become the subject of political, social, and sexual definition, debate, and even war.[27]

Lupton makes this claim against the grain of a long-established series of feminist critical readings of the marriage contract as an inherently one-sided tool of subjection. Recasting this very moment of female consent within the marriage vow as not merely spurious but actively damaging, in *The Sexual Contract* Carol Pateman quotes William Thompson's curt denunciation of the "gratuitous degradation of swearing to be slaves."[28] In the broader context of her work, Pateman's distinction between contract and consent in *The Problem of Political Obligation* leads her to argue that the very notion of "consent" arrives too late to redress or counter the constitutive, creative moment when the terms of the contract are constructed to favor the civil subordination of women to men.[29] Because the woman who pledges to serve and obey her husband was not present at the crucial moment when the terms of the marriage contract itself were articulated within a larger nexus of dominating, hierarchical forms, her "consent" is belated and nugatory. Whatever we might or might not make of Pateman's argument on its own merits, it can hardly apply to the exquisitely controlled negotiations of Elizabeth's counselors about the details of what she would and would not consent to were she to wed Alençon; unlike other women, to an exceptional degree Elizabeth's sovereignty meant that she really could "write her own ticket."[30] Yet the force of the Ephesian/Pauline text still stung.

Puritan pamphleteer John Stubbs hits exactly this point early on in his ill-fated protest against the French match, *The Discoverie of a Gaping Gulf*

Whereinto England is like to be Swallowed by an other French Marriage, if the Lord forbid not the banes, by letting her Maiestie see the sin and punishment thereof (1579). Certain that a Catholic husband will necessarily dictate terms to a Protestant wife, Stubbs insists upon the inherent hierarchy of the "head" metaphor central to the Ephesian passages within the marriage vow as a means to challenge Elizabeth's attachment to her sovereign prerogatives:

> And if the husband, which is the head, be drawn aside by his wife, over whom nevertheless he hath authority and rule, how much more easily shall the wife be perverted by her husband, to whom she is subject by the law of God and oweth both awe and obedience, howsoever the laws by prerogative or her place by pre-eminence may privilege her?[31]

Stubbs's text nettled Elizabeth for countless reasons, but in making this particular point he also presses upon a basic exception inherent in Bodin's ostensibly seamless definition of sovereignty: the supremacy of divine law.[32] The mandate that even the sovereign must yield to the will of God constitutes precisely the Achilles heel within sovereign indivisibility, and it is Stubbs's Puritan insistence upon the totalizing force and universal extent of that exception that effectively trumps sovereign power. As Stubbs reminds his readers and his queen, the position of marriage at the juncture of state power and divine law locates Elizabeth at once above all other subjects and yet beneath her husband in the eyes of God, and if we are to take the supremacy of divine law seriously then this corresponding vision of marriage as subjection allegedly upstages national interests as a consequence.

The unfair question to ask at this point is whether or not the woman who wrote out the Pauline maxim that "those who resist will bring judgment upon themselves" in her *Sententiae* was the same woman who ordered the execution of Stubbs as his reward for pointing this out, and settled for the public amputation of his hand?[33] Famously, Stubbs's own reaction to his public mutilation was his emphatic affirmation of allegiance on the other side of an irreversible sovereign cut: "Stubbs, having his right hand cut off, put off his hat with his left hand and said with a loud voice, 'God save the Queen.'"[34] One might expect that Stubbs's hand constitutes a grimly emblematic token of the absolute reach of Elizabethan sovereignty, but in fact it indexes rather the bureaucratic and procedural limitations upon that very power. The queen wanted Stubbs executed for his impertinence but was restrained from doing so by resistance from her counselors and the publicly embarrassing provenance of the law she used to sentence him (an anti-heretical edict that dated from the prior reign of her sister Mary that had been used to persecute Protestant martyrs).

4. The Marriage of Yes and No

This painful gap between absolute intentions and compromised acts was familiar ground to both monarch and theorist. As Schmitt realized full well,
definitions of sovereignty on the page had no necessary relationship to the
muddled contingencies operative in sixteenth century states, any more than
in twentieth century ones. He does not shy away from acknowledging the horizon that bounds his theoretical absolutes: "In political reality there is no irresistible highest or greatest power that operates according to the certainty of
a natural law."[35] The superlative nature of sovereignty as Bodin had framed
it need not correspond to the earthly entanglements of particular monarchs,
and Elizabeth's own experience of economic, religious, and political constraint as she pursued the possibility of marriage (and punished those who
tried to naysay her) vividly demonstrated her need to consult with others,
secure compromise, and ratify her judgments in the eyes of her counselors
and her people. A conservative mode of historicism would smugly announce
that the theoretical fantasies of infinite sovereignty definitively imposed by
political theology here meet the humbling kernel of the real. But Schmitt's
own framing in *Political Theology* already insists upon precisely this practical
limit to the utility of the "border concept" of sovereignty: "The connection
of actual power with the legally highest power is the fundamental problem
of sovereignty."[36] Yet the resolutely secular focus of Schmitt's own text upon
"actual power" suggests the potential limits of political theology as a formation: insofar as it relies upon the successful completion of secularization,
Schmitt's account cannot take seriously the theological exception nestled
within sovereignty itself, the exception that Stubbs took seriously enough to
stake his life and body upon its rhetorical force.

For all his supposed concessions to the distance between "actual power"
and "the legally highest power," Schmitt's account of the sovereign decision
is striking in the almost aesthetic seclusion in which he isolates the sovereign's
self-grounding mandate from any explanatory surroundings: "What is inherent in the idea of the decision is that there can never be absolutely declara-
tory decisions. That constitutive, specific element of a decision is, from the
perspective of the content of the underlying norm, new and alien. Looked at
normatively, the decision emanates from nothingness."[37] Schmitt is keen to
insist upon the separability of this groundlessness from all psychological facts,
contextual situatedness, or motivating forces. Qua juridical event, the decision
as pure decision cannot be routed through some bystanding explanatory force
or external agent. It is this hard, dark purity, this refusal to mix with the base
causal stew of its immediate surroundings, that lends the decision the pristine

oddity and reflective depthlessness of the monolith in Stanley Kubrick's film 2001. But it is difficult to square this doctrine with Schmitt's allegations that such definitions tell us nothing about the reality of political power.

In this respect, one might fruitfully compare Schmitt's account of the sovereign decision with the account of the decision put forward by his seemingly polar political opposite, Ernesto Laclau. The thunderclap of Schmitt's sovereign decision finds its reflection in the auto-generative force of Laclau's account of decision as the founding gesture of the subject. As J. Hillis Miller puts it, "For Laclau, . . . the subject does not precede the decision, but is brought into existence by the decision itself in an act of self-grounding or auto-generation. The subject, says Laclau, 'is the distance between the undecidability of the structure and the decision.'"[38] Above all, this self-generation is momentary: the deictic "now" of the decisive moment is also the deictic "I" of the subject who decides. Turning the Laclau definition of the subject's formation in and through a decision on its ear, Elizabeth (whether we view her as Great Procrastinator or as Virgin Queen) emerges as subject in the distance that she places between herself and the act of decision in the first place. Sovereign is she who makes others wait for her decision.

For all her sententious anticipation of the premise of *Political Theology*, Elizabeth seems exceptional, or at the very least eccentric, to such models of the sovereign decision. One searches in vain within the messy political scenario surrounding Elizabeth's decisions concerning Alençon's campaign for the absolute purity envisioned within Schmitt's text. Elizabeth's initial communications to Alençon were shot through with contradictory languages of desire and compulsion, policy and love, prudence and willfulness, a cautious performance which, far from being "new and alien," *sui generis*, was scrupulously managed and rehearsed. In part, the problem in squaring Schmitt with Elizabeth is a temporal disjunction between the narrative extensions of her history and the decisionist singularity of his theory: the lightning-like instantaneity of the decision for Schmitt can scarcely be detected within the malingering *durée* of Elizabeth and Alençon's affair. But it is not simply a matter of timing, but also of the difference between the solitude of the sovereign within Schmitt's scenario and the crowded stage/marketplace within which the French proposal of royal marriage was contracted, considered, and retracted. From the beginning, the intimations and counterproposals were conducted through intermediaries, with Elizabeth communicating with the queen mother of France, Catherine de Medici, and then with Alençon's primary representative, Jean de Simier, and modulating her tone and list of demands on the fly as circumstances shifted. This very intersubjective feedback loop suggests that her decisions emerged not from an occult and originary inward "nothingness" but were collaboratively brewed in a rich broth of intrigue, calculation, and guesswork.[39]

Pressing the issue, was there *ever* a moment when Queen Elizabeth did decide whether or not to marry Alençon? Perversely, it seems that the only honest answer is one that sounds like a ruse, and at the very least gives the standard historical narrative the slip: *Elizabeth never decided not to marry him.* Rather, on at least one occasion, November 22, 1581, at eleven in the morning, she did make the sovereign decision to do exactly that. In a vivid letter to Philip II, Mendoza described this momentary leap into the void:

> On the 22nd however, at eleven in the morning, the Queen and Alençon were walking together in a gallery, Leicester and Walsingham being present, when the French ambassador entered and said that he wished to write to his master, from whome he had received orders to hear from the Queen's own lips her intention with regard to marrying his brother. She replied "You may write this to the King: that the duke of Alençon shall be my husband," and at the same moment she turned to Alençon and kissed him on the mouth, drawing a ring from her own hand and giving it to him as a pledge. Alençon gave her a ring of his in return, and shortly afterwards the Queen summoned the ladies and gentlemen from the presence chamber to the gallery, repeating to them in a loud voice, in Alençon's presence, what she had previously said.[40]

If there ever was a moment of decision, this is the strongest possible candidate. Mendoza's tight focus in upon "the Queen's own lips" unleashes a torrent of activity: replying, turning, kissing, drawing, giving, summoning, repeating. Elizabeth's verbal promise occasions an expressive fireworks of matrimonial display. But the decisive nature of this decision already appears wanting when we attend to the remarkably stagy nature of this prompt from the absent brother (none other than her first French suitor, Henry, whose particularly staunch Catholicism, among other things, seemed to have placed him out of the race). It feels like theater deliberately staged for Walsingham, one of the most resistant of her inner circle to the marriage, and, in the decidedly supporting role in which Mendoza casts the husband, it plays like something of a surprise to Alençon himself. Most dissipating of all is the deadly grammatical dodge that reposes at the center of this romantic incident: the modal verb "shall be" connotes royal command, but slips towards futurity, a postponing gesture that will prove all too convenient. The "loud voice" and repetition already feels like self-persuasion, a kind of dazed insistence that this time, the sovereign has spoken, has made a decision.

It was not to be. The formal follow-through of this promissory gesture required that Alençon submit to the letter of a strongly framed marriage contract complete with stipulations that granted him the official title of King of England but forbid even private Catholic mass. Before the many roadblocks within that document had been fully discussed, let alone resolved, the outstanding issues of Elizabeth's loans to support his continental campaigns soured their fragile understanding. Within a year Alençon was to complain bitterly of his straits in the wake of his collapsed prospects: "Everything is falling apart in ruin, and the worst part of it is that I was given hopes which had led me too far to back down now."[41] This withering anticlimax allowed her to protest her enduring love while safely on the other side of his retreat from the country. Secure in her capacity to retroactively declare that it was his inability to negotiate, and his chronic need for money, that had finally led to the decisive collapse of negotiations, she spoke of her regrets at an outcome she never fully acknowledged as of her own making. On the defensive, she wrote letters and poems that mourn the evacuated possibility of the marriage from within a dense cover of financial, religious, and political overdetermination.

Supposedly the last resulting poem of complaint, "On Monsieur's Departure," supplies her absent suitor with a conciliatory display of amorous self-division exemplary in its irresolution. I quote it in its entirety:

> I grieve and dare not show my discontent;
> I love, and yet am forced to seem to hate;
> I do, yet dare not say I ever meant;
> I seem stark mute, but inwardly do prate.
> I am, and not; I freeze and yet am burned,
> Since from myself another self am turned.
>
> My care is like my shadow in the sun—
> Follows me flying, flies when I pursue it,
> Stands, and lies by me, doth what I have done,
> His too familiar care doth make me rue it.
> No means I find to rid him from my breast,
> Til by the end of things it be surprest.
>
> Some gentler passions slide into my mind,
> For I am soft, and made of melting snow;
> Or be more cruel, Love, and so be kind.
> Let me float or sink, be high or low;
> Or let me live with more sweet content,
> Or die and so forget what love e'er meant.[42]

To reiterate an all-too-common critical boast, it would be easy to deconstruct a text like this. One could invoke the love complaint conventions as
signs of its impossible gesture towards a sincerity that cannot be established,
and wheel out comparative evidence that ruthlessly reveals the standardiza-
tions in place within this verse as it "Englishes" the frozen fires of Petrarch
and glances towards Sidney's sonnets (from "I am not I, pity the tale of me"
to "since from myself another self am turned" is a faltering step down). If
one wanted to ironize its manifest protestations of remorse at Monsieur's
departure in search of a latent hostility to Alençon, one could simply read
the "shadow" image of the second stanza as a substitute prop for her now
discarded suitor. Pressing the psycho-biographical case, one cannot help
but hear a symptomatic sigh of relief at his timely exit in that stanza's final lines: "His too familiar care doth make me rue it. / No means I find to
rid him from my breast / Til by the end of things it be surprest." The fastidious refusal to disclose agent and object in the phrase "the end of things"
hits the appropriately vague and sour note, but exactly who suppressed
whom?

We cannot know. I am more interested in this poem's pronounced hostility to mediation: for my purposes what is compelling is not the encrypted
reality of the *roman à clef* surrounding the text but the insistence upon the
absolute decision of an "either/or" staged within it. I think we can read the
poem's compromised performance of that very insistence as an enactment
of what Horst Bredekamp has termed the "torsion of indecision" that ripples
across the baroque performance of sovereignty.[43] In longing to "be high or
low," what is precisely disavowed is the possibility of a laterally shared equiv-
alence between herself and another: true to Bodin's bitter recipe for sovereignty, companionship is voided. Bracketing the historicism that would not
cease to remind us that Elizabeth preserved and secured her power through
precisely the lukewarm settlement of a *via media* that eschewed extremes,
we have in her poetry evidence of an Elizabeth who longs for them. The
poem's stroboscopic ambitions formally enact Bodin's absolutist poetics of
an either/or, but they do so as an expression of longing and desire to be one
or the other, to be all or nothing, a desire that marks the subject as the lived
distance from a virtual experience of self-sovereignty that only texts can
imagine. The triple divagation of the three separate "Or . . ." lines within
the third stanza thus performs not a pendular swing between two distinct
stances, but a desperate, and repeatedly failed, attempt to push outwards,
to step forward and decide in favor of something. Life without reserve, or
death.

5. The Marriage of Queen Elizabeth and Alain Badiou

It is with Elizabeth's expressed longing to "die and so forget what love e'er meant" that I must end. What does this extravagantly positioned pronouncement accomplish? What usefully estranging context could rescue these lines from the hovering accusation of insincere, or all-too-sincere but simply histrionic, banality? As a closing gesture of my own, I wish to arrange one last marriage, between Queen Elizabeth and Alain Badiou. To do so, I shall map the position of this poem within the narrative of the French match via "The Four Subjective Destinations" proposed by Badiou's formal theory of the subject in *Logics of Worlds*, which defines a series of stances, or "figures," a subject may take in relation to the evental present: faithful, reactive, and obscure:

> The faithful subject organizes its *production*, the reactive subject its *denial* (in the guise of its deletion), and the obscure subject its *occultation* (the passage under the bar). We call *destination* of a subjective figure this synthetic operation in which the subject reveals itself as the contemporary of the evental present, without necessarily incorporating itself into it. . . . Let's say that the destinations proceed in a certain order (production to denial to occultation), for reasons that formalism makes altogether clear: the denial of the present presupposes its production, and its occultation supposes a formula of denial.[44]

In Badiou's formalism, the evental present of an amorous truth can be faithfully produced, and then reactively denied, and then obscurely occulted, at which point it awaits the decisive "act" of a de-occultation that would produce a new present. Mapping this sequence onto the evental site of the Queen Elizabeth/Alençon courtship, I want to suggest the following: Elizabeth's momentary decision in the gallery of her palace to announce to the assembled courtiers that "he shall be my husband" was the "production" of their marriage as present, a sovereign decision, a momentary expression of what Julia Lupton has termed "her consent to submit" to marriage. The resulting collapse of negotiations and disavowal of their relationship as the wrangling about loans and marriage contracts took over was the "denial" of that present, a turn from faithful to reactive subject, and thus the revocation of her fragile consent. The subsequent poems of apologia, flirtation, and suicidal/ impossible devotion constitute the terminal "occultation" of that present, its submersion into compensatory fantasies of possessive fusion in death. Elizabeth's serial movement across these subjective destinations defines a queen's progress from faithful subject, to reactive subject, to obscure subject. There was no "resurrection" of this present, and so we can say that the amorous/

political truth of the sovereign marriage of Queen Elizabeth and the Duke of Alençon died in obscurity, awaiting resurrection.

6. Conclusion and Honeymoon

What does it mean to identify Elizabeth as "obscure subject"? Does such a vision of Elizabeth constitute a point of departure from the prevalent spinster tropes and "Great Procrastinator" narratives, or merely a critical transposition of them? Badiou's startling paratactic list of the sorts of persons designated by the "obscure figure" slots rather well into this very stereotype:

> veterans of lost wars, failed artists, intellectuals perverted by bitterness, dried up matrons, illiterate muscle bound youths, shopkeepers ruined by Capital, desperate unemployed workers, rancid couples, bachelor informants, academicians envious of the success of poets, atrabilious professors, xenophobes of all stripes, Mafiosi greedy for decorations, vicious priests and cuckolded husbands.[45]

From the vantage point of this particular atrabilious professor, I am struck by the presence of both the "veteran of lost war" and the "dried up matron" within this hit list; Badiou's cruelly dismissive epithets potentially recast François Hercule, temporarily landed in England to beg for more money to pursue his doomed campaigns in the Netherlands, as "veteran of a lost war" and obscure supplicant to Elizabeth, the equally obscure "dried up matron," twice his age, striking her servants and amputating the hands of her Puritan critics.[46] Whether we regard this as a serendipitous stretch or a case of what Badiou terms "historical scansion," Badiou's grotesque grab-bag can at least potentially help us to read the gesture of Elizabeth's poem as more than a coldly calculating thank you note delivered to a no longer useful prop of her foreign policy.

What "On Monsieur's Departure" scorns absolutely is precisely the middling, the in-between-ness of process and becoming, the possibility of differences of degree between persons; it is not a case of love conquering all but of longing for an *all that is sovereign enough to conquer love.* Having fallen into "occultation," the all of love-as-production has given way to softer passions, melting snow. On the "occultation" of the amorous subject, Badiou notes:

> The obscure subject submits love to the fatal ordeal of a single fusional Body, an absolute knowledge of all things. . . . It demands an integrated originary destiny and consequently can only see a future for love in the chronic extortion of a detailed allegiance, a perpetual confession. Its vision of love is a *destined* one.[47]

Through this procedure of occultation, the amorous truth is not only submerged, or placed under a bar, but enters a fatal, tragic endgame, a "deadly possessive reciprocity" whose poem is, according to Badiou, Wagner's *Tristan und Isolde*.[48] I hope to have shown that another, less celebrated candidate for the poem of love's occultation would be Elizabeth's quietly suicidal revocation of her own sovereign dictate that Alençon "shall be my husband."

If the obscure subject's vision of love is a "destined one," we can see that vision souring and dying within that poem's very last line. But to shake loose the stern grip upon the historical imagination which the "obscure" Elizabeth has, forsaking all others, we who imagine this sovereign at the present moment as only ever the Great Procrastinator, the "dried up matron" who cannot choose because she did not love, might do well to return to the sovereign decision to marry and to love that *may* have occurred at the precise moment when Elizabeth's lips spoke the words "he shall be my husband." Badiou's formalism can usefully estrange the grip of the Great Procrastinator narrative by reminding us of other points in time at which other stances towards the evental site are possible. I want to arrest the procession of Elizabeth and Alençon at this point, before reaction and before occultation, to attend to their once-held stake in the futurity of a marriage that is only present insofar as we can say that it casts itself forwards towards the other shore of what was/is still, in that moment, perpetually to come. To sing a hymeneal hymn on behalf of the futurity still lodged within such dead moments, I shall leave the last word (why not?) to André Breton:

> People despair of love stupidly—I have despaired of it myself—they live in servitude to this idea that love is always behind them, never *before* them. . . . And yet for each, the promise of e.ach coming hour contains life's whole secret, perhaps about to be revealed one day, possibly in another being.[49]

Notes

1. Jean Bodin, *On Sovereignty: Four Chapters from The Six Books of the Commonwealth*, ed. Julian H. Franklin (Cambridge: Cambridge University Press, 1992), xxvii. Given the substantive differences between the first French edition of *Les six livres de la République* (1576) and the Latin translation *De Republica libri sex* (1586), in selecting passages in English I have opted for Julian Franklin's synthetic English edition over the first English translation by Knolles in 1606. When I quote the original French edition or the more extensive translation into English by M. J. Tooley, *Six Books of the Commonwealth* (Oxford: Basil Blackwell, 1955), this is noted.

2. Bodin, *On Sovereignty*, 1.

3. Lytton Strachey, *Elizabeth and Essex: A Tragic History* (New York: Harcourt, Brace and Company, 1928), 12. Strachey's reference to "Anjou" is, of course, a reference to François Hercule, Duke of Alençon, later also Duke of Anjou, and not to his brother Henry, also Duke of Anjou (later Henry III, the King of France). The fraternally transmitted title can induce referential con-

fusion between these two males in the Valois line who both courted Elizabeth at different times; in this paper I will be concentrating on the longer and more tumultuous courtship with François, and accordingly will use "Alençon," or the honorific "Monsieur," to designate this person.

4. Carolly Erickson, *The First Elizabeth* (New York: Summit Books, 1983), 316.

5. Wallace MacCaffrey, *The Shaping of the Elizabethan Regime: Elizabethan Policy* 1558–1572 (Princeton: Princeton University Press, 1971), 259.

6. Strachey, *Elizabeth and Essex,* 11.

7. As quoted in Natalie Mears, *Queenship and Political Discourse in the Elizabethan Realms* (Cambridge: Cambridge University Press, 2005), 33. I am indebted to her chapter "Elizabeth I and the Politics of Intimacy," 33–72. For an earlier consideration of Elizabeth within the matrix of political theology, see Frances Yates, "Queen Elizabeth as Astraea," *Journal of the Warburg and Courtauld Institutes* 10 (1947): 27–82, and Marie Axton, *The Queen's Two Bodies: Drama and the Elizabethan Succession* (London: The Royal Historical Society, 1977). More recently, an alternative vision of an inherently "secularized, mobile, incomplete" sovereignty nascent within Elizabeth's regime has been articulated by Jacques Lezra in his chapter "Phares; or, Divisible Sovereignty," *Wild Materialism: The Ethic of Terror and the Modern Republic* (New York: Fordham University Press, 2010), 63–87.

8. There is a kind of lingering refusal to decouple marriage from love that is implicit in such judgments, an error at once historical and theoretical, whereby the outer display of impulsive coquetry is instantly converted into the evident proof of an internal and carefully concealed "cold" inner core of calculation. Quite simply, the decision not to marry Anjou does not retroactively demonstrate that Elizabeth must never have loved him, nor would the decision to actually marry him have necessarily proved that she did. The repeated assurance that royal marriages were matters of international *Realpolitik* rather than "romance" is no sooner proffered than the negative outcomes of these negotiations are consolidated with the seemingly gratuitous announcement that she must not have loved him anyway. What is suspect is the sleight of hand by which aporia and consensus exchange places as we settle into the smugly counterfactual certitude that the things that did not happen definitely could not have happened.

9. Frances Dolan, *Marriage and Violence: The Early Modern Legacy* (Philadelphia: University of Pennsylvania Press, 2008), 139.

10. Susan Doran, *Monarchy and Matrimony: The Courtships of Elizabeth I* (London: Routledge, 1996), 11.

11. Bodin, *On Sovereignty,* 1.

12. Carl Schmitt, *Political Theology: Four Chapters on the Concept of Sovereignty,* trans. George Schwab (Chicago: University of Chicago Press, 2005), 8.

13. Ibid., 8.

14. Bodin, *On Sovereignty,* 11.

15. Julian Franklin, "Jean Bodin and the End of Medieval Constitutionalism," *Proceedings of the International Conference on Bodin* (Munich: Verlag C. H. Beck, 1973), 151.

16. Bodin, *On Sovereignty,* 59.

17. Jean Bodin, Livre première, chapitre X, *Les Six Livres De La République de J. Bodin, Angevin. A Monsieur du Faur, Seigneur de Pibrac, Conseiller du Roy en son privé Conseil. A Lyon, Par Gabriel Cartier* [1576] (Paris: Librairie Artheme Fayard, 1986), 309.

18. Jean Bodin, *Six Books of the Commonwealth,* trans. Tooley, 203.

19. Awkward moments of cultural misunderstanding (English resentment at Spanish wealth, Spanish disdain for English dances, cooking, and weather) gave way to theft and yet more violent interactions, until "by the last week of September there was fighting in the halls

of the palace nearly every day, and three Englishmen and a Spaniard were hanged following a murderous brawl" (Carolly Erickson, *Bloody Mary* [New York: St. Martin's Press, 1978], 384). The actual negotiations for the French match were relatively peaceful, with the exception of an unresolved, possible assassination attempt against Alençon's representative, Jean de Simier on July 17, 1579, when a shot was fired into Elizabeth's barge at the French courtier (Doran, *Monarchy and Matrimony*, 161).

20. Schmitt, *Political Theology*, 36.

21. The date, and even the very existence, of that dawn is not something we can safely assume. As Jacques Lezra asks by way of response to Derrida's remarks on sovereignty, "Was there not an 'aporetic of divisible sovereignty' before what we call the nation-state emerges—for instance, when Jean Bodin published *Les six livres de la république*?" (Lezra, *Wild Materialism*, 65). Far from constituting an account of historical relations and lineages, Lezra regards Schmitt's reading of Bodin as itself a "retrospective fantasy" (ibid., 67).

22. Elizabeth I, "Sententiae" [1563], *Elizabeth I: Translations, 1544–1589*, ed. Janel Mueller and Joshua Scodel (Chicago: University of Chicago Press, 2009), 346.

23. Here one might also want to consider whether or not a certain sententiousness haunts the dissemination of *Political Theology* itself via the memes of its eminently excerptable aphoristic pronouncements. Redolent of classical gravitas in the inverted syntax of its English translation, Schmitt's statement "Sovereign is he who decides the exception" has become a critical readymade.

24. Schmitt, *Political Theology*, 36, emphasis mine.

25. *The Book of Common Prayer* (1559), ed. John Booty (Charlottesville: University of Virginia Press, 2005), 290.

26. Ibid., 298.

27. Julia Lupton, *Citizen-Saints: Shakespeare and Political Theology* (Chicago: University of Chicago Press, 2005), 148.

28. Carole Pateman, *The Sexual Contract* (Cambridge: Polity Press, 1988), 159.

29. See Carole Pateman and Charles Mills, "On Critics and Contract," in *Contract and Domination* (Cambridge: Polity Press, 2008), 200–230, at 205.

30. But only, of course within the bounds prescribed by the preservation of the realm itself, and she and her council bitterly debated those very terms. Elizabeth was not free to grant whatever concessions she personally desired, and carefully hinged her negotiations upon the convenient escape clause that she would not be free to marry without the consent and approval of her people.

31. John Stubbs, *John Stubbs's Gaping Gulf with Letters and Other Relevant Documents*, ed. Lloyd E. Berry (Charlottesville: University Press of Virginia, 1968), 11.

32. There is a longstanding debate about the status of the references to the divine in Jean Bodin's *République*. J. W. Allen's remark that "you can eliminate from Bodin's *République* all his references to God, and to Princes as the lieutenants of God, and the whole structure will stand unaltered," constitutes the most strident attempt to enlist Bodin into a proto-secularist narrative (J. W. Allen, *A History of Political Thought in the Sixteenth Century* [London: Methuen, 1928], 415]. Yet it seems to intuitively mischaracterize the author of *De la démonomanie des sorciers* (1580) to suggest that his references to God's authority are, so to speak, optional. Stressing the function of divine will across Bodin's oeuvre as a whole, the strongest recent response to counter Allen's reading is made in Daniel Engster's chapter on Bodin in *Divine Sovereignty: The Origins of Modern State Power* (DeKalb: Northern Illinois University Press, 2001), 47–81.

33. Doran, *Monarchy and Matrimony*, 167.

34. Stubbs, *Gaping Gulf,* ed. Berry, xxxvi.

35. Schmitt, *Political Theology,* 17.

36. Ibid., 18.

37. Ibid., 32.

38. J. Hillis Miller, " 'Taking up a Task': Moments of Decision in Ernesto Laclau's Thought," in *Laclau: A Critical Reader,* ed. Simon Critchley and Oliver Marchart (London: Routledge, 2004), 217–26, at 223.

39. Doran, *Monarchy and Matrimony,* 157.

40. This version of Mendoza's text is quoted in Berry's edition, *John Stubbs's Gaping Gulf,* xxvii. One would do well to consider the Spanish source before crediting the unreality of this scene to Elizabeth's guile; this narrative's flimsy and impetuous quality may be a function of Elizabeth's promissory habits, or it may be a hostile embroidery onto something far more genuine.

41. R. J. Knecht, *The Rise and Fall of Renaissance France:* 1483–1610 (London: Fontana Press, 1996), 488.

42. Once attributed to the period of the Essex affair, this poem has generally been regarded as one of the queen's last communiqués with Alençon, but, fittingly, there remains some lingering mystery. Note the caution of her most recent editors: "Although this poem does not exist in any known manuscript version dating to the lifetime of Elizabeth, it is almost certainly hers, written in connection with Monsieur's final leave-taking in 1582 after a long and perplexing visit with the queen" (Elizabeth I, *Collected Works,* ed. Leah S. Marcus, Janel Mueller, and Mary Beth Rose [Chicago: University of Chicago Press], 302).

43. Horst Bredekamp, "From Walter Benjamin to Carl Schmitt, via Thomas Hobbes," *Critical Inquiry* 25.2 (1999): 247–66.

44. Alain Badiou, "Formal Theory of the Subject (Meta-Physics)," *Logics of Worlds,* trans. Alberto Toscano (London: Continuum, 2009), 62.

45. Ibid., 61.

46. As Doran notes, "By late September 1581, . . . the duke was running out of funds again and his army was starting to disband." On her end, the Queen was gradually admitting to her council members that the possibility of her being able to conceive a child as a result of this marriage was far from certain, and privately, there was speculation that an attempt to deliver a child might end both her life and that of her unborn child (Doran, *Monarchy and Matrimony,* 186).

47. Badiou, "Formal Theory," 74.

48. Ibid.

49. André Breton, *Mad Love,* trans. Mary Ann Caws (Lincoln: University of Nebraska Press, 1987), 42.

12

The Death of Christ in and as Secular Law

GREGORY KNEIDEL

It is doubtful whether a true power of testation was known to any original society
except the Roman.

SIR HENRY MAINE, *Ancient Laws* (1861)

In his groundbreaking 1516 edition of the New Testament, Erasmus renamed
the second part of the Christian Scriptures *Novum Instrumentum*. He would
revert back to *Novum Testamentum* just three years later, but by then he had
already broached a question that would perplex numerous critics in an age
of prolific biblical scholarship: How is it that each, and especially the second,
part of the Christian Scriptures can properly be called a testament?[1] At its
most basic level, this is a philological question involving three ancient languages (Hebrew, Greek, Latin), two distinct types of legal writing (the public
covenant and the private last will and testament), and, most surprisingly, the
single scriptural passage (Hebrews 9:15–18) upon which rested virtually the
entire case for placing the death of Christ on the cross within the competence
of Roman testamentary law. This essay examines Renaissance commentary
on this difficult passage and, by doing so, offers two distinct glimpses into
the emergence of secular law in early modern England. From the first, devout
humanist perspective, the Lutheran scholar Matthias Flacius Illyricus comments on Hebrews 9 in order to place the New Testament in a typological
relationship not with Judaic covenantal law but with Roman testamentary
law instead. From the second, more particularly English perspective, John
Donne invokes the problem of the Bible's "two wills" in order to protest
against the rise of English common law as an exclusively, even jealously, secular jurisdiction. Both Flacius and Donne take up Hebrews 9 as a problem of
jurisdictional pluralism and by doing so they transpose into a "minor key"
some major themes—concerning the origin, stability, and boundaries of law
and the institutional overlap between the secular and the spiritual—of Renaissance political theology.[2] That is, rather than isolating Christ's death as
a moment of exceptional or foundational legal violence, they figure it as a

more technical issue of deciding which of many existing laws obtains and, further, whether these plural laws can tolerate each other. Thus the crucial distinction is not between law and non-law, but between many laws and just one. In search of a proper jurisdictional framework for weighing the legal ramifications of Christ's death on the cross, both Flacius and Donne look past Jerusalem to Rome and its post-biblical legal tradition. There Flacius finds gentile law assuming its proper spiritual or ghostly jurisdiction; Donne, conversely, finds English common law, on the eve of its secularization, about to give up the ghost.

1. "A Testament is of Force after Men are Dead"

One way of wedging open the complex philological, doctrinal, and historical problems of the term 'testament' is to look at sixteenth-century commentaries on chapter 9 of the Epistle to the Hebrews. This epistle is a long, detailed, and sustained argument for the superiority of the New Testament over the Old, and chapter 9 begins (and ends) by rehearsing in great detail the regulations for ceremonial worship prescribed in Exodus 25, including the regulations for animal sacrifice. The chapter's middle verses then articulate its central comparative claim:

> For if the blood of bulls and of goats, and the ashes of an heifer sprinkling the unclean, sanctifieth to the purifying of the flesh: How much more shall the blood of Christ, who through the eternal Spirit offered himself without spot to God, purge your conscience from dead works to serve the living God? (Heb. 9:13–14; KJV)

Even this relatively short excerpt—with its structuring opposition of the sprinkled and the unspotted, flesh and conscience, dead works and eternal spirit—conveys something of the insistent typological logic of the Epistle of the Hebrews as a whole.[3] Christ is a sacrificial victim, but a superior victim; he is a sacrificing priest, but a superior sacrificing priest; and, of course, as God and man, Christ can be both priest and offering. Because Christ is presented as a single, superior, once-and-for-all sacrifice, these two verses underscore what would become the familiar, typologically warranted boast that liberal Christianity had abandoned the barbarism of bloody animal slaughter practiced by ancient Jews and pagans alike and adopted instead wholly spiritual or sacramental forms of sacrifice.[4]

The epistle's triumphant typologizing will continue for several more chapters but not before its author inserts four verses that figure centrally in most Renaissance attempts to explain if and how the Bible is a testament:

And for this cause he is the mediator of the new testament [Gr. *kainē diathēkē*],
that by means of death, for the redemption of the transgressions that were
under the first testament, they which are called might receive the promise
of eternal inheritance. For where a testament [*diathēkē*] is, there must also
of necessity be the death of the testator [*diathemenos*]. For a testament is of
force after men are dead: otherwise it is of no strength at all while the testator
liveth. Whereupon neither the first testament was dedicated without blood.
(Heb. 9:15–18; KJV)

Christ has been typologically identified with a sacrificial victim and a sacrificing priest; now, through the contrast between the "new testament" and the
"first testament" in verse 15, he is figured as Moses, who likewise mediates
between God and His people and gives laws in the form of a covenant. More
specifically, the author of Hebrews alludes to Exodus 24, in which Moses
sacrifices oxen and uses their blood to ratify or "dedicate" the "book of the
covenant" (Exod. 24:7) that he delivered from Mount Sinai.[5] But sixteenth-
century biblical scholars of all denominations, from Erasmus to Calvin, noticed a shift at verse 16 in the meaning of *diathēkē*.[6] This is the Greek word
used in the Septuagint to translate the Hebrew term *berit*, a public covenant
or treaty (*foedus* or *pactum* in Latin), one negotiated by an intermediary,
binding upon two or more parties, and ratified with the blood of a ritual
sacrifice. In Hebrew *berit* only means covenant in this sense; it never means
last will and testament (*voluntas ultima et testamentum* in Latin). In Greek,
however, *diathēkē* can mean either covenant *or* testament. Until verse 16,
diathēkē in Hebrews 9 clearly means something like covenant, as demanded
by the language of sacrificial rites borrowed first, in a ceremonial context,
from Exodus 25 and then, in a more legal, covenantal context, from Exodus
24. But verses 16 and 17, which postulate a kind of legal writing that does not
have any "force" until the "death of the testator," require *diathēkē* to be rendered as testament because a covenant, it was often noted, was nullified, not
given force, by the death of one of its consenting parties. Thus, in the whole
of Bèza's Latin translation of the New Testament, *diathēkē* is rendered as
testamentum only in Hebrews 9:16–17. Everywhere else, including everywhere
else in Hebrews, Bèza uses *foedus* or *pactum*.[7]

Several sixteenth-century commentators took this technical but significant change in the legal meaning of *diathēkē* as evidence that the Epistle to
the Hebrews was not, as church tradition had it, written by Paul. He was
both an educated and artful Greek-speaker and a "Hebrew among the Hebrews" (Phil. 3:5) with extensive training in Torah who frequently cited Roman law to his advantage. He would never have committed such a sloppy
semantic blunder. The Dominican cardinal Tomasso Cajetan, for example,

explains that at Heb 9:18 the author of this epistle either "changes from 'testament' properly so called to 'covenant'" or "errs in thinking that in Exodus there is talk of 'testament.' Each [possibility] is highly unbecoming to the apostle, especially [writing] to the Hebrews who know the peculiar quality of the words of the Hebrew text."[8] The epistle's original recipients, presumably Greek-speaking Jews living within the imperial sway of Rome, were already notorious for their arid legal rigidity and surely would have taken offense at the mishandling of the very term used to describe their unique legal relationship with God. Other commentators, in part to defend Paul's authorship, speculated that offense-giving was exactly the point. The Jesuit Francisco de Ribera, for example, conjectured that Paul's lexical miscue was actually a calculated rhetoric ploy, a trope by which he intentionally "turned his speech from the proper to an improper meaning" of *diathēkē* and by doing so overturned the semantic, legal, and theological presuppositions of his obstinate Jewish readers.[9]

Even apart from the controversy over Paul's authorship of the epistle, this central section of Hebrews 9 elicited commentary during the sixteenth century because it brings together the two possible legal meanings of *diathēkē* but strangely manages to do so *without* placing them in an explicitly typological arrangement. That is, for all of Hebrew's compulsive typological rhetoric and despite the fact that the epistle uses the term *diathēkē* more often than the rest of the New Testament combined, it does not treat the last will and testament as a form of legal writing that is typologically superior to the covenant or pact. The problem of the dual meanings of *diathēkē* was perfectly suited for Renaissance biblical commentators who, as Debora Kuller Shuger has masterfully demonstrated, had largely abandoned medieval criticism's obsession with typology and allegoresis in favor of a "doctrinal humanism" that deployed "the new philology in the service of doctrine."[10] This brand of humanism owed a huge debt not just to the flourishing of the classical arts of discourse (grammar, rhetoric, and logic) but also to the growth of post-Reformation legal historiography which asserted the alteriority of Roman civil and canon law and juxtaposed this Latin-based, transnational *ius commune* with the local, national, and vernacular legal traditions found throughout Europe. Shuger speculates that once the *Corpus Juris Civilis* and the *Corpus Juris Canonici* could be thought of as historical compilations rather than transcendent codes, it became easier to think of the Bible itself in similar, contextualizing ways.[11] As it developed over the sixteenth century, the challenge for doctrinal humanism was to maintain that the Bible was "simultaneously a manifestation of divine reason and a cultural artifact."[12] Thus, on the one hand, the Bible as testaments was, to use the official if recognizably bogus etymology offered in the *Corpus Juris Civilis* (cf. Inst. 2.10), a *testatio mentis*, a witness of God's mind, an infallible textual manifestation of His divine will. On the other hand, the very same idea begged for philological debunking: if the Bible was a testament, it was a cultural artifact with a knowable past, a legal form of primary importance whose principles were taught, theorized, and commented upon in an extensive body of legal literature, all of it extrabiblical.

2. *In politicis testamentis*

We can see the conflicting obligations of doctrinal humanism—to use philology to confirm immutable doctrine while almost but not quite recognizing the cultural specificity of its insights—in *Clavis Scripturae Sacrae* (1567), an influential treatise on scriptural hermeneutics by the Lutheran reformer Matthias Flacius Illyricus. The first part of this work is a lexicon of biblical terms, and in his entry on *testamentum* Flacius begins by arguing that the New Testament as a form of legal writing is most properly thought of as a mixed form (*mixtum ex foedere et testamento*) in which the testament is interior to or contained within the covenant so that Christ's death establishes a new covenantal bond between God and his chosen people. This would become a familiar formulation, especially among Protestant commentators, and coheres with Luther's Christological argument for the mixing of the two forms: "He who stays alive makes a covenant; he who is about to die makes a testament. Thus Jesus Christ, immortal God, made a covenant. At the same time He made a testament, because He was going to become mortal. Just as He is both God and man, so He made both a covenant and a testament."[13] Flacius is initially content to survey the various covenants of the Old Testament and to punctuate this survey occasionally with the typological argument, derived principally from Galatians 3, by which the Messianic covenant is said to be (1) identical to the Abrahamic covenant (cf. Gen. 12–15); and (2) both prior and superior to the intervening Mosaic covenant (Exod. 19–24).[14] When Flacius sets aside the Hebrew term *berit* and the major covenants of the Old Testament in order to consider the meaning of *diathēkē* in the New Testament, he turns immediately to the problem of Hebrews 9. In order to sort it out, he contrasts ten principal features (*proprietates*) of the covenant and ten features of the last will and testament. He argues that the New Testament possesses certain features indicative of each form: like a covenant, for example, the New Testament binds together two parties through the agency of a mediator (Christ); it makes promises, offers rewards, and threatens punishments; it is ratified by a sacrifice so that it cannot be altered without also being rendered void. Like a last will, the New Testament took effect upon the death of the testator and—a constant refrain among *sola gratia* Protestant commentators—offers a legacy, the free gift of grace, that places absolutely no obligation upon those who benefit from it. With compelling reasons to choose and to reject both formulations, Flacius reiterates his initial claim that the New Testament is a mixed legal form.[15]

Yet Flacius's analysis continues. He explains further that the Bible, our "spiritual testament," can also be thought of as a "kind of judicial compilation" featuring "those conditions which jurists usually require or prescribe in political testaments."[16] He then retells the story of Christian salvation through the legal definitions, rulings, and maxims of famous Roman *jurisprudentes*: from Ulpianus, he cites the canonical definition of *testamentum*; from Gaius, he affirms that the appointing of heirs (as opposed to the granting of legacies) was the original and primary purpose of the last will and testament; from Papinianus, he paraphrases the "broadest rule" (*generalissima regula*) about warrantees in good faith agreements. He notes that under Roman law an heir can be appointed, substituted, adopted, and—Flacius was no Calvinist—disinherited if shown to be unworthy. And he introduces Lucius Titius, the John Doe of Roman legal pedagogy and perpetual claimant in the inheritance disputes of the *Corpus Juris Civilis*, to clarify the exact legal basis for our salvation: just as Lucius Titius is appointed heir through a formulaic phrase expressing the will of the testator ("Lucius Titius mihi haeres esto"), so too we were made Christ's co-heirs when He said: "Father, I will that they also, whom thou hast given me, be with me where I am; that they may behold my glory, which thou hast given me" (John 17:24).[17]

Of course Flacius was not the first to use Roman law to clarify the basic terms and teachings of Christianity: it is cited often in the New Testament, especially by Luke and Paul, and throughout the teachings of the Latin Church Fathers (so much so that Tertullian the Church Father, who is often thought to have coined the terms *vetus* and *novum testamentum* in roughly their current usage, has sometimes been identified with Tertullian the jurist quoted in the Digest). Moreover, as Walter Ullman has argued, the reception of Roman imperial law made ready the way for the spread of Christianity throughout Europe.[18] What is remarkable, however, is how Flacius treats Christ as "the end" (cf. Rom. 10:4)—the *telos*, goal, purpose, fulfillment—not only of Jewish covenantal law but of Roman testamentary law as well. It may be that Flacius is deploying the common tactic of aligning Christianity with classical, Greco-Roman culture and, in doing so, partitioning both apart from Judaism. But it may be more appropriate to say Flacius seems to be replacing

Judaic law with Roman law, the Old Testament with the *Corpus Juris Civilis*, as the antecedent term of his typological reasoning. When he explains *testamentum* in terms of Roman law, Flacius re-uses many of the same rhetorical strategies—the extracting of scriptural phrases from their historical, narrative, or rhetorical contexts, the side-by-side proof-texting, the "so also" and "how much more" comparisons—he had used in the earlier section on *berit* in the Old Testament. Only now the purpose of his typological rhetoric is to demonstrate the validity of the New Testament as a testament, from the initial inquiry into Christ's legal capacity to make it (per Digest 28.1.4) to the final fulfillment of its terms, more surely and completely than any human testament, by His named executor, the Holy Spirit. Flacius's legal typology does not stop when he leaves aside Jewish covenant-making for Roman testament-making. It continues so that the New Testament is not just superior to the Old Testament, it is superior to the Roman testament as well. As a law-giver, Christ is not only a new Moses, but a new Justinian; as a testator and progenitor of God's chosen people, he is not only the equal of Abraham, but of the Roman *pater familias*.

Flacius is not making a historical argument: he is not treating Jesus and the earliest Christians as denizens of the Roman empire, nor is he asserting that the assorted legal maxims and rulings codified in the *Corpus Juris Civilis*, a sixth-century, Byzantine compilation, were in force in ancient Mediterranean cultures. What is interesting, however, is that the ambiguity of Hebrews 9—its imperfect typological shift from Christ's bloody covenantal sacrifice to His formal testamentary death—leads Flacius to align the spiritual with, not against, the political. In doing so, he provides further evidence for Julia Reinhard Lupton's recent argument that, because of the convergence of Pauline universalism and imperial Roman law in the New Testament and in Renaissance literature, "the saint is a citizen."[19] And if "citizenship requires sacrifice" and the citizen-saint must, as Lupton puts it, "die into citizenship"—die as the member of a local, particular tribe or nation to claim an imperial citizenship that transcends and so tolerates multiple memberships (and in doing so denies each membership's sacral claim of exclusivity)—then Christ's *testate* death becomes a foundational civic achievement.[20] From it are derived the normative "conditions" of participation in a this-worldly Christian *polis*: while many Protestants were drawn to the concept of the testament because it emphasized Christ's legacy, his free gift of grace bestowed upon humanity, Flacius emphasizes the more civic purpose of the testament, viz. the establishment of heirs.[21] Through the conditions of the testament, rather than the obligations and rewards and punishments of the covenant, the Bible establishes the godly community on earth as a *polis*.[22]

Flacius published his *Clavis* just before "a new sensitivity to historical discontinuity" developed in Renaissance biblical criticism, a moment around the 1580s when "the seamless fabric of typological time" was replaced "with the stratified divisions of a cultural archaeology" that emphasized "the underlying Semitic culture of the New Testament."[23] The ensuing shift from "patristics to orientalism" led to the monumental philological, legal, and anthropological treatises on biblical cultures by humanist polymaths such as Justus Lipsius, Daniel Heinsius, Johannes Drusius, Hugo Grotius, and John Selden. But even as the political constitution of the *Res Publica Hebraeorum* came into sharper focus, relatively little interest was given to the adoption or imposition of Roman testamentary law on ancient Jewish and early Christian culture.[24] So, for example, the fourth-century *Mosaicarum et Romanarum Legum Collatio*, discovered in manuscript in 1570 and first published in 1572, does indeed compare Mosaic and Roman legal codes. But it is almost wholly devoted to criminal law (e.g., the punishment of adulterers, cattleraiders, kidnappers, etc.); the exception is the final chapter, which interestingly concerns intestate succession.[25] Likewise, even though a few decades later Faustus Socinus and Grotius endeavored to determine the precise legal ramifications of Christ's bloody crucifixion in terms taken both from Hebrews 9 and from Roman penal and commercial law (*dominium, imperium, remissio, solutio, liberatio, novatio, satisfactio, acceptilatio*), they never contemplate it as a proper or valid testamentary succession.[26] And even though seventeenth-century Puritan divines were capable of excruciating grammatical rigor in their expatiation of the Covenant of Grace—e.g., what is the logical and legal force of "and" in God's words to Abraham, "Walk before me, and be thou upright, and I will make my covenant between me and thee" (Gen. 17:1–2)?—they showed relatively little interest in the formal problem of the Bible as a testament.[27] It is not until page 283 of his 383-folio-page treatise on *The Gospel-Covenant* that the Puritan Peter Bulkeley asks why the covenant is "otherwise called a testament" in Hebrews 9. In less than one page Bulkeley shows that this is, in essence, merely a figure of speech showing "the firmnesse, and inviolable and unchangeable nature" of the covenant because a last will and testament cannot be changed after the testator's death. Of course, in that regard, the Bible as executed testament is just like a covenant ratified with blood.

3. "Hee hath Made Two Wills"

So Roman testamentary law was never received by devout humanist scriptural commentators because, even after the 1580s, they could not quite bring themselves to acknowledge the obtrusion of gentile law into the quintessen-tially Judeo-Christian typological narrative of Hebrews 9. Instead, Scripture was received by Renaissance testamentary law, and, whether seen through either the receding civilian tradition or the ascendant common law tradition, the covenantal sacrifice of Judaism lapses not typologically into the bloodless sacrifice of Christianity but axiomatically into the dying testament of the Ro-man *civis* or of the English feudal tenant. In *A Briefe Treatise of Testaments and Last Willes* (first ed., 1591), "the first work of canon law to be published in English," the civilian lawyer Henry Swinburne sought to introduce the more erudite principles of Roman testamentary law to an English audience. In an early chapter, Swinburne takes up the same definition of testament that had prefaced Flacius's typological reading of Roman testamentary law: "A testa-ment is a just sentence of our will; touching that we would have done after our death."[28] Concerning the phrase "after our death" in specific, Swinburne explains: "For a Testament respecteth that which is to be performed after the death of the Testator, and therefore so long as he liveth, the Testament is of no force; but doth take his strength, and is confirmed by the Testators death."[29] This is a fairly direct paraphrase of Hebrews 9:16–17. It is not surpris-ing that Swinburne should paraphrase Scripture, but it is perhaps surprising that he should cite civilian glossators (Paulus de Castro, Diego de Covarru-bias, Matthaeus de Cracovia) as the source of this maxim. Similarly, Edward Coke paraphrases both Scripture and Roman law when he formulates what would become the standard version of this maxim in English common law. In a 1604 published report of a 1591 case, Coke gives the maxim as: *Nam omne testamentum morte consummatum est* ("Every testament is completed by death").[30] *Consummatum* is an unusual word in testamentary law, used in the *Corpus Juris Civlis* only once (cf. Codex 6). Coke's wording seems to echo instead Jesus' dying words on the cross: "it is finished" (John 19:30). But Coke cites neither Scripture nor the civilians.

As Peter Goodrich has argued in his analysis of the institutional uncon-scious of the Anglo-American common law tradition, this denial or repres-sion of sources is typical of Coke and other champions of the common law. They conceived of the common law as a unified, centralized, and rational system derived from immemorial custom even though, as Goodrich shows, it was instead "built upon the sacrifice, the devouring of other laws, not least those of conscience, of spirituality, and of the soul."[31] Writing at a pivotal juncture in the common law's emergence, John Donne's sonnet *HSPart* ("Father, part of his double interest") weighs in on the burgeoning secularity of English common law by linking the idea of the Bible as two testaments to the plurality of jurisdictions competing for preeminence in England. That is, Donne draws an analogy between the typological problem of the Bible as two testaments and the simultaneous arrogation and repression of spiritual authority by common law courts in seventeenth-century England.

HSPart has never ranked among John Donne's best loved or most anthologized poems, although the recent Variorum edition of *The Holy Sonnets* establishes its importance for any sequential reading of these poems (*HSPart* is fourth of twelve in the Original Sequence but last of twelve in the Revised). Its octet reads:

> Father, part of his double interest
> Unto thy kingdome, thy Sonne gives to mee,
> His Joincture in the knotty Trinity
> He keeps, and gives mee his Deaths Conquest.
> This Lambe, whose Death with life the world hath blest
> Was from the worlds beginning slayne: and hee
> Hath made two wills, which with the Legacie
> Of his, and thy kingdome, doth thy sonnes invest.[32]

It is difficult to dispute Richard Strier's conclusion that the poem "never generates any emotional intensity," no doubt because, though addressed to the Father, this opening seems to circle around and about the precise legal import of the Son's death.[33] Donne invokes four different jurisprudences or forms of law. Two of these are scripturally inspired. The first is imperial or colonial law, which stands behind Donne assertion of the Son's right to his kingdom derived from his messianic conquest (line 4). The second is ritual law, in relation to which Donne contrasts this conquering Son with a sacrificial victim, the slain Lamb of God (lines 5–6). But the last two refer to jurisdictions that were active in Donne's England: English common law is evoked by the Son's jointure (lines 1–4), affirming his eternal place in the "knotty Trinity," and the sons' "invest[ure]" (line 8), clarifying their stake in the eternal kingdom;[34] and civil law, which would have been the jurisdiction under which the problem (which does not yet appear to be a problem) of the Son's "two wills" (lines 7–8) would have traditionally fallen. Influenced partly by the reference to the Son as a sacrificial lamb, Donne's modern editors have glossed "two wills" as the two testaments of the Christian Bible and adduced Hebrews 9:15–18 as their scriptural warrant.

As in other post-Reformation passion narratives, Donne's Son is alarmingly "chimerical," though here his numerous divine and human selves are all legal actors (joint-holder, conqueror, sacrificial victim, testator).[35] As scriptural images, the conqueror and sacrificial victim oppose each other. As representatives of active jurisdictions, so too do the joint-holder and the

testator. The historian R. H. Helmholz notes, for instance, common lawyers had since the beginning of the Reformation been encroaching upon the
ecclesiastical court's jurisdiction concerning last wills and testaments, especially in mixed cases, like this one, that involve the devising of land (as opposed to the bequesting of personal property).[36] So what does Donne—who
descended from a line of prominent, Rome-leaning lawyers, most notably Sir
Thomas More and John Rastell—gain by evoking this jurisdictional conflict?
Why invoke the Son's "two wills"? Certainly, Donne keeps other theological
connotations of "two wills"—the Christological (i.e., the Son's dual nature),
the providential (i.e., God's divine decrees), and the anthropological (i.e., the
divided self)—in play throughout the poem.[37] But to cast the Son as a testator who has "made two wills" is also to situate the poem within a very well-
theorized area of testamentary law. In his survey of this law, Swinburne reiterates the key maxim that "no man can die with two Testaments," "because
the latter doth alwaies infringe the former."[38] Of course men often did die
with two (or more) written documents that had been or even still purport to
be testaments, so civilian jurists developed numerous procedural presumptions and interpretive rules of construction in order to determine which
document should be executed as the true expression of the testator's final
intentions. These presumptions and rules of construction gave huge leeway to
probate judges to recover the *animum testandi* within written texts because,
while the death of the testator confirms the testament, it is the "mind and
not the wordes of the testator" that "giveth" it "life" (324v). Equity, discretion, and what Swinburne calls "meaning" reign in testamentary law. Civilian jurists discussed all manner of scenarios—two written testaments are
produced; a latter testament revokes cancels, or amends an earlier will; the
significance of words (e.g., universal terms such as "all") change between the
time of the testament's making and of its execution; the physical document
is partly or wholly erased, over-scored, or destroyed; secret codes are devised
by the testator, such as the covert insertion of the Lord's Prayer in the text of
the testament, to designate his final intentions—and each scenario licensed
the probate judge to apply equity, use discretion, and above all heed the
testator's "meaning" rather than the testament's words. Testamentary law
also presumed that testators loved their children and supported (in their last
moments, at least) pious causes. When two wills exist and it is impossible to
determine which is latter, the testament that favors the testator's children or
that grants legacies "*ad pias causas*" is "presumed last" (315r-16r). Swinburne
even imagines a case in which a voided testament "made in favour of the testator's children, or some other person entirely beloved of the testator" might
"infringe[ ]" (he does not say exactly how) upon the execution of another,

more valid testament (329v). Perhaps no other arena of law better exemplifies Goodrich's point that Roman civil law, as it was recovered by medieval glossators and applied by Renaissance civilian jurists, should never be confused with secular law because it always treated the "text" as "secondary to the meaning (*mens legis*), the word to the spirit (*anima legis*), the language of law to the force, power, or virtue that underlies its enunciation" (225).

Goodrich has demonstrated that during the seventeenth century English common lawyers subsumed the civil law's "ghostly powers" and, by repressing them, effected the divorce of the law from "its spiritual essence" (225). As a civilian, Swinburne sought to prevent this secularization of the law. He wanted all the competing jurisdictions then operating in England—civil, canon, statutory, equity, and common law—to abide "peaceably amongst themselves," "shaking hands together like friends, and like loving brethren, saluting and embracing each other" (A4v). Swinburne urges the admission of Roman legal principles (which some perceived to be foreign and rooted in Roman Catholic dogma) insofar as they are "not repugnant" to either the New Testament or to the "statutes and customes of this Realme"; he locates the origin of the ecclesiastical courts' current probate authority in the statutes of Henry VIII, the founder of the Church of England and so unifier of England's diverse temporal and spiritual jurisdictions (3).[39] By contrast, the antiquarian and champion of the common law John Selden (1584–1654) would later argue that "the power which the Spiritual Courts have to exercise" "is meerly by the Common Law," although Selden unapologetically admits that "we find not when it came first to them, no more than we find divers of our setled Courses and Maxims in the Common Law."[40] Similarly, in inheritance cases tried under common law, the legal presumptions that enlarge judicial discretion in civilian judges are recast as the impersonal, rational operation of law. Thus, for example, a late Elizabethan case reported by William Noy recasts the presumption of love—the love of a parent for "his own blood"—as "nature and God's law" that legitimates the "sure and settled course" of common law primogeniture. Love still motives legal action. But it is no longer, as it was with Swinburne, a presumption "to be discretely handled by a grave Judge with leaden feete"; it is for Noy simply a "sure and settled course" of law that obviates discretion, ethics, emotion, and judgment itself.[41]

4. "All But Love"

Having confirmed the existence of the Son's "two wills" in line 7, Donne proceeds in the sonnet's sestet to situate them within a decidedly typological framework:

> Yet such are those lawes, that men argue yet
> Whether a man those statutes can fulfill;
> None doth; but all healing grace, and spirit
> Revive againe, what lawe and letter kill.
> Thy Lawes Abridgment, and thy last command
> Is all but Love, Oh lett that last will stand.

This section is cloyed with Pauline allusions: to the paradox that the law cannot be fulfilled (cf. Rom. 3:20); to the opposition of the reviving spirit of grace and killing letter of the law (cf. 2 Cor. 3:6); and to the "Abridgment" of God's "lawes" into a single "last command" (cf. Rom. 13:8–10).[42] Donne's terms also complicate the jurisdictional framework of the octet. The term "statutes" refers most directly to royal authority (technically to laws promulgated by the King-in-Parliament) that sometimes positioned itself with and sometimes against both common law and civilian courts. And Donne's phrasing is notably nondogmatic, as evidenced by the repetition of "yet," in both disjunctive and adverbial senses, that brackets line 9 (*epanalepsis* and *antanclasis*); by the plausible "men argue" in line 9, answered blandly by "None doth" in line 11 (Luther would have written that "None can"); and by the plea to "lett that last will stand" in line 14, the first and only admission in the poem that the Son's "two wills" are judicially problematic.

Bradin Cormack has argued that the concept of jurisdiction "exposes law's provisionality even as it opens a space of intensified literariness."[43] Even if they never generate any emotional intensity, the first thirteen lines of Donne's sonnet do much the same. By comparison, the climactic phrase "Is all but Love" is both more assertive and grammatically puzzling, in part because it captures something of the contradiction of Rom. 13:8 ("Owe no man any thing, but to love one another").[44] In terms of political theology, line 14 as a whole is probably best glossed by Slavoj Žižek's description of Paul's messianic progression "from law to love . . . and back," especially since the second half of line 14 refers back to the poem's earlier jurisdictional complexities and pleads, hesitatingly, for final, formal judgment.[45] In fact, a more apt summary of Donne's poem might be "from laws to love . . . and back," since it also imagines the homogenization of laws into an "all" only to posit "love" as a jurisprudential exception to it. In early modern legal discourse an "abridgement" was most often a book, an epitome or single-volume summary of existing laws; that is how critics have typically glossed Donne's use of the term in line 13. But, as Jeremy Maule astutely observed, when taken in a specifically common law context, the term could also signify the act of making "a declaration or count shorter by subtracting or severing some of the substance therein comprised."[46] According to this second sense, Donne's

point is that, in Maule's words, that "God . . . *subtracts* 'all but love' from
his 'lawes': He severs his severity."[47] Donne's sonnet thus parodies the campaign to unify law that led English common lawyers to adopt in their own
way the repressive logic of Christian typology: just as the New Testament
cancels, subsumes, and violently forgets the Old, so too, as Goodrich shows,
were common lawyers in the process of canceling, subsuming, and violently
forgetting their law's plural, emotional, and spiritual origins. So, for thirteen
lines, Donne slowly represses legal plurality. But in the last line, unhappy with
a unitary, impersonal "all," he singles out love as an exception that thwarts
the dream of a radically simplified and homogenized law. The reductive logic
of Christian typology falters as love exceeds the duality of law and grace. And
the "sure and settled course" of a homogenized, secularized English common law falters as love concedes one final plea for equitable, emotional, and
spiritual judgment.

Paul S. Coolidge once noted with some irony that the Bible of English
Protestants differed "in one all-important respect from scripture as Paul understood it: their scripture includes the Gospel and the preaching of Paul
himself."[48] Partly because Paul, limited as he was by his urgent and ultimately
frustrated messianic expectations, never thought of himself as *writing* either
a covenant or a testament, English Protestants struggled to explain how the
New Testament's unassailable spiritual authority could resist devolving into
rigid, loveless, scriptural legalism. As the examples of Flacius and Donne
show, Roman law helped to alleviate this struggle and break the typological
deadlock between law and grace, old and new, Judaism and Christianity. By
retelling the story of Christianity as the probation of testaments rather than
the succession (or restoration) of covenants, Flacius could imagine how, with
the logic of typology displaced from Jerusalem to Rome, Christ on the cross
gave up the ghost and at that moment inspired Roman law without weaken-
ing its civic, even imperial, institutional foundation. With the rest of Europe,
England had received this spiritualized Roman law, but Donne seemed to
be alert to the threat that England would give it up and sacrifice the law's
spirit in order to ensure its uniformity. Thus he found in the analogy between
Christian typology and English jurisdictional conflict a means to resist—to
make a last, willful stand against—the drive toward legal homogenization
and secularity in early modern England.

Notes

1. Erasmus defended *instrumentum* on two grounds: the patristic example of Augustine
and Jerome and the technical usage of the term in the *Corpus Juris Civilis*, which implied that
a *testamentum* did not have to be written in order to be valid while an *instrumentum* did. See

Erasmus, *Opus Epistolarum*, ed. P. S. Allen and H. M. Allen, vol. 7 (Oxford: Oxford University Press, 1928), Epistle 1858.519–38; and Henk Jan de Jonge, "Novum Testamentum a Nobis Versum: The Essence of Erasmus' Edition of the New Testament," *Journal of Theological Studies* 35 (1984): 394–413.

2. For jurisdiction as a "minor key" of political theology, see Bradin Cormack, *A Power to Do Justice* (Chicago: University of Chicago Press, 2008), 6. For political theology and last wills and testaments more broadly, see the suggestive connections made by Joseph Jenkins in "What Should Inheritance Be," *Cardozo Studies in Law and Literature* 20.2 (Summer 2008): 129–50.

3. For the aggressive logic, figurative aberrations, and literary afterlives of Christian typology, see Jill Robbins, *Prodigal Son/Elder Brother* (Chicago: University of Chicago Press, 1991); and Julia Reinhard Lupton, *The Afterlives of Saints* (Stanford: Stanford University Press, 1996). The classic study is Erich Auerbach, "Figura," in *Scenes from the Drama of European Literature* (Minneapolis: University of Minnesota Press, 1959), 11–76.

4. For a recent treatment of this subject, see Jonathan Sheehan, "Sacrifice Before the Secular," *Representations* 105 (Winter 2009): 12–36. See also Delbert R. Hillers, *Covenant: The History of a Biblical Idea* (Baltimore: Johns Hopkins University Press, 1969), 169–88.

5. For a nuanced reading of this moment, see Arthur J. Jacobson, "The Idolatry of Rules: Writing Law According to Moses, with Reference to Other Jurisprudences," *Cardozo Law Review* 11 (1989–90): 1079–32.

6. See Kenneth Hagen, *Hebrews Commenting from Erasmus to Bèze, 1516–1598* (Tübingen: J. C. B. Mohr, 1981), esp. 4–8 and 58–65.

7. In a marginal gloss, Bèza explains vv. 16–17 by arguing in effect that the *testamentum* put into force by Christ's death was a stipulation of a larger *foedus* (habet hoc foedus ratione Testamenti seu donationis mortis causa) (*Novum Testamentum* [London: 1579], ad loc.). The Geneva Bible's rather senseless translation of this gloss ignores the very distinction Bèza is trying to make: "This Testament hath the condition of a Testament or gift, which is made effectual by death" (*The Geneva Bible,* ed. Gerald T. Sheppard [Cleveland, Ohio: The Pilgrim Press, 1989], ad loc.).

8. Quoted in Hagen, *Hebrews Commenting,* 19. The translation is Hagen's.

9. "Ludit Paulus Rhetorum more, et vocem a proprio ad improprium significatum flecit" (in *Epistolam B. Pauli Apostoli ad Hebraeos commentarii* [Salamanca: 1598], quoted in Matthew Poole, *Synopsis Criticorum,* 2 vols. [London: 1667–71], 2:1321). The phrasing here echoes Quintilian's definition of a trope: "Tropos est verbi vel sermonis a propria significatione in aliam cum virtute mutatio" (*Institutio oratoria,* 8.6.1).

10. Debora Kuller Shuger, *The Renaissance Bible* (Berkeley and Los Angeles: University of California Press, 1994), 22.

11. For the possibility that sixteenth-century scriptural commentators followed the contextualizing lead of French legal historians, see ibid., 23 and 61–66. See also Donald R. Kelley, *Foundations of Modern Historical Scholarship* (New York: Columbia University Press, 1970).

12. Shuger, *Renaissance Bible,* 52.

13. Martin Luther, *Works,* 55 vols. (St. Louis, Minneapolis: Concordia Publishing House, Fortress Press, 1957–86), 27:268. See also Kenneth Hagen, "The Problem of Testament in Luther's 'Lectures on Hebrews,'" *The Harvard Theological Review* 63.1 (Jan. 1970): 61–90.

14. The Abrahamic and Messianic covenants "idem sunt" (Matthias Flacius Illyricus, *Clavis Scripturae Sacrae,* 2 vols. [Basil, 1567], 1.1612).

15. Ibid., 1.1621–23.

16. "Adscibam vero etiam iuridicam quandam collationem nostri istius spiritualis testamenti, cum iis conditionibus quas Jurisprudentes in politicis testamentis requirere ac praescribere solent" (ibid., 1.1623). For the various sorts of conditions that could and could not be attached to a last will and testament under Roman law, see Digest 28.7.

17. Ibid., 1.1623–25. Flacius's references are to: Digest 28.1.1 (attributed to Modestinus); Instit. 2.20.34; and Digest 5.1.41. Lucius Titius is forever being appointed, substituted, adrogated, adopted, and disinherited in, e.g., Digest 28 and 29.

18. See Walter Ullman, *Law and Politics in the Middle Ages* (Ithaca: Cornell University Press, 1975), esp. 23–50. For the praise of Roman civil law by magisterial reformers, see Shuger, *Renaissance Bible,* 61–65.

19. Julia Reinhard Lupton, *Citizen-Saints* (Chicago: University of Chicago Press, 2005), 30.

20. Ibid., 21.

21. As Michael Sheehan has noted, the medieval Catholic Church shifted the emphasis of testaments away from the establishment of heirs to the apportioning of legacies (*The Will in Medieval England* [Toronto: Pontifical Institute for Medieval Studies, 1963], 134). During the Reformation, Protestants challenged this emphasis as a matter of devotion (e.g., by no longer bequeathing money to pay for prayers and masses for the dead), but retained it as a matter of theology. As the spiritualist Puritan Richard Sibbes wrote: "A Testament bequeatheth good things merely of love. . . . A covenant requireth something to be done. In a testament, there is nothing but receiving the legacies given. In covenants, ofttimes it is for the mutual good one of another, but a testament is merely for their good for whom the testament is made, to whom the legacies are bequeathed" (*The Faithful Covenanter* [London, 1639], 6:4, quoted in Jason P. Rosenblatt, *Torah and Law in "Paradise Lost"* [Princeton: Princeton University Press, 1994], 78–79).

22. It is interesting to note that the term "political testament" (not yet adopted as a generic title by Enlightenment political theorists) is almost as much of an oddity as "spiritual testament": "Since jurisprudential axioms which the Digest embraced shaped the physiognomy and complexion of [medieval] Western Europe to a hitherto still not fully acknowledged extent, it is not indeed surprising to find that governmental practice and doctrine were unfamiliar with the very concept and term of 'political': the term did not occur in the vast body of the Roman law" (Ullmann, *Law and Politics in the Middle Ages,* 59).

23. Shuger, *Renaissance Bible,* 25.

24. For mutual influence in the post-biblical era, see Reuven Yaron, *Gifts in Contemplation of Death in Jewish and Roman Law* (Oxford: Clarendon Press, 1960).

25. See *Mosaicarum et Romanarum Legum Collatio,* ed. and trans. M. Hyamson (Oxford: Oxford University Press, 1913), 132–49.

26. For this debate, see Shuger, *Renaissance Bible,* 54–88; and Jonathan Sheehan, "Sacrifice Before the Secular," 20–25.

27. For this question and seventeenth-century treatises on the Covenant of Grace more generally, see John S. Coolidge, *The Pauline Renaissance in England* (Oxford: Oxford University Press, 1970), 99–140.

28. Henry Swinburne, *A Briefe Treatise of Testaments and Last Willes,* rev. ed. (London, 1611), 3v, quoting Digest 28.1.1.

29. Ibid., 12.

30. 3 Co. 29b, 32a, 34a; 4 Co. 61b; 6 Co. 76a; Co. Litt. 322b (not, as frequently found, Co. Litt. 112b). I have not been able to trace an earlier source for Coke's exact phrasing, but it

approximates sixteenth-century Latin translations of Heb. 9:17: Testamentum enim in mortuis confirmatum est (Vulgate); Nam testamentum in mortuis ratum est (Erasmus); Testamentum enim in mortuis ratum est (Bèza).

31. Peter Goodrich, *Oedipus Lex* (Berkeley and Los Angeles: University of California Press, 1995), 228 and 42. I have argued elsewhere that Donne's early satires evidence his attention to and disdain for the emerging English common law tradition; see "Coscus, Queen Elizabeth, and Law in Donne's 'Satyre II'" *Renaissance Quarterly* 61.1 (2008): 92–121.

32. I quote from *The Holy Sonnets*, vol. 7, part 1 of *The Variorum Edition of the Poetry of John Donne*, gen. ed. Gary A. Stringer (Bloomington: Indiana University Press, 2005), 110.

33. Richard Strier, "John Donne Awry and Squint: The 'Holy Sonnets,' 1608–10," *Modern Philology* 86 (1989): 379.

34. "*Iointure (Iunctura)* is a covenant, whereby the husband . . . assureth unto his wife, in respect of marriage, lands or tenements for terme of her life"; "*Vesture (vestitura)* is a French word signifying a garment: but in the vse of our common lawe, turned metaphorically to betoken a possession, or an admittance to a possession" (Thomas Blount, *The Interpreter* [London, 1607], s.vv.).

35. Shuger, *Renaissance Bible*, 113.

36. R. H. Helmholz, *Roman Canon Law in Reformation England* (Cambridge: Cambridge University Press, 1990), 79–89. Helmholz observes that civil and canon lawyers "knew, as the common lawyers reminded them, that there was nothing inherently spiritual about their testamentary jurisdiction" (88–89).

37. The Christological concept is invoked, e.g., by Thomas Bilson: "As then Christ had two contrary natures, yet knit and united in one person; so had he two contrary wills touching death, yet both agreeing and concurring in one end" (*The Survey of Christ's Sufferings for Mens Redemption* [London, 1604], 471). The providential question of whether or not God had "two wills" was a recurrent point of contention in debates over predestination (e.g. in 1581 Richard Hooker delivered his first public sermon, which was entitled "That in God there were two wills; an antecedent and a consequent will: his first will, That all mankind should be saved; but his second will was, That those only should be saved, that did live answerable to that degree of grace which he had offered or afforded them"; Izaak Walton reports that "this seemed to cross a late opinion of Mr. Calvin's" (Izaak Walton, *Lives* [London, 1670], 29). The anthropological notion of the individual's "two wills" (duae voluntates) was articulated most influentially in the Christian tradition by Augustine (cf. . *Confessions*, 8.5.10 and 8.9.21).

38. Swinburne, 15v; citing Inst. 2.17; cf. 315r and 326v. Further citations will be given parenthetically in the text. It should be noted that for Swinburne, there was a slight, formal difference between a testament and a last will: the former names an executor; the latter does not. For presumptions in Renaissance testamentary law, see Andrea Alicato's *De Praesumptionibus* (1542) and even more comprehensively Giacomo Menochio's 910-folio page *De Praesumptionibus, conjecturis, signis, et indiciis* (1588). On testamentary law and literary interpretation more generally, see Michael Hancher, "Dead Letters: Wills and Poems," in *Interpreting Law and Literature*, ed. Sanford Levinson and Steven Mailloux (Evanston: Northwestern University Press, 1988), 101–14.

39. Swinburne seems to have borrowed the phrase "not repugnant" from Richard Hooker and other conformist opponents of (what they mischaracterized as) rigid Puritan scripturalism (see Coolidge, *Pauline Renaissance in England*, 1–22).

40. John Selden, *Of the Original of Ecclesiastical Jurisdictions of Testaments*, 9, published posthumously with separate pagination in *Tracts* (London, 1683).

41. Swinburne, 320r; and 74 Eng. Rep. 1120. For the analogous case of evidentiary law, where the nuanced civil law calibrations of presumptions and proofs was adapted within common law courts (and the Renaissance stage), see Lorna Hutson, *The Invention of Suspicion* (Oxford: Oxford University Press, 2007).

42. Giorgio Agamben discusses Rom. 13:9 and especially Paul's term "recapitulation" (which may be compared to Donne's "Abridgment") as "the other facet of the typological relation established by messianic kairos between present and past" (*The Time that Remains*, trans., Patricia Dailey [Stanford: Stanford University Press, 2005], 76).

43. Cormack, *A Power to Do Justice*, 2–3.

44. A further analogy, if not source, may be found in the medieval Charter of Christ poems, which literalizes the language of Col. 2:14 and imagines the crucifixion as a legal document (Christ's body is the parchment, his blood is the ink, etc.). In one version of the Charter's reddendo (a "clause in a charter which specifies the duty to be paid to the superior" [*OED*]), Christ Himself is made to say: "Keep I no more for all my smart but true Love, and that thou be in charity" (Mary Caroline Spalding, ed., *The Middle English Charters of Christ* [Bryn Mawr: Bryn Mawr College, 1914], liv). For some uses of the Charter of Christ in later Protestant writings, see Janel Mueller, "Complications of Intertextuality: John Fisher, Katherine Parr, and The Book of the Crucifix," in *Representing Women in Renaissance England,* ed. Claude Summers and Ted-Larry Pebworth (Columbia: University of Missouri Press, 1997), 24–41.

45. See Slavoj Žižek, *The Puppet and the Dwarf* (Cambridge, Mass.: The MIT Press, 2003), 93–121; especially apt here is Žižek's discussion of "the paradoxical place of Love with regard to All" (115).

46. John Cowell, *The Interpreter* (1607), *sub* 'Abridge,' sig. A3r; quoted in Jeremy Maule, "Donne and the Words of the Law," in *John Donne's Professional Lives,* ed. David Colclough (Cambridge: D. S. Brewer, 2003), 19–36 at 33. Maule's brilliant but incomplete essay was published posthumously from his extended notes.

47. Maule, "Donne and the Words of the Law," 34 (italics original).

48. Coolidge, *Pauline Renaissance in England,* 142.

13

Samson Uncircumcised

JONATHAN GOLDBERG

> Targeting civilians is a negation of every possible school of Sunni Islam. Suicide bomb-
> ing is so foreign to the Quranic ethos that the Prophet Samson is entirely absent from
> our scriptures.
>
> ABDAL-HAKIM MURAD, *"Recapturing Islam from the Terrorists"*

In Milton's *Samson Agonistes*, the difference between the Israelites and the
Philistines is marked by circumcision. Milton does not invent this mode
of differentiation, of course; it can be found in various books of the Bible,
including Judges. Twice in the Samson chapters, but unemphatically, the
Philistines are called uncircumcised, first when Samson's parents complain
about his taking "a wife of the uncircumcised Philistines" in choosing the
woman of Timnath (14:3), later, when, after one of his victories, Samson
worries that he might die of thirst "and fall into the hand of the uncircumcised" (15:18). Milton uses the term more frequently in his poem, and with
greater emphasis.[1] Lambasting his fellow Israelites for delivering him up to
the Philistines, yielding him "To the uncircumcised a welcome prey" (260),
Samson's use of the epithet as a mode of derogation extends to his vilification
of the Israelites, who are represented as no less perfidious than the enemy to
whom they deliver their would-be deliverer. Similarly, when Samson declares
that his mission is "Against the uncircumcised, our enemies" (640), his statement occurs in the midst of a review of his career against them that is also
the story of his being "cast off" (641), a story, that is, in which he sees himself
as the enemy; it is among them that he perishes, "inmixed" and "tangled in
the fold," "a Nazarite in place abominable" (1658, 1665, 1359). But even before
he ends among the Philistines, as he is reminded by the Chorus, supposed
friends who nonetheless often add to Samson's miseries, his labor at the mill
at Gaza is service performed for the Philistines who are succinctly described
as "Idolatrous, uncircumcised, unclean" (1363). The three words are various
ways of saying the same thing and spell out what is condensed in being uncircumcised: standing against the worship of the true God and being filthy.
"Uncircumcised" is a metonym.

In perfect quid pro quo, the difference marked by the term "uncircum-cised" is flung back at Samson; Dalila answers his final charge that she will be reviled by saying that while her name "perhaps among the circumcised . . . may stand defamed" (975–77), the fickleness of fame does not give to "the circumcised" some special purchase on truth. The relativity that she under-scores is conveyed even more forcefully a bit later when Harapha wishes for a definitive Philistine victory over "the unforeskinned race, of whom [Sam-son] bear'st / The highest name for valiant acts" (1100–01). "Unforeskinned" marks something lacking in the condition of circumcision, which had been contrasted elsewhere to the something lacking in uncircumcision. The move-ment of the negative from "uncircumcised" to "unforeskinned" points to a parallel logic of part for whole, lack for completion. That meaning of circum-cision can be seen in the first passage marking Jewish/Philistine difference in the poem in what is undoubtedly the most provocative phrasing the poem offers. The Chorus is summoning up the great deeds of the now humili-ated, captive, and blind hero. His slaughter of the Philistines with the "trivial weapon" (142) of the jawbone of an ass is celebrated in this memorable line: "A thousand foreskins fell, the flower of Palestine" (144). This inquiry is prompted by that line.

It also prompted Roy Flannagan, editor of the 1998 Riverside Milton, to post an online query. Flannagan's posting lays out straightforwardly the quandary the line offers and also manages to suggest something of the charge it can have. "The subject," circumcision, Flannagan opines, "is no doubt painful," a delicious understatement, since it's not just the subject that hurts; "and especially to the uncircumcised," he continues:

> I have been wondering about it for years, ever since, in the fourth grade of an Episcopalian prep-school, my religion teacher told an awe-inspired class of all-boys that the Israelites in battle enumerated their slain and bragged about their kill by cutting off the foreskins of their enemies and displaying them in their tents after battle. My suggestible pre-teen mind immediately formed an image that I have never forgotten, of the inside of an Israelite battle tent with its little clothesline of foreskins . . . to brag about, a little like the lines of beads that count scores in a pool hall.

We could pause here, but as he turns to editorial business, affect is not left behind, so I continue: "I have to make a note on the passage in *Samson Ago-nistes*, for the edition I am working on," he writes:

> I am not embarrassed by the passage but I am confused. Do the foreskins stand for the fallen Philistines, by synecdoche, the (yuck!) part standing for the whole, as in Alastair Fowler's note (1968 Longman edition), in which he

identifies "foreskins" as "uncircumcised Philistines" (1968)? Or are those foreskins *real* foreskins that Samson bothered to cut off, rather fastidiously, after the battle?[2]

In his edition, Flannagan opted for what I suppose could be called the literal meaning of the line, imagining that Samson performed a postmortem operation on the thousand dead Philistines; the Riverside edition cites as a precedent the moment in 1 Samuel 18:27 when David delivers two hundred foreskins to oblige—and terrorize—Saul, who had demanded as brideprice for his daughter that David bring him one hundred foreskins from dead Philistines. Flannagan's literalizing decision accommodates his Episcopalian "all-boy" fantasy, which seems to combine a game of cowboys and Indians with male pool hall bravado. He much prefers this scene to the one he regards with distaste, the reading chosen by Fowler, in which the Philistines become their foreskins, a reductive synecdoche whose yuckiness for the Riverside editor presumably involves some of the distasteful uncleanness registered by the foreskin in Milton's poem. The painfulness of the subject, as Flannagan's posting suggests, cannot be separated from the worrisome prospect, from his normative male and Christian viewpoint, of being turned into the remnants of a mutilated penis. "I am not embarrassed by the passage," Flannagan insists, "but I am confused." Intellectually, the confusion is about the literal and the figurative, especially when the figure is synecdoche, and the whole person becomes an abject bit of skin; the intellectual dilemma is further exacerbated since the nomination "unforeskinned" serves as a vehicle of vituperation that is not merely verbal. And indeed, this is conveyed by the conjunction of foreskin and flower in the line, for when the foreskins fall so do "the flower of Palestine." The line conveys defloration even as it values the abject part as flower, "flower" itself a metonymy that metaphorizes the cut down enemy youth.[3] Flannagan's declared lack of embarrassment signals that he is untroubled by the sexual implications of this scene even as the forthright claim not to be embarrassed also fails to say what might be embarrassing in a confrontation in which one man faces another over the battlefield of the cut or uncut penis.

Perhaps the strangest thing the line does is have Samson circumcise the enemy; literally postmortem, if the line is literal, figuratively if not.[4] Killed, humiliated, the Philistines become physically equivalent to the Israelites. A painful operation marks them as among the chosen even as they are debased. This is congruent with the crossing of friend and enemy that we have noted already. If the marker of difference is not quite able to secure difference, this also might help explain the question of Milton's choice of subject for his final published poem, and his identification with Samson. Much of the criticism on *Samson Agonistes* assumes that the identification is entirely negative, that the strongman is condemned for his final act of violence as well as for succumbing to Dalila. Yet, Milton's identification with a blind hero who makes disastrous marriage choices and is alienated politically can't be simply negative; it is, crudely put, Milton's story too; moreover, the poem contains some of Milton's most powerful writing. Interpretively, the question of identification for Milton might be akin to Flannagan's: how is the Christian male, with his foreskin intact, to identify with the circumcised Jew? Or, to put it the other way round, what function can a Jewish hero play for a Christian writer? For, of course, it goes without saying—I am stating the obvious—that it is not only Jewish/Palestinian difference that is marked by circumcision; Jewish/Christian difference is as well.[5] In this doubling, the mark of difference passes from one of its negations to the other. Whereas in *Samson Agonistes*, uncircumcision is a sign of idolatry and filth, the opposite is the case in Christianity. How is Milton attached to his circumcised, foreskinless hero?

The simplest answer to this question would be that Samson is a type of Christ, the Nazarite an anticipation of the Nazarene.[6] Some critics of the poem countenance a typological reading of *Samson Agonistes*, others do not, but the existence of a typological connection cannot be disputed. The most commonplace (if startling) typology equates Samson carrying the gates with Christ's resurrection.[7] The Chorus in *Samson Agonistes* might not be indulging in typology when it passes seamlessly from the slaughter of the Philistines with the trivial weapon to carrying the gates; their narration connects the feats by way of a "then," "Then by main force pulled up, and on his shoulders bore / The gates of Azza" (146–47); two separate events seem simply connected to each other by a sequential logic. However, much as this appears to be the case, it is not straightforward chronology that moves the account from an "ass" to "Azza" (143, 147). *Samson Agonistes* is a poem in which most significant things happen twice. An angel descends twice to announce the extraordinary birth of the promised deliverer; Samson understands this figurally, believing that "all foretold" would "have been fulfilled" had he not failed (44–45). At the end of the play, an officer comes twice to command Samson's presence at the Philistine feast. Samson first refuses to go, then agrees. And, of course, the most spectacularly doubled events of the poem are Samson's two marriages, first to the woman of Timna, then to Dalila. The Chorus asks Samson why he seems to prefer sleeping with the enemy; he explains that the first marriage was prompted by an "intimate impulse" "of God" (221–22), while the second was a repetition of the first: "I thought it lawful from my former act" (231).

The difference between Jew and Christian is marked by the relation to the law; circumcision is a sign of the covenant attaching the Jews to the deity, binding them to God's law. The repetitions in *Samson Agonistes* may be offered as if they are merely a chronological and sequential one-two, but they cross the law. Indeed, the Chorus remarks of Samson's carrying of the gates that it was "no journey of a sabbath-day" (149), that it violates the injunction against labor on the Sabbath much in the way that the entire play, including Samson's final agon, takes place during a holiday. Samson balks at going with the officer, at first insisting to the Chorus that his labor for the Philistines at the mill is not the idolatrous labor being demanded of him on this holiday. "Our law forbids" such service, he tells the officer (1320), and then relents, claiming that God may "dispense" with him as he chooses (1378). The model for this dispensation is precisely the new dispensation under which, as the Chorus puts it, contemplating Samson's untoward marriages, God "with his own laws can best dispense" (314). The seconding of an event would seem to be at once its repetition and its undoing, often bearing the further implication that the first instance was governed by the rule of the second. Samson carries the gates in violation of the law; he marries against the law; and what he thinks was lawful by the precedent was lawful precisely by not being so.

Another way to put this would be to say that the first event, even as it is literally what it is, also figures the second. This means that what appears to be happening, indeed what does happen in the most visible and apparent way, is not from a typological perspective what it appears to be. "Who are these?" (110), Samson asks of the enemies he imagines he hears approaching, who turn out to be his fellow Israelites, nominally his friends. "This is he," they report of Samson, but within ten lines they take it back; "Can this be he," they ask (116, 124). "Is this the man, / The invincible Samson," his father also asks when he appears (340). The figure who serves as the object of every gaze, available to be seen precisely because he cannot see, seems also to be invisible. This is a condition that extends beyond himself.[8] "But who is this" is the first question raised by the arrival of Dalila; in the eyes of the Chorus she is some "thing of sea or land" ("Female of sex it seems," they continue [710–11]). So, too with Harapha, the last to appear: the Chorus announces Harapha's arrival as a storm, and Samson counters, "Be less abstruse, my riddling days are past" (1064). It would simplify things to say that the one-two of *Samson Agonistes* is riddle and then solution; for the solution remains a riddle. As Milton cryptically declares in the headnote to the text, "It suffices if the whole drama be found not produced beyond the fifth act" (p. 672). The redeemer does not appear; the play remains as an obscure figure. This might be another way of saying that the play remains literal. Or that in its typology it renders moot the difference between the literal and the figurative. And, of course, so doing, it remains within the vexed orbit of circumcision. For however real circumcision is, it also is a sign; in Pauline accounts, which proved decisive for marking Jewish-Christian difference, literal circumcision is no longer required but a circumcision of the heart is instead. This would be a matter of simple replacement of spirit for flesh, inward for outward, were it not for the fact that circumcision is, from the first, a figure.

Moreover, Jewish circumcision cannot be entirely effaced, turned into Christian uncircumcision, or entirely metaphorized as a spiritual condition, if only because Jesus himself, according to Luke 2:21, was circumcised. Early in his career, Milton attempted and failed to complete a poem on the central event of Christianity, the crucifixion; he did succeed with "Upon the Circumcision." The poem presents the circumcision as a figure of the crucifixion; the infant "now bleeds to give us ease" (11) in anticipation of the final "wounding smart" (25) to be delivered on the cross. The riddle presented by the event is precisely the place where figure becomes fulfillment: "O more exceeding love or law more just? / Just law indeed, but more exceeding love" (15–16). Somehow by asking and answering the question in the same words, the equation of law and love also displaces the terms in a movement of "more" that is more than a mark of quantification. Circumcision, as Jill Robbins has put the point succinctly, "serves as both the literal and that which makes possible the difference between the literal and the figurative."[9] Or, to go one step further, it makes impossible that difference even as it serves to mark it and secure it.

The circumcision sets the Son onto the violent path of expiation for human sin, and the return of Son to Father. In English poetry, the double affect of the event is best found in one of Crashaw's poems on the circumcision, "Our Lord in his Circumcision to his Father." In this poem, the infant speaks, inviting the father to "tast" (3) "these first fruits of my growing death" (1).[10] The offer of blood, "these purple buds of blooming death" (9), of course, is part of the circumcision—the mohel stanches the wound by taking the bloody penis in his mouth. Crashavian erotics do not stop here; the mohel's knife makes its way into the final line of Crashaw's poem, sealing the typological thrust of the event: "this knife may be the speares *Proeludium*" (12), the poem concludes. Cutting off becomes penetrating; outside becomes inside. Sucking the penis and thrusting in the spear seem congruent with each other.

"This, this is he; softly awhile, / Let us not break in upon him" (115–16).

"Out of the eater came forth meat, and out of the strong came forth sweetness" (Judges 14:14).

Is the second event already in the first? Circumcision figures crucifixion; removal of the foreskin—to go no further—is its restitution. This can be seen most spectacularly in the images that fill Leo Steinberg's *The Sexuality of Christ in Renaissance Art and Modern Oblivion.*[11] Steinberg's book is not so much about sexuality as it is about genitality, how the embodiment of Jesus is marked insistently by the genital. Steinberg gathers numerous images of the baby Jesus, his penis always on display. (And always, it seems, uncircumcised.) Most stunning are the images of the crucified Christ, where resurrection is more than intimated by the erect penis. Yet even in these images of an aroused Jesus what is shown is not his penis but elaborate folds, and despite the exuberance of images of swirling, flying, voluminous drapery, the penis remains covered. These paintings therefore do not quite deliver what Steinberg claims, "a phallic erection" (298), or, if they do, it is because "phallic" here is being used figuratively. Drapery for phallus; folds of cloth for foreskin: metonymic relations. A veil covers, one whose folds might just as easily suggest, in the logic of the fetish, the absence of the penis, just as the folds might read as labial, the female prepuce, the clitoral hood:

> But who is this, what thing of sea or land?
> Female of sex it seems,
> That so bedecked, ornate, and gay,
> Comes this way sailing . . .
> With all her bravery on, and tackle trim,
> Sails filled, and streamers waving,
> Courted by all the winds that hold them play . . .
> (710–13, 717–19)

Dalila's role continues the thematics of circumcision, for her shearing Samson's hair and his blinding are castrative gestures, and circumcision might well figure castration; removal of the part could figure removal of the organ entirely. Samson's special relation to God is marked, we know, in his hair; as a person separate to God, he has been enjoined from cutting it. On his head the uncut hair functions much as the circumcised penis does to mark the special relationship of the Jews to God. In doubling this relationship, the cut is reversed since it is the uncut hair that functions as will the uncircumcised uncut penis in the new dispensation. In revealing his secret to Dalila, he makes himself doubly vulnerable even as his double condition is intimated; for Samson's fault is the revelation of a secret within that is not evidently connected to his uncut hair.

He is his riddle.

Mantegna's painting of the slack hero, head buried in Dalila's lap, that adorns the cover of the Riverside Milton, whether chosen or not by Roy Flannagan, perhaps registers, in displaced form, what he felt no embarrassment about thinking about circumcision. The painting answers to Milton's imagery when Samson describes his fall to "fair fallacious looks, venereal trains" to "lay [his] head and hallowed pledge / Of all [his] strength in the lascivious lap / Of a deceitful concubine who shore me / Like a tame wether" (533, 534–37).[12] Samson literalizes his haircut as castration by way of the wether who also figures the lamb; the metaphorization of the shearing of his head as castration perhaps metaphorizes circumcision. Indeed, it has been claimed that when biblical texts refer to circumcision—as in the scene of David removing foreskins—they euphemize a less fastidious battle practice (to recall Flannagan's nice term), the castration of the enemy.[13] The scene of castration in *Samson Agonistes* becomes a scene of displaced phallic discharge. For it is when he is "swoll'n with pride" (532) that Samson falls into the snare and is cut off. Phallically swollen, he reveals himself as a woman, blabbing his secret relationship to God.

Samson laments the "effeminacy" (410) that yokes him in sexual enslavement to Dalila; she, like the Philistines, as a Philistine, is "unclean" (323), unclean as a foreskin. In sleeping with the enemy, Samson undergoes an experience like that of the Sechemites whose history is told in Genesis 34. They had asked to marry Israeli women.[14] Pretending to agree to this enemy alliance, the Israelites insist that their future sons-in-law be circumcised; once the operation has been performed, and the men have been made proper men, fellows to the tribe of the circumcised, they are also debilitated; the Israelites finish the act by killing them. Sexual potency and impotence cross, as they do when Samson and Dalila argue about their shared condition of weakness; to be effeminate is to be overinvested in women. It is to be a woman or to want women too much; for the male, arousal, phallic strength is its register; perhaps for the female too who comes sailing into the play.

"How could I once look up, or heave the head, / Who like a foolish pilot have shipwrecked my vessel" (197–99): Samson's question is answered, as is the case throughout the poem, by the crossing of the imagery into enemy territory when Dalila sails into view. Samson, pledged to God, pledges him his hair; as a sign of their relationship, he gives it to him by not giving it up; it remains uncut. But the hair, like circumcision, is also a sign of a secret that lies within. It is not just literal, although it is literally the case that without his hair Samson cannot perform. When Dalila shears his head, she also reveals his "capital secret" (394). That is, she unsheathes him, and shows what the sign covered. Shows, that is, that the literal is a sign. Revealing his head, she reveals what was otherwise not to be seen. In effect—in fact?—she circumcises him.

And, as usual, in these heady exchanges, the valences by which we would know the difference between the figurative and the literal, circumcision and castration, male and female, cross. Dalila's betrayal mirrors her husband's way of loving his enemies, marrying them. The argument that he makes to Dalila, and again to Harapha, that he loves the enemy, seems more like the way the Israelites loved the Sechemites: loved them to destroy them as enemies. Circumcision is the sign to Abraham of a potency that is figured as generative, and not merely figured since the aged "father of many nations" (Gen. 17:5) also fathers Isaac as a sign of the promise. Yet, circumcision is a sign of a potency that requires impotence. Samson apparently gives himself to God, but is prompted to marry the enemy. The "intimate impulse" for the woman of Timna (223) is a motion of God. In keeping him for himself, God is nonetheless willing to share him—with unclean women, with unclean men. The bond with God would seem at the same time to violate the very specialness and separateness of the Nazarite condition, not to mention the marking of the chosen people. Much as Samson refuses to touch Dalila, Harapha refuses to touch him, although Samson yearns for his touch as much as he does for Dalila's (it is because of his desire for her that he would not touch her, because his desire for her would lead him to destroy her). These impulses of desire and their violent repudiation can be associated with circumcision as, at once, a limitation of sex and of sexual pleasure, and, at the same time, a guarantee of sex, of potency for God. As Daniel Boyarin notes, circumcision is the sign of the Jewish male's erotic relationship with God; as he also says, it carries with it a threat of effeminization.[15] This may be Boyarin's way of stating and sidestepping the homoerotics of the relationship. For, as we have already seen, at least in Milton's poem, erection can be the sign of effeminacy.

When we first see Samson, the Chorus notes his "languished head unpropped" (119); when we first see Dalila, the Chorus surveys her "head declined / Like a fair flower surcharged with dew" (729). The Philistine flower has migrated here, the flaccid head a sign of a previous discharge, a sign thereby of potency. In the crossing represented by circumcision, some kind of generative strength is promised precisely by a cut. Weakness and strength cross, and with them the signs of gendered difference. Undoubtedly, Milton's poem is filled with a hatred of women, but as in *Paradise Lost*, it also attempts to turn that hatred upon the masculine self. But in so doing, it marks what is hateful in the male as feminine, his "effeminization," and thereby continues its assault. This is, at least, what is most apparent in the poem. But in the logic I have been seeking to expose by way of circumcision, gendered difference, like Jewish-Philistine difference, remains less easily differentiated.

As his "thorn intestine" (1037) and "bosom snake" (763–64), as the one who has shown the way to love the enemy, Dalila is interchangeable with Samson, his repetition and his self-difference, the difference between inner and outer which is the structure of the riddle, of typological sequence, of the relationship between circumcision and uncircumcison, friend and enemy, Israel and its other.[16] William Empson remains almost the only critic to side entirely with Dalila. Empson fastens on the moment when Dalila likens herself to Jael, "who with inhospitable guile / Smote Sisera sleeping through temples nailed" (989–90), as "decisive proof . . . that [Milton] alleged no moral superiority for Jehovah's religion over Dagon's."[17] Dalila, for Empson, is preferable as a wronged wife giving her husband what he deserved. Dalila takes her cue from Samson; Samson takes his from his religious fanaticism, from the "rebel doctrine of the Inner Light" (217), as Empson puts it, pointing to the antinomianism that clings to the lawbreaking hero that defines that place in which opposites cross into each other in the play.

We approach here what has been the major point of critical controversy about *Samson Agonistes* ever since John Carey, in an issue of *TLS* commemorating the first anniversary of 9/11, declared that Milton's Samson was akin to the terrorist hijackers who brought down the twin towers.[18] Such a sentiment echoes Empson, who also has no use for Milton's hero—he calls him a lunatic—and it is echoed by many other critics as well for whom Samson's final act, bringing down the roof on thousands of innocent Philistines, is unforgivable—or, if forgivable is so only if understood as divinely sanctioned. The understanding adduced may be attributed to Milton, or may be the critic's own belief. Critics who are sure that the final cataclysm of the poem can't be countenanced by Milton assert that Milton's humanism would not tolerate intolerable Jewish violence. Critics who view the final catastrophe with equanimity define a good Christian form of lawbreaking to be contrasted with bad antinomianism.[19] Feisal Mohamed in an essay that appeared in *PMLA* in 2005 handily answers Milton's critics—both those who find Samson deplorable as well as those who find him free of negative judgment insofar as the inscrutable mystery of the play is placed in God's hands.[20] For Mohamed, God is not so inscrutable; he is the justifying name for a deplorable religious violence that Mohamed wishes to extend beyond Islamic terrorism to its Christian counterpart. *Samson Agonistes* can be read to further such an argument, even if the intention of the poem is to give support to a Christian violence that would render moot the difference between loving your enemy and destroying him. This, indeed, would correspond to the structure of typology as Kathleen Biddick has recently described it, in which the Jews have a place in Christian history only to be annihilated and replaced, to become merely figural.[21] Biddick finds circumcision to figure the cutting off of the Jews even as she insists that "no cut is ever a clean one" (75). A remnant remains to trouble the figural design, not merely in the literal existence that supersedes the violent removal but also within the typological imaginary itself, haunted by the continual process of figuration. The time of typology is not one.[22]

Such an understanding must trouble readings of the play like Julia Lupton's that regard Dalila as Samson's "accomplished snare," as a form of the flesh tantamount to a Jewish carnality that can never deliver on the promise of a Pauline universality. "When Samson . . . suffers trimming at the hands of Dalila, the motif of circumcision continues to sharpen the brutal edge of the law at the expense of its symbolic functioning," Lupton writes.[23] For Lupton, Pauline universality is assimilable to democratic citizenship, whereas the Judaism of the play represents a particularism and tribalism that she deplores. This view is congruent with Carey's; for him, as Mohamed points out, Samson is an "'outmoded' Jewish hero denounced in a Christian poem."[24] It's not Milton's humanism that separates him from Samson but his disgust for the Old Testament figure; Milton's Jewish hero is *eo ipse* insupportable. Adding a further twist to this, Carey's likening of Samson to Arab terrorists extends the anti-Semitic argument. But Mohamed's argument, even as he deplores the assumption that Christianity is incapable of violence, supports the notion that Milton's poem must offer a Samson who breaks with the Old Law and with a carnality found in his relationship with Dalila. "We are reminded in the flyting between the circumcised and the uncircumcised," Mohamed writes of Samson's confrontation with Harapha, "that Samson's achievements are those of the flesh rather than the spirit" (331). Like Lupton, Mohamed insists that for Samson to be a Christian hero he must transcend "tribal, legalistic terms" to achieve "the universality of the gospels" (331). Unlike Lupton, however, Mohamed refuses this universality, seeing it as an ideological ploy that requires vilification of the Other (338) for a violence that, Mohamed insists, is to be found in Milton's radical Christian beliefs.

Lupton holds up Pauline citizenship as the political good to be contrasted with Samson's terroristic behavior. Other critics of Milton extol his republicanism. Republicanism is not democracy, however, rather a form of government that posits an elite that knows best; it is manifest in Milton's *Ready and Easy Way* when he advocates minority rule; the minority is for Milton those who have the inner light and who are thereby relieved of any law but the Christian liberty that is the new dispensation. Milton's position derives from Paul—his assurance that to the pure all things are pure. This is not the universalist Pauline citizenship that Lupton admires. If Christian violence is the most immediate source for Milton's politics, it's not merely religious violence, as Mohamed suggests, that is the question posed by terrorism. Mohamed handily links Milton's republicanism to an elitism that is defined by religious beliefs, and extends it in essays subsequent to and related to his *PMLA* piece to the defense of violence that was the hallmark of the Bush administration's war on terror.[25] In this work he gestures tentatively to secular humanism as the answer to the divisions wrought by religion. However, as Benedict Robinson argues persuasively in *Islam and Early Modern English Literature*, such a gesture of differentiation on the basis of religious difference is a founding one for political difference.[26] In the early modern period, Robinson writes, "Islamic fanaticism helped to invent modern politics" (147). The state claims its power precisely in the state of exception, its power to abrogate the law, as Carl Schmitt argued, and as Robinson reminds us (168); the foundational violence at the heart of state sovereignty is entangled in religious violence. Although the state—in the name of law and order—seeks to mark its difference from the irrationality of religious violence, it cannot secure that difference, for it is its complicity with it that marks the state's formation, and its blindness to that complicity that allows it to condemn in others what is its own support, what Robinson succinctly states as "the secret complicity of political modernity with the sacred violence it claimed to expel" (147).

Milton, in *Tenure of Kings and Magistrates*, argues that no ruler is safe from the people. The tract could seem to simply enunciate democratic politics, but Milton is also adamant about dividing the people into those who have the right to rule and separating them from those who don't. He instances Ehud, the man who under pretense of hospitality kills the enemy, to insist that what Ehud exemplifies is not a division between friend and enemy, but a division within:

> He, therefore, that keeps peace with me, near or remote, of whatsoever nation, is to me, as far as all civil and human offices, an Englishman and a neighbour: but if an Englishman, forgetting all laws, human, civil and religious, offend against life and liberty, to him offended, and to the law in his behalf, though born of the same womb, he is no better than a Turk, a Saracen, a heathen. (285)

Milton would seem to be affirming a universality, a brotherhood beyond nation: but it is a brotherhood that is based on a difference so violent that someone who might literally be my brother or sister is here expelled to the nonexistence of the Turk. National belonging and coming from "the same womb," shared humanity and mortal existence, are repudiated in the name of a universality that is itself a figure for a saving remnant. Milton's contemplation of what the story of Ehud signifies for a revolutionary politics explains how *Samson Agonistes* can be a play that traffics in the most violent and invidious differences and yet constantly suggests that difference is unsustainable. Ehud's story is both Samson's and Dalila's. The reading that I have been offering seizes upon the promise of indifference, of difference within sameness, but in the hope of thinking it without the violence that produces sameness by obliterating difference.

To conclude this inquiry in the orbit of circumcision, its relationship to the penis and its various substitutes—in *Samson Agonistes*, the head in which the secret is found and revealed and covered—ponder the image in *Areopagitica* of revolutionary violence: "Methinks I see in my mind a noble and puissant nation rousing herself like a strong man after sleep, and shaking her invincible locks" (267). Samson gendered as Dalila. This figuration goes beyond supposed natural difference. At the end of the play Samson feels again "rousing motions" (1382) that are akin to the "intimate impulse" that had led him to the woman of Timna, and then again to Dalila; the law of his member is impossible to distinguish from his giving of himself—in what Manoa imagines as filial submission (Manoa does not know that Samson's father is in heaven; critics who worry whether Samson's final act is a murderous and deplorable human desire or a divine prompting wish to separate what the play cannot).[27] "At last, with head erect" (1639), the "one who prayed, / Or some great matter in his mind revolved" (1637–38) speaks in defiant double-speak, riddler again, to the Philistines:

> Hitherto, lords, what your commands imposed
> I have performed, as reason was, obeying,
> Not without wonder or delight beheld.
> Now of my own accord such o ther trial
> I mean to how you of my strength, yet greater;
> As with amaze shall strike all who behold.
>
> (1640–45)

This is the moment when Samson is about to pay "the rigid score" (510), offering a "rigid satisfaction" (*Paradise Lost* 3.212) akin to what the Father demands from the Son. It was this Christian violence that Empson so powerfully saw in Milton and could not believe that Milton did not see and deplore. The Father wants the Son dead, fully. For him this lasts but three days, until the resurrection; for us, we are dead until the end of time, and in any case, life after death is not life. Milton's play does not get past the fifth act, for were it to do that, it would be at that ultimate end, and the figures would finally be fulfilled in an ending that would also be total obliteration. Earl on could not come through on a poem on the crucifixion, nor could he at the end of his career face more directly the unspeakable act at the heart of Christianity. He comes as close as he can bear in his last published poem when the final erect Samson strains to break the pillars. Dalila dreamt of bringing Samson home to have him once again all to herself, "whole to myself" (809) is how she puts it. "I should enjoy thee day and night, / Mine and love's prisoner" (807–8). In the past, too, she had wanted nothing more than to "hold thee to me firmest" (795). Dalila says she speaks "love's law" (811), and that law might also be the way the Father loves the Son. In Milton's poem, Manoa dreams Dalila's dream too, enunciating a "father's love" (1506) in which the son, blind, infantilized, would be nursed; Manoa dreams this dream even as he sees without seeing what sprouts on his son's head, "hair . . . like a camp of faithful soldiery" (1576–77), Milton's dream in *Areopagitica;* no dream there, he had an army to back him, as he did a few years later advocating cutting off the king's head. Terroristic violence and this erotic scene are inextricable in Milton. Hard for God.

Notes

1. Thomas Luxon, *Single Imperfection* (Pittsburgh: Duquesne University Press, 2005) notes that Samson is "significantly" circumcised (158); the significance consists in his manly relationship to God, as contrasted to his relationship to Dalila. All Milton citations are from *John Milton: The Major Works,* ed. Stephen Orgel and Jonathan Goldberg (Oxford: Oxford University Press, 1991), line numbers for verse, page numbers for prose.

2. http://digitalhumanities.org/humanist/Archives/Converted_Text/humanist.1990-1991.txt; accessed 28 October 2011.

3. Gordon Teskey, *Delirious Milton* (Cambridge, Mass.: Harvard University Press, 2006), 194–95, comments on this figurative conjunction as pointing to a contamination of the figurative by the literal, where literality is a heap of the dead, or a heap of dead (fore)skins. The combination of death and circumcision may also relate to the widespread claim, documented by James Shapiro, *Shakespeare and the Jews* (New York: Columbia University Press, 1996), 113, that Jews circumcised Christian boys before killing them.

4. Michael Lieb, "'A Thousand Fore-Skins': Circumcision, Violence, and Selfhood in Milton," *Milton Studies* 36 (2000) declares Samson "the greatest *mohel* of all time" (198) in performing this act upon the Philistines; he makes clear that he means this ironically, participating in the conflicted view of violence he ascribes to Milton (see 211 especially, where ironic connections between circumcising Jews and slaughtering Philistines are posited in order not to make identifications between the acts). Julia Reinhard Lupton, *Citizen-Saints* (Chicago: University of Chicago Press, 2005) likewise views Samson's act as "a kind of mass enforced circumcision" tied to "the brutal edge of the law" (190) that makes Samson a fully negative exemplar of an unredeemed and unredeemable violence.

5. On "uncircumcision" as a Pauline figure, see Shapiro, *Shakespeare and the Jews,* 128–30. In "'The People of Asia and with Them the Jews': Israel, Asia, and England in Milton's Writings," in *Milton and the Jews,* ed. Douglas A. Brooks (Cambridge: Cambridge University Press, 2008), 172–77, Rachel Trubowitz notes the identifications of Jew and Philistine in *Samson Agonistes,* which she reads as pointing to a Christian universalism that would overcome difference, and which she sees as the explanation of Milton's ambivalent antipathy to "others."

6. F. Michael Krouse, *Milton's Samson and the Christian Tradition* (Princeton: Princeton University Press, 1949), 42, provides the basic information, including Isidore of Seville's paral-

leling Nazarite and Nazarene. In *Milton and the Rabbis* (New York: Columbia University Press, 2001), 243, Jeffrey Shoulson notes Milton's uses of typology both to posit a metonymic continuity from Old to New Testaments and as a metaphoric substitution to mark the break between old and new dispensations; Shoulson sees this use of typology as in the service of "homogeneity and heterogeneity," a point congruent with the argument I offer.

7. For this, see Rosemond Tuve, *A Reading of George Herbert* (Chicago: University of Chicago Press, 1952), 160, by way of an explanation of Herbert's "Sunday"; Krouse indicates the Augustinian invention of the connection between carrying the doors and resurrection after the harrowing of Hell (*Milton's Samson*, 41; the equivalent of Hell in the Samson story is the harlot's bed from which Samson leaves exiting Gaza).

8. On blindness as a making vulnerable to the gaze, see Jacques Derrida, *Memoirs of the Blind* (Chicago: University of Chicago Press, 1993), 106–9, a discussion of Samson that includes Milton's poem and treats such availability to be seen under the sign of castration.

9. Jill Robbins, "Circumcising Confession: Derrida, Autobiography, Judaism," *diacritics* 25.4 (1995): 34. As Robbins points out, the Pauline turning of circumcision into a figure is already to be found in Old Testament uses of the circumcision of the heart and mouth.

10. Citations from *The Poems of Richard Crashaw*, ed. L. C. Martin (Oxford: Clarendon Press, 1957), 99.

11. Citations from Leo Steinberg, *The Sexuality of Christ in Renaissance Art and Modern Oblivion*, 2d ed. (Chicago: University of Chicago Press, 1996). As part of his argument how "the genuineness of the Incarnation is put to proof in the sexual member" (57), Steinberg discusses Christ's circumcision on 49–64, emphasizing its typological meaning in Christian patristics beginning with Augustine and how the circumcised penis figures the weakness of the flesh sacrificed on the cross. He examines one Renaissance painting of the circumcision, Mantegna's, noting the double logic of fulfilling and abrogating the law, and interprets the typological thrust of a number of texts, including Milton's and Crashaw's poems.

12. Shapiro, *Shakespeare and the Jews*, argues that Shylock's bond of flesh could involve a castrative cut, matched by Antonio calling himself a "'tainted wether' or castrated ram" (120), Samson's figure as well for himself.

13. David L. Gollaher, *Circumcision* (New York: Basic Books, 2000), 12.

14. In *Blood Relations* (Chicago: University of Chicago Press, 2008), 104, Janet Adelman notes by way of this biblical story that circumcision is meant to be a mark forbidding marriage outside the tribe.

15. Daniel Boyarin, "'This We Know to be the Carnal Israel': Circumcision and the Erotic Life of God and Israel," *Critical Inquiry* 18.3 (spring 1992): 495; Boyarin writes here as if the possibility of an erotic life for Israel and God can be understood as male effeminacy, circumcision as castration.

16. For considerations of the intimate relationship of Samson and Dalila, see Herman Rapaport, *Milton and the Postmodern* (Lincoln: University of Nebraska Press, 1983), chap. 5, where the connection is made by way of castration, and Jackie DiSalvo, "Intestine Thorn: Samson's Struggle with the Woman Within," in *Milton and the Idea of Woman*, ed. Julia M. Walker (Urbana: University of Illinois Press, 1988), 211–29, where Samson (and Milton) are shown to be in the grips of a patriarchal refusal of the feminine.

17. William Empson, *Milton's God* (Cambridge: Cambridge University Press, 1981), chap. 6, at 221.

18. John Carey, "A Work in Praise of Terrorism?" *TLS* (Sept. 6, 2002): 16–17. Alan Rudrum, "Milton Scholarship and the *Agon* over *Samson Agonistes*," *Huntington Library Quarterly* 65.3–4 (2002): 465–88, reviews scholarship from what he regards as Carey's misguided position, to argue for a Christian view that finds Samson exemplary.

19. See, for example, Norman T. Burns, "'Then Stood Up Phinehas': Milton's Antinomianism, and Samson's," *Milton Studies* 33 (1996): 27–46.

20. Feisal Mohamed, "Confronting Religious Violence: Milton's *Samson Agonistes*," *PMLA* 120.2 (2005): 327–40.

21. Kathleen Biddick, *The Typological Imaginary* (Philadelphia: University of Pennsylvania Press, 2003). In "Returning to Egypt: 'The Jew,' 'the Turk,' and the English Republic," in *Milton and the Jews*, Benedict Robinson links a typology of replacement to Milton's republicanism, in which Jewish bondage to the law is bondage tout court, and identical to the Oriental despotism that the Christian republic opposes (198–99). Trubowitz, "The People of Asia," makes a similar point about the equation of Jewish backsliding into Philistine slavery in *Samson Agonistes, Milton and the Jews*, 174.

22. This is a point that Biddick makes, *The Typological Imaginary*, 104; it is also the central argument of Giorgio Agamben, *The Time That Remains*, trans. Patricia Dailey (Stanford: Stanford University Press, 2005).

23. Lupton, *Citizen-Saints*, 190.

24. Mohamed, "Confronting Religious Violence," 329.

25. In "Reading *Samson* in the New American Century," *Milton Studies* 46 (2007): 149–64, Mohamed advocates a position that would allow humanity to the Other, a position not to be found either in Islamic extremism or U.S. ideology (the latter is attached to Milton's position). In "Liberty before and after Liberalism: Milton's Shifting Politics and the Current Crisis in Liberal Theory," *University of Toronto Quarterly* 77.3 (Summer 2008): 940–60, Mohamed attempts to distinguish a religiously-based liberalism (which he associates with Milton's republicanism and its aim "of securing liberty for a religiously enlightened minority" [951], a position Mohamed characterizes as illiberal) from a secular liberalism.

26. Benedict S. Robinson, *Islam and Early Modern English Literature* (London: Palgrave Macmillan, 2007). Robinson handily shows that Stanley Fish (whom Mohamed demonstrates as misguidedly targeted by Carey as a supporter of Samson-as-terrorist when he rather shares with Carey a humanist distance from religious extremism) bases his supposedly apolitical reading of Milton within the foundational politics of the exception; this is even more evident in Victoria Kahn's *Wayward Contracts* (Princeton: Princeton University Press, 2004), an avowed brief for liberalism. Fish's work on *Samson Agonistes* is gathered in *How Milton Works* (Cambridge, Mass.: Harvard University Press, 2001), chaps. 12 and 13, and continued in "'There is Nothing He Cannot Ask': Milton, Liberalism, and Terrorism," in *Milton in the Age of Fish*, ed. Michael Lieb and Albert C. Labriola (Pittsburgh: Duquesne University Press, 2006), 243–64. In "The Wit of Circumcision, the Circumcision of Wit," in *The Wit of Seventeenth-Century Poetry*, ed. Claude J. Summers and Ted-Larry Pebworth (Columbia: University of Missouri Press, 1995), 62–77, Jim Ellis tackles some "unseemly" texts (his characterization of Herrick's "To his Saviour: The New yeers gift," 63) in which the literal circumcision of Christ is equated with figurative circumcision of the heart, correlating this witty translation with typological readings of the literal as figurative (69) and this in turn with spiritual readings of the body that do not serve to reject the body per se but perform an act that Ellis correlates with the working of the liberal social contract in which "dangerous individuality" is "pared away" for the sake of "community" (76). This

regime of turning the unseemly into the socially acceptable parallels what I have examined in this essay; however, Ellis does not problematize the various translations upon which his analysis rests. *Samson Agonistes* is treated to the bland and evasive commonplaces of republican criticism in the new *Complete Works of John Milton*, vol. 2, ed. Laura Lunger Knoppers (Oxford: Oxford University Press, 2008), who writes in the "General Introduction": "While the violent action of *Samson Agonistes* seems to contrast with the restrained piety and refusal to act in *Paradise Regain'd*, both poems focus on inner faith (whether maintained or regained), and individual endurance under persecution, the witness of the faithful, and the knowledge and willingness to act when the time is right" (lvii).

27. Shoulson, *Milton and the Rabbis*, 255, notes the erotics of divine arousal at this point. When, in "The Secret of *Samson Agonistes*," *Milton Studies* 33 (1996): 111–32, John Rogers opts for Samson's final act as an individual act that shows the displacement of the divine for a divinized humanity, while he usefully points to Milton's monism, he also shows how liberal individualism is the product of a religious vision of antinomian exceptionalism. Rogers thinks he has replaced an unacceptable religious view with a secular one but he has simply displaced and occluded it.

The Idea of "New Enlightenment" [Nouvelles Lumières] and the Contradictions of Universalism

ÉTIENNE BALIBAR

Translated by Vivian Folkenflik

I am taking the expression "new Enlightenment"—"nouvelles Lumières"—from the philosopher Jacques Derrida, who used it emphatically if somewhat enigmatically in his written and spoken work during the 1990s and early years of the twenty-first century, especially the second part of *Voyous* (2003), which he devoted to the future of reason.[1] Indeed, he had already remarked at the 1994 *Parlement international des Ecrivains* in Lisbon: "What is at stake [in the effort to invent new forms of expression, communication, and independence for intellectuals—and particularly for writers] is the Enlightenment of to-morrow, democracy to come, and every instance of literature's relationship to the theological-political. . . ."[2] Again, more obliquely, in the 1996 Capri seminar on Faith and Knowledge: "Everywhere light dictates that which even yesterday was naively construed to be pure of all religion or even opposed to it and whose future must today be rethought (*Aufklärung, Lumières,* Enlightenment, *Illuminismo . . .*)."[3] And lastly, in an article written in 1994 but reissued on 11 October 2004, the day after his death, in the newspaper *L'Humanité*: "Plural humanity is also the issue for the old and young humanities, which are under threat more than ever before in secondary education, research, and the humanities. The humanities . . . remain the last place where the principles of free speech or free thought can still *be presented* as such. The same is true of the principle of a 'question of man,' freed from old presuppositions; it is true of new Enlightenments, of a *forever irredentist resistance* to the powers of economic, media, and political appropriation, to dogmatism of every kind."[4]

I call Derrida's expression "new Enlightenment" enigmatic because, in context, like the already-dated term "cultural crisis" (Hazard, Simmel, Arendt) which it seems to echo, this formulation—evoking an indefinite future conjoined with an injunction to act, to construct an enterprise in the immediacy of politics and history—seems to me capable of being interpreted in several different ways that may, at their limits, be mutually contradictory.

Why? In the first place, because the word "new" is equivocal. "New" can signify radical alterity: a new Enlightenment would then be different from everything our historiographic tradition has circumscribed within this word (including the partially equivalent terms *Aufklärung, Lumières, Enlightenment, Illuminismo*). A new enlightenment might even reverse its course. But the word "new" also points to a renewal or return to sources. In that sense, "new Enlightenment" would imply a reprise—three centuries later—of the intellectual and social movement that decisively traced, at the dawn of early modern times, lines of demarcation between "reason" and irrationality or "superstition"; between "free thought" and intolerance, whether religious or not; between human beings' "equality" or "equal dignity" and the idea of a "natural" hierarchy of individuals or the "sacred" authority of the rulers: all lines that would have to be redrawn today against old and new "adversaries" of emancipation and free thought. Which might raise fewer difficulties if the formation of the term "Lumières" for enlightenment were presented more clearly in histories and encyclopedias. It apparently involves a *reaction* to the debate on Enlightenment proposed in 1783 by the *Berlinische Monatsschrift*, prompting the famous contributions of Mendelssohn and Kant. The expression "Lumières" would then be a "retranslation" into French of the noun *Die Aufklärung*, itself coined to include the idea common to ordinary usage of the adjective "enlightened" and an antithesis between the "light of faith" and the "light of reason" in French and English philosophers, based on a great (Gnostic) antithesis between Light and Darkness.[5] Such return trips across the intellectual geography of pre-revolutionary Europe seem to cover up evident ideological fractures: between deism and atheism (the "Radical Enlightenment"), between constitutional republicanism and "enlightened despotism" (and its counterpoint, the myth of "Oriental despotism").

Then, too, there is the multiplicity—even incompatibility—of the possible contents covered by the term "Enlightenment" according to various historical schools and philosophies, and similar gaps among whatever temporal and geographical landmarks are used to identify its referent historically: ranging from a unique Western tendency at the dawn of "modernity" to an ideal type applicable to every epoch and to all great civilizations. Furthermore, if—using Habermas's formulation, to which I will return—Enlightenment is to be identified as an "unfinished project," should this project be considered the culmination of a characteristically Western tendency (one whose "source" it would, under these conditions, be tempting to locate in a specific invention or in an originary encounter, from which to derive Enlightenment's capacity for "civilization" itself)? Or, as suggested by the "post-colonial" studies clustered today under the rubric "alternative modernities," should this project be considered as a *différance* or "differential" capable of appearing at various times and places, in "cultures" that might not even know or "wish to know" anything about each other (one possible interpretation, let us note in passing, of the idea *Nicht-wissen*)? In this sense, each culture would have its own "Enlightenment," or its own way of thinking the/an enlightenment (though also, correlatively, its "dark ages").

Nevertheless, however difficult it may be to interpret, the expression "new Enlightenment" bears brilliant witness to the liveliness of a debate on the *present-day value* of ideals, principles, and institutions which we see as originating in the "Age of Enlightenment" and classical rationalism. In Europe, the debate takes on a particular tonal quality because it intersects with an interrogation into the identity of our subcontinent, in search of cultural borders and a new form of political organization. However, the debate is not merely European: it is worldwide. And this means that it bears witness also to the complexity of the symbolic relationships between Europe and the world it "conquered" and "civilized" according its own model, then to be "displaced" and "provincialized."[6] The only debate characterized by such characteristic intensity and generality is the one about the value of Christianity and religious monotheism in general. Nor, to be sure, is this any coincidence, since these two "structures" have in common, fifteen centuries apart, that they knit together abstract speculation with the concretion of social and institutional reform affecting both individual education (*Bildung*) and the legitimation of political power. And these two structures immediately joined in close combat, term-for-term, though within their contestation we may also, and paradoxically, read a shared profound epistemological affinity, as has been shown by historians who, following Franco Venturi, Isaiah Berlin, and Jean Deprun, and before them Hegel's famous chapter of the *Phenomenology of Spirit*, have studied the interrelationship of "Enlightenment" and "Counter-Enlightenment" in the eighteenth and nineteenth centuries.[7]

I would now like to concentrate this debate on the theme of *universalism*, which, to tell the truth, implies all the other aspects of the "quarrel of the Enlightenment": validity of the idea of "progress" for the interpretation of history; possibility of basing encyclopedic and critical knowledge, but also the regulation of behavior and institutions, on the evidence of "reason"; subordination of beliefs and their expression to a principle of "secularization" of community life; foundation of politics on a teleology of "human rights" whose natural consequence would be a democratic regime, and whose ideal horizon would be cosmopolitanism. Approaching the discussion from this angle seems to me the most appropriate way to distinguish between our present-day controversies about the model of civilization represented by "the Enlightenment" and the historic debates of the past involving "Enlightenment," "Counter-Enlightenment," and "Romanticism," as stylized for us by allegorical masterpieces such as Thomas Mann's *The Magic Mountain*: in the "duel" between the characters Settembrini and Naphta, who are fighting each other to conquer the soul of hero Hans Castorp (but he chooses the woman, who is like the line of escape out of this ideational conflict, before reentering the "real world" of history, which is to say the war).[8]

Yet even if these past debates bequeathed us many theoretical "commonplaces" that are still alive and well today, their application in practice changed radically once it became clear not only that the ideals and programs supported by the expansive movement of capitalist society and a dominant Western civilization were also factors in violence and destruction, but that they comprised an internal self-contradiction: their tendency to *exclude* minority or subjugated groups from "normal," "rational," "civilized" humanity, while simultaneously *including* virtually any and every creature who bore "the face of man" (Fichte) within the domain of citizenship, political rights, and the "right to have rights."[9] By institutionalizing itself, universalism not only "particularizes" itself, but denies itself as well.

Horkheimer and Adorno formulated this paradox notably in their *Dialectic of Enlightenment,* where they present the very notion of the disappearance of irrational powers as a "myth" dating from earliest Western culture. Taking as its point of departure the "dark side" of naturalism (exemplified by the marquis de Sade), their work analyzes the conversion of inclusion into exclusion through the phenomenologies of anti-Semitism and, more generally, racism—a communitary delirium reducing the status of individuals to instruments—and industrial mass culture *(Kulturindustrie)*, where universal "availability" of knowledge for one and all is turned into a conditioning of individuals by the manufacture of audiovisual simulacra.[10] But although we may debate the philosophy underlying their descriptions and predictions, we cannot claim—despite Habermas's impassioned and sustained critique of his former teachers—that the problem they are posing is a false problem inspired by irrational pessimism and skepticism, or that it would quite simply be better to revert to the authenticity of the "unfinished project of modernity."[11]

For my own part, therefore, I will maintain that the contradictions in the universalism of Enlightenment are inherent to it, and in that sense irreversible; and indeed, that these contradictions cannot be resolved by inverting them, in the sense of promulgating "principles" that would represent their simple negation. We must instead "tarry" within the contradiction so as to clarify its terms and produce its displacement: which can happen only through continued efforts to deconstruct both the classical theoretical formulas and the apparatuses of power in which they have been invested.

This holds good also for the idea of *progress*—whose "decadence" was first proclaimed in the late nineteenth century[12]—whether in the field of technological applications of science, or a gradual "constitutionalization of human rights" with no end in sight.[13] The economic and political premises of capitalism subjecting scientific research to the production of a healthcare market or the militarization of space are no more external to the practice of knowledge, than are ideologies delegating power to the "elites" and universal competition external to the constitution of democracy. We now know that there is no such thing as the definitive acquisition of liberty; no preestablished harmony of individual and collective rights; no conflict-free or residue-free repression of anthropological difference (whether relating to sexualities or cultures). This does not mean that knowledge and citizenship are themselves illusions; but rather that the adventure of learning and the affirmation of the equal liberty of human beings are indissociable from intellectual and moral risk, and from perennial transgression against established order and received wisdom.

This approach holds good also for the idea of secularization, now more than ever vacillating between a liberal model of "tolerance" and a republican model of "civil religion," neither of which truly leads to the construction of a global public sphere—and this, at the very moment when communitarian ideas founded on national sovereignty are wavering, and when religious ideologies are reappearing in the field of politics and ethics as the expression of spiritual identities, feelings of existential distress, or a will to power. Which does not imply that the idea of neutralizing, at least relatively, the intolerance necessarily associated with belief is a meaningless one. But such an idea must no longer coincide with abstract and equivocal boundaries between public and private, or with fixed *a priori* educational norms postulating the point they are trying to make: the "disenchantment of the world." It must instead simultaneously include (as Spinoza proposed at the dawn of the Enlightenment) an internal critique of religion together with a recognition of its symbolic power of socialization.[14] And it must actively hunt out the "theological" in its apparent adversaries, whether in the state or the marketplace or the media (as already shown by Marx and Nietzsche, in their different ways).

And finally, this approach holds good for the idea of *cosmopolitanism*—the ultimate geopolitical figure of universalism—about which the Encyclopedists themselves were already so deeply divided.[15] Not only will there be no real cosmopolitanism without a radical critique of both eurocentrism and the inequality instituted by modernity among the peoples of the world; but also, there will be no egalitarian international law or collective security without a vibrant cosmopolitan utopia, translatable into the languages of the entire world (instead of being formulated in a single idealized "universal language"),[16] and taking into account, as Kofi Annan has proposed, the irreducible plurality of "threats" to happiness and self-determination. In this sense, Enlightenment universalism, like that of revealed religion and alongside socialist internationalism, faces a choice: either to dissolve, or to reformulate itself more dialogically and more effectively.

Embryonic as they may be, these formulations are related in their own way to Michel Foucault's reflection in his commentary on Kant's opuscule *What is Enlightenment?*—that Enlightenment be interpreted not as a historic tradition, however important and valuable, but rather as an unresolved *present-day problem* on which depends the very definition of "what we are."[17] This idea stands out in particular relief at a moment when universalism is being tested by the globalization of the historical conditions of human existence. And it connects, in my view, with the most disturbing and indeed, most demanding interpretation of Derrida's injunction: Enlightenment is always already "new"—and yet, in another sense, it will never be new enough.

Notes

Contribution to the colloquium "Formen des Nichtwissens der Aufklärung," Martin-Luther-Universität Halle-Wittenberg, 20–22 August 2008. This contribution takes up and develops some of the ideas put forward in my essay "Quelle universalité des Lumières?" in *Le Bottin des Lumières*, ed. Nadine Descendre (Ville de Nancy: Communauté urbaine du Grand Nancy, 2005).

1. Jacques Derrida, *Rogues: Two Essays on Reason*, trans. Pascale-Anne Brault and Michael Naas (Stanford: Stanford University Press, 2005).

2. Jacques Derrida, Parlement international des Ecrivains, September 28–29, 1994; published in *Libération*, 4 November 1994. My translation.

3. Jacques Derrida, *Foi et savoir*, 1996, republished 2000; first published in France as *La Religion, Séminaire de Capri* (Paris: Editions du Seuil et Editions Laterza); published in English translation as "Faith and Religion," trans. Samuel Weber, in *Religion*, ed. Jacques Derrida and Gianni Vattimo (Stanford: Stanford University Press, Polity Press, 1998); translation republished as "Faith and Religion: The Two Sources of 'Religion' at the Limits of Reason Alone," in *Acts of Religion*, ed. Gil Anidjar (Routledge: New York, 2002), 46.

4. Jacques Derrida, "My Sunday 'Humanities,'" trans. Rachel Bowlby, *Paper Machine* (Stanford: Stanford University Press, 2005), 107. (Omissions in Balibar's text.)

5. See Pascal David, "Lumière," in *Vocabulaire européen des Philosophies*, ed. Barbara Cassin (Paris: Editions du Seuil, 2004).

6. According to the thought-provoking expression put in circulation by Dipesh Chakrabarty's book *Provincializing Europe: Postcolonial Thought and Historical Difference* (Princeton: Princeton University Press, 2000).

7. Hegel, *Phenomenology of Spirit*, trans. A. V. Miller (Oxford: Clarendon Press, 1977), Part VI. Spirit. B: "Self-alienated Spirit. Culture."

8. For Romanticism, see the definition of "ideal-typical" in Michael Löwy and Robert Sayre, *Romanticism Against the Tide of Modernity*, trans. Catherine Porter (Durham: Duke University Press, 2001).

9. The expression "right to have rights" as the political limit of the human being, in the positive as well as negative sense, and thus what is fundamentally at stake in any "politics of human rights" in the Enlightenment tradition, was first used by Hannah Arendt in the second volume of her *Origins of Totalitarianism* (New York: Harcourt, Brace, 1951), devoted to imperialism and the "crisis of the nation-state."

10. The German title is explicit: *Dialektik der Aufklärung.* Cf. the French translation by Eliane Kaufholz, *La dialectique de la raison: fragments philosophiques* (Paris: Gallimard, 1989).

11. See especially Habermas, *The Philosophical Discourse of Modernity: Twelve Lectures*, trans. Frederick Lawrence (Cambridge, Mass: MIT Press, 1987); *Der Philosophische Diskurs der Moderne: Zwölf Vorlesungen* (Frankfurt: Suhrkamp Verlag, 1985) and his acceptance speech for the *Theodor-W.-Adorno-Preis*, in *Die Moderne—en unvollendetes Projekt: Philosophisch-politische Aufsätze, 1977–1990* (Frankfurt: Surhkamp, 1994).

12. See Georges Canguilhem, "La décadence de l'idée de progrès," *Revue de Métaphysique et de Morale* 92.4 (October-December 1987): 437–54.

13. According to the expression of Gerald Stourzh, *Wege der Grundrechtsdemokratie: Studien zur Begriffs- und Institutionengeschichte des liberalen Verfassungsstaates* (Wien: Böhlau Verlag, 1989).

14. See Jonathan I. Israel, *Radical Enlightenment: Philosophy and the Making of Modernity 1650–1750* (Oxford: Oxford University Press, 2001).

15. See Franco Venturi, *Italy and the Enlightenment: Studies in a Cosmopolitan Century*, Trans. Susan Corsi (Longman: London, 1972).

16. See Umberto Eco, *The Search for the Perfect Language*, trans. James Fentress (Oxford and Cambridge, Mass.: Blackwell, 1995).

17. Michel Foucault, "What Is Enlightenment ?" ("Qu'est-ce que les Lumières?" in *Dits et Écrits* [Paris: Gallimard, 1984]), in Paul Rabinow, *The Foucault Reader* (New York: Pantheon, 1984), 32–50.

Contributors

ÉTIENNE BALIBAR is Distinguished Professor of French and Italian and of comparative literature at the University of California, Irvine and Emeritus Professor of Philosophy at the University of Paris-Nanterre. His most recent books in English are *Politics and the Other Scene* (2002), and *We, the People of Europe? Reflections on Transnational Citizenship* (2003).

KATHLEEN BIDDICK is professor of history at Temple University and cofounder of the Temple Premodern Studies Colloquium. She authored *The Other Economy* (1989), *The Shock of Medievalism* (1998), and *The Typological Imaginary* (2003).

DREW DANIEL is assistant professor of English at the Johns Hopkins University. He is the author of *The Melancholy Assemblage* (forthcoming).

CARLO GALLI is professor of history of political thought at the Faculty of Humanities, University of Bologna. His most recent books are *Political Spaces and Global War* (2010) and *Genealogia della Politica: Carl Schmitt e la Crisi del Pensiero Politico Moderno* (reprint, 2010).

JONATHAN GOLDBERG is Arts and Sciences Distinguished Professor at Emory University. His most recent books are *The Seeds of Things: Theorizing Sexuality and Materiality in Renaissance Representations* (2009) and *Sodometries: Renaissance Texts, Modern Sexualities* (reprint, 2010).

GRAHAM HAMMILL is professor of English and comparative literature at the University at Buffalo, State University of New York. His publications include *Sexuality and Form: Caravaggio, Marlowe, and Bacon* (2000) and *The Mosaic Constitution: Political Theology and Imagination from Machiavelli to Milton* (2012).

VICTORIA KAHN is the Katharine Bixby Hotchkis Chair in English and professor of comparative literature at the University of California, Berkeley. Her publications include *Wayward Contracts: The Crisis of Political Obligation in England, 1640–1674* (2004) and *Machiavellian Rhetoric from the Counter-Reformation to Milton* (1994).

GREGORY KNEIDEL is associate professor of English at the University of Connecticut. His publications include *Rethinking the Turn to Religion in Early Modern English Literature: The Poetics of All Believers* (2008).

PAUL A. KOTTMAN is associate professor of comparative literature at the New School for Liberal Arts and Eugene Lang College, the New School for Liberal Arts. He has most recently authored *Tragic Conditions in Shakespeare* (2009) and *A Politics of the Scene* (2008) and edited *Philosophers on Shakespeare* (2009).

JACQUES LEZRA is professor of Spanish and Portuguese and chair of comparative literature at New York University. He authored *Wild Materialism: The Ethic of Terror and the Modern Republic* (2010) and *Unspeakable Subjects: The Genealogy of the Event in Early Modern Europe* (1997).

JULIA REINHARD LUPTON is professor of English and comparative literature at the University of California, Irvine. Her most recent books are *Thinking with Shakespeare: Essays on Politics and Life* (2011) and *Citizen-Saints: Shakespeare and Political Theology* (2005).

JANE O. NEWMAN is professor of comparative literature at the University of California, Irvine. Her books include *Benjamin's Library: Modernity, Nation, and the Baroque* (2011) and *The Intervention of Philology: Gender, Learning, and Power in Lohenstein's Roman Plays* (2000).

JENNIFER RUST is assistant professor of English at Saint Louis University. She is completing *The Body in Mystery: Political Theology and Its Fictions in Post-Reformation England*.

ADAM SITZE is assistant professor of law, jurisprudence, and social thought at Amherst College.

Index